Collins

gem

Collins
gem

Hockey Facts & Stats

Andrew Podnieks

HarperCollins*PublishersLtd*

Collins Gem Hockey Facts & Stats
Copyright © 2006 by Andrew Podnieks.
All rights reserved.

First edition

Published by Collins, an imprint of HarperCollins Publishers Ltd.

HarperCollins books may be purchased for educational, business, or sales
promotional use through our Special Markets Department.

HarperCollins Publishers Ltd
2 Bloor Street East, 20th Floor
Toronto, Ontario, Canada
M4W 1A8

www.harpercollins.ca

Library and Archives Canada Cataloguing in Publication

Podnieks, Andrew
Collins Gem hockey facts & stats / Andrew Podnieks—1st ed.

ISBN-13: 978-0-00-639328-3
ISBN-10: 0-00-639328-4

1. National Hockey League-Miscellanea. 2. Hockey-Miscellanea.
I. Title. II. Title: Collins Gem hockey facts and stats.

GV847.8.N3P573 2006   796.962´64   C2006-903985-2

RRD 9 8 7 6 5 4 3 2 1

Printed and bound in Canada

Contents

INTERNATIONAL HOCKEY

Introduction

A season that started with uncertainty ended with a game-seven flourish. A year of potentially dubious new rule changes ended with emphatic success. The 2005–06 NHL season was quickly dubbed the "new NHL," the "new" referring to a fresh start after a year without hockey as well as a fresh attempt to breathe life into a near-moribund game. The result was energetic, exciting hockey climaxing with a narrow 2–1 win by Carolina over Edmonton in the deciding game for the Stanley Cup. Wow!

Collins GEM Hockey Facts & Stats provides essential statistics that will help explain, summarize, and contribute to a better understanding of the 2005–06 season and the history of hockey. The book also includes data that hasn't been tracked before such as statistics on shootouts, which are new because the NHL introduced the format in 2005–06. This section allows fans to see every skater's record against every goalie, and every goalie's performance against every shooter. No more detailed information is available anywhere else.

The NHL has become an increasingly international league with more players from around the world. *Collins GEM Hockey Facts & Stats* considers this aspect of the game in depth. First, there is a listing of all the players in the NHL in 2005–06 by nationality. Canada leads the way, as always, but the representation of other countries is interesting, to say the least. There are more Americans than one might have thought, far fewer Russians, and at least one player from 18 countries. In Canada, the breakdown continues by province and then by city. The First Games Played section takes this one step further, showing how players fared in their first game and which players played their first game in 2005–06. It also identifies these newcomers by nationality so we can see whether the overall trend of, for instance, Canada providing the majority of players continued this past season (it does).

While many sources separate NHL and international hockey, *Collins GEM Hockey Facts & Stats* does not. This past year saw two important international tournaments dominated by NHL players—the Olympics in Torino and the World Championships in Riga, Latvia. The truth is, just as the NHL is becoming more international, international hockey is increasing its NHL content. For lovers of the NHL and NHL players, it is no longer good enough to follow just that league—you must follow the World Junior Championships, to get a clear sense of who tomorrow's stars will be. You must watch the World Championships to see which players love the game and are honoured by representing their country. You must follow the Olympics to see which players rise to the occasion of playing best-on-best. Only then can you know hockey completely nowadays.

Of course, in addition to new and international statistics, *Collins GEM Hockey Facts & Stats* has the most complete historical statistics available in one place and in a handy format—all-time standings, every playoff game ever played (with overtime winners and shutouts included), All-Star Games, the 2006 draft, and much more.

Enjoy.

Andrew Podnieks
Toronto, 2006

GLOSSARY OF ABBREVIATIONS

NHL Teams

ANA= Anaheim Ducks, ATL=Atlanta Thrashers, BOS=Boston Bruins, BUF=Buffalo Sabres, CAL=Calgary Flames, CAR=Carolina Hurricanes, CHI=Chicago Blackhawks, COL=Colorado Avalanche, CBJ=Columbus Blue Jackets, DAL=Dallas Stars, DET=Detroit Red Wings, EDM=Edmonton Oilers, FLO=Florida Panthers, LA=Los Angeles Kings, MIN=Minnesota Wild, MON=Montreal Canadiens, NAS=Nashville Predators, NJ=New Jersey Devils, NYI=New York Islanders, NYR=New York Rangers, OTT=Ottawa Senators, PHI=Philadelphia Flyers, PHO=Phoenix Coyotes, PIT=Pittsburgh Penguins, STL=St. Louis Blues, SJ=San Jose Sharks, TB=Tampa Bay Lightning, TOR=Toronto Maple Leafs, VAN=Vancouver Canucks, WAS=Washington Capitals

International

AUT	Austria	RUS	Russia
BLR	Belarus	SLO	Slovenia
CAN	Canada	SUI	Switzerland
CZE	Czech Republic	SVK	Slovakia
FIN	Finland	SWE	Sweden
FRA	France	UKR	Ukraine
GBR	Great Britain	USA	United States
GER	Germany		
IRL	Ireland		
KAZ	Kazakhstan		
LAT	Latvia		
LTU	Lithuania		
NOR	Norway		
POL	Poland		

ANAHEIM DUCKS

(name changed from Mighty Ducks of Anaheim on June 22, 2006)
First Game Played: October 8, 1993
Detroit Red Wings 7 at Mighty Ducks of Anaheim 2
Nickname Provenance: Owners, Disney, named team after a
popular kids' movie, *The Mighty Ducks* (1992)
Mascot: Wild Thing
Arena History: Arrowhead Pond, 1993–present (capacity 17,174)
Retired Numbers: none
Hall of Famers: Players (1): Jari Kurri
Website: www.anaheimducks.com
Minor League Affiliate(s): Portland Pirates (AHL)
Stanley Cups: none
Hosted All-Star Game: none
2006 Olympians: Ilja Bryzgalov (RUS), Sandis Ozolinsh (LAT),
Samuel Pahlsson (SWE), Teemu Selanne (FIN)
1st Overall Draft Choices: none

ATLANTA THRASHERS

First Game Played: October 2, 1999
New Jersey Devils 4 at Atlanta Thrashers 1
Nickname Provenance: The Brown Thrasher is the state bird
of Georgia
Mascot: Thrash (b. September 4, 1999)
Arena History: Philips Arena, 1999–present (capacity 18,545)
Retired Numbers: Dan Snyder (43, unofficial)
Hall of Famers: none
Website: www. atlantathrashers.com
Minor League Affiliate(s): Chicago Wolves (AHL), Gwinnett
Gladiators (ECHL)
Stanley Cups: none

Hosted All-Star Game: none
2006 Olympians: Peter Bondra (SVK), Niclas Havelid (SWE), Marian Hossa (SVK), Ilya Kovalchuk (RUS), Ronald Petrovicky (SVK)
1st Overall Draft Choices: 1999 (Patrik Stefan), 2001 (Ilya Kovalchuk)

BOSTON BRUINS

First Game Played: December 1, 1924
Montreal Maroons 1 at Boston Bruins 2
Nickname Provenance: Named by owner Art Ross for the brown bear
Mascot: Blades (b. October 9, 2000)
Arena History: Boston Arena, 1924–28; Boston Garden, 1928–95; FleetCenter, 1995–2003; TD Banknorth Garden (formerly known as the FleetCenter), 2005–present (capacity 17,565)
Retired Numbers: Eddie Shore (2), Lionel Hitchman (3), Bobby Orr (4), Dit Clapper (5), Phil Esposito (7), Cam Neely (8), Johnny Bucyk (9), Milt Schmidt (15), Terry O'Reilly (24), Ray Bourque (77)
Hall of Famers: Players (45): Marty Barry, Bobby Bauer, Leo Boivin, Ray Bourque, Frank Brimsek, Johnny Bucyk, Billy Burch, Gerry Cheevers, Dit Clapper, Sprague Cleghorn, Paul Coffey, Roy Conacher, Bun Cook, Bill Cowley, Cy Denneny, Woody Dumart, Phil Esposito, Fern Flaman, Frank Fredrickson, Harvey Jackson, Tom Johnson, Duke Keats, Guy Lapointe, Harry Lumley, Mickey MacKay, Sylvio Mantha, Joe Mullen, Cam Neely, Harry Oilver, Bobby Orr, Bernie Parent, Brad Park, Jacques Plante, Babe Pratt, Bill Quackenbush, Jean Ratelle, Art Ross (inducted as Player, associated with Boston as Builder), Terry Sawchuk, Milt Schmidt, Eddie Shore, Babe Siebert, Hooley Smith, Allan Stanley, Nels Stewart, Tiny Thompson, Cooney Weiland; Builders (5): Charles Adams, Weston Adams, Walter Brown, Bud Poile (played with Boston, inducted as Builder), Glen Sather (played with Boston, inducted as Builder), Harry Sinden
Website: www.bostonbruins.com

Minor League Affiliate(s): Providence Bruins (AHL)
Stanley Cups: (5) 1928–29, 1938–39, 1940–41, 1969–70, 1971–72
Hosted All-Star Game: (2) 1971, 1996
2006 Olympians: P-J Axelsson (SWE), Milan Jurcina (SVK)
1st Overall Draft Choices: 1982 (Gord Kluzak), 1997 (Joe Thornton)

BUFFALO SABRES

First Game Played: October 10, 1970
Buffalo Sabres 2 at Pittsburgh Penguins 1
Nickname Provenance: a contest determined the name Sabres
Mascot: Sabre-Tooth
Arena History: Memorial Auditorium ("The Aud"), 1970–96;
Marine Midland Bank Arena, 1996–2000; HSBC Arena (formerly
known as the Marine Midland Bank Arena), 2000–present
(capacity 18,690)
Retired Numbers: Tim Horton (2), Rick Martin (7), Gilbert Perreault
(11), Rene Robert (14), Pat LaFontaine (16), Danny Gare (18)
Hall of Famers: Players (8): Dick Duff, Tim Horton, Gilbert
Perreault, Dale Hawerchuk, Clark Gillies, Grant Fuhr, Pat
LaFontaine, Marcel Pronovost (inducted as Player, associated
with Buffalo as Builder); Builders (4): Scotty Bowman, Punch
Imlach, Seymour Knox III, Roger Neilson
Website: www.sabres.com
Minor League Affiliate(s): Rochester Americans (AHL—shared
with Florida)
Stanley Cups: none
Hosted All-Star Game: 1978
2006 Olympians: Maxim Afinogenov (RUS), Chris Drury (USA),
Ales Kotalik (CZE), Toni Lydman (FIN), Teppo Numminen (FIN)
1st Overall Draft Choices: 1970 (Gilbert Perreault), 1987 (Pierre
Turgeon)

CALGARY FLAMES

First Game Played:
As Atlanta Flames: October 7, 1972
Atlanta Flames 3 at New York Islanders 2
As Calgary Flames: October 9, 1980
Quebec Nordiques 5 at Calgary Flames 5
Nickname Provenance: Flames was chosen by contest, representative of Atlanta during the Civil War when much of it was burned to the ground
Mascot: Harvey the Hound
Arena History: The Omni (Atlanta), 1972–80; Stampede Corral, 1980–83; Olympic Saddledome, 1983–95; Canadian Airlines Saddledome, 1995–2001; Pengrowth Saddledome (same building as previous two Saddledomes), 2001–present (capacity 17,439)
Retired Numbers: Lanny McDonald (9)
Hall of Famers: Players (3): Lanny McDonald, Joe Mullen, Grant Fuhr; Builders (2): Cliff Fletcher, Harley Hotchkiss
Website: www.calgaryflames.com
Minor League Affiliate(s): Omaha Ak-Sar-Ben Knights (AHL), Las Vegas Wranglers (ECHL)
Stanley Cups: (1) 1988–89
Hosted All-Star Game: 1985
2006 Olympians: Jarome Iginla (CAN), Jordan Leopold (USA), Robyn Regehr (CAN)
1st Overall Draft Choices: none

CAROLINA HURRICANES

First Game Played:
As Hartford Whalers: October 11, 1979
Hartford Whalers 1 at Minnesota North Stars 4
As Carolina Hurricanes: October 1, 1997
Carolina Hurricanes 2 at Tampa Bay Lightning 4
Nickname Provenance: Whalers adopted because it contained the letters of the WHA and it was emblematic of the region

Mascot: Stormy
Arena History: Springfield Civic Center (Hartford), 1979–80; Hartford Civic Center (Hartford), 1980–97; Greensboro Coliseum, 1997–99; Raleigh Entertainment & Sports Arena, 1999–2003; RBC Center, 2003–present (capacity 18,730)
Retired Numbers: Ron Francis (10)
Hall of Famers: Players (4): Paul Coffey (Hartford/Carolina), Gordie Howe (Hartford), Bobby Hull (Hartford), Dave Keon (Hartford)
Website: www.carolinahcanes.com
Minor League Affiliate(s): Lowell Lock Monsters (AHL—shared with Colorado), Florida Everblades (ECHL—shared with Florida)
Stanley Cups: 2005–06
Hosted All-Star Game: 1986 (as Hartford Whalers)
2006 Olympians: Erik Cole (USA), Martin Gerber (SUI), Bret Hedican (USA), Frantisek Kaberle (CZE)
1st Overall Draft Choices: no

CHICAGO BLACKHAWKS

First Game Played: November 17, 1926
Toronto St. Pats 1 at Chicago Blackhawks 4
Nickname Provenance: (spelling changed from "Black Hawks" to "Blackhawks" in 1986)
Mascot: none
Arena History: Chicago Coliseum, 1926–32; Chicago Stadium, 1932–94, United Center, 1995–present (opening of United Center delayed by disruption of 1994–95 NHL season, capacity 20,500)
Retired Numbers: Glenn Hall (1), Bobby Hull (9), Denis Savard (18), Stan Mikita (21), Tony Esposito (35)
Hall of Famers: Players (37): Sid Abel, Doug Bentley, Max Bentley, Georges Boucher, Frank Brimsek, Billy Burch, Paul Coffey, Lionel Conacher, Roy Conacher, Art Coulter, Babe Dye, Phil Esposito, Tony Esposito, Bill Gadsby, Charlie Gardiner, Herb Gardiner, Michel Goulet, Glenn Hall, George Hay, Bobby Hull, Duke Keats,

Hugh Lehman, Ted Lindsay, Harry Lumley, Mickey MacKay, Stan Mikita, Howie Morenz, Bill Mosienko, Bert Olmstead, Bobby Orr, Pierre Pilote, Denis Savard, Earl Seibert, Clint Smith, Allan Stanley, Barney Stanley, Jack Stewart, Carl Voss (played for Chicago, inducted as Builder), Harry Watson; Builders (10): Al Arbour, Emile Francis (played for Chicago, inducted as Builder), Dick Irvin (played for Chicago, inducted as Builder), Tommy Ivan, John Mariucci (also played for Chicago), Major Frederic McLaughlin, James Norris, James Norris, Jr., Rudy Pilous, Bud Poile (played for Chicago, inducted as Builder), Arthur Wirtz, William Wirtz

Website: www.chicagoblackhawks.com
Minor League Affiliate(s): Norfolk Admirals (AHL), Greenville Grrrowl (ECHL—shared with Edmonton)
Stanley Cups: (3) 1933–34, 1937–38, 1960–61
Hosted All-Star Game: (4) 1948, 1961, 1974, 1991
2006 Olympians: none
1ˢᵗ Overall Draft Choices: none

COLORADO AVALANCHE

First Game Played:
As Quebec Nordiques: October 10, 1979
Atlanta Flames 5 at Quebec Nordiques 3
As Colorado Avalanche: October 6, 1995
Detroit Red Wings 2 at Colorado Avalanche 3
Nickname Provenance: Team owners polled fans. Out of 8 names offered, Avalanche was the most popular.
Mascot: Howler
Arena History: McNichols Sports Arena, 1995–99; Pepsi Center, 1999–present (capacity 18,007)
Retired Numbers: J-C Tremblay (3), Marc Tardif (8), Michel Goulet (16), Patrick Roy (33), Ray Bourque (77)
Hall of Famers: Players (6): Ray Bourque, Patrick Roy, Michel Goulet (Quebec), Jari Kurri, Guy Lafleur (Quebec), Peter Stastny (Quebec)

Website: www.coloradoavalanche.com
Minor League Affiliate(s): Lowell Lock Monsters (AHL—shared with Carolina)
Stanley Cups: (2) 1995–96, 2000–01
Hosted All-Star Game: 2001
2006 Olympians: David Aebischer (SUI), Rob Blake (CAN), Peter Budaj (SVK), Milan Hejduk (CZE), Vitaliy Kolesnik (KAZ), Antti Laaksonen (FIN), John-Michael Liles (USA), Joe Sakic (CAN), Karlis Skrastins (LAT), Marek Svatos (SVK)
1st Overall Draft Choices: 1989 (Mats Sundin—Quebec Nordiques), 1990 (Owen Nolan—Quebec), 1991 (Eric Lindros—Quebec)

COLUMBUS BLUE JACKETS

First Game Played: October 7, 2000
Chicago Blackhawks 5 at Columbus Blue Jackets 3
Nickname Provenance: reflects patriotism and history of the Civil War
Mascot: Stinger
Arena History: Nationwide Arena, 2000–present (capacity 18,136)
Retired Numbers: none
Hall of Famers: none
Website: www. bluejackets.com
Minor League Affiliate(s): Syracuse Crunch (AHL), Dayton Bombers (ECHL)
Stanley Cups: none
Hosted All-Star Game: none
2006 Olympians: Adam Foote (CAN), Rick Nash (CAN), Radoslav Suchy (SVK), David Vyborny (CZE)
1st Overall Draft Choices: 2002 (Rick Nash)

DALLAS STARS

First Game Played:

As Minnesota North Stars: October 11, 1967

Minnesota North Stars 2 at St. Louis Blues 2

As Dallas Stars: October 5, 1993

Detroit Red Wings 4 at Dallas Stars 6

Nickname Provenance: shortening of North Stars, consistent with Texas as the Lone Star state

Mascot: none

Arena History: Metropolitan Sports Center (also known as the Met Center), 1967–93; Reunion Arena, 1993–2001; American Airlines Center, 2001–present (capacity 18,532)

Retired Numbers: Neal Broten (7), Bill Goldsworthy (8), Bill Masterton (19)

Hall of Famers: Players (5): Mike Gartner (Minnesota), Harry Howell (Minnesota), Larry Murphy (Minnesota), Gump Worsley (Minnesota), Leo Boivin (Minnesota); Builders (3): Herb Brooks (coached Minnesota), Glen Sather (played for Minnesota, inducted as Builder), John Mariucci (played for Minnesota, inducted as Builder)

Website: www.dallasstars.com

Minor League Affiliate(s): Iowa Stars (AHL—shared with Edmonton), Idaho Steelheads (ECHL)

Stanley Cups: 1998–99

Hosted All-Star Game: 1972 (as North Stars); they will also host in 2007

2006 Olympians: Bill Guerin (USA), Niklas Hagman (FIN), Jussi Jokinen (FIN), Niko Kapanen (FIN), Jere Lehtinen (FIN), Mike Modano (USA), Marty Turco (CAN—did not play)

1st Overall Draft Choices: 1978 (Bobby Smith—Minnesota North Stars), 1983 (Brian Lawton—Minnesota), 1988 (Mike Modano—Minnesota)

DETROIT RED WINGS

First Game Played:

As Detroit Cougars: November 18, 1926
Boston Bruins 2 at Detroit Cougars 0
As Detroit Falcons: November 13, 1930
New York Rangers 0 at Detroit Falcons 1
As Detroit Red Wings: November 10, 1932
Chicago Blackhawks 1 at Detroit Red Wings 3

Nickname Provenance: Owner James Norris, a Montreal native, used the Winged Wheel from his hometown and combined it with Detroit's place in America as a car-making centre

Mascot: none

Arena History: Windsor Arena (Border Cities Arena), 1926–27; Olympia, 1929–79; Joe Louis Arena, 1979–present (capacity 20,066)

Retired Numbers: Terry Sawchuk (1), Ted Lindsay (7), Gordie Howe (9), Alex Delvecchio (10), Sid Abel (12)

Hall of Famers: Players (45): Sid Abel, Jack Adams (inducted as Player, associated with Detroit as builder), Marty Barry, Andy Bathgate, Johnny Bucyk, Paul Coffey, Charlie Conacher, Roy Conacher, Alec Connell, Alex Delvecchio, Marcel Dionne, Bernie Federko, Slava Fetisov, Frank Foyston, Frank Fredrickson, Bill Gadsby, Ed Giacomin, Ebbie Goodfellow, Glenn Hall, Doug Harvey, George Hay, Harry Holmes, Gordie Howe, Syd Howe, Duke Keats, Red Kelly, Brian Kilrea (played for Detroit, inducted as Builder), Herbie Lewis, Ted Lindsay, Harry Lumley, Frank Mahovlich, Larry Murphy, Reg Noble, Brad Park, Bud Poile (played for Detroit, inducted as Builder), Marcel Pronovost, Bill Quackenbush, Borje Salming, Terry Sawchuk, Earl Seibert, Darryl Sittler, Jack Stewart, Tiny Thompson, Norm Ullman, Jack Walker, Harry Watson, Cooney Weiland; Builders (9): Al Arbour (played for Detroit, inducted as Builder), Leo Boivin (played for Detroit, inducted as Builder), Scotty Bowman, Tommy Ivan, Bruce Norris, James Norris, James Norris, Jr., Carl Voss (played for Detroit, inducted as Builder)

Website: www.detroitredwings.com
Minor League Affiliate(s): Grand Rapids Griffins (AHL), Toledo Storm (ECHL)
Stanley Cups: (10) 1935–36, 1936–37, 1942–43, 1949–50, 1951–52, 1953–54, 1054–55, 1996–97, 1997–98, 2002–02
Hosted All-Star Game: (5) 1950, 1952, 1954, 1955, 1980
2006 Olympians: Chris Chelios (USA), Pavel Datsyuk (RUS), Kris Draper (CAN), Tomas Holmstrom (SWE), Niklas Kronwall (SWE), Robert Lang (CZE), Nicklas Lidstrom (SWE), Mikael Samuelsson (SWE), Mathieu Schneider (USA)
1st Overall Draft Choices: 1977 (Dale McCourt), 1986 (Joe Murphy)

EDMONTON OILERS

First Game Played: October 10, 1979
Edmonton Oilers 2 at Chicago Black Hawks 4
Nickname Provenance: from Alberta Oilers and later Edmonton Oilers of WHA, to refer to Alberta's place as an oil capital in Canada
Mascot: none
Arena History: Northlands Coliseum, 1979–99; Skyreach Centre, 1999–2003; Rexall Place, 2005–present (all three are the same building, capacity 16,839)
Retired Numbers: Al Hamilton (3), Paul Coffey (7), Jari Kurri (17), Grant Fuhr (31), Wayne Gretzky (99—leaguewide recognition)
Hall of Famers: Players (4): Paul Coffey, Grant Fuhr, Wayne Gretzky, Jari Kurri; Builders (1): Glen Sather
Website: www.edmontonoilers.com
Minor League Affiliate(s): Hamilton Bulldogs (AHL—shared with Montreal), Iowa Stars (AHL—shared with Dallas), Greenville Grrrowl (ECHL—shared with Chicago), Odessa Jackalopes (CHL)
Stanley Cups: (5) 1983–84, 1984–85, 1986–87, 1987–88, 1989–90
Hosted All-Star Game: 1989
2006 Olympians: Ales Hemsky (CZE), Chris Pronger (CAN), Ryan Smyth (CAN), Jaroslav Spacek (CZE)
1st Overall Draft Choices: none

FLORIDA PANTHERS

First Game Played: October 6, 1993
Florida Panthers 4 at Chicago Blackhawks 4
Nickname Provenance: named for the animal, which is common in Florida
Mascot: Stanley C. Panther
Arena History: Miami Arena, 1993–99; National Car Rental Center, 1999–2002; Office Depot Center, 2002–03; BankAtlantic Center, 2005–present (previous three are the same building, capacity 19,250)
Retired Numbers: none
Hall of Famers: none
Website: www.floridapanthers.com
Minor League Affiliate(s): Rochester Americans (AHL—shared with Buffalo), Florida Everblades (ECHL—shared with Carolina)
Stanley Cups: none
Hosted All-Star Game: 2003
2006 Olympians: Jay Bouwmeester (CAN), Olli Jokinen (FIN), Roberto Luongo (CAN), Rostislav Olesz (CZE), Jozef Stumpel (SVK)
1ˢᵗ Overall Draft Choices: 1994 (Ed Jovanovski)

LOS ANGELES KINGS

First Game Played: October 14, 1967
Philadelphia Flyers 2 at Los Angeles Kings 4
Nickname Provenance: named by owner Jack Kent Cooke to give the team a royal (i.e., important) sound to it
Mascot: none
Arena History: Long Beach Arena, October 1967; Los Angeles Sports Arena, November–December 1967; The Forum, 1967–88; Great Western Forum, 1988–99 (same building as The Forum); Staples Center, 1999–present (capacity 18,118)
Retired Numbers: Marcel Dionne (16), Dave Taylor (18), Rogie Vachon (30), Wayne Gretzky (99—leaguewide recognition)

Hall of Famers: Players (13): Paul Coffey, Marcel Dionne, Dick Duff, Grant Fuhr, Wayne Gretzky, Harry Howell, Jari Kurri, Larry Murphy, Bob Pulford, Larry Robinson, Terry Sawchuk, Steve Shutt, Billy Smith; Builders (1): Brian Kilrea (played for Los Angeles, inducted as Builder)
Website: www.lakings.com
Minor League Affiliate(s): Manchester Monarchs (AHL), Reading Royals (ECHL)
Stanley Cups: none
Hosted All-Star Game: (2) 1981, 2002
2006 Olympians: Craig Conroy (USA), Pavol Demitra (SVK), Alexander Frolov (RUS), Ronnie Sundin (SWE), Lubomir Visnovsky (SVK)
1st Overall Draft Choices: none

MINNESOTA WILD

First Game Played: October 6, 2000
Minnesota Wild 1 at Mighty Ducks of Anaheim 3
Nickname Provenance: selected by fan contest
Mascot: none
Arena History: Xcel Energy Center, 2000–present (capacity 18,064)
Retired Numbers: none
Hall of Famers: none
Website: www.wild.com
Minor League Affiliate(s): Houston Aeros (AHL), Texas Wildcatters (ECHL)
Stanley Cups: none
Hosted All-Star Game: (1) 2004
2006 Olympians: Marian Gaborik (SVK), Mikko Koivu (FIN), Filip Kuba (CZE), Brian Rolston (USA), Daniel Tjarnqvist (SWE)
1st Overall Draft Choices: none

MONTREAL CANADIENS

First Game Played:
In NHA: January 19, 1910
Montreal Canadiens 4 at Renfrew Millionaires 9
In NHL: December 19, 1917
Ottawa Senators 4 at Montreal Canadiens 7

Nickname Provenance: as a Canadian team based in Quebec, simply called Canadians in French (they are also known as "the Habs," short for "*les habitants*," a name given to the early settlers of the province)

Mascot: Youppi

Arena History: Westmount Arena, 1909–1918; Jubilee Arena, 1918–20; Mount Royal Arena, 1920–24; Montreal Forum, 1924–96 (refurbished in 1968); Molson Centre, 1996–2002; Bell Centre, 2002–present (same building as Molson Centre, capacity 21,273)

Retired Numbers: Jacques Plante (1), Doug Harvey (2), Jean Beliveau (4), Bernie Geoffrion (5), Howie Morenz (7), Maurice Richard (9), Guy Lafleur (10), Yvan Cournoyer (12), Henri Richard (16)

Hall of Famers: Players (43): Marty Barry, Harry Cameron, Gord Drillon, Dick Duff, Tony Esposito, Rod Langway, Roy Worters, Dick Irvin (inducted as Player, associated with Montreal as Builder), Howie Morenz, Georges Vezina, Aurel Joliat, Newsy Lalonde, Joe Malone, Sprague Cleghorn, Herb Gardiner, Sylvio Mantha, Joe Hall, George Hainsworth, Maurice Richard, Jack Laviolette, Didier Pitre, Bill Durnan, Babe Siebert, Toe Blake, Emile Bouchard, Elmer Lach, Ken Reardon, Tom Johnson, Jean Beliveau, Bernie Geoffrion, Doug Harvey, Dickie Moore, Jacques Plante, Henri Richard, Patrick Roy, Gump Worsley, Frank Mahovlich, Yvan Cournoyer, Ken Dryden, Jacques Lemaire, Bert Olmstead, Serge Savard, Jacques Laperriere, Guy Lafleur, Buddy O'Connor, Bob Gainey, Guy Lapointe, Steve Shutt, Larry Robinson, Denis Savard; Builders (11): Cliff Fletcher, William Northey, Hon. Donat Raymond, Frank Selke, Ambrose O'Brien, Leo Dandurand, Tommy Gorman, Hon. Hartland de Montarville Molson, Joseph

Cattarinich, Sam Pollock, Scotty Bowman, Glen Sather (played with Montreal, inducted as Builder)

Website: www.canadiens.com

Minor League Affiliate(s): Hamilton Bulldogs (AHL—shared with Edmonton), Long Beach Ice Dogs (ECHL)

Stanley Cups: (23) 1923–24, 1929–30, 1930–31, 1943–44, 1945–46, 1952–53, 1955–56, 1956–57, 1957–58, 1958–59, 1959–60, 1964–65, 1065–66, 1967–68, 1968–69, 1970–71, 1972–73, 1975–76, 1976–77, 1977–78, 1978–79, 1985–86, 1992–93

Hosted All-Star Game: (11) 1953, 1956, 1957, 1958, 1959, 1960, 1965, 1967, 1969, 1975, 1993

2006 Olympians: Jan Bulis (CZE), Saku Koivu (FIN), Alexei Kovalev (RUS), Andrei Markov (RUS), Mark Streit (SUI), Richard Zednik (SVK)

1st Overall Draft Choices: 1969 (Rejean Houle), 1971 (Guy Lafleur), 1980 (Doug Wickenheiser)

NASHVILLE PREDATORS

First Game Played: October 10, 1998
Florida Panthers 1 at Nashville Predators 0

Nickname Provenance: selected by fans

Mascot: Gnash

Arena History: Gaylord Entertainment Center, 1998–present (capacity 17,113)

Retired Numbers: none

Hall of Famers: none

Website: www.nashvillepredators.com

Minor League Affiliate(s): Milwaukee Admirals (AHL)

Stanley Cups: none

Hosted All-Star Game: none

2006 Olympians: Martin Erat (CZE), Daniil Markov (RUS), Kimmo Timonen (FIN), Tomas Vokoun (CZE), Marek Zidlicky (CZE)

1st Overall Draft Choices: none

NEW JERSEY DEVILS

First Game Played:
As Kansas City Scouts: October 9, 1974
Kansas City Scouts 2 at Toronto Maple Leafs 6
As Colorado Rockies: October 5, 1976
Toronto Maple Leafs 2 at Colorado Rockies 4
As New Jersey Devils: October 5, 1982
Pittsburgh Penguins 3 at New Jersey Devils 3
Nickname Provenance: selected by fans in reference to legend of a demonic baby produced by one Mrs. Leeds in 1735, her 13th child
Mascot: The Devil
Arena History: Kemper Arena (Kansas City), 1974–76; McNichols Sports Arena (Colorado), 1976–82; Brendan Byrne Arena, 1982–83; Byrne Meadowlands Arena, 1983–92 (same building as Brendan Byrne Arena); Meadowlands Arena (same building as Byrne Meadowlands Arena), 1992–96; Continental Airlines Arena (same building as Meadowlands Arena), 1996–present (capacity 19,040)
Retired Numbers: Ken Daneyko (3), Scott Stevens (4)
Hall of Famers: Players (3): Slava Fetisov, Lanny McDonald (Colorado Rockies), Peter Stastny; Builders (1): Herb Brooks
Website: www.newjerseydevils.com
Minor League Affiliate(s): Albany River Rats (AHL)
Stanley Cups: (3) 1994–95, 1999–2000, 2002–03
Hosted All-Star Game: 1984
2006 Olympians: Martin Brodeur (CAN), Patrik Elias (CZE), Brian Gionta (USA), Scott Gomez (USA), Viktor Kozlov (RUS), Brian Rafalski (USA)
1st Overall Draft Choices: 1979 (Rob Ramage—Colorado Rockies)

NEW YORK ISLANDERS

First Game Played: October 7, 1972
Atlanta Flames 3 at New York Islanders 2
Nickname Provenance: named, simply, because the team is located on Long Island, New York

Mascot: none
Arena History: Nassau Veterans' Memorial Coliseum, 1972–present (capacity 16,234)
Retired Numbers: Denis Potvin (5), Clark Gillies (9), Bryan Trottier (19), Mike Bossy (22), Bob Nystrom (23), Billy Smith (31)
Hall of Famers: Players (6): Mike Bossy, Pat LaFontaine, Denis Potvin, Billy Smith, Bryan Trottier, Clark Gillies; Builders (2): Al Arbour, Bill Torrey
Website: www.newyorkislanders.com
Minor League Affiliate(s): Bridgeport Sound Tigers (AHL)
Stanley Cups: (4) 1979–80, 1980–81, 1981–82, 1982–83
Hosted All-Star Game: 1983
2006 Olympians: Jason Blake (USA), Rick DiPietro (USA), Mark Parrish (USA), Miroslav Satan (SVK), Vitali Vishnevski (RUS), Alexei Yashin (RUS)
1st Overall Draft Choices: 1972 (Billy Harris), 1973 (Denis Potvin), 2000 (Rick DiPietro)

NEW YORK RANGERS

First Game Played: November 16, 1926
Montreal Maroons 0 at New York Rangers 1
Nickname Provenance: Emerged when sportswriters in New York called the new franchise Tex's Rangers, in reference to Tex Rickard, the president of Madison Square Garden and the man who assembled the executive for the team in 1926
Mascot: none
Arena History: Madison Square Garden, 1926–68; Madison Square Garden, 1968–present (newly built, capacity 18,200)
Retired Numbers: Ed Giacomin (1), Rod Gilbert (7), Mark Messier (11)
Hall of Famers: Players (41): Dick Duff, Howie Morenz, Lester Patrick, Bill Cook, Frank Boucher, Ching Johnson, Babe Siebert, Earl Seibert, Doug Bentley, Max Bentley, Babe Pratt, Neil Colville, Bryan Hextall, Bill Gadsby, Terry Sawchuk, Bernie Geoffrion, Doug Harvey, Charlie Rayner, Art Coulter, Johnny Bower, Tim

Horton, Andy Bathgate, Jacques Plante, Harry Howell, Lynn Patrick, Pat LaFontaine, Harry Lumley, Gump Worsley, Allan Stanley, Rod Gilbert, Phil Esposito, Jean Ratelle, Ed Giacomin, Guy Lafleur, Buddy O'Connor, Brad Park, Clint Smith, Marcel Dionne, Edgar Laprade, Bun Cook, Wayne Gretzky, Mike Gartner, Jari Kurri; Builders (7): Herb Brooks, Bud Poile (played with Rangers, inducted as Builder), Emile Francis (also played for Rangers), William Jennings, John Kilpatrick, Roger Neilson, Craig Patrick, Glen Sather (played with Rangers, inducted as Builder), Carl Voss (played with Rangers, inducted as Builder)
Website: www.newyorkrangers.com
Minor League Affiliate(s): Hartford Wolf Pack (AHL), Charlotte Checkers (ECHL—shared with Ottawa)
Stanley Cups: (4) 1927–28, 1932–33, 1939–40, 1993–94
Hosted All-Star Game: (2) 1973, 1994
2006 Olympians: Marcel Hossa (SVK), Jaromir Jagr (CZE), Darius Kasparaitis (RUS), Henrik Lundqvist (SWE), Marek Malik (CZE), Ville Nieminen (FIN), Martin Rucinsky (CZE), Martin Straka (CZE), Fedor Tyutin (RUS)
1st Overall Draft Choices: none

OTTAWA SENATORS

First Game Played: October 8, 1992
Montreal Canadiens 3 at Ottawa Senators 5
Nickname Provenance: from original team of same name from 1917–34
Mascot: Spartacat
Arena History: Civic Centre, 1992–96; Palladium, 1996; Corel Centre, 1996–2006; Scotiabank Place, 2006–present (same building as Palladium and Corel Centre, capacity 18,500)
Retired Numbers: Frank Finnigan (8)
Hall of Famers: none
Website: www.ottawasenators.com

Minor League Affiliate(s): Binghampton Senators (AHL), Charlotte Checkers (ECHL—shared with NY Rangers)
Stanley Cups: none
Hosted All-Star Game: none
2006 Olympians: Daniel Alfredsson (SWE), Zdeno Chara (SVK), Dominik Hasek (CZE), Dany Heatley (CAN), Andrej Meszaros (SVK), Wade Redden (CAN), Christoph Schubert (GER), Anton Volchenkov (RUS)
1st Overall Draft Choices: 1993 (Alexandre Daigle), 1995 (Bryan Berard), 1996 (Chris Phillips)

PHILADELPHIA FLYERS

First Game Played: October 11, 1967
Philadelphia Flyers 1 at Oakland Seals 5
Nickname Provenance: named by a nine-year-old in a fan contest
Mascot: none
Arena History: The Spectrum, 1967–96; CoreStates Center, 1996–98; First Union Center, 1998–2003 (same building as CoreStates Center); Wachovia Center, 2003–present (same building as First Union Center, capacity 19,523)
Retired Numbers: Bernie Parent (1), Barry Ashbee (4), Bill Barber (7), Bobby Clarke (16)
Hall of Famers: Players (4): Paul Coffey, Bernie Parent, Bobby Clarke, Bill Barber, Dale Hawerchuk, Darryl Sittler, Allan Stanley; Builders (2): Ed Snider, Keith Allen
Website: www.philadelphiaflyers.com
Minor League Affiliate(s): Philadelphia Phantoms (AHL), Trenton Titans (ECHL)
Stanley Cups: (2) 1973–74, 1974–75
Hosted All-Star Game: (2) 1976, 1992
2006 Olympians: Robert Esche (USA), Peter Forsberg (SWE), Simon Gagne (CAN), Derian Hatcher (USA), Mike Knuble (USA), Antero Niittymaki (FIN)
1st Overall Draft Choices: 1975 (Mel Bridgman)

PHOENIX COYOTES

First Game Played:

As Winnipeg Jets: October 10, 1979

Winnipeg Jets 2 at Pittsburgh Penguins 4

As Phoenix Coyotes: October 5, 1996

Phoenix Coyotes 0 at Hartford Whalers 1

Nickname Provenance: the logo depicts a Kachina coyote, indigenous to the region

Mascot: none

Arena History: Winnipeg Arena (Winnipeg), 1979–96; America West Arena, 1996–98; Cellular One Ice Den (same building as America West Arena), 1998–99; America West Arena, 1999–2000; ALLTEL Ice Den, 2000–03; Glendale Arena, 2003–present (capacity 17,799)

Retired Numbers: Bobby Hull (9), Thomas Steen (25)

Hall of Famers: Players (3): Mike Gartner, Bobby Hull (Winnipeg), Dale Hawerchuk (Winnipeg), Serge Savard (Winnipeg)

Website: www.phoenixcoyotes.com

Minor League Affiliate(s): San Antonio Rampage (AHL), Stockton Thunder (ECHL), Laredo Bucks (CHL)

Stanley Cups: none

Hosted All-Star Game: none

2006 Olympians: Shane Doan (CAN), Dennis Seidenberg (GER)

1st Overall Draft Choices: 1981 (Dale Hawerchuk—Winnipeg Jets)

PITTSBURGH PENGUINS

First Game Played: October 11, 1967

Montreal Canadiens 2 at Pittsburgh Penguins 1

Mascot: Iceburgh

Arena History: Civic Arena ("The Igloo"), 1967–2000; Mellon Arena, 2000–present (same building as Civic Arena, capacity 16,940)

Retired Numbers: Michel Briere (21), Mario Lemieux (66)

Hall of Famers: Players (8): Leo Boivin, Paul Coffey, Tim Horton, Red Kelly (inducted as Player, associated with Pittsburgh as

Builder), Andy Bathgate, Mario Lemieux, Larry Murphy, Bryan
Trottier, Joe Mullen; Builders (4): Scotty Bowman, Bob Johnson,
Craig Patrick, Glen Sather (played for Pittsburgh, inducted as
Builder)

Website: www.pittsburghpenguins.com

Minor League Affiliate(s): Wilkes-Barre/Scranton Penguins
(AHL), Wheeling Nailers (ECHL)

Stanley Cups: (2) 1990–91, 1991–92

Hosted All-Star Game: 1990

2006 Olympians: Sergei Gonchar (RUS), Tomas Surovy (SVK)

1st Overall Draft Choices: 1984 (Mario Lemieux), 2003 (Marc-
Andre Fleury), 2005 (Sidney Crosby)

ST. LOUIS BLUES

First Game Played: October 11, 1967
Minnesota North Stars 2 at St. Louis Blues 2

Nickname Provenance: named to remember the city's place in
the history of music

Mascot: none

Arena History: St. Louis Arena, 1967–94; Kiel Center, 1994–2000;
Savvis Center, 2000–present (same building as Kiel Center, capacity
19,022)

Retired Numbers: Al MacInnis (2), Bob Gassoff (3), Barclay Plager
(8), Brian Sutter (11), Bernie Federko (24)

Hall of Famers: Players (11): Grant Fuhr, Bernie Federko, Dale
Hawerchuk, Joe Mullen, Wayne Gretzky, Peter Stastny, Guy
Lapointe, Jacques Plante, Glenn Hall, Dickie Moore, Doug Harvey;
Builders (5): Roger Neilson, Al Arbour, Scotty Bowman, Emile
Francis, Craig Patrick (played for St. Louis, inducted as Builder),
Lynn Patrick, Glen Sather (played for St. Louis, inducted as Builder)

Website: www.stlouisblues.com

Minor League Affiliate(s): Peoria Rivermen (AHL),
Alaska Aces (ECHL)

Stanley Cups: none

Hosted All-Star Game: (2) 1970, 1988
2006 Olympians: Christian Backman (SWE), Petr Cajanek (CZE),
Keith Tkachuk (USA), Doug Weight (USA)
1st Overall Draft Choices: none

SAN JOSE SHARKS

First Game Played: October 4, 1991
San Jose Sharks 3 at Vancouver Canucks 4
Nickname Provenance: named by team owners after a fan contest
Mascot: S.J. Sharkie (b. January 1992)
Arena History: Cow Palace, 1991–93; San Jose Arena, 1993–2001;
Compaq Center, 2001–03; HP Pavilion, 2003–present (same build-
ing as Compaq Center and San Jose Arena, capacity 17,496)
Retired Numbers: none
Hall of Famers: none
Website: www.sjsharks.com
Minor League Affiliate(s): Cleveland Barons (AHL), Fresno
Falcons (ECHL), Toledo Storm (ECHL)
Stanley Cups: none
Hosted All-Star Game: 1997
2006 Olympians: Christian Ehrhoff (GER), Marcel Goc (GER),
Evgeni Nabokov (RUS), Joe Thornton (CAN)
1st Overall Draft Choices: none

TAMPA BAY LIGHTNING

First Game Played: October 7, 1992
Chicago Blackhawks 3 at Tampa Bay Lightning 7
Mascot: Thunder Bug
Arena History: Expo Hall, 1992–93; ThunderDome, 1993–96
(five home games played at Orlando Arena); Ice Palace,
1998–2003; *St. Pete Times* Forum, 2003–present (same building as
Ice Palace, capacity 19,758)
Retired Numbers: none

Hall of Famers: Players (1): Denis Savard
Website: www.tampabaylightning.com
Minor League Affiliate(s): Springfield Falcons (AHL), Johnstown Chiefs (ECHL)
Stanley Cups: 2003–04
Hosted All-Star Game: 1999
2006 Olympians: John Grahame (USA), Pavel Kubina (CZE), Vincent Lecavalier (CAN), Fredrik Modin (SWE), Vaclav Prospal (CZE), Brad Richards (CAN), Martin St. Louis (CAN)
1st Overall Draft Choices: 1992 (Roman Hamrlik), 1998 (Vincent Lecavalier)

TORONTO MAPLE LEAFS

First Game Played:
As Toronto Arenas: December 19, 1917
Toronto Arenas 9 at Montreal Wanderers 10
As Toronto St. Pats: December 23, 1919
Toronto St. Pats 0 at Ottawa Senators 5
As Toronto Maple Leafs: February 17, 1927
New York Americans 1 at Toronto Maple Leafs 4
Nickname Provenance: named by owner Conn Smythe after a World War I regiment
Mascot: Carlton the Bear
Arena History: Arena Gardens (Mutual Street Arena), 1917–31; Maple Leaf Gardens, 1931–99; Air Canada Centre, 1999–present (capacity 18,819)
Retired Numbers: Bill Barilko (5), Ace Bailey (6)
Honoured Numbers: Turk Broda (1), Johnny Bower (1), King Clancy (7), Tim Horton (7), Charlie Conacher (9), Ted Kennedy (9), Syl Apps (10), George Armstrong (10), Frank Mahovlich (27), Darryl Sittler (27)
Hall of Famers: Players (58): Jack Adams, Syl Apps, Al Arbour, George Armstrong, Ace Bailey, Andy Bathgate, Max Bentley, Leo

Boivin, Johnny Bower, Turk Broda, Harry Cameron, Gerry Cheevers, King Clancy, Sprague Cleghorn, Charlie Conacher, Rusty Crawford, Hap Day, Gord Drillon, Dick Duff, Babe Dye, Fern Flaman, Grant Fuhr, Mike Gartner, Eddie Gerard, George Hainsworth, Harry Holmes, Red Horner, Tim Horton, Syd Howe, Harvey Jackson, Red Kelly, Ted Kennedy, Dave Keon, Harry Lumley, Frank Mahovlich, Lanny McDonald, Dickie Moore, Larry Murphy, Frank Nighbor, Reg Noble, Bert Olmstead, Bernie Parent, Pierre Pilote, Jacques Plante, Babe Pratt, Joe Primeau, Marcel Pronovost, Bob Pulford, Borje Salming, Terry Sawchuk, Sweeney Schriner, Darryl Sittler, Allan Stanley, Norm Ullman, Carl Voss, Harry Watson; Builders (9): Harold Ballard, J.P. Bickell, Cliff Fletcher, Foster Hewitt, William Hewitt, Punch Imlach, Dick Irvin (played for Toronto, inducted as Builder), Frank Mathers (played for Toronto, inducted as Builder), Rudy Pilous, Bud Poile (played for Toronto, inducted as Builder), Frank Selke, Conn Smythe
Website: www.torontomapleleafs.com
Minor League Affiliate(s): Toronto Marlies (AHL), Pensacola Ice Pilots (ECHL)
Stanley Cups: (13) 1917–18, 1921–22, 1931–32, 1941–42, 1944–45, 1946–47, 1947–48, 1948–49, 1950–51, 1961–62, 1962–63, 1963–64, 1966–67
Hosted All-Star Game: (8) 1947, 1949, 1951, 1962, 1963, 1964, 1968, 2000
2006 Olympians: Nikolai Antropov (KAZ), Aki Berg (FIN), Tomas Kaberle (CZE), Bryan McCabe (CAN), Mats Sundin (SWE), Mikael Tellqvist (SWE)
1st Overall Draft Choices: 1985 (Wendel Clark)

VANCOUVER CANUCKS

First Game Played: October 9, 1970
Los Angeles Kings 3 at Vancouver Canucks 1
Nickname Provenance: continuation of WHL franchise nickname
Mascot: none

Arena History: Pacific Coliseum, 1970–95; General Motors (GM) Place, 1995–present (capacity 18,630)

Retired Numbers: Wayne Maki (11, unofficial, later worn by Mark Messier but not before or since), Stan Smyl (12)

Hall of Famers: Cam Neely

Website: www.canucks.com

Minor League Affiliate(s): Manitoba Moose (AHL), Columbia Inferno (ECHL)

Stanley Cups: none

Hosted All-Star Game: (2) 1977, 1998

2006 Olympians: Todd Bertuzzi (CAN), Mattias Ohlund (SWE), Jarkko Ruutu (FIN), Sami Salo (FIN), Daniel Sedin (SWE), Henrik Sedin (SWE)

1st Overall Draft Choices: none

WASHINGTON CAPITALS

First Game Played: October 9, 1974
Washington Capitals 3 at New York Rangers 6

Nickname Provenance: so called because the team plays in the capital city of the USA

Mascot: Slapshot

Arena History: Capital Center, 1974–93; US Air Arena, 1993–95; MCI Center, 1995–present (same building as US Air Arena, capacity 18,277)

Retired Numbers: Rod Langway (5), Yvon Labre (7), Dale Hunter (32)

Hall of Famers: Players (3): Mike Gartner, Rod Langway, Larry Murphy; Builders (1): Craig Patrick (played for Washington, inducted as Builder)

Website: www.washingtoncaps.com

Minor League Affiliate(s): Hershey Bears (AHL), South Carolina Stingrays (ECHL)

Stanley Cups: none

Hosted All-Star Game: 1982

2006 Olympians: Olaf Kolzig (GER), Ivan Majesky (SVK), Alexander Ovechkin (RUS)
1st Overall Draft Choices: 1974 (Greg Joly), 1976 (Rick Green), Alexander Ovechkin (2005)

FINAL STANDINGS, REGULAR SEASON, 2005–06

EASTERN CONFERENCE

Northeast Division	GP	W	L	OTL	SOL	GF	GA	P
Ottawa Senators	82	52	21	3	6	314	211	113
Buffalo Sabres	82	52	24	1	5	281	239	110
Montreal Canadiens	82	42	31	6	3	243	247	93
Toronto Maple Leafs	82	41	33	1	7	257	270	90
Boston Bruins	82	29	37	8	8	230	266	74

Atlantic Division								
New Jersey Devils	82	46	27	5	4	242	229	101
Philadelphia Flyers	82	45	26	5	6	267	259	101
New York Rangers	82	44	26	8	4	257	215	100
New York Islanders	82	36	40	3	3	230	278	78
Pittsburgh Penguins	82	22	46	8	6	244	316	58

Southeast Division								
Carolina Hurricanes	82	52	22	6	2	294	260	112
Tampa Bay Lightning	82	43	33	2	4	252	260	92
Atlanta Thrashers	82	41	33	3	5	281	275	90
Florida Panthers	82	37	34	6	5	240	257	85
Washington Capitals	82	29	41	6	6	237	306	70

WESTERN CONFERENCE

Central Division	GP	W	L	OTL	SOL	GF	GA	P
Detroit Red Wings	82	58	16	5	3	305	209	124
Nashville Predators	82	49	25	5	3	259	227	106
Columbus Blue Jackets	82	35	43	1	3	223	279	74
Chicago Blackhawks	82	26	43	7	6	211	285	65
St. Louis Blues	82	21	46	6	9	197	292	57

Northwest Division	GP	W	L	OTL	SOL	GF	GA	P
Calgary Flames	82	46	25	4	7	218	200	103
Colorado Avalanche	82	43	30	3	6	283	257	95
Edmonton Oilers	82	41	28	4	9	256	251	95
Vancouver Canucks	82	42	32	4	4	256	255	92
Minnesota Wild	82	38	36	5	3	231	215	84

Pacific Division	GP	W	L	OTL	SOL	GF	GA	P
Dallas Stars	82	53	23	5	1	265	218	112
San Jose Sharks	82	44	27	4	7	266	242	99
Mighty Ducks of Anaheim	82	43	27	5	7	254	229	98
Los Angeles Kings	82	42	35	4	1	249	270	89
Phoenix Coyotes	82	38	39	2	3	246	271	81

SCORING LEADERS & GOALIE LEADERS, 2005–06

(Nationality and NHL affiliation in brackets)

Points

	GP	G	A	P	PIM
Joe Thornton (CAN–BOS/SJ)	81	29	96	125	61
Jaromir Jagr (CZE–NYR)	82	54	69	123	72
Alexander Ovechkin (RUS–WAS)	81	52	54	106	52
Dany Heatley (CAN–OTT)	82	50	53	103	86
Daniel Alfredsson (SWE–OTT)	77	43	60	103	50
Sidney Crosby (CAN–PIT)	81	39	63	102	110
Eric Staal (CAN–CAR)	82	45	55	100	81
Ilya Kovalchuk (RUS–ATL)	78	52	46	98	68
Marc Savard (CAN–ATL)	82	28	69	97	100
Jonathan Cheechoo (CAN–SJ)	82	56	37	93	58

Goals

Jonathan Cheechoo (CAN–SJ)	56
Jaromir Jagr (CZE–NYR)	54
Alexander Ovechkin (RUS–WAS)	52
Ilya Kovalchuk (RUS–ATL)	52
Dany Heatley (CAN–OTT)	50
Brian Gionta (USA–NJ)	48
Simon Gagne (CAN–PHI)	47
Eric Staal (CAN–CAR)	45
Daniel Alfredsson (SWE–OTT)	43
Teemu Selanne (FIN–ANA)	40
Brendan Shanahan (CAN–DET)	40

Assists

Joe Thornton (CAN–BOS/SJ)	96
Jason Spezza (CAN–OTT)	71
Jaromir Jagr (CZE–NYR)	69
Marc Savard (CAN–ATL)	69
Brad Richards (CAN–TB)	68
Nicklas Lidstrom (SWE–DET)	64
Sidney Crosby (CAN–PIT)	63
Daniel Alfredsson (SWE–OTT)	60
Pavel Datsyuk (RUS–DET)	59
Ales Hemsky (CZE–EDM)	58
Sergei Zubov (RUS–DAL)	58
Tomas Kaberle (CZE–TOR)	58

Penalty Minutes

Sean Avery (CAN–LA)	257
Brendan Witt (CAN–NAS)	209
Chris Neil (CAN–OTT)	204
Brenden Morrow (CAN–DAL)	183
Steve Ott (CAN–DAL)	178
Matthew Barnaby (CAN–CHI)	178
Todd Fedoruk (CAN–ANA)	174
Donald Brashear (USA–PHI)	166
Jody Shelley (CAN–CBJ)	163
Darcy Hordichuk (CAN–NAS)	163

Most Wins, Goalie

Martin Brodeur (CAN–NJ)	43
Miikka Kiprusoff (FIN–CAL)	42
Marty Turco (CAN–DAL)	41
Martin Gerber (SUI–CAR)	38
Manny Legace (CAN–DET)	37
Tomas Vokoun (CZE–NAS)	36

Roberto Luongo (CAN–FLO)   35
Alexander Auld (CAN–VAN)   33
Curtis Joseph (CAN–PHO)   32
Mathieu Garon (CAN–LA)   31

Most Losses, Goalie

Roberto Luongo (CAN–FLO)   30
Olaf Kolzig (GER–WAS)   28
Marc-Andre Fleury (CAN–PIT)   27
Alexander Auld (CAN–VAN)   26
Mathieu Garon (CAN–LA)   26
Nikolai Khabibulin (RUS–CHI)   26
Marc Denis (CAN–CBJ)   25
Rick DiPietro (USA–NYI)   24
Dwayne Roloson (CAN–EDM)   24
Martin Brodeur (CAN–NJ)   23

Best GAA

Miikka Kiprusoff (FIN–CAL)   2.07
Dominik Hasek (CZE–OTT)   2.09
Manny Legace (CAN–DET)   2.19
Cristobal Huet (FRA–MON)   2.20
Henrik Lundqvist (SWE–NYR)   2.24
Manny Fernandez (CAN–MIN)   2.29
Ilja Bryzgalov (RUS–ANA)   2.51
Marty Turco (CAN–DAL)   2.55
Vesa Toskala (FIN–SJ)   2.56
Martin Brodeur (CAN–NJ)   2.57

GOALIE SCORING STATISTICS, 2005-06

Goalie	G	A	P	Pim
David Aebischer	0	3	3	16
Craig Anderson	0	1	1	14
J-S Aubin	0	0	0	0
Alexander Auld	0	2	2	4
Jason Bacashihua	0	1	1	0
Ed Belfour	0	1	1	12
Adam Berkhoel	0	0	0	0
Martin Biron	0	1	1	10
Brian Boucher	0	0	0	2
Martin Brodeur	0	3	3	4
Ilja Bryzgalov	0	2	2	4
Peter Budaj	0	1	1	4
Sean Burke	0	1	1	10
Sebastien Caron	0	1	1	0
Frederic Cassivi	0	0	0	0
Scott Clemmensen	0	0	0	0
Dan Cloutier	0	0	0	4
Gerald Coleman	0	0	0	0
Ty Conklin	0	0	0	2
Corey Crawford	0	0	0	0
Yann Danis	0	0	0	0
Marc Denis	0	1	1	2
Rick DiPietro	0	1	1	28
Reinhard Divis	0	0	0	0
Wade Dubielewicz	0	0	0	0
Mike Dunham	0	0	0	0
Brian Eklund	0	0	0	0
Ray Emery	0	1	1	2
Robert Esche	0	3	3	4

Goalie	G	A	P	Pim
Manny Fernandez	0	3	3	6
Brian Finley	0	0	0	0
Marc-Andre Fleury	0	1	1	0
Michael Garnett	0	2	2	0
Mathieu Garon	0	3	3	8
Martin Gerber	0	2	2	4
J-S Giguere	0	0	0	20
John Grahame	0	1	1	14
Josh Harding	0	0	0	0
Dominik Hasek	0	0	0	16
Adam Hauser	0	0	0	0
Johan Hedberg	0	2	2	6
Chris Holt	0	0	0	0
James Howard	0	0	0	0
Cristobal Huet	0	0	0	0
Brent Johnson	0	0	0	14
Curtis Joseph	0	1	1	18
Nikolai Khabibulin	0	1	1	0
Miikka Kiprusoff	0	2	2	10
Vitaliy Kolesnik	0	1	1	2
Olaf Kolzig	0	3	3	14
Jason LaBarbera	0	1	1	0
Patrick Lalime	0	0	0	0
Pascal Leclaire	0	1	1	2
Manny Legace	0	1	1	0
Kari Lehtonen	0	1	1	4
David Leneveu	0	0	0	0
Henrik Lundqvist	0	2	2	0
Roberto Luongo	0	3	3	2
Jussi Markkanen	0	1	1	0
Chris Mason	1	0	1	0
Jamie McLennan	0	0	0	0

Goalie	G	A	P	Pim
Rob McVicar	0	0	0	0
Ryan Miller	0	2	2	0
Michael Morrison	0	1	1	2
Adam Munro	0	1	1	0
Evgeni Nabokov	0	1	1	18
Antero Niittymaki	0	1	1	0
Mika Noronen	0	0	0	2
Chris Osgood	0	0	0	8
Maxime Ouellet	0	0	0	2
Martin Prusek	0	0	0	0
Andrew Raycroft	0	0	0	0
Pekka Rinne	0	0	0	0
Dwayne Roloson	0	1	1	8
Dany Sabourin	0	0	0	0
Curtis Sanford	0	0	0	0
Philippe Sauve	0	0	0	21
Nolan Schaefer	0	0	0	2
Steve Shields	0	0	0	0
Jordan Sigalet	0	0	0	0
Garth Snow	0	0	0	2
Mikael Tellqvist	0	0	0	0
Jose Theodore	0	1	1	2
Jocelyn Thibault	0	0	0	2
Tim Thomas	0	1	1	4
Hannu Toivonen	0	0	0	6
Vesa Toskala	0	1	1	4
Marty Turco	0	2	2	28
Tomas Vokoun	0	2	2	26
Cam Ward	0	2	2	0
Kevin Weekes	0	1	1	4

PLAYER SHOOTOUT STATISTICS, 2005–06

Here is an A–Z guide of all shootout shots by player. A letter W or L after the goalie's name indicates that the shot was a deciding one. An asterisk (∗) after "goal" means that the shooter scored the game-winning shot. At the end of each player's complete list are his final stats: goals–misses–total shots.

					TOTALS
Afanasenkov	Dimitry	TB	Olaf Kolzig (WAS)	miss	0–1–1
Afinogenov	Maxim	BUF	Antero Niittymaki (PHI) L	goal∗	
			Brian Boucher (PHO)	miss	
			Martin Gerber (CAR)	goal	
			Henrik Lundqvist (NYR)	miss	
			J-S Aubin (TOR) L	goal∗	3–2–5
Alfredsson	Daniel	OTT	Ed Belfour (TOR) L	goal∗	
			Ed Belfour (TOR)	miss	
			Alexander Auld (VAN)	goal	
			Cristobal Huet (MON) W	miss	
			J-S Giguere (ANA)	miss	
			Ryan Miller (BUF) W	miss	
			Tim Thomas (BOS)	miss	
			Martin Brodeur (NJ) W	miss	2–6–8
Allison	Jason	TOR	Dominik Hasek (OTT)	miss	
			Dominik Hasek (OTT) W	miss	
			Andrew Raycroft (BOS)	miss	0–3–3
Amonte	Tony	CAL	Nolan Schaefer (SJ)	miss	
			Peter Budaj (COL) L	goal∗	
			Mike Morrison (EDM)	miss	
			Antero Niittymaki (PHI)	miss	
			Alexander Auld (VAN)	goal	
			Curtis Sanford (STL)	goal	
			Marc Denis (CBJ)	miss	
			Jason LaBarbera (LA)	miss	3–5–8
Arnason	Tyler	CHI	Peter Budaj (COL)	goal	
			John Grahame (TB) W	miss	

35

Arnason	*(cont'd)*		Martin Brodeur (NJ) W	miss	1–2–3
Arnott	Jason	DAL	Nikolai Khabibulin (CHI)	miss	0–1–1
Asham	Arron	NYI	Jocelyn Thibault (PIT)	miss	0–1–1
Axelsson	P-J	BOS	Henrik Lundqvist (NYR)	miss	0–1–1
Balastik	Jaroslav	CBJ	Manny Fernandez (MIN) L	goal*	
			Chris Osgood (DET)	goal	
			David Aebischer (COL)	goal	
			Curtis Sanford (STL)	miss	
			Miikka Kiprusoff (CAL) L	goal*	
			Jussi Markkanen (EDM)	goal	
			J-S Giguere (ANA)	miss	
			Chris Osgood (DET) L	goal*	
			Manny Legace (DET)	miss	6–3–9
Barnaby	Matthew	CHI	Johan Hedberg (DAL)	goal	
			Chris Mason (NAS)	miss	1–1–2
Bates	Shawn	NYI	Jocelyn Thibault (PIT)	goal	
			Martin Brodeur (NJ)	miss	
			Sebastien Caron (PIT)	goal	2–1–3
Bell	Mark	CHI	John Grahame (TB)	miss	
			Johan Hedberg (DAL)	miss	0–2–2
Berard	Bryan	CBJ	Dwayne Roloson (MIN)	miss	0–1–1
Bergeron	Patrice	BOS	Ed Belfour (TOR) W	miss	
			Marty Turco (DAL)	miss	
			Henrik Lundqvist (NYR)	goal	
			Martin Gerber (CAR)	miss	
			Mikael Tellqvist (TOR)	miss	
			Ray Emery (OTT) L	goal*	
			Kari Lehtonen (ATL)	miss	
			Roberto Luongo (FLO)	miss	
			J-S Aubin (TOR)	miss	2–7–9
Bernier	Steve	SJ	Marty Turco (DAL)	miss	0–1–1
Bertuzzi	Todd	VAN	Jussi Markkanen (EDM) W	miss	
			Dominik Hasek (OTT)	goal	
			Mathieu Garon (LA)	miss	

			Miikka Kiprusoff (CAL) W	miss	
			Dwayne Roloson (EDM) L	goal*	2–3–5
Betts	Blair	NYR	Olaf Kolzig (WAS)	miss	0–1–1
Blake	Jason	NYI	Jocelyn Thibault (PIT) L	goal*	
			Martin Biron (BUF) W	miss	
			Jussi Markkanen (EDM)	miss	
			Martin Brodeur (NJ)	miss	
			Sebastien Caron (PIT)	goal	2–3–5
Bondra	Peter	ATL	Olaf Kolzig (WAS) W	miss	
			Jose Theodore (MON)	miss	
			Tim Thomas (BOS)	miss	0–3–3
Bouchard	Pierre-Marc	MIN	Martin Prusek (CBJ)	miss	0–1–1
Bourque	Rene	CHI	Michael Garnett (ATL)	miss	
			John Grahame (TB)	goal	
			Curtis Sanford (STL)	miss	
			Johan Hedberg (DAL)	miss	
			Alexander Auld (VAN)	miss	1–4–5
Boyes	Brad	BOS	Henrik Lundqvist (NYR)	miss	
			Martin Gerber (CAR)	goal	
			Mikael Tellqvist (TOR)	miss	
			Kari Lehtonen (ATL)	miss	
			Roberto Luongo (FLO) W	miss	
			J-S Aubin (TOR) L	goal*	2–4–6
Bradley	Matt	WAS	Henrik Lundqvist (NYR) W	miss	0–1–1
Briere	Daniel	BUF	John Grahame (TB) L	goal*	
			Kevin Weekes (NYR)	goal	
			Henrik Lundqvist (NYR)	miss	
			J-S Aubin (TOR)	miss	2–2–4
Brind'Amour	Rod	CAR	Antero Niittymaki (PHI) L	goal*	
			Roberto Luongo (FLO)	miss	
			Tim Thomas (BOS)	miss	
			Ryan Miller (BUF)	miss	1–3–4
Brunette	Andrew	COL	Martin Brodeur (NJ)	miss	0–1–1

Brylin	Sergei	NJ	Vitaly Kolesnik (COL)	miss	
			Rick DiPietro (NYI)	miss	
			Olaf Kolzig (WAS) L	goal*	1–2–3
Byfuglien	Dustin	CHI	Johan Hedberg (DAL)	miss	0–1–1
Cajanek	Peter	STL	Tomas Vokoun (NAS)	miss	
			Evgeni Nabokov (SJ) L	goal*	
			Olaf Kolzig (WAS)	miss	
			Miikka Kiprusoff (CAL)	miss	
			Mathieu Garon (LA)	miss	
			Josh Harding (MIN) W	miss	1–5–6
Calder	Kyle	CHI	Johan Hedberg (DAL) W	miss	0–1–1
Cammalleri	Mike	LA	J-S Giguere (ANA)	miss	0–1–1
Carter	Anson	VAN	David Aebischer (COL)	miss	0–1–1
Carter	Jeff	PHI	Miikka Kiprusoff (CAL)	miss	
			Ryan Miller (BUF)	miss	
			Martin Gerber (CAR) W	miss	0–3–3
Cassels	Andrew	WAS	Henrik Lundqvist (NYR)	goal	
			Michael Garnett (ATL)	miss	1–1–2
Cheechoo	Jonathan	SJ	Miikka Kiprusoff (CAL)	miss	
			Marty Turco (DAL) W	miss	
			Mike Morrison (EDM) W	miss	
			Jason Bacashihua (STL)	goal	
			Manny Fernandez (MIN)	miss	
			Marty Turco (DAL)	miss	1–5–6
Chimera	Jason	CBJ	Jussi Markkanen (EDM) L	goal*	1–0–1
Chouinard	Marc	MIN	Martin Prusek (CBJ)	miss	0–1–1
Christensen	Erik	PIT	Rick DiPietro (NYI)	goal	1–0–1
Clark	Chris	WAS	Henrik Lundqvist (NYR)	miss	0–1–1
Clymer	Ben	WAS	Henrik Lundqvist (NYR)	miss	
			Martin Brodeur (NJ) W	miss	0–2–2
Cole	Erik	CAR	Roberto Luongo (FLO) L	goal*	
			Tim Thomas (BOS)	miss	
			Ryan Miller (BUF)	miss	1–2–3
Comrie	Mike	PHO	Evgeni Nabokov (SJ)	goal	
			Martin Biron (BUF)	miss	

			Jussi Markkanen (EDM)	miss	
			Mike Morrison (EDM)	miss	1–3–4
Connolly	Tim	BUF	John Grahame (TB)	miss	
			Rick DiPietro (NYI)	goal	
			Brian Boucher (PHO)	miss	
			Antero Niittymaki (PHI)	goal	
			J-S Aubin (TOR)	miss	2–3–5
Conroy	Craig	LA	J-S Giguere (ANA)	miss	0–1–1
Corvo	Joe	LA	Alexander Auld (VAN)	miss	
			J-S Giguere (ANA) L	goal*	
			Patrick Lalime (STL)	miss	1–2–3
Crosby	Sidney	PIT	Cam Ward (CAR)	miss	
			Jose Theodore (MON) L	goal*	
			Rick DiPietro (NYI)	goal	
			Wade Dubielewicz (NYI)	miss	
			John Grahame (TB) W	miss	
			Rick DiPietro (NYI)	miss	2–4–6
Cullen	Mark	CHI	Johan Hedberg (DAL)	miss	0–1–1
		CAR	Sebastien Caron (PIT)	miss	
			Mikael Tellqvist (TOR)	goal	
			Johan Hedberg (DAL)	goal	
			Antero Niittymaki (PHI)	goal	
			Roberto Luongo (FLO)	miss	
			Ryan Miller (BUF)	goal	
			Antero Niittymaki (PHI)	miss	
			Brent Johnson (WAS) L	goal*	
			Sean Burke (TB) L	goal*	6–3–9
Czerkawski	Mariusz	BOS	Ray Emery (OTT)	miss	
			Kari Lehtonen (ATL)	miss	0–2–2
Dagenais	Pierre	MON	Dominik Hasek (OTT) L	goal*	
			Steve Shields (ATL) L	goal*	2–0–2
Daigle	Alexandre	MIN	Martin Prusek (CBJ) W	miss	0–1–1
Datsyuk	Pavel	DET	Pascal Leclaire (CBJ)	goal	
			Marty Turco (DAL)	miss	
			Dwayne Roloson (EDM)	miss	

Datsuk	*(cont'd)*		Tomas Vokoun (NAS)	goal	
			Pascal Leclaire (CBJ)	miss	
			Miikka Kiprusoff (CAL) L	goal*	3–3–6
Demitra	Pavol	LA	Tomas Vokoun (NAS) L	goal*	
			J-S Giguere (ANA) L	goal*	
			Alexander Auld (VAN)	miss	
			Curtis Joseph (PHO)	miss	
			Miikka Kiprusoff (CAL) L	goal*	3–2–5
de Vries	Greg	ATL	Nikolai Khabibulin (CHI)	miss	
			Tim Thomas (BOS)	miss	0–2–2
Dimitrakos	Niko	SJ	Mike Morrison (EDM)	miss	
			Curtis Joseph (PHO)	goal	
			Manny Fernandez (MIN)	miss	1–2–3
Doan	Shane	PHO	Evgeni Nabokov (SJ)	miss	
			Mike Morrison (EDM)	goal	
			Mathieu Garon (LA)	miss	1–2–3
Drury	Chris	BUF	Kevin Weekes (NYR)	miss	0–1–1
Dumont	J-P	BUF	Martin Gerber (CAR)	miss	0–1–1
Dvorak	Radek	EDM	Curtis Joseph (PHO) L	goal*	
			Marc Denis (CBJ)	miss	1–1–2
Eaves	Patrick	OTT	J-S Giguere (ANA) W	miss	0–1–1
Ekman	Nils	SJ	Miikka Kiprusoff (CAL) L	goal*	
			Curtis Joseph (PHO) W	miss	
			Jason Bacashihua (STL) W	miss	
			Mike Morrison (EDM)	goal	
			Manny Fernandez (MIN)	miss	
			Marty Turco (DAL) W	miss	2–4–6
Elias	Patrik	NJ	Rick DiPietro (NYI)	goal	
			Adam Munro (CHI)	goal	
			Tomas Vokoun (NAS)	miss	
			Olaf Kolzig (WAS)	miss	
			Ray Emery (OTT)	miss	2–3–5
Eminger	Steve	WAS	Henrik Lundqvist (NYR)	miss	0–1–1
Erat	Martin	NAS	Manny Legace (DET) L	goal*	
			Craig Anderson (CHI) L	goal*	2–0–2

Fedorov	Sergei	ANA	Tomas Vokoun (NAS)	miss	
		CBJ	Manny Fernandez (MIN)	miss	
			Rick DiPietro (NYI)	miss	
			Chris Osgood (DET) W	miss	
			Jussi Markkanen (EDM)	miss	0–5–5
Fedotenko	Ruslan	TB	Olaf Kolzig (WAS)	miss	0–1–1
Fisher	Mike	OTT	Alexander Auld (VAN) W	miss	
			Ryan Miller (BUF)	miss	0–2–2
Fleischmann	Tomas	WAS	John Grahame (TB) W	miss	
			Henrik Lundqvist (NYR)	miss	0–2–2
Forsberg	Peter	PHI	Ryan Miller (BUF)	goal	
			Roberto Luongo (FLO)	miss	
			Olaf Kolzig (WAS) W	miss	
			Martin Brodeur (NJ) W	miss	
			Cristobal Huet (MON)	goal	
			Martin Gerber (CAR)	goal	
			Kevin Weekes (NYR)	miss	3–4–7
Fritsche	Dan	CBJ	Dwayne Roloson (MIN)	miss	0–1–1
Frolov	Alexander	LA	J-S Giguere (ANA)	goal	
			Alexander Auld (VAN) L	goal*	
			J-S Giguere (ANA)	goal	
			Curtis Joseph (PHO)	miss	3–1–4
Gaborik	Marian	MIN	Pascal Leclaire (CBJ) W	miss	
			Martin Brodeur (NJ)	miss	
			Vesa Toskala (SJ)	miss	
			Alexander Auld (VAN)	miss	
			Reinhard Divis (STL)	miss	
			Dwayne Roloson (EDM)	miss	0–6–6
Gagne	Simon	PHI	Tomas Vokoun (NSH)	miss	
			Roberto Luongo (FLO)	miss	
			Martin Gerber (CAR)	miss	
			Cristobal Huet (MON)	miss	
			Martin Gerber (CAR) L	goal*	
			Kevin Weekes (NYR)	goal	2–4–6

Gamache	Simon	NAS	David LeNeveu (PHO)	miss	
			Jason LaBarbera (LA)	miss	0–2–2
Gelinas	Martin	FLO	Martin Gerber (CAR) W	miss	0–1–1
Getzlaf	Ryan	ANA	Manny Fernandez (MIN) W	miss	
			Mathieu Garon (LA) W	miss	0–2–2
Gionta	Brian	NJ	Kevin Weekes (NYR)	goal	
			Vitaly Kolesnik (COL)	miss	
			Ty Conklin (EDM)	goal	
			Adam Munro (CHI)	miss	
			Tomas Vokoun (NAS)	goal	
			Rick DiPietro (NYI)	miss	
			Rick DiPietro (NYI)	miss	
			Olaf Kolzig (WAS)	miss	
			Ray Emery (OTT)	miss	
			Hannu Toivonen (BOS) L	goal*	4–6–10
Gomez	Scott	NJ	Vitaly Kolesnik (COL)	miss	
			Olaf Kolzig (WAS)	goal	
			Ray Emery (OTT) L	goal*	2–1–3
Gonchar	Sergei	PIT	Rick DiPietro (NYI)	goal	1–0–1
Guerin	Bill	DAL	Curtis Joseph (PHO)	goal	1–0–1
Halpern	Jeff	WAS	John Grahame (TB)	miss	
			Henrik Lundqvist (NYR)	miss	0–2–2
Handzus	Michal	PHI	Roberto Luongo (FLO) L	goal*	
			Olaf Kolzig (WAS)	miss	
			Martin Gerber (CAR)	miss	
			Kevin Weekes (NYR) W	miss	2–2–4
Hartigan	Mark	CBJ	Dwayne Roloson (MIN)	goal	
			Manny Legace (DET)	miss	1–1–2
Havlat	Martin	OTT	Ed Belfour (TOR)	miss	0–1–1
Heatley	Dany	OTT	Ed Belfour (TOR)	goal*	
			Ed Belfour (TOR)	goal*	
			Alexander Auld (VAN)	miss	
			Cristobal Huet (MON)	miss	
			J-S Giguere (ANA)	miss	

			Ryan Miller (BUF)	miss	
			Tim Thomas (BOS)	miss	
			Martin Brodeur (NJ)	miss	2–6–8
Hedstrom	Jonathan	ANA	Dominik Hasek (OTT)	miss	
			Marty Turco (DAL)	goal	1–1–2
Hejduk	Milan	COL	Marty Turco (DAL)	miss	
			Philippe Sauve (CAL)	miss	
			Martin Brodeur (NJ)	miss	
			Pascal Leclaire (CBJ)	miss	
			Alexander Auld (VAN) W	miss	
			Curtis Sanford (STL) L	goal*	
			Dwayne Roloson (EDM)	miss	1–6–7
Hemsky	Ales	EDM	Dan Cloutier (VAN)	goal	
			Evgeni Nabokov (SJ)	goal	
			Miikka Kiprusoff (CAL)	miss	
			Rick DiPietro (NYI)	goal	
			Martin Brodeur (NJ) W	miss	
			Vesa Toskala (SJ)	miss	
			Curtis Joseph (PHO) W	miss	
			Curtis Joseph (PHO)	goal	
			Marc Denis (CBJ)	goal	
			J-S Giguere (ANA)	miss	
			Curtis Sanford (STL)	miss	
			Marty Turco (DAL)	miss	
			Alexander Auld (VAN)	miss	
			Manny Fernandez (MIN)	miss	5–9–14
Heward	Jamie	WAS	Henrik Lundqvist (NYR)	miss	0–1–1
Hilbert	Andy	PIT	Rick DiPietro (NYI)	miss	0–1–1
Hollweg	Ryan	NYR	Olaf Kolzig (WAS)	miss	0–1–1
Holmqvist	Mikael	CHI	Michael Garnett (ATL) L	goal*	
			Martin Brodeur (NJ)	goal	
			Curtis Sanford (STL) W	miss	
			Johan Hedberg (DAL)	miss	
			Alexander Auld (VAN) W	miss	2–3–5

Holmstrom	Tomas	DET	Marc Denis (CBJ) L	goal*	
			Tomas Vokoun (NAS)	miss	1–1–2
Horcoff	Shawn	EDM	Marc Denis (CBJ) W	miss	0–1–1
Horton	Nathan	FLO	Antero Niittymaki (PHI)	miss	
			Olaf Kolzig (WAS)	goal	
			Martin Gerber (CAR)	miss	
			Kari Lehtonen (ATL)	miss	
			Kevin Weekes (NYR)	goal	
			Tim Thomas (BOS)	miss	
			Brent Johnson (WAS)	miss	2–5–7
Hossa	Marcel	NYR	Olaf Kolzig (WAS)	miss	0–1–1
Hossa	Marian	ATL	Olaf Kolzig (WAS)	miss	
			Jose Theodore (MON) W	miss	
			Nikolai Khabibulin (CHI)	goal	
			Brent Johnson (WAS)	miss	
			Tomas Vokoun (NAS) L	goal*	
			Cristobal Huet (MON)	miss	
			Roberto Luongo (FLO)	miss	
			Henrik Lundqvist (NYR) L	goal*	
			Sean Burke (TB) W	miss	3–6–9
Hrdina	Jan	CBJ	Dwayne Roloson (MIN)	miss	
			Jussi Markkanen (EDM)	miss	0–2–2
Hunter	Trent	NYI	Marc-Andre Fleury (PIT)	goal	
			Martin Brodeur (NJ)	goal	
			Martin Brodeur (NJ) L	goal*	
			Ed Belfour (TOR) L	miss	
			Sebastien Caron (PIT)	miss	
			Jocelyn Thibault (PIT)	goal	
			Jussi Markkanen (EDM) L	goal*	
			Martin Brodeur (NJ) W	miss	
			Sebastien Caron (PIT)	miss	5–4–9
Huselius	Kristian	FLO	Henrik Lundqvist (NYR) W	miss	
		CAL	Antero Niittymaki (PHI) W	miss	
			Curtis Sanford (STL)	miss	0–3–3

Iginla	Jarome	CAL	Nolan Schaefer (SJ)		goal	
			Peter Budaj (COL)		miss	
			Mike Morrison (EDM)		miss	
			Antero Niittymaki (PHI)		miss	
			Alexander Auld (VAN)		miss	
			Curtis Sanford (STL)		miss	
			Marc Denis (CBJ)	W	miss	
			Chris Osgood (DET)	W	miss	
			Jason LaBarbera (LA)	W	miss	1–8–9
Isbister	Brad	BOS	Henrik Lundqvist (NYR)	W	miss	0–1–1
Jagr	Jaromir	NYR	Rick DiPietro (NYI)		miss	
			Scott Clemmensen (NJ)		miss	
			Roberto Luongo (FLO)		miss	
			Martin Biron (BUF)	L	goal*	
			Olaf Kolzig (WAS)		miss	
			Tim Thomas (BOS)		goal	
			Roberto Luongo (FLO)	W	miss	
			John Grahame (TB)		miss	2–6–8
Johnson	Mike	PHO	Mike Morrison (EDM)	W	miss	0–1–1
Jokinen	Jussi	DAL	Peter Budaj (COL)		goal	
			Evgeni Nabokov (SJ)		goal	
			Martin Gerber (CAR)		goal	
			J-S Giguere (ANA)		goal	
			Tim Thomas (BOS)	L	goal*	
			Curtis Sanford (STL)		goal	
			Peter Budaj (COL)	L	goal*	
			Manny Legace (DET)		goal	
			Mike Morrison (EDM)		goal	
			Vesa Toskala (SJ)		miss	
			Nikolai Khabibulin (CHI)		miss	
			J-S Giguere (ANA)	W	miss	
			Curtis Joseph (PHO)	L	goal*	10–3–13
Jokinen	Olli	FLO	Henrik Lundqvist (NYR)		miss	
			Antero Niittymaki (PHI)		miss	

Jokinen	*(cont'd)*		Olaf Kolzig (WAS)	miss	
			Martin Gerber (CAR)	goal	
			Kari Lehtonen (ATL)	miss	
			Olaf Kolzig (WAS)	miss	
			Kevin Weekes (NYR) L	goal*	
			Tim Thomas (BOS) L	goal*	
			Brent Johnson (WAS)	goal	4–5–9
Kapanen	Niko	DAL	Nikolai Khabibulin (CHI)	miss	0–1–1
Kariya	Paul	NAS	J-S Giguere (ANA) L	goal*	
			David LeNeveu (PHO) L	goal*	
			Antero Niittmaki (PHI)	goal*	
			Kari Lehtonen (ATL)	miss	
			Martin Brodeur (NJ) W	miss	
			Manny Legace (DET)	goal	
			Craig Anderson (CHI)	goal	5–2–7
Kesler	Ryan	VAN	Dominik Hasek (OTT)	miss	
			David Aebischer (COL)	miss	0–2–2
Klepis	Jakub	WAS	Mike Dunham (ATL)	miss	
			Henrik Lundqvist (NYR)	miss	0–2–2
Knuble	Mike	PHI	Tomas Vokoun (NSH)	miss	
			Ryan Miller (BUF) W	miss	0–2–2
Kobasew	Chuck	CAL	Nolan Schaefer (SJ) W	miss	
			Peter Budaj (COL)	miss	
			Mike Morrison (EDM) W	miss	
			Curtis Sanford (STL) W	miss	0–4–4
Koivu	Mikko	MIN	J-S Giguere (ANA)	goal	
			Pascal Leclaire (CBJ)	miss	
			Vesa Toskala (SJ)	miss	
			Reinhard Divis (STL)	goal	
			Dwayne Roloson (EM)	goal	
			Alexander Auld (VAN) L	goal*	4–2–6
Kolnik	Juraj	FLO	Henrik Lundqvist (NYR)	miss	0–1–1
Koltsov	Konstantin	PIT	Rick DiPietro (NYI)	miss	0–1–1
Kondratiev	Maxim	NYR	Olaf Kolzig (WAS)	miss	0–1–1

Kotalik	Ales	BUF	Kevin Weekes (NYR)	goal	
			Rick DiPietro (NYI) L	goal*	
			Antero Niittymaki (PHI)	miss	
			Ed Belfour (TOR)	miss	
			Dominik Hasek (OTT)	miss	
			Martin Gerber (CAR)	miss	2–4–6
Kovalchuk	Ilya	ATL	Olaf Kolzig (WAS)	miss	
			Jose Theodore (MON)	miss	
			Nikolai Khabibulin (CHI)	goal	
			Brent Johnson (WAS)	miss	
			Tomas Vokoun (NAS)	miss	
			Cristobal Huet (MON)	miss	
			Roberto Luongo (FLO)	miss	
			Henrik Lundqvist (NYR)	miss	
			Tim Thomas (BOS)	miss	
			Sean Burke (TB)	miss	1–9–10
Kovalev	Alexei	MON	Jocelyn Thibault (PIT)	miss	
			Dominik Hasek (MON)	goal	
			Kari Lehtonen (ATL)	miss	
			Robert Esche (PHI)	miss	1–3–4
Kozlov	Slava	ATL	Nikolai Khabibulin (CHI) W	miss	
			Brent Johnson (WAS) W	miss	
			Roberto Luongo (FLO) L	goal*	
			Henrik Lundqvist (NYR)	goal	
			Sean Burke (TB)	goal	
			Tim Thomas (BOS)	goal	
			Cristobal Huet (MON) L	goal*	5–2–7
Kozlov	Viktor	NJ	Rick DiPietro (NYI)	goal	
			Olaf Kolzig (WAS)	goal	
			Vitaly Kolesnik (COL)	miss	
			Ty Conklin (EDM) L	goal*	
			Hannu Toivonen (BOS)	goal	
			Kevin Weekes (NYR)	miss	
			Manny Fernandez (MIN) L	goal*	

Kozlov	*(cont'd)*		Adam Munro (CHI) L	goal*	
			Tomas Vokoun (NAS) L	goal*	
			Rick DiPietro (NYI)	miss	
			Robert Esche (PHI) L	goal*	
			Rick DiPietro (NYI)	miss	8–4–12
Kuba	Filip	MIN	Martin Prusek (CBJ)	miss	0–1–1
Kubina	Pavel	TB	Brent Johnson (WAS) W	miss	0–1–1
Kunitz	Chris	ANA	Curtis Sanford (STL) L	goal*	
			Johan Hedberg (DAL)	miss	
			Dominik Hasek (OTT) L	goal*	
			Mathieu Garon (LA)	miss	
			Mike Morrison (EDM)	miss	
			Pascal Leclaire (CBJ)	miss	2–4–6
Laaksonen	Antti	COL	Martin Brodeur (NJ) L	goal*	
			Curtis Sanford (STL)	miss	
			Dwayne Roloson (EDM)	miss	1–2–3
Laich	Brooks	WAS	Henrik Lundqvist (NYR)	miss	
			Roberto Luongo (FLO)	goal	
			Curtis Sanford (STL)	miss	
			Martin Brodeur (NJ)	goal	
			Martin Gerber (CAR) W	miss	
			Jamie McLennan (FLO)	miss	2–4–6
Lang	Robert	DET	Marty Turco (DAL) W	miss	
			Marc Denis (CBJ)	miss	0–2–2
Langenbrunner	Jamie	NJ	Kevin Weekes (NYR) W	miss	
			Vitaly Kolesnik (COL) W	miss	
			Rick DiPietro (NYI) W	miss	0–3–3
Lecavalier	Vincent	TB	Olaf Kolzig (WAS)	goal	
			Brent Johnson (WAS)	miss	
			Olaf Kolzig (WAS)	miss	
			Craig Anderson (CHI) L	goal	
			Ed Belfour (TOR) L	goal*	
			Marc-Andre Fleury (PIT)	miss	
			Henrik Lundqvist (NYR)	miss	
			Mike Dunham (ATL)	goal	

			Martin Gerber (CAR)	miss	4–5–9
LeClair	John	PIT	Rick DiPietro (NYI)	miss	0–1–1
Lehtinen	Jere	DAL	Nikolai Khabibulin (CHI)	miss	0–1–1
Lemieux	Mario	PIT	Cam Ward (CAR)	miss	
			Jose Theodore (MON)	miss	
			Rick DiPietro (NYI)	miss	0–3–3
Letowski	Trevor	CBJ	Dwayne Roloson (MIN) L	goal*	
			Manny Fernandez (MIN)	miss	
			Jussi Markkanen (EDM)	goal	
			Manny Legace (DET)	miss	2–2–4
Lindros	Eric	TOR	Dominik Hasek (OTT) W	miss	
			Dominik Hasek (OTT)	miss	
			Andrew Raycroft (BOS) L	goal*	1–2–3
Lombardi	Matt	CAL	Curtis Sanford (STL)	goal	
			Chris Osgood (DET)	miss	
			Jason LaBarbera (LA)	miss	1–2–3
Lundmark	Jamie	PHO	Mike Morrison (EDM)	miss	0–1–1
Lupul	Joffrey	ANA	Curtis Sanford (STL)	miss	
			Johan Hedberg (DAL)	miss	0–2–2
Madden	John	NJ	Vitaly Kolesnik (COL)	miss	
			Rick DiPietro (NYI) W	miss	0–2–2
Malik	Marek	NYR	Olaf Kolzig (WAS) L	goal*	1–0–1
Malone	Ryan	PIT	Wade Dubielewicz (NYI) W	miss	
			Rick DiPietro (NYI) W	miss	0–2–2
Marleau	Patrick	SJ	Miikka Kiprusoff (CAL)	miss	
			Marty Turco (DAL)	miss	
			Curtis Joseph (PHO)	miss	
			Jason Bacashihua (STL)	miss	
			Mike Morrison (EDM) W	miss	0–5–5
McAmmond	Dean	STL	Evgeni Nabokov (SJ)	miss	
			J-S Giguere (ANA)	miss	
			Olaf Kolzig (WAS)	goal	
			Marc Denis (CBJ)	miss	
			Miikka Kiprusoff (CAL)	miss	
			Josh Harding (MIN)	miss	1–5–6

McClement	Jay	STL	Miikka Kiprusoff (CAL)	goal	
			Corey Crawford (CHI)	goal	
			Mike Morrison (EDM)	miss	
			David Aebischer (COL)	miss	2–2–4
McDonald	Andy	ANA	Tomas Vokoun (NAS) W	miss	
			Manny Fernandez (MIN)	miss	
			Johan Hedberg (DAL)	goal	
			Dominik Hasek (OTT)	miss	
			Mathieu Garon (LA)	goal	
			Pascal Leclaire (CBJ)	miss	2–4–6
Michalek	Milan	SJ	Curtis Joseph (PHO)	miss	
			Marty Turco (DAL)	goal	1–1–2
Miettinen	Antti	DAL	J-S Giguere (ANA) L	goal*	
			Manny Legace (DET)	miss	
			Vesa Toskala (SJ) L	goal*	
			Nikolai Khabibulin (CHI)	miss	
			J-S Giguere (ANA)	miss	2–3–5
Modano	Mike	DAL	Martin Gerber (CAR) L	goal*	
			J-S Giguere (ANA)	miss	
			Tim Thomas (BOS)	miss	
			Peter Budaj (COL)	miss	
			Manny Legace (DET) L	goal*	
			Vesa Toskala (SJ)	goal	
			Nikolai Khabibulin (CHI)	miss	3–4–7
Mogilny	Alexander	NJ	Hannu Toivonen (BOS)	miss	
			Kevin Weekes (NYR)	miss	
			Manny Fernandez (MIN)	miss	
			Vitaly Kolesnik (COL)	miss	0–4–4
Moore	Dominic	NYR	Olaf Kolzig (WAS)	miss	0–1–1
Morrow	Brenden	DAL	Nikolai Khabibulin (CHI) Lgoal*		1–0–1
Muir	Bryan	WAS	Henrik Lundqvist (NYR)	goal	1–0–1
Murray	Glen	BOS	Ed Belfour (TOR)	miss	
			Scott Clemmensen (NJ) W	miss	
			Kari Lehtonen (ATL)	goal	

			Roberto Luongo (FLO)	miss	
			Martin Gerber (CAR)	miss	1–4–5
Nagy	Ladislav	PHO	Chris Mason (NAS) W	miss	
			Evgeni Nabokov (SJ)	miss	
			Martin Biron (BUF)	miss	
			Jussi Markkanen (EDM) L	goal*	
			Mike Morrison (EDM)	miss	1–4–5
Nash	Rick	CBJ	Chris Osgood (DET)	miss	
			David Aebischer (COL)	miss	
			Curtis Sanford (STL) L	goal*	
			Miikka Kiprusoff (CAL)	goal	
			Jussi Markkanen (EDM)	miss	
			J-S Giguere (ANA) L	goal*	
			Chris Osgood (DET)	miss	
			Manny Legace (DET)	miss	3–5–8
Naslund	Markus	VAN	Jussi Markkanen (EDM)	miss	
			Dominik Hasek (OTT)	miss	
			Mathieu Garon (LA) W	miss	
			Miikka Kiprusoff (CAL)	miss	
			Craig Anderson (CHI) L	goal*	
			Dwayne Roloson (EDM)	goal	
			Manny Fernandez (MIN)	miss	2–5–7
Nedved	Petr	PHO	Chris Mason (NAS)	miss	
		PHI	Martin Brodeur (NJ)	miss	
			Cristobal Huet (MON) L	goal*	
			Martin Gerber (CAR)	miss	1–3–4
Niedermayer Rob		ANA	Marty Turco (DAL) L	goal*	1–0–1
Niedermayer Scott		ANA	Mathieu Garon (LA) W	miss	0–1–1
Nieminen Ville		NYR	Olaf Kolzig (WAS)	goal	1–0–1
Nieuwendyk Joe		FLO	Antero Niittymaki (PHI)	miss	
			Olaf Kolzig (WAS) L	goal*	
			Martin Gerber (CAR)	miss	
			Kari Lehtonen (ATL) W	miss	
			Olaf Kolzig (WAS) L	goal*	

Nieuwendyk	*(cont'd)*		Tim Thomas (BOS)	miss	
			Brent Johnson (WAS)	miss	2–5–7
Nilsson	Robert	NYI	Jocelyn Thibault (PIT)	miss	
			Sebastien Caron (PIT) L	goal*	1–1–2
Nylander	Michael	NYR	Roberto Luongo (FLO)	miss	
			Martin Biron (BUF)	goal	
			Tim Thomas (BOS)	miss	
			Roberto Luongo (FLO)	miss	
			John Grahame (TB) W	miss	
			Ryan Miller (BUF)	miss	
			Robert Esche (PHI) L	goal*	
			Rick DiPietro (NYI) W	miss	
			Scott Clemmensen (NJ)	goal	
			Olaf Kolzig (WAS)	goal	
			Kari Lehtonen (ATL)	goal	5–6–11
Olesz	Rastislav	FLO	Olaf Kolzig (WAS)	miss	0–1–1
O'Neill	Jeff	TOR	Martin Gerber (CAR) W	miss	0–1–1
Ortmeyer	Jed	NYR	Olaf Kolzig (WAS)	miss	0–1–1
Ouellet	Maxime	PIT	Wade Dubielewicz (NYI)	miss	
			Rick DiPietro (NYI) W	miss	
			Rick DiPietro (NYI)	goal	1–2–3
Ovechkin	Alexander	WAS	Sean Burke (TB)	goal	
			Mike Dunham (ATL) L	goal*	
			Sean Burke (TB) L	goal*	
			John Grahame (TB)	goal	
			Henrik Lundqvist (NYR)	miss	
			Michael Garnett (ATL) L	goal*	
			Antero Niittymaki (PHI)	miss	
			Roberto Luongo (FLO)	miss	
			Curtis Sanford (STL)	goal	
			Martin Brodeur (NJ)	miss	
			Roberto Luongo (FLO)	miss	
			Martin Gerber (CAR)	miss	
			Jamie McLennan (FLO)	miss	6–7–13

Palffy	Zigmund	PIT	Cam Ward (CAR)	miss	
			Rick DiPietro (NYI)	miss	0–2–2
Parise	Zach	NJ	Adam Munro (CHI)	miss	
			Robert Esche (PHI)	miss	
			Rick DiPietro (NYI) L	goal*	1–2–3
Park	Richard	VAN	Craig Anderson (CHI)	miss	0–1–1
Parrish	Mark	NYI	Jocelyn Thibault (PIT)	miss	
		LA	Patrick Lalime (STL)	miss	
		NYI	Henrik Lundqvist (NYR)	miss	0–3–3
Peca	Michael	EDM	Vesa Toskala (SJ)	goal	
			Curtis Joseph (PHO)	miss	
			Marc Denis (CBJ)	miss	
			Alexander Auld (VAN) W	goal	
			Peter Budaj (COL)	miss	2–3–5
Perezhogin	Alexander	MON	Jocelyn Thibault (PIT) W	miss	
			Kari Lehtonen (ATL)	miss	
			Robert Esche (PHI) W	miss	0–3–3
Perry	Corey	ANA	Mathieu Garon (LA)	miss	
			Mike Morrison (EDM) W	miss	0–2–2
Petrovicky	Ronald	ATL	Tim Thomas (BOS)	miss	0–1–1
Pettinger	Matt	WAS	John Grahame (TBL)	miss	
			Henrik Lundqvist (NYR)	miss	
			Antero Niittymaki (PHI)	goal	
			Curtis Sanford (STL)	goal*	
			Martin Brodeur (NJ)	miss	
			Roberto Luongo (FLO)	miss	
			Jamie McLennan (FLO) L	goal*	3–4–7
Phaneuf	Dion	CAL	Mike Morrison (EDM)	miss	0–1–1
Pirjeta	Lasse	PIT	Rick DiPietro (NYI)	miss	0–1–1
Pisani	Fernando	EDM	Miikka Kiprusoff (CAL) L	goal*	
			Rick DiPietro (NYI)	miss	
			Curtis Joseph (PHO)	miss	
			Marc Denis (CBJ)	goal	
			J-S Giguere (ANA) L	goal*	

Pisani	*(cont'd)*		Curtis Sanford (STL) W	miss	
			Manny Legace (DET)	miss	3–4–7
Pominville	Jason	BUF	Brian Boucher (PHO) W	miss	
			Martin Gerber (CAR) W	miss	0–2–2
Ponikarovsky	Alexei	TOR	Martin Biron (BUF)	goal	
			Sean Burke (TB) W	miss	
			Rick DiPietro (NYI)	miss	
			Martin Biron (BUF) W	miss	
			Tim Thomas (BOS) W	miss	1–4–5
Prospal	Vaclav	TB	Brent Johnson (WAS)	miss	
			Olaf Kolzig (WAS) L	goal*	
			Marc-Andre Fleury (PIT) L	goal*	2–1–3
Prucha	Petr	NYR	Olaf Kolzig (WAS)	miss	
			Tim Thomas (BOS)	miss	
			Rick DiPietro (NYI)	miss	
			Scott Clemmensen (NJ) L	goal*	
			Roberto Luongo (FLO) L	goal*	2–3–5
Reasoner	Marty	BOS	Kari Lehtonen (ATL)	miss	0–1–1
Recchi	Mark	PIT	Jose Theodore (MON)	miss	
			Rick DiPietro (NYI)	miss	
			Rick DiPietro (NYI)	miss	
		CAR	Brent Johnson (WAS)	miss	0–4–4
Reinprecht	Steve	CAL	Nolan Schaefer (SJ)	miss	
			Alexander Auld (VAN) L	goal*	
		PHO	Mathieu Garon (LA) L	goal*	2–1–3
Ribeiro	Mike	MON	Robert Esche (PHI)	goal	1–0–1
Richards	Brad	TB	Ryan Miller (BUF) W	miss	
			Olaf Kolzig (WAS) W	miss	
			Olaf Kolzig (WAS)	goal	
			Craig Anderson (CHI)	goal*	
			Ed Belfour (TOR)	goal	
			Marc-Andre Fleury (PIT)	goal	
			Henrik Lundqvist (NYR) L	goal*	
			Mike Dunham (ATL) L	goal*	
			Martin Gerber (CAR)	miss	6–3–9

Richards	Mike	PHI	Roberto Luongo (FLO)	miss	
			Martin Brodeur (NJ)	miss	
			Cristobal Huet (MON)	miss	
			Martin Gerber (CAR)	miss	
			Miikka Kiprusoff (CAL) L	goal*	
			Olaf Kolzig (WAS)	goal	
			Martin Gerber (CAR)	goal	3–4–7
Rita	Jani	PIT	John Grahame (TB)	miss	0–1–1
Robitaille	Luc	LA	J-S Giguere (ANA)	goal	
			Patrick Lalime (STL) L	goal*	
			Miikka Kiprusoff (CAL)	miss	2–1–3
Robitaille	Randy	MIN	Martin Prusek (CBJ)	miss	
			Pascal Leclaire (CBJ)	miss	
			Vesa Toskala (SJ)	miss	
			J-S Giguere (ANA) L	goal*	1–3–4
Roenick	Jeremy	LA	Tomas Vokoun (NAS)	goal	
			Curtis Joseph (PHO) W	miss	1–1–2
Rolston	Brian	MIN	J-S Giguere (ANA)	miss	
			Martin Brodeur (NJ)	miss	
			Vesa Toskala (SJ) L	goal*	
			Martin Prusek (CBJ)	miss	
			Alexander Auld (VAN)	miss	
			Reinhard Divis (STL) L	goal*	
			Dwayne Roloson (EDM) L	goal*	3–4–7
Roy	Derek	BUF	Martin Gerber (CAR)	miss	
			Henrik Lundqvist (NYR) W	miss	1–1–2
Rozsival	Michal	NYR	Olaf Kolzig (WAS)	miss	0–1–1
Rucinsky	Martin	NYR	Tim Thomas (BOS)	miss	
			Kari Lehtonen (ATL)	miss	0–2–2
Ruutu	Jarkko	VAN	David Aebischer (COL) L	goal*	
			Craig Anderson (CHI)	miss	
			Dwayne Roloson (EDM)	goal	
			Manny Fernandez (MIN)	miss	2–2–4
Ruutu	Tuomo	CHI	Peter Budaj (COL) L	goal*	1–0–1

Ryder	Michael	MON	Jocelyn Thibault (PIT)	miss	
			Steve Shields (ATL)	miss	
			Kari Lehtonen (ATL) W	miss	
			Robert Esche (PHI)	miss	0–4–4
St. Louis	Martin	TB	Martin Gerber (CAR) W	miss	
			Ryan Miller (BUF)	miss	
			Olaf Kolzig (WAS)	miss	0–3–3
Sakic	Joe	COL	Philippe Sauve (CAL)	miss	
			Martin Brodeur (NJ)	miss	
			Pascal Leclaire (CBJ)	miss	
			Marty Turco (DAL)	miss	
			Alexander Auld (VAN)	miss	
			Curtis Sanford (STL)	miss	
			Dwayne Roloson (EDM) W	miss	0–7–7
Samsonov	Sergei	BOS	Scott Clemmensen (NJ)	miss	
			Marty Turco (DAL) W	miss	
			Martin Gerber (CAR) W	miss	
		EDM	Manny Legace (DET) W	miss	
			Peter Budaj (COL) L	goal*	
			Manny Fernandez (MIN)	goal	2–4–6
Samuelsson	Mikael	DET	Marc Denis (CBJ)	miss	0–1–1
Sanderson	Geoff	PHO	Evgeni Nabokov (SJ) L	goal*	
			Martin Biron (BUF) L	goal*	
			Jussi Markkanen (EDM)	goal	
			Mathieu Garon (LA)	goal	
			Johan Hedberg (DAL) W	miss	3–2–5
Saprykin	Oleg	PHO	Chris Mason (NAS)	miss	
			Mike Morrison (EDM)	miss	0–2–2
Satan	Miroslav	NYI	Henrik Lundqvist (NYR) L	goal*	
			Jocelyn Thibault (PIT)	miss	
			Pascal Leclaire (CBJ)	miss	
			Martin Brodeur (NJ)	goal	
			Sebastien Caron (PIT) L	goal*	
			Marc-Andre Fleury (PIT) L	goal*	

			Martin Brodeur (NJ) L	goal*	
			Martin Brodeur (NJ)	goal	
			Ed Belfour (TOR)	goal*	
			Sebastien Caron (PIT)	miss	7–3–10
Savard	Marc	ATL	Nikolai Khabibulin (CHI)	miss	
			Henrik Lundqvist (NYR)	goal	
			Tim Thomas (BOS)	miss	1–2–3
Sedin	Daniel	VAN	Dominik Hasek (OTT) L	goal*	
			Mathieu Garon (LA)	miss	
			Manny Fernandez (MIN) W	miss	1–2–3
Selanne	Teemu	ANA	Tomas Vokoun (NAS)	miss	
			Manny Fernandez (MIN)	goal	
			Mathieu Garon (LA)	miss	
			Johan Hedberg (DAL) W	miss	
			Mathieu Garon (LA)	goal	
			Mike Morrison (EDM)	miss	
			Pascal Leclaire (CBJ) W	miss	2–5–7
Shanahan	Brendan	DET	Tomas Vokoun (NAS) W	miss	0–1–1
Sharp	Patrick	CHI	Michael Garnett (ATL)	miss	
			Chris Mason (NAS) W	miss	0–2–2
Sillinger	Mike	STL	Evgeni Nabokov (SJ)	miss	
			J-S Giguere (ANA) W	miss	
			Marc Denis (CBJ) W	miss	
			Marty Turco (DAL)	miss	
		NAS	Manny Legace (DET)	goal	1–4–5
Sim	Jon	PHI	Ryan Miller (BUF)	miss	0–1–1
Slater	Jim	ATL	Tim Thomas (BOS) L	goal*	1–0–1
Smyth	Ryan	EDM	Evgeni Nabokov (SJ) L	goal*	
			Miikka Kiprusoff (CAL)	miss	
			Rick DiPietro (NYI) W	miss	
			Vesa Toskala (SJ) L	goal*	
			Curtis Joseph (PHO)	goal	
			Curtis Joseph (PHO)	miss	
			Marc Denis (CBJ)	miss	

Smyth	*(cont'd)*		J-S Giguere (ANA)	miss	
			Curtis Sanford (STL)	miss	
			Marty Turco (DAL) W	miss	
			Alexander Auld (VAN)	goal	
			Peter Budaj (COL)	miss	
			Manny Fernandez (MIN) W	miss	4–9–13
Spacek	Jaroslav	CHI	Michael Garnett (ATL)	goal	1–0–1
Spezza	Jason	OTT	Alexander Auld (VAN)	miss	
			Tim Thomas (BOS) W	miss	0–2–2
Staal	Eric	CAR	Antero Niittymaki (PHI)	miss	
			Ryan Miller (BUF) L	goal*	
			Antero Niittymaki (PHI) W	miss	
			Sean Burke (TB)	miss	1–3–4
Stempniak	Lee	STL	Miikka Kiprusoff (CAL) L	goal*	
			Corey Crawford (CHI) L	goal*	
			Mathieu Garon (LA) W	miss	2–1–3
Stevenson	Grant	SJ	Manny Fernandez (MIN) W	miss	0–1–1
Stillman	Cory	CAR	Sebastien Caron (PIT) L	goal*	
			Johan Hedberg (DAL)	miss	
			Brent Johnson (WAS)	miss	1–2–3
Stoll	Jarret	EDM	Martin Brodeur (NJ)	miss	
			Curtis Joseph (PHO)	miss	
			Marc Denis (CBJ)	goal	1–2–3
Straka	Martin	NYR	Mika Noronen (BUF)	goal	
			Scott Clemmensen (NJ)	miss	
			Roberto Luongo (FLO)	miss	
			Olaf Kolzig (WAS)	miss	
			Tim Thomas (BOS)	miss	
			Kari Lehtonen (ATL) W	miss	1–5–6
Strudwick	Jason	NYR	Olaf Kolzig (WAS)	goal	1–0–1
Stuart	Brad	BOS	Kari Lehtonen (ATL) W	miss	0–1–1
Stumpel	Josef	FLO	Antero Niittymaki (PHI) W	miss	
			Kevin Weekes (NYR)	miss	
			Brent Johnson (WAS) W	miss	0–3–3

Sturm	Marco	SJ	Miikka Kiprusoff (CAL)	goal	
			Mike Morrison (EDM)	goal	
		BOS	Marty Turco (DAL)	miss	
			Henrik Lundqvist (NYR)	miss	
			Mikael Tellqvist (TOR) W	miss	
			Kari Lehtonen (ATL)	miss	2–4–6
Sullivan	Steve	NAS	J-S Giguere (ANA)	miss	
			David LeNeveu (PHO)	miss	
			Patrick Lalime (STL) L	goal*	
			Antero Niittymaki (PHI)	goal	
			Kari Lehtonen (ATL)	miss	
			Martin Brodeur (NJ)	miss	
			Manny Legace (DET)	goal	3–4–7
Sundin	Mats	TOR	Martin Gerber (CAR)	miss	
			Martin Biron (BUF) L	goal*	
			Sean Burke (TB)	miss	
			Rick DiPietro (NYI)	miss	
			Tim Thomas (BOS)	miss	
			Martin Biron (BUF)	miss	
			Tim Thomas (BOS)	miss	1–6–7
Sutherby	Brian	WAS	Henrik Lundqvist (NYR)	miss	0–1–1
Svatos	Marek	COL	Nikolai Khabibulin (CHI) W	miss	
			Martin Brodeur (NJ)	miss	
			Pascal Leclaire (CBJ)	goal	
			Marty Turco (DAL)	goal	
			Alexander Auld (VAN)	miss	2–3–5
Sykora	Petr	WAS	Sean Burke (TB) L	goal*	1–0–1
Sykora	Petr	ANA	Curtis Sanford (STL)	miss	
		NYR	Tim Thomas (BOS) L	goal*	
			Roberto Luongo (FLO)	goal	
			Kari Lehtonen (ATL)	goal	
			John Grahame (TB)	miss	
			Ryan Miller (BUF) L	goal*	
			Robert Esche (PHI)	goal	5–2–7

Tanguay	Alex	COL	Nikolai Khabibulin (CHI)	goal	
			Marty Turco (DAL) W	miss	
			Philippe Sauve (CAL) W	miss	
			Martin Brodeur (NJ)	miss	
			Pascal Leclaire (CBJ) L	goal*	
			Marty Turco (DAL) W	miss	2–4–6
Thomas	Bill	PHO	Johan Hedberg (DAL)	miss	0–1–1
Thornton	Joe	BOS	Ed Belfour (TOR)	miss	
			Scott Clemmensen (NJ)	goal	
		SJ	Jason Bacashihua (STL)	miss	
			Mike Morrison (EDM)	miss	
			Manny Fernandez (MIN)	miss	1–4–5
Timonen	Kimmo	NAS	Manny Legace (DET)	miss	0–1–1
Tjarnqvist	Daniel	MIN	Vesa Toskala (SJ)	miss	0–1–1
Tkachuk	Keith	STL	Mike Morrison (EDM)	miss	
			David Aebischer (COL)	miss	
			Josh Harding (MIN)	goal	1–2–3
Torres	Raffi	EDM	Dan Cloutier (VAN) L	goal*	
			Evgeni Nabokov (SJ)	miss	
			Miikka Kiprusoff (CAL)	miss	
			Curtis Joseph (PHO)	miss	
			Marc Denis (CBJ)	miss	1–4–5
Tucker	Darcy	TOR	Rick DiPietro (NYI) W	miss	
			Tim Thomas (BOS) L	goal*	
			Martin Biron (BUF)	miss	
			Tim Thomas (BOS)	miss	1–3–4
Turgeon	Pierre	COL	Martin Brodeur (NJ)	miss	0–1–1
Vanek	Thomas	BUF	John Grahame (TB)	goal	
			Rick DiPietro (NYI)	miss	
			Antero Niittymaki (PHI)	miss	
			Ed Belfour (TOR) W	miss	
			Dominik Hasek (OTT) L	goal*	
			Martin Gerber (CAR)	miss	2–4–6
Vermette	Antoine	OTT	Martin Brodeur (NJ)	miss	0–1–1

Vorobiev	Pavel	CHI	Michael Garnett (ATL)	goal	
			Martin Brodeur (NJ)	miss	
			Peter Budaj (COL)	goal	2–1–3
Vrbata	Radim	CAR	Mikael Tellqvist (TOR) L	goal*	
			Johan Hedberg (DAL) W	miss	
		CHI	Martin Brodeur (NJ)	miss	
			Curtis Sanford (STL)	goal	
			Alexander Auld (VAN)	miss	
			Johan Hedberg (DAL)	miss	2–4–6
Vyborny	David	CBJ	Dwayne Roloson (MIN)	miss	
			Rick DiPietro (NYI) L	goal*	
			David Aebischer (COL)	miss	
			Jussi Markkanen (EDM)	miss	
			J-S Giguere (ANA)	miss	
			Chris Osgood (DET)	miss	
			Manny Legace (DET) W	miss	1–6–7
Walter	Ben	BOS	Henrik Lundqvist (NYR)	miss	0–1–1
Walz	Wes	MIN	Martin Prusek (CBJ)	miss	0–1–1
Ward	Jason	NYR	Olaf Kolzig (WAS)	miss	0–1–1
Weight	Doug	STL	Tomas Vokoun (NAS) W	miss	
			Evgeni Nabokov (SJ)	goal	
			J-S Giguere (ANA)	miss	
			Olaf Kolzig (WAS)	miss	
			Marc Denis (CBJ)	miss	
		CAR	Tim Thomas (BOS) L	goal*	2–4–6
Weiss	Stephen	FLO	Henrik Lundqvist (NYR)	miss	0–1–1
Wellwood	Kyle	TOR	Dominik Hasek (OTT)	miss	0–1–1
White	Todd	MIN	Martin Prusek (CBJ)	goal	
			Martin Brodeur (NJ) W	miss	1–1–2
Whitney	Ray	CAR	Antero Niittymaki (PHI)	goal	
			Roberto Luongo (FLO)	goal	
			Tim Thomas (BOS)	goal	
			Ryan Miller (BUF)	miss	
			Antero Niittymaki (PHI)	goal	4–1–5

Whitney	Ryan	PIT	Rick DiPietro (NYI) W	miss	
			Rick DiPietro (NYI)	goal	1–1–2
Wideman	Dennis	STL	Marty Turco (DAL) W	miss	
			Miikka Kiprusoff (CAL)	goal	
			Corey Crawford (CHI)	miss	
			Mike Morrison (EDM) L	goal*	
			David Aebischer (COL)	miss	
			Mathieu Garon (LA)	miss	2–4–6
Williams	Jason	DET	Pascal Leclaire (CBJ) L	goal*	
			Marty Turco (DAL)	goal	
			Dwayne Roloson (EDM) L	goal*	
			Tomas Vokoun (NAS)	goal	
			Pascal Leclaire (CBJ)	miss	
			Miikka Kiprusoff (CAL)	goal	
			Marc Denis (CBJ)	miss	5–2–7
Williams	Justin	CAR	Ryan Miller (BUF)	goal	
			Antero Niittymaki (PHI)	miss	1–1–2
Willsie	Brian	WAS	Sean Burke (TB)	miss	
			John Grahame (TBL)	miss	
			Henrik Lundqvist (NYR)	goal	
			Michael Garnett (ATL)	miss	
			Antero Niittymaki (PHI) L	goal*	
			Roberto Luongo (FLO) W	miss	
			Martin Brodeur (NJ)	goal	
			Roberto Luongo (FLO) W	miss	
			Martin Gerber (CAR)	miss	3–6–9
Wright	Tyler	CBJ	Dwayne Roloson (MIN)	miss	0–1–1
Yashin	Alexei	NYI	Henrik Lundqvist (NYR)	miss	
			Jocelyn Thibault (PIT)	miss	
			Martin Biron (BUF)	miss	
			Pascal Leclaire (CBJ) W	miss	
			Jussi Markkanen (EDM)	goal	
			Martin Brodeur (NJ)	miss	
			Sebastien Caron (PIT)	goal	2–5–7

York	Mike	NYI	Jocelyn Thibault (PIT)	miss	
			Pascal Leclaire (CBJ)	miss	0–2–2
Young	Scott	STL	Olaf Kolzig (WAS) W	miss	0–1–1
Yzerman	Steve	DET	Tomas Vokoun (NAS)	goal	
			Marc Denis (CBJ)	miss	1–1–2
Zetterberg	Henrik	DET	Marty Turco (DAL)	goal	
			Dwayne Roloson (EDM)	goal	
			Tomas Vokoun (NAS)	goal	
			Pascal Leclaire (CBJ) W	miss	2–2–4
Zherdev	Nikolai	CBJ	Dwayne Roloson (MIN)	miss	
			David Aebischer (COL) W	miss	
			Jussi Markkanen (EDM)	goal	1–2–3
Zidlicky	Marek	NAS	J-S Giguere (ANA)	miss	
			Patrick Lalime (STL)	goal	
			Jason LaBarbera (LA) W	miss	
			Kari Lehtonen (ATL) W	miss	
			Manny Legace (DET)	miss	1–4–5
Zubov	Sergei	DAL	Peter Budaj (COL) L	goal*	
			Evgeni Nabokov (SJ) L	goal*	
			Martin Gerber (CAR)	miss	
			J-S Giguere (ANA)	miss	
			Tim Thomas (BOS)	miss	
			Curtis Sanford (STL) L	goal*	
			Manny Legace (DET)	goal	
			Mike Morrison (EDM) L	goal*	
			Vesa Toskala (SJ)	miss	
			Nikolai Khabibulin (CHI)	goal	
			Curtis Joseph (PHO)	miss	
			Peter Budaj (COL)	goal	7–5–12
Zubrus	Dainius	WAS	Curtis Sanford (STL)	miss	
			Jamie McLennan (FLO)	goal	1–1–2

GAMES PLAYED, 2005–06

(arranged by most games, team, alphabetical)

Player	GP
Niklas Hagman (FLO–DAL)	84
Mark Recchi (PIT–CAR)	83
Andy McDonald (ANA)	82
Scott Niedermayer (ANA)	82
Samuel Pahlsson (ANA)	82
Vitaly Vishnevski (ANA)	82
Greg de Vries (ATL)	82
Niclas Havelid (ATL)	82
Slava Kozlov (ATL)	82
Marc Savard (ATL)	82
Brad Boyes (BOS)	82
Travis Green (BOS)	82
Ales Kotalik (BUF)	82
Henrik Tallinder (BUF)	82
Andrew Ference (CAL)	82
Jarome Iginla (CAL)	82
Daymond Langkow (CAL)	82
Dion Phaneuf (CAL)	82
Kevyn Adams (CAR)	82
Eric Staal (CAR)	82
Justin Williams (CAR)	82

Player	GP
Matthew Barnaby (CHI)	82
Mark Bell (CHI)	82
Martin Lapointe (CHI)	82
Andrew Brunette (COL)	82
Ian Laperriere (COL)	82
John-Michael Liles (COL)	82
Brett McLean (COL)	82
Joe Sakic (COL)	82
Karlis Skrastins (COL)	82
Steve Ott (DAL)	82
Andreas Lilja (DET)	82
Kirk Maltby (DET)	82
Brendan Shanahan (DET)	82
Steve Staios (EDM)	82
Jarret Stoll (EDM)	82
Raffi Torres (EDM)	82
Jay Bouwmeester (FLO)	82
Martin Gelinas (FLO)	82
Olli Jokinen (FLO)	82
Brian Rolston (MIN)	82
Wes Walz (MIN)	82
Mathieu Dandenault (MON)	82
Craig Rivet (MON)	82
Dan Hamhuis (NAS)	82
Paul Kariya (NAS)	82

Player	GP
Sergei Brylin (NJ)	82
Brian Gionta (NJ)	82
Scott Gomez (NJ)	82
John Madden (NJ)	82
Jay Pandolfo (NJ)	82
Brian Rafalski (NJ)	82
Trent Hunter (NYI)	82
Miroslav Satan (NYI)	82
Alexei Yashin (NYI)	82
Jaromir Jagr (NYR)	82
Dominic Moore (NYR)	82
Michal Rozsival (NYR)	82
Martin Straka (NYR)	82
Dany Heatley (OTT)	82
Chris Kelly (OTT)	82
Andrej Meszaros (OTT)	82
Peter Schaefer (OTT)	82
Antoine Vermette (OTT)	82
Mike Knuble (PHI)	82
Keith Ballard (PHO)	82
Shane Doan (PHO)	82
Zbynek Michalek (PHO)	82
Jonathan Cheechoo (SJ)	82
Patrick Marleau (SJ)	82
Nolan Pratt (TB)	82
Brad Richards (TB)	82

Player	GP
Cory Sarich (TB)	82
Tim Taylor (TB)	82
Tomas Kaberle (TOR)	82
Todd Bertuzzi (VAN)	82
Ryan Kesler (VAN)	82
Trevor Linden (VAN)	82
Brendan Morrison (VAN)	82
Jarkko Ruutu (VAN)	82
Daniel Sedin (VAN)	82
Henrik Sedin (VAN)	82
Brian Willsie (WAS)	82

PLAYERS WHO PLAYED IN 2003–04, BUT NOT IN 2005–06

Player	2005–06 Status
Johnathan Aitken	played in AHL
Mel Angelstad	played in England
Denis Arkhipov	played in Russia
Chris Armstrong	played in Germany
Magnus Arvedson	retired
Donald Audette	retired
Ryan Barnes	played in AHL & UHL
Murray Baron	retired
Bates Battaglia	played in AHL
Ryan Bayda	played in AHL
Eric Beaudoin	played in Sweden
Jaroslav Bednar	played in Czech Republic
Derek Bekar	played in Switzerland
Drake Berehowsky	played in AHL & Germany
Marc Bergevin	retired
Christian Berglund	played in Switzerland
Rick Berry	played in AHL
Goran Bezina	played in Switzerland
Jiri Bicek	played in Sweden
Zac Bierk	did not play
Mike Bishai	played in AHL
Patrick Boileau	played in Germany
Brad Bombardir	played briefly in AHL
Dennis Bonvie	played in AHL
Darryl Bootland	played in AHL
Jason Botterill	rertired
Josef Boumedienne	played in Switzerland & Sweden
Christoph Brandner	played in Sweden
Fred Brathwaite	played in Russia
Travis Brigley	played in AHL

Player	2005–06 Status
Aris Brimanis	played in Switzerland
Martin Brochu	did not play
Brad Brown	played in AHL
Kelly Buchberger	retired
Valeri Bure	retired
Garrett Burnett	played in AHL & ECHL
Dan Bylsma	retired
Sebastien Charpentier	played in Russia
Brad Chartrand	did not play
Andy Chiodo	played in AHL & ECHL
Stanislav Chistov	played in Russia
Mathieu Chouinard	played in ECHL
Artem Chubarov	played in Russia
Ivan Ciernik	played in Germany
Carl Corazzini	played in AHL
Daniel Corso	played in Germany
Shayne Corson	unsigned all season
Jim Cummins	retired
Jakub Cutta	played in AHL
Andreas Dackell	played in Sweden
Byron Dafoe	retired
Vincent Damphousse	retired
Mike Danton	serving jail sentence
Craig Darby	played in AHL
Mathieu Darche	played in Germany
Adam Deadmarsh	did not play—concussion
Jason Doig	played in AHL
Ted Donato	retired
Harold Druken	played in Switzerland
Gord Dwyer	played in AHL
Karl Dykhuis	played in Germany
Mike Eastwood	retired

Player	2005–06 Status
Dan Ellis	played in AHL
Anders Eriksson	played in AHL & Russia
Brennan Evans	played in AHL
Mike Farrell	did not play
Brad Fast	played in AHL
Brad Ference	played in AHL
Jeff Finley	played in Germany
Dan Focht	played in AHL
J-F Fortin	played in AHL
Ron Francis	retired
Owen Fussey	played in AHL
Ken Gernander	retired
Jonathan Girard	played briefly in AHL
Ray Giroux	played in Russia
Jean-Luc Grand-Pierre	played in Germany
Benoit Gratton	played in Germany
Martin Grenier	played in AHL
Michal Grosek	played in Switzerland & Russia
John Gruden	did not play
Jeff Hackett	retired
Riku Hahl	played in Switzerland
Chris Hajt	played in AHL
Casey Hankinson	did not play
Pierre Hedin	played in Germany
Jeff Heerema	played in AHL
Shawn Heins	played in Germany
Bryan Helmer	played in AHL
Darby Hendrickson	played in Austria
Burke Henry	played in Austria
Jan Hlavac	played in Switzerland
Milan Hnilicka	played in Czech Republic
Josh Holden	played in Switzerland

Player	2005–06 Status
Jason Holland	played in Germany
Brian Holzinger	did not play
Jody Hull	did not play
Ivan Huml	played in Czech Republic & Finland
Arturs Irbe	played in Austria
Doug Janik	played in AHL
Jason Jaspers	played in AHL
Andreas Johansson	played in Switzerland
Calle Johansson	retired
Craig Johnson	played in Germany
Matt Johnson	did not play
Ty Jones	retired
Kenny Jonsson	played in Sweden
Joe Juneau	retired
Mike Keane	played in AHL
Steve Kelly	played in Germany
Trevor Kidd	played briefly in Germany
Jason King	played in AHL
Trent Klatt	retired
Espen Knutsen	retired
Zenith Komarniski	played in AHL
Igor Korolev	played in Russia
Alexander Korolyuk	played in Russia
Milan Kraft	played in Czech Republic & Russia
Jordan Krestanovich	played in Sweden & Italy
Jason Krog	played in Switzerland
Kristian Kudroc	played in Finland
Lasse Kukkonen	played in Finland
Tomas Kurka	played in Finland
Zdenek Kutlak	played in Czech Republic
Maxim Kuznetsov	played in Russia
Scott Lachance	played in Switzerland

Player	2005–06 Status
Christian Laflamme	played in Germany
Quintin Laing	played in AHL
Marc Lamothe	played in Russia
Claude Lapointe	retired
Igor Larionov	retired
Cory Larose	played in Switzerland
Kirby Law	played in AHL
Brad Leeb	played in AHL
Mike Leighton	played in AHL
Curtis Leschyshyn	retired
Mats Lindgren	retired
Bill Lindsay	played in Germany
David Ling	played in Russia
Neil Little	played in Finland
Reed Low	played in UHL & AHL
Dave Lowry	retired
Mikko Luoma	played in Sweden
Doug Lynch	played in ECHL
Brett Lysak	played in AHL & Italy
Jason MacDonald	played in AHL
Al MacInnis	retired
Jeff MacMillan	played in AHL
Eric Manlow	played in AHL
Justin Mapletoft	played in Sweden & Finland
Tony Martensson	played in Sweden
Greg Mauldin	played in AHL
Chris McAllister	played in AHL
Sandy McCarthy	did not play
Kent McDonell	played in AHL
Steve McKenna	played in Italy
Jim McKenzie	did not play
Steve McLaren	played in AHL

Player	**2005–06 Status**
Grant McNeill	played in AHL & ECHL
Eric Meloche	played in AHL
Eric Messier	did not play
Mark Messier	retired
Kevin Miller	did not play
Kip Miller	played in AHL
Boris Mironov	did not play
Steve Moore	missed season due to injury
Brad Moran	played in Switzerland
Gavin Morgan	played in AHL
Aleksey Morozov	played in Russia
Marty Murray	played in Germany
Anders Myrvold	played briefly in Switzerland
Stan Neckar	played in Sweden
Andrej Nedorost	played in Czech Republic & Germany
Vaclav Nedorost	did not play
Andrei Nikolishin	played in Russia
Owen Nolan	missed season due to injury
Ivan Novoseltsev	did not play
Pasi Nurminen	retired
Lawrence Nycholat	played in AHL
Adam Oates	retired
Josh Olson	played in AHL
Mike Pandolfo	played in Germany
Justin Papineau	played in AHL
Steve Passmore	played in Finland
James Patrick	retired
Scott Pellerin	retired
Jean-Marc Pelletier	played in AHL
Mike Peluso	did not play
Eric Perrin	played in Switzerland

Player	2005–06 Status
Karel Pilar	played in Czech Republic
Kamil Piros	played in Russia
Domenic Pittis	played in Switzerland
Libor Pivko	played in AHL
Andrei Podkonicky	played in Czech Republic
Jame Pollock	played in Germany
Felix Potvin	unsigned all season
Sean Pronger	retired
Dale Purinton	played in NHL
Deron Quint	played in Germany & Switzerland
Stephane Quintal	retired
Karel Rachunek	played in Russia
Igor Radulov	played in Russia
Marcus Ragnarsson	retired
Rob Ray	retired
Jeremy Reich	played in AHL
Robert Reichel	played in Czech Republic
Brandon Reid	played in Switzerland
Todd Reirden	played in Germany
Mikael Renberg	played in Sweden
Travis Roche	played in AHL
Todd Rohloff	played in AHL
Cliff Ronning	retired
Kyle Rossiter	played in Finland & Italy
Darren Rumble	retired
Tony Salmelainen	played in Finland
Tommy Salo	played in Sweden
Martin Samuelsson	played in Sweden
Tommi Santala	played in Finland
Petr Schastlivy	played in Russia
Robert Schnabel	played in Finland
Corey Schwab	retired

Player	2005–06 Status
Richard Scott	did not play
Darrel Scoville	played in Austria
Lubomir Sekeras	did not play
Alexander Semin	played in Russia
Denis Shvidki	played in Russia
Mike Siklenka	played in Austria
Reid Simpson	played in Russia
Rob Skrlac	retired
John Slaney	played in AHL
Blake Sloan	played in Sweden
Alexei Smirnov	played in Russia
Radovan Somik	played in Russia
Martin Sonnenberg	played in AHL
Rastislav Stana	played in Sweden
Charlie Stephens	played in AHL
Scott Stevens	retired
P.J. Stock	retired
Jamie Storr	played in AHL
Martin Strbak	played in Russia
Garret Stroshein	played in ECHL
Mike Stutzel	played in Finland
Damian Surma	played in UHL
Alexander Svitov	played in Russia
Brian Swanson	played in Germany
Don Sweeney	retired
Chris Tamer	played in AHL
Chris Taylor	played in AHL
Joey Tetarenko	played in AHL
Steve Thomas	unsigned all season
Mattias Timander	played in Sweden
Yannick Tremblay	played in Germany
John Tripp	played in Germany

Player	2005–06 Status
Pavel Trnka	played in Sweden & Czech Republic
Ron Tugnutt	retired
Roman Turek	played in Czech Republic
Roman Tvrdon	played in Czech Republic
Matt Underhill	played in ECHL
Layne Ulmer	played in AHL
Rob Valicevic	played in Germany
Stephen Valiquette	played in Russia
Shaun Van Allen	retired
Julien Vauclair	played in Switzerland
Kris Vernarsky	played in UHL
Darcy Verot	played in AHL
Rickard Wallin	played in Sweden
Derrick Walser	played in Germany
Lance Ward	played in AHL
Steve Webb	did not play
Peter White	played in Finland
Shane Willis	played in Switzerland
Landon Wilson	played in Switzerland
Peter Worrell	played in ECHL
Jeremy Yablonski	played in AHL & ECHL
Matthew Yeats	played in ECHL
Jason York	played in Switzerland
Miroslav Zalesak	played in Sweden
Rob Zamuner	played in Italy & Switzerland
Sergei Zholtok	deceased
Dwayne Zinger	played in AHL
Sergei Zinoviev	played in Russia
Tomas Zizka	played in Czech Republic

2006 PLAYOFF RESULTS

Eastern Conference Quarter-finals

April 21   Tampa Bay 1 at Ottawa 4 (Tampa Bay led 1–0
             after 1st & 2nd)
April 23   Tampa Bay 4 at Ottawa 3 (Ottawa led 3–2 early in 3rd)
April 25   Ottawa 8 at Tampa Bay 4 (Ottawa led 3–0, 5–1)
April 27   Ottawa 5 at Tampa Bay 2 (Tampa Bay led 2–1 after 1st)
April 29   Tampa Bay 2 at Ottawa 3 (Ottawa led 2–0 after 1st)
Ottawa wins best-of-seven 4–1

April 22   Montreal 6 at Carolina 1
April 24   Montreal 6 at Carolina 5 (Ryder 2:32 2OT) (Montreal led
             3–0, trailed 4–3, led 5–4; Carolina tied game at 18:30
             of 3rd)
April 26   Carolina 2 at Montreal 1 (Staal 3:38 pp OT)
April 28   Carolina 3 at Montreal 2 (Carolina scored only goal
             of 3rd)
April 30   Montreal 1 at Carolina 2 (no scoring in 3rd)
May 2   Carolina 2 at Montreal 1 (Stillman 1:19 OT) (both regula-
             tion goals in 1st)
Carolina wins best-of-seven 4–2

April 22   NY Rangers 1 at New Jersey 6 (game tied 1–1 after 1st;
             Elias two goals, four assists)
April 24   NY Rangers 1 at New Jersey 4 (Devils led 3–0 after 2nd)
April 26   New Jersey 3 at NY Rangers 0 (Brodeur)
April 29   New Jersey 4 at NY Rangers 2 (Rangers led 1–0 after 1st)
New Jersey wins best-of-seven 4–0

April 22   Philadelphia 2 at Buffalo 3 (Briere 7:31 2OT)
April 24   Philadelphia 2 at Buffalo 8 (Dumont & Pominville each
             had hat tricks)

April 26   Buffalo 2 at Philadelphia 4
April 28   Buffalo 4 at Philadelphia 5 (Buffalo led 2–0 midway
           through 1st)
April 30   Philadelphia 0 at Buffalo 3 [Miller] (Buffalo scored in
           every period)
May 2   Buffalo 7 at Philadelphia 1 (Buffalo led 5–0 in 2nd)
Buffalo wins best-of-seven 4–2

Western Conference Quarter-finals

April 21   Edmonton 2 at Detroit 3 (Maltby 2:39 2OT)
April 23   Edmonton 4 at Detroit 2 (Edmonton led 3–2 after 2nd)
April 25   Detroit 2 at Edmonton 3 (Stoll 8:44 2OT)
April 27   Detroit 4 at Edmonton 2 (game tied 2–2 after 2nd)
April 29   Edmonton 3 at Detroit 2 (Edmonton led 3–0 midway
           through 2nd)
May 1   Detroit 3 at Edmonton 4 (Detroit led 2–0 after 2nd;
           Hemsky scored series winner at 18:54 of 3rd)
Edmonton wins best-of-seven 4–2

April 22   Colorado 5 at Dallas 2 (Colorado scored only three
           goals of 2nd to overcome 2–1 Dallas lead)
April 24   Colorado 5 at Dallas 4 (Sakic 4:36 OT; his seventh career
           overtime goal, most in NHL history)
April 26   Dallas 3 at Colorado 4 (Tanguay 1:09 OT) (Brunette
           [Col] tied game at 19:03 pp 3rd)
April 28   Dallas 4 at Colorado 1 (Colorado scored first)
April 30   Colorado 3 at Dallas 2 (Brunette 13:55 OT)
Colorado wins best-of-seven 4–1

April 21   Anaheim 1 at Calgary 2 (McCarty 9:45 OT)
April 23   Anaheim 4 at Calgary 3 (Anaheim led 3–0 early in 2nd)
April 25   Calgary 5 at Anaheim 2 (game tied 2–2 midway
           through 2nd)

April 27   Calgary 2 at Anaheim 3 (O'Donnell 1:36 OT)
April 29   Anaheim 2 at Calgary 3 (Calgary led 3–0 after 2nd)
May 1   Calgary 1 at Anaheim 2 (Scott Niedermayer [Ana] scored only goal of 3rd)
May 3   Anaheim 3 at Calgary 0 [Bryzgalov]
Anaheim wins best-of-seven 4–3

April 21   San Jose 3 at Nashville 4 (Hall broke 3–3 tie at 12:06 pp of 3rd)
April 23   San Jose 3 at Nashville 0 [Toskala]
April 25   Nashville 1 at San Jose 4 (Nashville led 1–0 after 1st)
April 27   Nashville 4 at San Jose 5 (San Jose led 1–0, trailed 2–1, led 5–2)
April 30   San Jose 2 at Nashville 1 (San Jose led 2–0 after 2nd)
San Jose wins best-of-seven 4–1

Eastern Conference Semi-finals

May 5   Buffalo 7 at Ottawa 6 (Drury 0:18 OT) (Buffalo led 1–0, trailed 2–1, 3–2, 4–3, 5–4, 6–5, tied game at 19:49 of 3rd)
May 8   Buffalo 2 at Ottawa 1 (all goals in 2nd)
May 10   Ottawa 2 at Buffalo 3 (Dumont 5:05 OT) (Buffalo led 1–0, 2–1)
May 11   Ottawa 2 at Buffalo 1 (Ottawa scored only goal of 3rd)
May 13   Buffalo 3 at Ottawa 2 (Pominville 2:26 sh OT)
Buffalo wins best-of-seven 4–1

May 6   New Jersey 0 at Carolina 6
May 8   New Jersey 2 at Carolina 3 (Wallin 3:09 OT) (New Jersey tied game at 19:39 of 3rd)
May 10   Carolina 3 at New Jersey 2 (game tied 2–2 midway through 3rd)
May 13   Carolina 1 at New Jersey 5 (New Jersey led 5–0 midway through game)

May 14   New Jersey 1 at Carolina 4 (game tied 1–1 after 1st)
Carolina wins best-of-seven 4–1

Western Conference Semi-finals

May 7   Edmonton 1 at San Jose 2 (no scoring in 3rd)
May 8   Edmonton 1 at San Jose 2 (Edmonton 0–2 on pp; no
         scoring in 3rd)
May 10   San Jose 2 at Edmonton 3 (Horcoff 42:24 OT) (shots
         58–34 Edmonton)
May 12   San Jose 3 at Edmonton 6 (Edmonton scored last five
         goals of game)
May 14   Edmonton 6 at San Jose 3 (game tied 3–3 early in 3rd)
May 17   San Jose 0 at Edmonton 2 [Roloson] (San Jose 0–8
         on pp)
Edmonton wins best-of-seven 4–2

May 5   Colorado 0 at Anaheim 5 [Bryzgalov] (Anaheim scored
         four goals in 2nd)
May 7   Colorado 0 at Anaheim 3 [Bryzgalov] (no scoring in 3rd)
May 9   Anaheim 4 at Colorado 3 (Lupul 16:30 OT) (Anaheim
         trailed 1–0, 2–1, led 3–2)
May 11   Anaheim 4 at Colorado 1 (Colorado scored early in 1st)
Anaheim wins best-of-seven 4–0

Eastern Conference Finals

May 20   Buffalo 3 at Carolina 2 (Buffalo led 3–1 midway
         through 3rd)
May 22   Buffalo 3 at Carolina 4 (Carolina led 4–1 early in 3rd)
May 24   Carolina 3 at Buffalo 4 (Buffalo led 4–1 midway
         through 2nd)
May 26   Carolina 4 at Buffalo 0 [Gerber]
May 28   Buffalo 3 at Carolina 4 (Stillman 8:46 pp OT)
May 30   Carolina 1 at Buffalo 2 (Briere 4:22 pp OT)

June 1   Buffalo 2 at Carolina 4 (Buffalo led 2–1 after 2nd)
Carolina wins best-of-seven 4–3

Western Conference Finals

May 19   Edmonton 3 at Anaheim 1 (game tied 1–1 after 1st)
May 21   Edmonton 3 at Anaheim 1 (game tied 1–1 midway
          through 2nd)
May 23   Anaheim 4 at Edmonton 5 (Edmonton led 1–0 after 1st &
          2nd; led 4–0 early in 3rd)
May 25   Anaheim 6 at Edmonton 3
May 27   Edmonton 2 at Anaheim 1 (Anaheim led 1–0 after 1st)
Edmonton wins best-of-seven 4–1

Stanley Cup Finals

June 5   Edmonton 4 at Carolina 5 (Edmonton led 3–0 early in
          2nd; Carolina won game in final minute of regulation)
June 7   Edmonton 0 at Carolina 5 [Ward]
June 10   Carolina 1 at Edmonton 2 (Smyth scored game winner
          at 17:45 of 3rd)
June 12   Carolina 2 at Edmonton 1 (Oilers 1–25 on pp in the
          series to date)
June 14   Edmonton 4 at Carolina 3 (Pisani 3:31 sh OT)
June 17   Carolina 0 at Edmonton 4 [Markkanen]
June 19   Edmonton 1 at Carolina 3 (Carolina led 2–0 after 2nd)
Carolina wins Stanley Cup 4–3

PLAYER STATISTICS BY TEAM, 2006 PLAYOFFS

Mighty Ducks of Anaheim

	GP	G	A	P	Pim
Teemu Selanne	16	6	8	14	6
Todd Marchant	16	3	10	13	14
Joffrey Lupul	16	9	2	11	31
Scott Niedermayer	16	2	9	11	14
Dustin Penner	13	3	6	9	12
Francois Beauchemin	16	3	6	9	11
Andy McDonald	16	2	7	9	10
Chris Kunitz	16	3	5	8	8
Ryan Getzlaf	16	3	4	7	13
Ruslan Salei	16	3	2	5	18
Sean O'Donnell	16	2	3	5	23
Samuel Pahlsson	16	2	3	5	18
Jeff Friesen	16	3	1	4	6
Rob Niedermayer	16	1	3	4	10
Vitaly Vishnevski	16	0	4	4	10
Corey Perry	11	0	3	3	16
Travis Moen	9	1	0	1	10
Jonathan Hedstrom	3	0	1	1	2
Todd Fedoruk	12	0	0	0	16
Joe Dipenta	16	0	0	0	13
Ilya Bryzgalov	11	0	0	0	2
J-S Giguere	6	0	0	0	0

Goalies	GP	W-L	Mins	GA	SO	GAA
Ilya Bryzgalov	11	6–4	659	16	3	1.46
J-S Giguere	6	3–3	318	18	0	3.40

Buffalo Sabres

	GP	G	A	P	Pim
Daniel Briere	18	8	11	19	12
Chris Drury	18	9	9	18	10
Derek Roy	18	5	10	15	16
J-P Dumont	18	7	7	14	14
Tim Connolly	8	5	6	11	0
Ales Kotalik	18	4	7	11	8
Jason Pominville	18	5	5	10	8
Maxim Afinogenov	18	3	5	8	10
Mike Grier	18	3	5	8	2
Henrik Tallinder	14	2	6	8	16
Jochen Hecht	15	2	6	8	8
Brian Campbell	18	0	6	6	12
Jay McKee	17	2	3	5	30
Toni Lydman	18	1	4	5	18
Taylor Pyatt	14	0	5	5	10
Rory Fitzpatrick	11	0	4	4	16
Paul Gaustad	18	0	4	4	14
Thomas Vanek	10	2	0	2	6
Teppo Numminen	12	1	1	2	4
Dmitri Kallinin	8	0	2	2	2
Doug Janik	5	1	0	1	2
Ryan Miller	18	0	0	0	2
Jeff Jillson	4	0	0	0	0
Jiri Novotny	4	0	0	0	0
Adam Mair	3	0	0	0	0
Nathan Paetsch	1	0	0	0	0

Goalie	GP	W-L	Mins	GA	SO	GAA
Ryan Miller	18	11-7	1,122	48	1	2.56

Calgary Flames

	GP	P	A	P	Pim
Jarome Iginla	7	5	3	8	11
Kristian Huselius	7	2	4	6	4
Daymond Langkow	7	1	5	6	6
Robyn Regehr	7	1	3	4	6
Andrew Ference	7	0	4	4	12
Tony Amonte	7	2	1	3	10
Darren McCarty	7	2	0	2	15
Roman Hamrlik	7	0	2	2	2
Matt Lombardi	7	0	2	2	2
Stephane Yelle	7	1	0	1	8
Dion Phaneuf	7	1	0	1	7
Chuck Kobasew	7	1	0	1	0
Chris Simon	6	0	1	1	7
Jamie Lundmark	4	0	1	1	7
Jordan Leopold	7	0	1	1	4
Mike Leclerc	3	0	0	0	2
Rhett Warrener	7	0	0	0	14
Shean Donovan	7	0	0	0	6
Miikka Kiprusoff	7	0	0	0	2
Byron Ritchie	7	0	0	0	0
Craig MacDonald	1	0	0	0	0

Goalie	GP	W-L	Mins	GA	SO	GAA
Miikka Kiprusoff	7	3–4	427	16	0	2.24

Carolina Hurricanes

	GP	G	A	P	Pim
Eric Staal	25	9	19	28	8
Corey Stillman	25	9	17	26	14
Rod Brind'Amour	25	12	6	18	16
Justin Williams	25	7	11	18	34
Matt Cullen	25	4	14	18	12
Mark Recchi	25	7	9	16	18
Doug Weight	23	3	13	16	20
Ray Whitney	24	9	6	15	14
Frantisek Kaberle	25	4	9	13	8
Bret Hedican	25	2	9	11	42
Aaron Ward	25	2	3	5	18
Andrew Ladd	17	2	3	5	4
Niclas Wallin	25	1	4	5	14
Mike Commodore	25	2	2	4	33
Glen Wesley	25	0	2	2	16
Chad LaRose	21	0	1	1	10
Cam Ward	23	0	1	1	0
Kevyn Adams	25	0	0	0	14
Craig Adams	25	0	0	0	10
Martin Gerber	6	0	0	0	4
Josef Vasicek	8	0	0	0	2
Oleg Tverdovsky	5	0	0	0	0
Erik Cole	2	0	0	0	0

Goalies	GP	W-L	Mins	GA	SO	GAA
Cam Ward	23	15–8	1,320	47	2	2.14
Martin Gerber	6	1–1	221	13	1	3.53

Colorado Avalanche

	GP	G	A	P	Pim
Joe Sakic	9	4	5	9	6
Andrew Brunette	9	3	6	9	8
Milan Hejduk	9	2	6	8	2
Alex Tanguay	9	2	4	6	12
Jim Dowd	9	2	3	5	20
Rob Blake	9	3	1	4	8
Brett Clark	9	2	2	4	2
Wojtek Wolski	8	1	3	4	2
John-Michael Liles	9	1	2	3	6
Dan Hinote	9	1	1	2	31
Pierre Turgeon	5	0	2	2	6
Antti Laaksonen	9	0	2	2	2
Brad Richardson	9	1	0	1	6
Ian Laperriere	9	0	1	1	27
Karlis Skrastins	9	0	1	1	10
Patrice Brisebois	9	0	1	1	4
Brett McLean	8	0	1	1	4
Kurt Sauer	9	0	0	0	4
Steve Konowalchuk	2	0	0	0	4
Jose Theodore	9	0	0	0	0
Brad May	3	0	0	0	0
Ossi Vaananen	1	0	0	0	0

Goalie	GP	W-L	Mins	GA	SO	GAA
Jose Theodore	9	4–5	573	29	0	3.04

Dallas Stars

	GP	G	A	P	Pim
Brenden Morrow	5	1	5	6	6
Sergei Zubov	5	1	5	6	6
Bill Guerin	5	3	1	4	0
Jere Lehtinen	5	3	1	4	0
Mike Modano	5	1	3	4	4
Niklas Hagman	5	2	1	3	4
Jussi Jokinen	5	2	1	3	0
Jason Arnott	5	0	3	3	4
Stu Barnes	5	1	1	2	0
Stephane Robidas	5	0	2	2	4
Jon Klemm	5	1	0	1	0
Niko Kapanen	5	0	1	1	10
Antti Miettinen	5	0	1	1	8
Janne Niinimaa	4	0	1	1	8
Philippe Boucher	5	0	1	1	2
Steve Ott	5	0	1	1	2
Willie Mitchell	5	0	0	0	2
Marty Turco	5	0	0	0	2
Jaroslav Svoboda	2	0	0	0	2
Trevor Daley	3	0	0	0	0
Jeremy Stevenson	1	0	0	0	0

Goalie	GP	W-L	Mins	GA	SO	GAA
Marty Turco	5	1–4	319	18	0	3.39

Detroit Red Wings

	GP	G	A	P	Pim
Mathieu Schneider	6	1	7	8	6
Henrik Zetterberg	6	6	0	6	2
Robert Lang	6	3	3	6	2
Steve Yzerman	4	0	4	4	4
Kirk Maltby	6	2	1	3	4
Tomas Holmstrom	6	1	2	3	12
Johan Franzen	6	1	2	3	4
Niklas Kronwall	6	0	3	3	2
Pavel Datsyuk	5	0	3	3	0
Brendan Shanahan	6	1	1	2	6
Jason Williams	6	1	1	2	6
Niklas Lidstrom	6	1	1	2	2
Daniel Cleary	6	0	1	1	6
Andreas Lilja	6	0	1	1	6
Mikael Samuelsson	6	0	1	1	6
Chris Chelios	6	0	0	0	6
Kris Draper	6	0	0	0	6
Brett Lebda	6	0	0	0	4
Manny Legace	6	0	0	0	0
Mark Mowers	3	0	0	0	0

Goalie	GP	W-L	Mins	GA	SO	GAA
Manny Legace	6	2–4	407	18	0	2.65

Edmonton Oilers

	GP	G	A	P	Pim
Chris Pronger	24	5	16	21	26
Shawn Horcoff	24	7	12	19	12
Fernando Pisani	24	14	4	18	10
Ales Hemsky	24	6	11	17	14
Ryan Smyth	24	7	9	16	22
Sergei Samsonov	24	4	11	15	14
Jaroslav Spacek	24	3	11	14	24
Michael Peca	24	6	5	11	20
Raffi Torres	22	4	7	11	16
Jarret Stoll	24	4	6	10	24
Steve Staios	24	1	5	6	28
Jason Smith	24	1	4	5	16
Rem Murray	24	0	4	4	2
Ethan Moreau	21	2	1	3	19
Marc-Andre Bergeron	18	2	1	3	14
Brad Winchester	10	1	2	3	4
Georges Laraque	15	1	1	2	44
Todd Harvey	10	1	1	2	4
Dwayne Roloson	18	0	2	2	14
Dick Tarnstrom	12	0	2	2	10
Radek Dvorak	16	0	2	2	4
Toby Petersen	2	1	0	1	0
Matt Greene	18	0	1	1	34
Jussi Markkanen	6	0	0	0	0
Ty Conklin	1	0	0	0	0

Goalies	GP	W-L	Mins	GA	SO	GAA
Dwayne Roloson	18	12–5	1,159	45	1	2.33
Jussi Markkanen	6	3–3	360	13	1	2.17
Ty Conklin	1	0–1	5	1	0	12.00

Montreal Canadiens

	GP	G	A	P	Pim
Alexei Kovalev	6	4	3	7	4
Sheldon Souray	6	3	2	5	8
Michael Ryder	6	2	3	5	0
Chris Higgins	6	1	3	4	0
Tomas Plekanec	6	0	4	4	6
Francis Bouillon	6	1	2	3	10
Mathieu Dandenault	6	0	3	3	4
Niklas Sundstrom	5	0	3	3	4
Richard Zednik	6	2	0	2	4
Radek Bonk	6	2	0	2	2
Alexander Perezhogin	6	1	1	2	4
Jan Bulis	6	1	1	2	2
Craig Rivet	6	0	2	2	2
Saku Koivu	3	0	2	2	2
Mike Ribeiro	6	0	2	2	0
Andrei Markov	6	0	1	1	4
Michael Komisarek	6	0	0	0	10
Steve Begin	2	0	0	0	2
Cristobal Huet	6	0	0	0	0
Garth Murray	6	0	0	0	0
Aaron Downey	1	0	0	0	0
Mark Streit	1	0	0	0	0

Goalie	GP	W-L	Mins	GA	SO	GAA
Cristobal Huet	6	2–4	385	15	0	2.33

Nashville Predators

	GP	G	A	P	Pim
Paul Kariya	5	2	5	7	0
Kimmo Timonen	5	1	3	4	4
Mike Sillinger	5	2	1	3	12
Shea Weber	4	2	0	2	8
Martin Erat	5	1	1	2	6
Dan Hamhuis	5	0	2	2	2
Steve Sullivan	5	0	2	2	0
Scott Hartnell	5	1	0	1	4
Adam Hall	5	1	0	1	0
David Legwand	5	0	1	1	8
Greg Johnson	5	0	1	1	2
Marek Zidlicky	2	0	1	1	2
Vernon Fiddler	2	0	1	1	0
Brendan Witt	5	0	0	0	12
Mark Eaton	5	0	0	0	8
Danny Markov	5	0	0	0	6
Scott Walker	5	0	0	0	6
Jerred Smithson	3	0	0	0	4
Scott Nichol	3	0	0	0	2
Yanic Perreault	1	0	0	0	2
Chris Mason	5	0	0	0	0
Jordin Tootoo	3	0	0	0	0
Scottie Upshall	2	0	0	0	0

Goalie	GP	W-L	Mins	GA	SO	GAA
Chris Mason	5	1–4	295	17	0	3.45

New Jersey Devils

	GP	G	A	P	Pim
Patrik Elias	9	6	10	16	4
Jamie Langenbrunner	9	3	10	13	16
Scott Gomez	9	5	4	9	6
Brian Rafalski	9	1	8	9	2
Brian Gionta	9	3	4	7	2
John Madden	9	4	1	5	8
Jay Pandolfo	9	1	4	5	0
Zach Parise	9	1	2	3	2
Paul Martin	9	0	3	3	4
Sergei Brylin	9	2	0	2	2
David Hale	8	0	2	2	12
Ken Klee	6	1	0	1	6
Grant Marshall	7	0	1	1	8
Cam Janssen	9	0	0	0	26
Jason Wiemer	8	0	0	0	16
Erik Rasmussen	9	0	0	0	8
Brad Lukowich	9	0	0	0	4
Richard Matvichuk	7	0	0	0	4
Colin White	4	0	0	0	4
Martin Brodeur	9	0	0	0	2
Tommy Albelin	2	0	0	0	2
Viktor Kozlov	3	0	0	0	0
Scott Clemmensen	1	0	0	0	0

Goalies	GP	W-L	Mins	GA	SO	GAA
Scott Clemmensen	1	0–0	6	0	0	0.00
Martin Brodeur	9	5–4	532	20	1	2.25

New York Rangers

	GP	G	A	P	Pim
Blair Betts	4	1	1	2	2
Jed Ortmeyer	4	1	0	1	4
Petr Prucha	4	1	0	1	0
Steve Rucchin	4	1	0	1	0
Ryan Hollweg	4	0	1	1	19
Michal Rozsival	4	0	1	1	8
Marek Malik	4	0	1	1	6
Jaromir Jagr	3	0	1	1	2
Martin Rucinsky	2	0	1	1	2
Michael Nylander	4	0	1	1	0
Fedor Tyutin	4	0	1	1	0
Marcel Hossa	4	0	0	0	6
Sandis Ozolinsh	3	0	0	0	6
Dominic Moore	4	0	0	0	2
Tom Poti	4	0	0	0	2
Martin Straka	4	0	0	0	2
Henrik Lundqvist	3	0	0	0	2
Colton Orr	1	0	0	0	2
Jason Ward	1	0	0	0	2
Chad Wiseman	1	0	0	0	2
Petr Sykora	4	0	0	0	0
Jason Strudwick	3	0	0	0	0
Darius Kasparaitis	2	0	0	0	0
Kevin Weekes	1	0	0	0	0

Goalies	GP	W-L	Mins	GA	SO	GAA
Kevin Weekes	1	0–1	59	4	0	4.00
Henrik Lundqvist	3	0–3	177	13	0	4.41

Ottawa Senators

	GP	G	A	P	Pim
Jason Spezza	10	5	9	14	2
Martin Havlat	10	7	6	13	4
Dany Heatley	10	3	9	12	11
Wade Redden	9	2	8	10	10
Daniel Alfredsson	10	2	8	10	4
Peter Schaefer	10	2	5	7	14
Bryan Smolinski	10	3	3	6	2
Mike Fisher	10	2	2	4	12
Zdeno Chara	10	1	3	4	23
Anton Volchenkov	9	0	4	4	8
Brian Pothier	8	2	1	3	2
Chris Phillips	9	2	0	2	6
Antoine Vermette	10	2	0	2	4
Vaclav Varada	8	0	2	2	12
Andrej Meszaros	10	1	0	1	18
Chris Neil	10	1	0	1	14
Patrick Eaves	10	1	0	1	10
Christoph Schubert	7	0	1	1	4
Ray Emery	10	0	1	1	0
Chris Kelly	10	0	0	0	2

Goalie	GP	W-L	Mins	GA	SO	GAA
Ray Emery	10	5–5	604	29	0	2.88

Philadelphia Flyers

	GP	G	A	P	Pim
Peter Forsberg	6	4	4	8	6
Simon Gagne	6	3	1	4	2
Mike Knuble	6	1	3	4	8
Eric Desjardins	6	1	3	4	6
Petr Nedved	6	2	0	2	8
Derian Hatcher	6	0	2	2	10
Michal Handzus	6	0	2	2	2
Joni Pitkanen	6	0	2	2	2
Brian Savage	6	1	0	1	4
R.J. Umberger	5	1	0	1	2
Branko Radivojevic	5	1	0	1	0
Denis Gauthier	6	0	1	1	19
Freddy Meyer	6	0	1	1	8
Mike Richards	6	0	1	1	0
Ben Eager	2	0	0	0	26
Jeff Carter	6	0	0	0	10
Mike Rathje	6	0	0	0	6
Robert Esche	6	0	0	0	2
Sami Kapanen	6	0	0	0	2
Niko Dimitrakos	5	0	0	0	2
Antero Niittymaki	2	0	0	0	0
Donald Brashear	1	0	0	0	0

Goalies	GP	W-L	Mins	GA	SO	GAA
Robert Esche	6	2–4	314	22	0	4.20
Antero Niittymaki	2	0–0	72	5	0	4.11

San Jose Sharks

	GP	G	A	P	Pim
Patrick Marleau	11	9	5	14	8
Jonathan Cheechoo	11	4	5	9	8
Joe Thornton	11	2	7	9	12
Christian Ehrhoff	11	2	6	8	18
Tom Preissing	11	1	6	7	4
Steve Bernier	11	1	5	6	8
Milan Michalek	9	1	4	5	8
Nils Ekman	11	2	2	4	8
Mark Smith	11	3	0	3	6
Pat Rissmiller	11	2	1	3	6
Matt Carle	11	0	3	3	4
Kyle McLaren	11	0	3	3	4
Marcel Goc	11	0	3	3	0
Scott Thornton	11	2	0	2	6
Ville Nieminen	11	0	2	2	24
Scott Hannan	11	0	1	1	6
Josh Gorges	11	0	1	1	4
Alyn McCauley	6	0	1	1	4
Grant Stevenson	5	0	0	0	4
Vesa Toskala	11	0	0	0	0
Ryane Clowe	1	0	0	0	0
Rob Davison	1	0	0	0	0
Evgeni Nabokov	1	0	0	0	0

Goalies	GP	W-L	Mins	GA	SO	GAA
Vesa Toskala	11	6–5	686	28	1	2.45
Evgeni Nabokov	1	0–0	11	1	0	5.00

Tampa Bay Lightning

	GP	G	A	P	Pim
Brad Richards	5	3	5	8	6
Paul Ranger	5	2	4	6	0
Martin St. Louis	5	4	0	4	2
Vincent Lecavalier	5	1	3	4	7
Dan Boyle	5	1	3	4	6
Pavel Kubina	5	1	1	2	26
Vaclav Prospal	5	0	2	2	0
Evgeni Artyukhin	5	1	0	1	6
Cory Sarich	5	0	1	1	4
Dimitry Afanasenkov	5	0	1	1	2
Darryl Sydor	5	0	1	1	0
Ruslan Fedotenko	5	0	0	0	20
Chris Dingman	3	0	0	0	19
Ryan Craig	5	0	0	0	10
Nolan Pratt	5	0	0	0	7
Fredrik Modin	5	0	0	0	6
Tim Taylor	5	0	0	0	2
Martin Cibak	5	0	0	0	0
John Grahame	4	0	0	0	0
Sean Burke	3	0	0	0	0
Rob DiMaio	2	0	0	0	0

Goalies	GP	W-L	Mins	GA	SO	GAA
John Grahame	4	1–3	188	15	0	4.79
Sean Burke	3	0–1	109	7	0	3.85

GAME SUMMARY, 2005–06

October 5, 2005

Colorado 4 at Edmonton 3 (Horcoff scored game winner at 16:32 of 3rd)

Phoenix 2 at Vancouver 3 (coaching debut for Wayne Gretzky)

Calgary 3 at Minnesota 6

San Jose 3 at Nashville 3 (Nashville trailed 2–1 after 2nd)

Atlanta 0 at Florida 2 (both goals in 3rd) [Luongo]

Montreal 2 at Boston 1 (Ryder scored game winner at 19:48 of 3rd on pp)

Anaheim 5 at Chicago 3

Los Angeles 4 at Dallas 5 (Kings led 4–0 after 1st)

NY Islanders 4 at Buffalo 6

Columbus 2 at Washington 3 (all goals in 2nd; Columbus led 1–0 and 2–1)

NY Rangers 5 at Philadelphia 3 (Flyers led 3–1 midway through game)

Pittsburgh 1 at New Jersey 5 (New Jersey led 4–0 early in 3rd)

Carolina 2 at Tampa Bay 5 (Lightning hoist Stanley Cup banner)

St. Louis 1 at Detroit 5 (Detroit outshot St. Louis 37–14)

Ottawa 3 at Toronto 2 (Alfredsson [Ott] tied game at 18:58 of 3rd and scored winning goal in first-ever shootout in NHL)

October 6, 2005

Montreal 4 at NY Rangers 3 (Ryder 2:10 OT)

Phoenix 2 at Los Angeles 3

Detroit 4 at St. Louis 3 (Detroit led 4–1 after 2nd)

October 7, 2005

Atlanta 7 at Washington 3

Pittsburgh 2 at Carolina 3 (Stillman SO)

New Jersey 2 at Philadelphia 5 (New Jersey led 2–0 early in 2nd)
Tampa Bay 0 at Florida 2 (both goals in 3rd) [Luongo]
Calgary 3 at Columbus 1 (game tied 1–1 early in 3rd)
San Jose 3 at Chicago 6 (Chicago led 4–0 early in 2nd)
Boston 1 at Buffalo 4

October 8, 2005

Buffalo 0 at Ottawa 5 [Hasek] (Ottawa led 2–0 after 2nd)
Carolina 2 at NY Islanders 3
Washington 1 at Atlanta 8 (Atlanta scored five goals in 3rd; Atlanta
    4–15 on pp)
NY Rangers 2 at New Jersey 3 (Rafalski 3:17 OT)
Boston 7 at Pittsburgh 6 (Murray 1:23 OT) (Pittsburgh led 1–0, 2–1,
    4–2, 6–4)
Florida 1 at Tampa Bay 2
Vancouver 3 at Edmonton 4 (Torres SO)
San Jose 7 at St. Louis 6 (San Jose led 2–0, trailed 4–2, 5–3, 6–5;
    Cheechoo scored game winner at 18:06 of 3rd)
Anaheim 2 at Nashville 3 (Kariya SO)
Colorado 3 at Dallas 2 (Svatos scored game winner at 18:03 of 3rd
    on pp)
Minnesota 1 at Phoenix 2
Montreal 5 at Toronto 4 (Montreal trailed 2–1, 4–3)

October 9, 2005

Minnesota 1 at Los Angeles 2 (Demitra 3:31 OT)
Calgary 3 at Detroit 6 (Detroit led 3–0 after 1st)
Columbus 3 at Chicago 2

October 10, 2005

Calgary 3 at Colorado 7 (Colorado led 5–0 late in 2nd)
Edmonton 4 at Anaheim 2 (Anaheim led 2–0 after 1st)
NY Rangers 2 at Washington 3 (Rangers led 1–0, 2–1)
Florida 3 at NY Islanders 1 (Islanders led 1–0 after 1st)

Boston 4 at Tampa Bay 2
Pittsburgh 2 at Buffalo 3 (Hecht 4:39 OT)
Vancouver 4 at Detroit 2
Toronto 5 at Ottawa 6 (Heatley SO) (Ottawa led 1–0, trailed 2–1, led 4–2, trailed 5–4)

October 11, 2005

Ottawa 4 at Montreal 2 (game tied 2–2 after 2nd)
Chicago 1 at St. Louis 4 (St. Louis led 4–0 early in 3rd)
Phoenix 2 at Dallas 3
Edmonton 1 at Los Angeles 3 (game tied 1–1 after 1st)
Philadelphia 2 at Toronto 4 (game tied 2–2 after 2nd)

October 12, 2005

Washington 2 at Carolina 7 (Washington led 1–0 after 1st)
Montreal 2 at Atlanta 0 [Danis] (Danis records shutout in first NHL game)
Vancouver 0 at Minnesota 6 [Roloson]
Nashville 5 at Colorado 4 (Colorado led 3–0 midway through game)
Columbus 1 at San Jose 4 (San Jose led 4–0 after 2nd)

October 13, 2005

Nashville 5 at Phoenix 4 (Kariya SO)
Detroit 5 at Los Angeles 2 (game tied 1–1 after 2nd)
Buffalo 4 at Tampa Bay 3 (Briere SO)
Dallas 3 at Calgary 2 (Boucher 4:05 OT)
New Jersey 1 at NY Rangers 4 (NY Rangers led 3–0 after 1st and 2nd)
Boston 5 at Florida 2
NY Islanders 5 at Washington 3

October 14, 2005

Columbus 3 at Anaheim 4
Pittsburgh 5 at Philadelphia 6 (Rathje 3:17 pp OT) (Philadelphia led 2–0, 5–1)

Vancouver 5 at Minnesota 3 (Vancouver led 1–0, trailed 2–1, led 3–2; game tied 3–3 after 2nd)

Chicago 3 at Colorado 2 (Ruutu SO)

Toronto 9 at Atlanta 1 (Toronto led 1–0 after 1st, 4–0 after 2nd) (Toronto 7–16 on pp)

October 15, 2005

Chicago 3 at San Jose 4 (no scoring in 3rd)

Nashville 4 at St. Louis 1

Edmonton 0 at Calgary 3 [Kiprusoff] (Calgary led 2–0 after 1st & 2nd)

Detroit 2 at Phoenix 0 [Legace]

Atlanta 1 at NY Rangers 5 (NY Rangers led 4–0 after 2nd)

Boston 1 at Ottawa 5 (Ottawa led 5–0 early in 3rd) (Dominik Hasek wins 300th NHL game)

NY Islanders 1 at Philadelphia 5 (teams a combined 3–20 on pp)

Carolina 6 at New Jersey 1 (Carolina led 5–1 after 2nd, chased Martin Brodeur from New Jersey goal)

Tampa Bay 3 at Pittsburgh 1 (Tampa Bay led 3–0 after 2nd) (Pittsburgh only winless team in NHL at 0–2–4)

Buffalo 2 at Florida 3

Toronto 3 at Montreal 2

October 16, 2005

Tampa Bay 2 at Washington 3 (Sykora SO)

Anaheim 1 at Minnesota 4 (Minnesota led 4–0 early in 3rd)

Dallas 2 at Vancouver 5 (game tied 2–2 after 2nd)

Columbus 1 at Los Angeles 3 (L.A. led 3–0 after 2nd)

October 17, 2005

Florida 0 at NY Rangers 4 [Lundqvist] (no scoring in 3rd)

Phoenix 2 at Calgary 0 [Joseph] (both goals in 3rd)

San Jose 2 at Detroit 3 (Fischer 4:09 OT)

October 18, 2005

Florida 3 at New Jersey 4 (New Jersey trailed 1–0, led 2–1, trailed 3–2)
Boston 3 at Montreal 4 (Boston led 2–0 after 1st, 3–2 after 2nd)
Chicago 2 at Vancouver 6 (Vancouver led 4–1 after 2nd)
Phoenix 4 at Edmonton 3 (Morris 1:00 pp OT) (Edmonton retired
    Paul Coffey's #7 sweater) (Phoenix led 3–1 early in 3rd)

October 19, 2005

Los Angeles 5 at Colorado 4 (Conroy scored game winner at 19:01
    of 3rd)
Anaheim 2 at St. Louis 3 (Brewer scored game winner at 19:03 of 3rd)
San Jose 1 at Minnesota 6 (game tied 1–1 after 2nd)
NY Islanders 3 at NY Rangers 2 (Satan SO)

October 20, 2005

Los Angeles 7 at Dallas 2 (no scoring in 3rd)
Edmonton 1 at Calgary 3 (Edmonton led 1–0 after 1st)
Phoenix 2 at Vancouver 3 (game tied 2–2 after 2nd)
New Jersey 6 at Pittsburgh 3 (Pittsburgh still winless to start
    season)
Tampa Bay 6 at Atlanta 0 [Grahame]
Buffalo 4 at Boston 3 (game tied 2–2 after 2nd)
Washington 2 at Florida 3 (Ovechkin scored both Washington
    goals to start his career with a point in each of his first eight
    games)
NY Rangers 4 at NY Islanders 5 (Jagr [NYR] hat trick—Islanders led
    3–0 by 2:47 of 1st)
St. Louis 2 at Nashville 3 (Sullivan SO)
Carolina 4 at Toronto 5 (Klee 4:44 pp OT)

October 21, 2005

Ottawa 4 at Tampa Bay 1 (game tied 1–1 after 1st) (Ottawa 6–0–0 to
    start season)
Anaheim 2 at Detroit 3

San Jose 1 at Columbus 4
Colorado 7 at Edmonton 1 (Colorado led 7–0 after 2nd)

October 22, 2005

Philadelphia 5 at Toronto 2 (game tied 2–2 early in 3rd)
Pittsburgh 3 at Boston 6 (Pittsburgh now winless in first eight games)
NY Islanders 3 at Montreal 4 (Begin scored game winner at 18:15 of 3rd)
Carolina 4 at Washington 0 [Ward/Gerber]
New Jersey 3 at Atlanta 4 (New Jersey led 3–1 midway through 3rd)
Detroit 6 at Columbus 0 [Legace] (Detroit led 4–0 after 1st & 2nd)
NY Rangers 1 at Buffalo 3 (Rangers led 1–0 after 1st)
Minnesota 3 at St. Louis 2 (Chouinard [Min] scored only goal of 3rd)
San Jose 1 at Nashville 2 (Hartnell [NAS] scored only goal of 3rd)
Calgary 1 at Dallas 2 (Morrow [DAL] scored only goal of 3rd)
Colorado 4 at Vancouver 6 (Vancouver led 5–1 midway through 3rd)
Ottawa at Florida (postponed to December 5 because of Hurricane Wilma)

October 23, 2005

Phoenix 3 at Anaheim 5 (Anaheim led 3–0 after 1st)
Minnesota 2 at Chicago 4 (game tied 2–2 after 2nd)
Calgary 3 at Los Angeles 2 (Simon scored game winner at 19:30 of 3rd on pp)

October 24, 2005

Ottawa 2 at Carolina 3 (Ottawa led 2–0 after 1st)
Detroit 6 at Columbus 2 (game tied 1–1 after 1st) (Detroit 5–0–0 on road)
Boston 4 at Toronto 5 (Lindros SO) (Boston 0–10 on pp)

October 25, 2005

Atlanta 3 at NY Islanders 4 (Islanders scored three goals in 2nd)

Florida 4 at Pittsburgh 3 (Weiss 0:53 pp OT)

Philadelphia 2 at Montreal 3 (Ribeiro 2:28 OT)

Vancouver 3 at Minnesota 1 (game tied 1–1 after 1st)

Chicago 3 at Nashville 5 (Nashville led 3–0 after 1st) (Chicago 1–13 on pp)

Edmonton 3 at Colorado 5 (Brisebois scored game winner at 19:11 of 3rd)

St. Louis 4 at Phoenix 5 (Nedved 1:51 OT) (Phoenix led 1–0, 2–1, trailed 3–2, 4–3)

Anaheim 1 at Los Angeles 3

October 26, 2005

Washington 3 at Buffalo 2

Boston 3 at Carolina 4 (Cullen 3:24 OT)

Nashville 2 at Columbus 3 (Foote 0:35 sh OT) (Nashville lost for the first time this season)

Tampa Bay 6 at New Jersey 3 (game tied 2–2 after 2nd)

San Jose 5 at Dallas 4 (Sturm [SJ] tied game at 19:40 of 3rd on pp) (Marleau 3:20 OT)

Calgary 1 at Anaheim 4 (Anaheim led 2–0 after 2nd)

October 27, 2005

Toronto 1 at Boston 2 (Boston led 2–0 early in 3rd)

NY Islanders 1 at NY Rangers 3 (Rangers led 2–0 after 1st and 2nd)

Florida 4 at Philadelphia 5 (Pitkanen 1:13 OT) (Florida led 1–0, 2–1, 3–2)

Montreal 3 at Ottawa 4 (Spezza 3:48 OT)

Atlanta 5 at Pittsburgh 7 (Atlanta led 4–0 midway through 1st) (Pittsburgh went 6–11 on pp; Mario Lemieux two goals, five points)

Chicago 2 at Detroit 5 (game tied 2–2 after 2nd)

Vancouver 2 at Colorado 6 (first game for Todd Bertuzzi [VAN] in Colorado after his attack on Steve Moore [COL] a year and a half previous)

Calgary 2 at Phoenix 3 (Comrie scored game winner at 18:32 of 3rd)

October 28, 2005

Philadelphia 6 at Carolina 8 (Philadelphia led 2–0, 3–2, 5–3) (Staal [CAR] hat trick)

Minnesota 1 at Columbus 2 (Letowski SO, 5th sudden-death) (Foote [COL] tied game at 19:18 of 3rd)

Buffalo 2 at New Jersey 3

Washington 2 at Tampa Bay 4 (game tied 2–2 after 2nd)

Edmonton 5 at Dallas 3

St. Louis 4 at Anaheim 6 (St. Louis led 2–0 early in 3rd)

San Jose 5 at Los Angeles 4 (San Jose led 2–0, trailed 3–2, led 4–3, game tied 3–3 early in 3rd)

October 29, 2005

Washington at Florida (postponed by hurricane)

New Jersey 5 at Boston 4 (Gionta SO)

Ottawa 8 at Toronto 0 [Hasek] (Heatley four goals)

NY Rangers 5 at Montreal 2 (Rangers led 3–0 after 1st & 2nd)

Tampa Bay 3 at Atlanta 2 (Atlanta led 2–0 midway through game)

Buffalo 6 at NY Islanders 4 (Islanders led 1–0, 2–1, 4–3)

Carolina 5 at Pittsburgh 3 (Pittsburgh led 3–1 after 2nd)

Columbus 1 at Minnesota 3 (game tied 1–1 after 1st)

Edmonton 5 at Nashville 1 (game tied 1–1 after 1st)

Detroit 4 at Chicago 2

Dallas 5 at Phoenix 3 (Phoenix led 2–1 after 1st, 3–2 after 2nd)

Vancouver 3 at Colorado 4 (Laperriere 1:55 OT) (game tied 1–1 after 1st, 2–2 after 2nd, 3–3 after 3rd)

Calgary 2 at San Jose 3 (Ekman SO, 1st sudden death) (Flames led 2–0 midway through 3rd; Stuart [SJ] tied game at 19:37 of 3rd)

St. Louis 2 at Los Angeles 5 (game tied 2–2 after 1st)

October 30, 2005

Philadelphia 5 at Ottawa 3 (game tied 2–2 midway through game)
Phoenix 2 at Anaheim 3 (game tied 2–2 early in 3rd)

October 31, 2005

Montreal 4 at NY Rangers 1 (game tied 0–0 after 2nd)
Florida 1 at Toronto 2 (Ponikarovsky [TOR] scored only goal of 3rd)

November 1, 2005

Boston 3 at NY Islanders 4 (Bates 4:31 OT)
Chicago 1 at Detroit 3 (Detroit won 9th in a row)
Florida 4 at Montreal 5 (Ryder 3:19 pp OT) (Begin [MON] tied game
at 19:51 of 3rd on pp)
Pittsburgh 4 at New Jersey 3 (Gonchar 1:01 OT) (New Jersey led 1–0
midway through game)
Atlanta 6 at Tampa Bay 4 (Tampa Bay led 1–0, 2–1, 3–2)
Minnesota 0 at Calgary 3 [Kiprusoff]
Columbus 1 at Edmonton 5 (game tied 1–1 after 1st)
Nashville 1 at Anaheim 4 (Nashville led 1–0 after 1st)

November 2, 2005

Ottawa 10 at Buffalo 4 (Havlat and Alfredsson each scored four
goals for Ottawa)
Chicago 6 at St. Louis 5 (Seabrook 0:35 OT) (Chicago led 5–2 early
in 3rd)
Los Angeles 6 at Dallas 3 (Visnovsky [LA] hat trick)
Minnesota 1 at Vancouver 2 (Vancouver led 2–0 midway through
game)
Nashville 2 at San Jose 3 (McCauley 1:44 sh OT)

November 3, 2005

Florida 1 at Boston 3 (Boston led 3–0 early in 3rd)
Pittsburgh 5 at NY Islanders 1 (Crosby two goals, one assist)
Washington 1 at Philadelphia 8 (game tied 1–1 midway through 1st)

Toronto 3 at Carolina 4 (Toronto led 1–0, 3–2) (Cole scored game winner at 18:26 of 3rd)

Tampa Bay 2 at Ottawa 4 (game tied 2–2 early in 3rd)

NY Rangers 4 at New Jersey 2

Edmonton 4 at Detroit 3 (Torres 1:51 OT) (Edmonton led 1–0, 2–1, 3–2)

Anaheim 3 at Colorado 4

Columbus 1 at Calgary 2 (Columbus led 1–0 after 2nd)

Los Angeles 0 at Phoenix 4 [Joseph] (no goals in 3rd)

November 4, 2005

Atlanta 2 at Washington 3 (Ovechkin SO)

Montreal 3 at Buffalo 2 (Buffalo led 1–0, 2–1; Sundstrom scored game winner at 17:08 of 3rd)

Edmonton 7 at St. Louis 2 (Edmonton wins fifth straight; St. Louis loses seventh straight)

Chicago 1 at Dallas 9 (Stu Barnes hat trick)

Columbus 3 at Vancouver 5 (Columbus led 1–0 after 1st)

San Jose 1 at Anaheim 0 [Schaefer] (Goc 0:51 pp OT)

November 5, 2005

New Jersey 2 at NY Rangers 3 (Prucha 1st–sudden death SO) (New Jersey led 2–0 midway through game)

Nashville 2 at Los Angeles 3 (Nashville led 2–0 after 1st & 2nd) (Demitra SO)

Pittsburgh 3 at Boston 6 (Boston led 3–0 midway through 1st)

Tampa Bay 3 at Toronto 5 (Hockey Hall of Fame game)

Buffalo 2 at Montreal 3

NY Islanders 0 at Ottawa 6 [Hasek]

Atlanta 3 at Philadelphia 4 (Simon Gagne [PHI] hat trick, giving him 15 goals, tops in NHL)

Florida 0 at Carolina 2 [Gerber] (both goals in 3rd)

Phoenix 4 at Detroit 1 (game tied 1–1 after 1st) (Detroit outshot Phoenix 19–1 in 3rd)

Dallas 3 at Colorado 2 (Zubov SO) (Colorado led 2–1 after 1st)
Vancouver 0 at Calgary 1 [Kiprusoff] (Nilson 10:28 1st)
Minnesota 3 at San Jose 1 (Brian Rolston hat trick)

November 6, 2005

Toronto 4 at Washington 5
Phoenix 1 at Chicago 2 (Seabrook 4:21 OT)
Detroit 4 at St. Louis 1 (Detroit 7–0–0 on road)
Minnesota 4 at Anaheim 3 (Robitaille SO)

November 7, 2005

Pittsburgh 3 at NY Rangers 2 (Pittsburgh led 3–0 early in 3rd;
    Rangers 0–7 on pp)
Edmonton 0 at Dallas 4 [Turco]
Vancouver 0 at Calgary 4 (Phaneuf scored game winner at 17:40 of
    3rd on pp)

November 8, 2005

Boston 3 at Philadelphia 4 (Pitkanen 1:55 OT; Pitkanen [PHI] tied
    game at 19:36 of 3rd)
Washington 4 at Toronto 6 (game tied 2–2 after 2nd)
Tampa Bay 2 at Montreal 3 (Tampa Bay led 2–1 after 2nd)
NY Islanders 4 at New Jersey 1
Edmonton 2 at Nashville 3 (Hartnell scored game winner at 19:37
    of 3rd; Smyth [EDM] tied game at 19:01 of 3rd)
Phoenix 4 at Minnesota 2 (Phoenix led 3–0 after 1st)
San Jose 2 at Colorado 5

November 9, 2005

Carolina 5 at Buffalo 3 (Erik Cole [CAR] first player ever to have two
    penalty shots in one game (one goal))
Pittsburgh 0 at Atlanta 5 [Dunham] (game tied 0–0 after 1st)
NY Rangers 4 at Florida 3 (Prucha 1st sudden-death SO)
St. Louis 1 at Columbus 3 (St. Louis 1–9 on pp)

Los Angeles 4 at Detroit 5 (Lang 1:39 OT) (Detroit led 4–2 midway through 3rd)

November 10, 2005

Ottawa 5 at Boston 2 (Heatley [OTT] sets team record with points in 14 straight games)

NY Islanders 2 at Philadelphia 3 (Islanders led 2–0 after 1st)

Montreal 2 at Pittsburgh 3 (Crosby SO)

NY Rangers 5 at Tampa Bay 2 (game tied 1–1 after 1st)

Chicago 4 at St. Louis 2 (St. Louis lost team record 10th in a row)

Dallas 3 at Nashville 5 (Dallas led 1–0, 2–1, 3–2)

Calgary 4 at Phoenix 3 (Iginla scored eventual game winner in 3rd on penalty shot)

Colorado 5 at Vancouver 3

November 11, 2005

New Jersey 4 at Washington 3 (New Jersey led 4–1 early in 3rd)

Tampa Bay 4 at Atlanta 5 (Tampa Bay led 2–0 late in 1st)

Edmonton 3 at Columbus 1 (game tied 1–1 after 1st & 2nd)

Carolina 1 at Florida 0 [Gerber] (Staal 17:16 pp 2nd)

Minnesota 1 at Detroit 3 (Detroit led 2–0 after 2nd)

Toronto 2 at Buffalo 5 (game tied 2–2 after 2nd)

Los Angeles 4 at Chicago 2 (Chicago led 1–0 late in 1st)

November 12, 2005

Washington 2 at New Jersey 3 (New Jersey 3–8 on pp)

Toronto 5 at Montreal 4 (O'Neill 4:13 pp OT) (Toronto led 2–0, 3–2, trailed 4–3)

Buffalo 1 at Ottawa 6 (Ottawa led 6–0 midway through 3rd)

Boston 2 at NY Islanders 5 (game tied 2–2 early in 3rd)

Florida 4 at Philadelphia 5 (Knuble scored game winner at 19:56 of 3rd sh)

Atlanta 9 at Carolina 0 [Dunham/Berkhoel] (Atlanta led 5–0 after 1st)

NY Rangers 6 at Pittsburgh 1 (Jagr hat trick)

St. Louis 1 at Nashville 3 (St. Louis led 1–0 after 1st)
Anaheim 1 at Phoenix 2 (Michalek 3:09 OT)
Colorado 3 at Calgary 5 (Calgary led 4–0 after 1st & won sixth in a row)
Dallas 3 at San Jose 2 (Zubov SO)

November 13, 2005

Los Angeles 8 at Columbus 2 (Frolov & Conroy hat tricks)
Edmonton 1 at Chicago 3 (Chicago led 3–0 after 1st)
Dallas 3 at Anaheim 1 (Dallas led 3–0 after 2nd)
Detroit 1 at Vancouver 4 (Bertuzzi hat trick)

November 14, 2005

NY Islanders 3 at Pittsburgh 2 (Jason Blake 6th sudden-death SO)
Philadelphia 2 at Tampa Bay 5 (Prospal hat trick; game tied 2–2 midway through 2nd)
Edmonton 5 at Colorado 2 (game tied 2–2 midway through 2nd)
Minnesota 2 at Calgary 3 (Minnesota led 2–0 after 2nd; Iginla scored game winner at 18:53 of 3rd on pp)

November 15, 2005

New Jersey 1 at Buffalo 4 (game tied 1–1 after 1st)
Tampa Bay 3 at Washington 4 (Ovechkin SO) (Ovechkin tied game at 18:45 of 3rd)
NY Rangers 1 at Toronto 2 (game tied 1–1 after 2nd)
Florida 3 at Montreal 4 (Koivu 4:56 OT) (Montreal led 3–0 after 2nd)
Carolina 2 at Ottawa 1 (Ottawa 0–8 on pp)
Los Angeles 2 at Nashville 3

November 16, 2005

Pittsburgh 3 at Philadelphia 2 (Crosby 4:13 OT) (all other goals in 3rd)
NY Islanders 7 at Atlanta 3 (NYI 3–12 on pp)
St. Louis 2 at Columbus 0 [Sanford] (both goals in 3rd)
Detroit 1 at Calgary 3 (game tied 1–1 after 1st)

Colorado 3 at Phoenix 1 (game tied 1–1 after 2nd)
Dallas 4 at Anaheim 2 (Anaheim led 2–1 after 1st & 2nd)
Vancouver 3 at San Jose 1 (game tied 1–1 after 2nd)

November 17, 2005

Toronto 4 at Boston 1 (game tied 1–1 after 2nd)
Washington 5 at Buffalo 8 (Pyatt [BUF] hat trick
NY Rangers 1 at Carolina 5 (game tied 1–1 after 1st)
Florida 1 at Ottawa 4 (Florida led 1–0 after 1st & 2nd)
NY Islanders 2 at Tampa Bay 3 (M. St. Louis scored game winner
    at 18:17 of 3rd)
Detroit 5 at Edmonton 6 (Stoll 0:33 pp OT) (Edmonton led 1–0,
    trailed 3–1, led 5–3)
Vancouver 4 at Los Angeles 5

November 18, 2005

Atlanta 6 at Philadelphia 5 (de Vries 3:05 OT) (Atlanta trailed 1–0,
    led 3–1, trailed 5–3; Stefan tied game at 19:53 of 3rd on pp)
Montreal 3 at New Jersey 5 (New Jersey led 2–0, trailed 3–2)
Columbus 3 at Dallas 5 (game tied 2–2 after 2nd)
Chicago 5 at Calgary 2 (Calgary led 2–1 after 1st; Chi 1–1 on pp, Cal
    2–9 on pp)
Colorado 3 at Anaheim 2 (game tied 1–1 after 1st & 2nd)

November 19, 2005

Carolina 3 at NY Rangers 4 (Rangers led 4–1 midway through 3rd)
Buffalo 3 at Boston 2 (Tallinder scored game winner at 15:39 of 3rd)
Atlanta 1 at Toronto 5 (no scoring in 3rd)
Washington 5 at Montreal 1 (Montreal 1–8 on pp)
New Jersey 4 at Ottawa 5 (New Jersey 2–10 on pp)
Philadelphia 6 at Pittsburgh 3 (game tied 3–3 after 2nd)
NY Islanders at Florida 3 (game tied 1–1 after 1st; Florida lost 11th
    straight game)
St. Louis 3 at Detroit 2

Nashville 2 at Minnesota 4
Chicago 4 at Edmonton 3
Colorado 3 at Los Angeles 4 (Demitra [LA] hat trick)
Phoenix 4 at San Jose 3 (Sanderson SO)

November 20, 2005

Vancouver 3 at Anaheim 2
Boston 2 at NY Rangers 3 (Rangers led 1–0 after 2nd)
Tampa Bay 5 at Carolina 2
Columbus 1 at Phoenix 5

November 21, 2005

Nashville 1 at Detroit 0 (not completed—late in 1st period, Detroit's Jiri Fischer collapsed at the Detroit bench and with Nashville leading 1–0 the game was cancelled)
Calgary 3 at Colorado 2 (Amonte SO)
San Jose 1 at Edmonton 2 (Ryan Smyth SO) (both regulation goals in 2nd)

November 22, 2005

NY Rangers 3 at Buffalo 2 (Jagr SO) (Buffalo led 1–0 & 2–1)
Tampa Bay 4 at Philadelphia 2
Ottawa 5 at Carolina 3
Atlanta 2 at Montreal 3 (Dagenais SO) (all regulation goals in 2nd)
Washington 4 at Pittsburgh 5 (Pittsburgh led 4–0 after 1st)
Los Angeles 6 at St. Louis 3 (game tied 3–3 after 2nd) (Demitra 4 assists)
Anaheim 2 at Phoenix 1 (all goals in 1st)
Chicago 1 at Vancouver 3 (Chicago led 1–0 after 1st)

November 23, 2005

Buffalo 4 at NY Islanders 3 (Connolly SO)
Tampa Bay 4 at Washington 3 (Prospal 2nd sudden-death SO) (Washington led 3–0 early in 2nd)

New Jersey 5 at Florida 1 (New Jersey led 5–0 midway through game; Florida's 12th straight loss)

Nashville 4 at Columbus 2

Boston 5 at Toronto 1 (Boston led 4–0 after 2nd)

Colorado 3 at Detroit 7 (game tied 2–2 midway through 2nd)

Edmonton 4 at Minnesota 3 (Moreau scored game winner at 19:10 of 3rd)

Anaheim 1 at Dallas 3 (Anaheim led 1–0 after 1st)

San Jose 2 at Calgary 3

November 24, 2005

NY Rangers 6 at Atlanta 3 (game tied 3–3 late in 2nd)

Los Angeles 3 at Nashville 4 (Nashville led 4–0 after 2nd)

San Jose 2 at Vancouver 3 (Vancouver trailed 2–1 early in 3rd)

November 25, 2005

Philadelphia 5 at Boston 3 (Philadelphia led 2–0, trailed 3–2 in 2nd)

Ottawa 6 at NY Islanders 2 (Heatley [OTT] remained the only player to have a point in every game this year so far [20])

St. Louis 3 at Minnesota 5 (Minnesota led 1–0, 2–1, trailed 3–2 after 2nd)

Detroit 1 at Anaheim 3 (game tied 1–1 after 2nd)

Toronto 3 at Carolina 4 (Vrbata SO)

Colorado 5 at Columbus 0 (Aebischer)

New Jersey 8 at Tampa Bay 2 (New Jersey led 4–1 after 1st)

Pittsburgh 3 at Florida 6 (Florida led 4–1 after 1st)

Montreal 1 at Buffalo 3 (Buffalo led 2–0 after 2nd)

Phoenix 4 at Dallas 1 (Dallas 1–12 on pp)

Edmonton 2 at Calgary 1 (Pisani 1st sudden-death SO)

November 26, 2005

NY Islanders 4 at Philadelphia 2 (Islanders scored only two goals of 3rd)

Boston 2 at Ottawa 4

Montreal 3 at Toronto 4 (Sundin 0:29 pp OT)

Florida 4 at Atlanta 7 (Atlanta led 3–0 after 1st, scored only three goals of 3rd)

Washington 2 at NY Rangers 3 (Malik 12th sudden-death SO)

Columbus 4 at St. Louis 3 (Columbus scored only two goals of 3rd)

Dallas 3 at Nashville 1 (Dallas 2–12 on pp, Nashville 1–9 on pp)

Vancouver 1 at Phoenix 2 (Phoenix led 2–0 after 1st & 2nd)

Chicago 2 at Los Angeles 3 (LA 0–9 on pp) (no scoring in 3rd)

Detroit 7 at San Jose 6 (Detroit led 1–0, trailed 2–1, led 3–2, led 4–3, led 5–4, trailed 6–5)

November 27, 2005

Buffalo 3 at Washington 2

Atlanta 5 at Carolina 4 (Atlanta scored only three goals of 3rd)

Pittsburgh 1 at Tampa Bay 4 (Tampa Bay led 4–0 early in 3rd)

Chicago 1 at Anaheim 3 (all goals in 3rd) (teams combined 0–16 on pp)

Vancouver 2 at Colorado 6 (Colorado led 4–0 after 1st)

November 28, 2005

Toronto 2 at Florida 1 (Toronto scored only goal of 3rd)

Detroit 5 at Los Angeles 2 (Chelios [DET] scored for the first time in 57 games)

November 29, 2005

Philadelphia 4 at NY Islanders 3 (Philadelphia scored only goal of 3rd)

Carolina 4 at Atlanta 3 (Kaberle 0:32 OT) (Carolina trailed 2–0, led 3–2)

Montreal 0 at Ottawa 4 [Emery] (Emery won for 9th straight time to start his career—new NHL record)

Boston 2 at New Jersey 3 (Mogilny scored game winner at 19:28 of 3rd after Madden won faceoff cleanly from Joe Thornton, who was traded the next day)

Buffalo 3 at Pittsburgh 2
Calgary 0 at Nashville 2 [Vokoun]
Colorado 3 at Edmonton 2 (Colorado led 2–0 after 1st; game tied
2–2 after 2nd)

November 30, 2005

New Jersey 1 at Philadelphia 2 (Philadelphia led 2–0 after 2nd)
Toronto 1 at Tampa Bay 2 (Tampa Bay scored only goal of 3rd)
Columbus 3 at Minnesota 2 (Balastik SO)
Los Angeles 2 at Chicago 3 (Chicago led 3–0 after 2nd)
San Jose 1 at Dallas 4 (Dallas led 2–1 after 1st & 2nd)
Colorado 2 at Vancouver 5 (game tied 2–2 midway through 2nd)
Phoenix 1 at Anaheim 6 (Anaheim led 4–0 after 2nd)

December 1, 2005

Washington 2 at Florida 3
Ottawa 0 at Boston 3 [Toivonen]
Pittsburgh 1 at NY Rangers 2 (no scoring in 3rd)
Toronto 4 at Atlanta 0 [Tellqvist]
Buffalo 3 at Montreal 2 (Campbell 2:15 OT) (Montreal led 2–0
midway through game)
Calgary 3 at Detroit 2 (Calgary scored only goal of 3rd)
Columbus 1 at St. Louis 4 (St. Louis 3–11 on pp)
Minnesota 1 at Nashville 2 (both teams 1–8 on pp)
Vancouver 3 at Edmonton 5 (Vancouver led 1–0 after 0:18 of 1st)

December 2, 2005

Los Angeles 1 at Ottawa 5
Chicago 2 at Tampa Bay 3 (Richards SO) (both teams scored once
each in 1st & 2nd)
San Jose 5 at Buffalo 0 [Nabokov/Schaefer] (no scoring in 3rd)
Carolina 4 at Dallas 5 (Modano SO) (Carolina scored only two goals
of 3rd)

December 3, 2005

Minnesota 2 at New Jersey 3 (Kozlov SO)

NY Rangers 1 at Washington 5 (Washington led 5–0 early in 3rd)
(Ovechkin one goal, three assists)

San Jose 5 at Toronto 4 (Toronto led 3–1 after 1st)

Los Angeles 2 at Montreal 3 (Montreal scored only goal of 3rd)

Calgary 3 at Pittsburgh 2 (game tied 1–1 after 2nd)

Chicago 3 at Florida 4 (Jokinen 3:57 OT)

Philadelphia 2 at Nashville 3

Carolina 4 at Phoenix 8

Boston 5 at Edmonton 4 (Tanabe 4:30 OT) (Edmonton led 3–0
early in 2nd)

Atlanta 1 at Anaheim 2 (McDonald scored game winning goal at
15:31 of 3rd)

December 4, 2005

NY Islanders 2 at Detroit 1 (Islanders scored only goal of 3rd)

Buffalo 6 at Colorado 4 (Buffalo led 4–1 after 1st; game tied 4–4
midway through 3rd)

Boston 2 at Vancouver 5 (Vancouver led 2–0 after 1st; game tied 2–2
after 2nd)

December 5, 2005

Minnesota 1 at NY Rangers 3 (game tied 1–1 after 2nd)

Ottawa 6 at Florida 3 (Bochenski [OTT] first career hat trick)

Atlanta 2 at Phoenix 5 (Atlanta led 2–0 midway through 2nd)

December 6, 2005

Calgary 0 at Philadelphia 1 [Kiprusoff (CAL)/Niittymaki (PHI)]
(Richards SO) (for the first time in NHL history, a goalie lost a
game in which he recorded a shutout. Miikka Kiprusoff (CAL)
was credited with a shutout but also a loss after the Flames
lost the shootout)

Los Angeles 2 at Toronto 1 (no scoring in 3rd)

New Jersey 2 at Detroit 5 (game tied 2–2 midway through 2nd)

NY Islanders 6 at St. Louis 3 (Islanders led 3–0 after 1st)

Carolina 6 at Anaheim 2 (Kevyn Adams natural hat trick)

Atlanta 3 at San Jose 5 (San Jose 3–0 since acquiring Thornton)

December 7, 2005

Nashville 5 at Washington 2 (Washington 1–10 on pp)

Calgary 4 at New Jersey 1 (Calgary scored three goals on first four shots)

NY Rangers 1 at Chicago 2 (Arnason 1:20 pp OT) (both regulation goals in 2nd)

Florida 3 at Dallas 4 (Lehtinen scored game winner at 19:44 of 3rd on pp)

Boston 1 at Colorado 4 (game tied 1–1 after 1st)

December 8, 2005

Anaheim 2 at Buffalo 3 (Afinogenov 2:11 pp OT)

Edmonton 3 at Philadelphia 2 (Moreau [EDM] scored two sh goals)

NY Islanders 3 at Columbus 4 (Vyborny SO) (Parrish [NYI] tied game at 19:23 of 3rd)

Minnesota 5 at Pittsburgh 0 [Fernandez]

St. Louis 3 at Tampa Bay 5 (St. Louis led 3–2 after 2nd)

NY Rangers 5 at Nashville 1 (Rangers led 5–0 after 2nd)

Carolina 3 at Los Angeles 2 (Carolina led 3–0 after 2nd)

Florida 6 at San Jose 2 (San Jose scored four goals in 2nd)

December 9, 2005

Detroit 4 at Washington 3 (game tied 2–2 after 2nd)

Columbus 2 at Atlanta 5 (Ronald Petrovicky first career hat trick)

Colorado 2 at New Jersey 3 (Laaksonen 4th sudden-death SO) (Colordao led 3–0 after 1st)

Ottawa 3 at Vancouver 4 (D. Sedin 1st sudden-death SO)

December 10, 2005

Minnesota 2 at Philadelphia 3 (Radivojevic scored game winner at 19:07 of 3rd)

Florida 1 at Los Angeles 3 (LA led 3–0 early in 3rd; Florida lost 12th road game in a row)

Dallas 2 at Toronto 1 (Dallas led 2–0 after 1st & 2nd)

Anaheim 5 at Montreal 3

Edmonton 2 at NY Islanders 3 (Hunter SO)

Colorado 3 at Pittsburgh 4 (Pittsburgh ended six-game losing streak)

Nashville 3 at Tampa Bay 4 (Nashville had 16 total shots)

NY Rangers 5 at St. Louis 4 (Rucinsky 1:37 OT) (Rangers trailed 1–0, led 2–1, led 3–2 and 4–3; Sillinger [STL] tied game at 19:52 of 3rd)

Ottawa 1 at Calgary 2 (Langkow 3:38 OT)

Carolina 3 at San Jose 4

December 11, 2005

Chicago 5 at Atlanta 4 (Holmqvist 2nd sudden-death SO) (Chicago led 3–0 midway through 1st)

Phoenix 2 at Boston 1 (Nagy 0:30 OT)

New Jersey 2 at Columbus 3 Berard 4:46 OT)

Buffalo 3 at Minnesota 2 (Grier broke 2–2 tie at 16:28 of 3rd)

December 12, 2005

Pittsburgh 1 at Detroit 3 (Pittsburgh scored in final minute)

Anaheim 2 at Toronto 3 (Anaheim 0–8 on pp)

Ottawa 6 at Colorado 2 (Colorado led 1–0 & 2–1)

December 13, 2005

Minnesota 4 at NY Islanders 3 (no scoring in 3rd)

Vancouver 3 at NY Rangers 2 (Cooke broke 2–2 tie at 15:29 of 3rd)

Chicago 3 at Carolina 5 (Chicago led 2–0 midway through 1st)

Detroit 6 at Atlanta 7 (Detroit trailed 6–2 after 2nd, scored four in 3rd to tie game; Stefan scored game winner at 15:49 of 3rd)

Nashville 3 at Florida 7 (Florida scored four unanswered goals in 2nd)
Philadelphia 3 at Columbus 1 (Columbus scored opening goal)
Phoenix 2 at Montreal 5 (Montreal led 3–0 after 2nd)
Edmonton 1 at New Jersey 2 (Kozlov SO)
Pittsburgh 0 at St. Louis 3 [Sanford]

December 14, 2005

Dallas 3 at Buffalo 4 (Buffalo goalie Biron won 11th straight game)
Tampa Bay 2 at Anaheim 4
Washington 3 at Los Angeles 2 (LA led 2–1 after 2nd)

December 15, 2005

Vancouver 5 at Philadelphia 4 (Vancouver trailed 1–0, 2–1, 3–2, scored three goals early in 3rd)
Columbus 1 at Carolina 2 (Columbus scored only goal of 3rd)
Dallas 2 at Ottawa 0 [Turco]
Atlanta 3 at New Jersey 2 (Savard 4:55 pp OT)
Detroit 2 at Florida 3 (Jokinen 1:36 pp OT)
Chicago 3 at Nashville 5 (Chicago 0–9 on pp)
Boston 2 at Minnesota 3 (Sturm [BOS] scored only goal of 3rd)
Montreal 3 at Edmonton 5 (Montreal led 3–1 early in 2nd)
Tampa Bay 3 at Phoenix 1 (Tampa Bay led 3–0 early in 3rd)

December 16, 2005

Buffalo 4 at Pittsburgh 3 (Drury 1:32 pp OT)
St. Louis 1 at Chicago 5 (Chicago led 2–0 after 1st)
Los Angeles 4 at Anaheim 3 (Demitra SO)
Washington 1 at San Jose 4 (San Jose led 3–0 after 2nd; teams combined 0–11 on pp)

December 17, 2005

Pittsburgh 3 at Buffalo 4 (Buffalo led 3–1 after 1st)
Toronto 2 at Ottawa 8 (game tied 1–1 after 1st; Belfour surrendered all eight goals)

Colorado 4 at NY Islanders 5 (Islanders led 3–0 early in 2nd)

New Jersey 1 at Carolina 4 (Carolina scored only three goals of 3rd to break 1–1 tie)

Florida 1 at Atlanta 2 (Atlanta scored only two goals of 3rd)

Detroit 6 at Tampa Bay 3 (game tied 3–3 after 2nd)

Philadelphia 5 at St. Louis 2 (Philadelphia led 4–1 early in 2nd)

Columbus 3 at Nashville 7 (Nashville scored six goals in 2nd)

Montreal 3 at Minnesota 4 (Foster 3:13 OT)

Boston 0 at Calgary 3 [Kiprusoff] (all goals in 1st)

Edmonton 5 at Vancouver 4 (Peca 4:08 OT)

Phoenix 1 at Los Angeles 4 (Gretzky not coaching Phoenix to attend to gravely ill mother)

December 18, 2005

Colorado 2 at NY Rangers 1 (all goals in 2nd)

Florida 3 at Washington 2

Dallas 5 at Chicago 3 (Dallas led 3–0 after 1st)

San Jose 4 at Anaheim 5 (first loss for San Jose since Joe Thornton joined team seven games ago)

December 19, 2005

Buffalo 2 at Philadelphia 1 (Afinogenov 1st sudden-death SO)

NY Islanders 6 at Toronto 9 (game tied 4–4 after 1st)

Dallas 1 at Minnesota 2 (Minnesota scored only two goals of 3rd)

Calgary 4 at Edmonton 5 (Edmonton scored only two goals of 3rd)

Los Angeles 4 at Vancouver 3 (Frolov SO)

December 20, 2005

New Jersey 3 at NY Rangers 1 (New Jersey scored only three goals of 3rd in first game for Lou Lamoriello as team's interim coach)

Tampa Bay 4 at Carolina 6 (Carolina scored only two goals of 3rd)

Ottawa 3 at Montreal 4 (Dagenais SO)

Columbus 3 at Detroit 4 (Williams SO)

Colorado 2 at Nashville 3 (Nashville led 2–1 after 1st & 2nd)

St. Louis 5 at Phoenix 4 (Phoenix led 1–0, 2–1, 3–2)
Anaheim 2 at San Jose 4 (Anaheim 2–9 on pp; Cheechoo hat trick)

December 21, 2005

Dallas 5 at Columbus 3 (Dallas scored only three goals of 3rd)
New Jersey 2 at NY Islanders 4 (teams combined 2–18 on pp)
Nashville 6 at Chicago 1 (game tied 1–1 midway through 1st; attendance 10,545 in Chicago)
Los Angeles 5 at Calgary 2 (Calgary led 2–0 after 1st)
Edmonton 7 at Vancouver 6 (game tied 2–2 after 1st, 5–5 after 2nd)
St. Louis 3 at Anaheim 6 (Anaheim led 4–1 after 1st)

December 22, 2005

Toronto 1 at Boston 4 (Boston scored only two goals of 3rd)
Tampa Bay 2 at NY Rangers 4 (Rangers led 2–0 after 2nd; game tied 2–2 early in 3rd)
Ottawa 3 at Philadelphia 4 (Philadelphia led 4–0 midway through game)
Washington 6 at Atlanta 5 (Ovechkin SO) (Ovechkin also had one goal, three assists)
Buffalo 1 at Florida 4
Minnesota 3 at Colorado 4 (Colorado led 2–0, 3–2; game tied 3–3 after 2nd)
San Jose 1 at Phoenix 2 (game tied 1–1 after 1st & 2nd)

December 23, 2005

Boston 1 at Toronto 2 (Toronto scored only goal of 3rd)
Ottawa 4 at NY Islanders 2 (Ottawa led 3–0 after 1st)
Montreal 2 at Washington 4 (game tied 2–2 midway through 3rd)
Florida 3 at Carolina 4 (game tied 1–1 after 1st, 2–2 after 2nd)
Nashville 5 at Columbus 4 (Nashville led 4–2 after 1st)
Atlanta 1 at New Jersey 0 [Garnett] (Hossa 9:03 pp 2nd)
Philadelphia 5 at Pittsburgh 4 (Philadelphia led 3–0, trailed 4–3)

Buffalo 4 at Tampa Bay 1 (game tied 1–1 after 1st; Tampa Bay 0–7 on pp)

Colorado 3 at Minnesota 5 (game tied 2–2 midway through 3rd)

Detroit 3 at Chicago 2 (Datsyuk 4:59 pp OT) (Detroit scored twice in final minute of 3rd to tie game)

Phoenix 3 at Dallas 2 (both teams scored twice in 3rd; Phoenix won despite having just 13 total shots, two in 3rd)

Los Angeles 3 at Edmonton 5 (Edmonton scored only three goals of 3rd)

Calgary 6 at Vancouver 5 (Reinprecht SO) (Calgary led 1–0, 2–1, trailed 3–2, led 4–3, 5–4)

St. Louis 2 at San Jose 1 (Cajanek SO) (both regulation goals in 3rd)

December 26, 2005

NY Islanders 3 at Buffalo 6 (Islanders led 3–1 after 1st)

Montreal 0 at Atlanta 4 [Garnett]

Philadelphia 3 at Florida 2 (Handzus 1st sudden-death SO)

Chicago 3 at Columbus 4 (Balastik 2:35 OT) (Zherdev [CBJ] tied game at 19:36 of 3rd)

New Jersey 1 at Toronto 2 (all goals in 1st)

NY Rangers 2 at Ottawa 6 (Redden two goals, two assists)

Carolina 4 at Tampa Bay 5 (Boyle 4:26 OT)

Dallas 6 at St. Louis 1 (Dallas led 6–0 late in 3rd)

Phoenix 4 at Colorado 7 (Phoenix led 3–0 in 1st; game tied 3–3 end of 1st; Phoenix led 4–3 after 2nd)

Minnesota 4 at Edmonton 1 (Edmonton scored only goal of 1st)

Calgary 1 at Vancouver 2

San Jose 3 at Los Angeles 4 (LA led 4–1 early in 3rd)

December 27, 2005

Boston 4 at Washington 3 (Stuart 2:04 OT) (Washington led 3–1 midway through 3rd)

Toronto 3 at Pittsburgh 2 (Kaberle 2:26 OT)

Detroit 4 at Dallas 1 (game tied 1–1 after 1st)
Nashville 4 at Calgary 3 (Nashville scored only two goals of 3rd)

December 28, 2005

NY Rangers 6 at NY Islanders 2 (game tied 2–2 after 1st & 2nd)
    (Jagr four points)
Philadelphia 4 at Atlanta 3 (Kapanen 0:13 OT)
Boston 4 at Florida 6 (game tied 3–3 after 1st)
Anaheim 0 at Columbus 1 (Chimera 16:53 3rd) [Denis]
Carolina 2 at Ottawa 6 (Carolina 1–11 on pp)
Washington 2 at New Jersey 7 (Washington scored first, then
    trailed 4–1 by 3rd)
Montreal 4 at Tampa Bay 3 (Montreal ended nine-game road
    losing streak)
Minnesota 4 at Edmonton 2
St. Louis 2 at Chicago 1 (St. Louis led 2–0 after 1st & 2nd)
Los Angeles 5 at Colorado 3
Nashville 3 at Vancouver 4 (Nashville led 2–0, 3–2; Vancouver
    scored only goal of 3rd)
Phoenix 5 at San Jose 4 (Phoenix scored four goals in 2:58 early in 3rd)

December 29, 2005

Philadelphia 4 at Carolina 3 (Kapanen 1:27 OT)
Buffalo 3 at Toronto 4 (Sundin SO)
New Jersey 2 at Pittsburgh 6 (Pittsburgh ends six–game losing
    streak)
St. Louis 0 at Dallas 3 [Turco]
Los Angeles 5 at Phoenix 6 (Ballard 3:52 sh OT) (Armstrong [LA]
    tied game at 18:49 of 3rd)
Minnesota 2 at Calgary 4 (game tied 2–2 after 2nd)

December 30, 2005

NY Islanders 3 at Ottawa 4 (Islanders led 3–1 midway through 2nd;
    Smolinski scored game winner at 18:14 of 3rd)

Boston 2 at Tampa Bay 1 (game tied 0–0 after 1st, 1–1 after 2nd)
Montreal 1 at Florida 2 (Nieuwendyk both Florida goals)
Atlanta 1 at Buffalo 4 (Atlanta 0–8 on pp)
Columbus 3 at Chicago 2 (Columbus led 3–0 after 1st)
Nashville 2 at Edmonton 4
Colorado 2 at San Jose 5 (game tied 2–2 midway through 2nd)

December 31, 2005

NY Rangers 3 at Pittsburgh 4 (Crosby 3:31 pp OT)
Philadelphia 3 at Washington 4 (Willsie SO)
Anaheim 5 at St. Louis 4 (Kunitz SO)
Vancouver 3 at Minnesota 4
Toronto 6 at New Jersey 3 (Toronto trailed 2–1 early in 2nd)
Columbus 2 at Detroit 5 (Columbus led 2–0 early in 2nd)
Montreal 3 at Carolina 5 (Carolina scored two goals in last two
   minutes of 3rd to break 3–3 tie)
Los Angeles 3 at Dallas 2 (LA led 3–0 after 2nd)
Colorado 5 at Phoenix 2
Edmonton 5 at Calgary 6 (Huselius broke 5–5 tie with game winner
   at 18:45 of 3rd)

January 1, 2006

Atlanta 5 at Washington 2 (Atlanta led 3–0 midway through 2nd)
Florida 2 at Buffalo 1 (Florida scored only goal of 3rd)
Anaheim 4 at Nashville 2 (Anaheim led 3–2 after 1st)

January 2, 2006

Philadelphia 1 at Boston 0 (Carter 6:25 2nd) [Niittymaki]
Chicago 2 at Calgary 3 (Calgary scored only goal of 3rd)
Tampa Bay 2 at NY Islanders 1 (Tampa Bay scored only goal of 3rd)
Ottawa 3 at Atlanta 8 (first game in Atlanta for Dany Heatley since
   being traded, and he was booed all night; worst loss of the
   season for Ottawa)
Pittsburgh 2 at Toronto 3 (McCabe 1:02 OT)

Vancouver 1 at St. Louis 4 (St. Louis led 3–1 after 1st & 2nd)

Dallas 2 at Los Angeles 3 (Norstrom 2:29 pp OT)

January 3, 2006

Minnesota 4 at Detroit 2 (Minnesota led 2–0 after 1st; Roloson [MIN]) stopped 43 of 45 shots)

Tampa Bay 1 at NY Rangers 0 (Prospal 3:47 OT) [Grahame]

Pittsburgh 6 at Montreal 4 (Crosby two goals in first game in Montreal, his boyhood favourite team; game tied 4–4 after 2nd)

Florida 0 at New Jersey 3 [Brodeur] (New Jersey scored in each period)

Nashville 0 at Colorado 3 [Aebischer] (Colorado scored in each period)

Chicago 0 at Edmonton 5 [Conklin]

January 4, 2006

Florida 3 at NY Islanders 4 (Parrish 2:15 OT)

Ottawa 3 at Washington 1 (Ottawa led 2–0 after 2nd; teams combined 1–17 on pp)

Atlanta 3 at Carolina 4 (Atlanta led 3–1 early in 3rd)

Nashville 4 at St. Louis 3 (game tied 2–2 after 1st; Nashville scored only two goals of 2nd)

Vancouver 1 at Dallas 3 (Dallas trailed 1–0 after 2nd)

January 5, 2006

Ottawa 2 at Boston 4 (game tied 2–2 midway through 3rd)

Tampa Bay 1 at Buffalo 3

Philadelphia 4 at NY Rangers 3 (Gagne 0:07 OT)

Montreal 4 at New Jersey 5 (Montreal scored only two goals of 3rd)

St. Louis 0 at Detroit 3 [Legace] (Detroit led 2–0 after 1st & 2nd)

Colorado 4 at Minnesota 2

Vancouver 3 at Chicago 2

Phoenix 0 at Los Angeles 4 [Garon] (LA led 3–0 after 1st & 2nd)

Columbus 3 at San Jose 6 (Cheechoo [SJ] hat trick)

January 6, 2006

Philadelphia 3 at Washington 1 (Washington led 1–0 after 1st)
NY Islanders 1 at Carolina 4 (game tied 1–1 midway through 2nd)
Pittsburgh 4 at Atlanta 6 (Kovalchuk [ATL] hat trick; Atlanta led 5–0 after 2nd)
Detroit 3 at Nashville 1 (Nashville led 1–0 after 1st)
Anaheim 3 at Dallas 4 (Miettinen 1st round sudden-death SO) (Anaheim led 3–0 after 1st)
Toronto 0 at Calgary 1 (Amonte 4:24 2nd) [Kiprusoff]

January 7, 2006

Florida 0 at NY Rangers 4 [Lundqvist]
Ottawa 1 at Montreal 4 (Montreal led 4–0 after 1st)
Columbus 2 at Colorado 3 (Tanguay 1st sudden-death SO) (Colorado led 2–0 after 1st)
Tampa Bay 3 at Boston 6 (Boston scored last five goals of game)
Carolina 3 at NY Islanders 0 (all goals in 2nd) [Gerber]
Toronto 3 at Edmonton 2 (Toronto led 2–0 after 1st)
New Jersey 3 at Buffalo 2
Atlanta 4 at Pittsburgh 3 (Atlanta scored only goal of 3rd)
Anaheim 1 at Minnesota 4
Calgary 3 at Vancouver 4 (Morrison 2:53 pp OT) (Salo [VAN] tied game at 19:30 of 3rd)
Los Angeles 2 at San Jose 3 (L.A. led 2–0 midway through 1st)

January 8, 2006

Florida 4 at Washington 3 (Nieuwendyk SO)
Dallas 6 at Detroit 3 (Detroit led 3–0 early in 3rd)
Nashville 5 at Chicago 1 (Nashville led 5–0 early in 3rd)
Columbus 5 at Phoenix 2 (Berard hat trick)

January 9, 2006

Philadelphia 0 at New Jersey 3 (New Jersey scored in each period) [Brodeur]

Dallas 2 at Minnesota 1 (no scoring in 3rd)
St. Louis 1 at Colorado 6 (Svatos hat trick)
Los Angeles 2 at Anaheim 6 (game tied 2–2 early in 2nd)

January 10, 2006

San Jose 6 at Boston 2 (first game vs. Boston for the recently traded
    Joe Thornton)
Calgary 2 at NY Rangers 4 (Calgary led 2–0 after 1st)
Chicago 4 at Washington 3 (Calder 2:01 OT)
Detroit 2 at Carolina 3 (Carolina led 3–0 late in 1st)
Phoenix 2 at Ottawa 7 (game tied 1–1 midway through 1st)
Edmonton 3 at Pittsburgh 1 (Horcoff hat trick)
NY Islanders 1 at Nashville 2 (Nashville scored only goal of 3rd)
Toronto 3 at Vancouver 4 (Toronto led 2–1 after 1st)

January 11, 2006

Nashville 3 at Atlanta 4 (Marian Hossa SO)
Pittsburgh 1 at Columbus 6 (no scoring in 3rd)
Philadelphia 5 at Chicago 2 (Philadelphia scored only three goals
    of 3rd)
Montreal 1 at Colorado 2 (Colorado scored only two goals of 3rd)

January 12, 2006

Los Angeles 6 at Boston 0 (Frolov hat trick) [Garon]
Phoenix 2 at Buffalo 1 (Sanderson SO)
Calgary 2 at NY Islanders 3 (Calgary led 2–1 after 1st)
Edmonton 4 at NY Rangers 5 (Jagr 0:14 OT)
St. Louis 1 at Florida 3
San Jose 2 at Ottawa 0 [Nabokov]
Philadelphia 3 at Detroit 6 (game tied 1–1 after 2nd)
Washington 1 at Dallas 4 (Dallas led 3–0 after 1st)

January 13, 2006

Nashville 4 at Carolina 5 (Kaberle 2:31 OT penalty shot)
St. Louis 0 at Atlanta 2 [Lehtonen]
Vancouver 0 at New Jersey 3 (all goals in 3rd) [Brodeur]
Columbus 2 at Tampa Bay 4
Pittsburgh 1 at Chicago 4 (fifth successive loss for Pittsburgh)
Washington 3 at Anaheim 2 (Ovechkin 3:04 OT; Ovechkin hat trick)

January 14, 2006

Dallas 2 at Boston 1 (Jokinen SO; Jokinen now 5–5 in shootouts)
Colorado 4 at Philadelphia 3 (Tanguay 4:14 pp OT)
NY Rangers 3 at Detroit 4 (game tied 2–2 after 2nd)
Phoenix 4 at Toronto 3 (Toronto led 3–0 after 1st)
San Jose 2 at Montreal 6 (Montreal scored all six goals in 2nd)
Vancouver 8 at NY Islanders 1 (Bertuzzi hat trick)
Los Angeles 1 at Buffalo 10 (Drury one goal & three assists)
Columbus 5 at Florida 4 (Vyborny 4:48 pp OT) (Horton [FLO] tied
     game at 19:13 of 3rd)
Calgary 4 at Minnesota 1 (Calgary scored only three goals of 3rd)
Ottawa 5 at Edmonton 3 (Edmonton led 2–1 after 1st)

January 15, 2006

St. Louis 2 at Carolina 4 (St. Louis led 2–0 after 1st)
New Jersey 3 at Chicago 2 (Kozlov 1st sudden-death SO)
Pittsburgh 4 at Nashville 5 (Nashville led 5–1 midway through
     game)

January 16, 2006

Anaheim 3 at Boston 4 (Bergeron 1:55 OT)
Washington 6 at Phoenix 1 (game tied 1–1 after 1st)
NY Rangers 3 at Columbus 4 (Nash broke 3–3 tie at 13:22 of 3rd)
Dallas 2 at Montreal 4 (Montreal had just 15 shots in total)
Vancouver 4 at Pittsburgh 2 (Pittsburgh 1–8 on pp)

Ottawa 6 at Minnesota 1 (Minnesota scored game's first goal)
Tampa Bay 1 at San Jose 3
Buffalo 3 at Edmonton 1 (game tied 1–1 after 1st & 2nd)

January 17, 2006

Carolina 4 at Philadelphia 3 (Brind'Amour 1st sudden-death SO)
New Jersey 5 at St. Louis 3 (New Jersey led 3–0; St. Louis tied game
    3–3 in 3rd)
NY Islanders 2 at Chicago 1 (Kvasha 3:02 OT)
Toronto 3 at Colorado 5 (Colorado scored four goals in 2nd)
Tampa Bay 4 at Los Angeles 1 (1,000th regular-season game in
    Tampa Bay history)

January 18, 2006

Detroit 4 at Columbus 0 [Osgood]
Toronto 3 at Minnesota 5 (game tied 2–2 late in 2nd)
Atlanta 5 at Dallas 2 (Dallas led 2–0 midway through 2nd)

January 19, 2006

Boston 5 at Philadelphia 2 (Philadelphia's fourth straight loss)
St. Louis 4 at Washington 5 (Eminger 1st sudden-death shootout)
NY Islanders 3 at Carolina 4 (Islanders 0–7 on pp)
Anaheim 4 at Ottawa 3 (Kunitz SO)
NY Rangers 4 at Pittsburgh 2 (game tied 2–2 midway through 3rd)
New Jersey 4 at Nashville 3 (Kozlov SO)
Colorado 2 at Chicago 4 (no scoring in 3rd)
Montreal 2 at Calgary 3 (Montreal scored first)
Florida 3 at Phoenix 6 (Phoenix 5–8 on pp)
Buffalo 1 at Vancouver 4 (Vancouver scored only three goals of 3rd)
Atlanta 6 at Los Angeles 8 (Robitaille [LA] hat trick) (LA led 2–0,
    3–2, trailed 5–3, led 6–5)
Edmonton 3 at San Jose 2 (Smyth SO)

January 20, 2006

St. Louis 3 at Columbus 4 (Nash SO)

Chicago 1 at Minnesota 4

Tampa Bay 6 at Dallas 3 (Tampa Bay led 4–1 after 1st)

January 21, 2006

NY Islanders 2 at New Jersey 3 (Parise 2nd sudden-death SO) (New Jersey led 2–0 early in 3rd)

Philadelphia 2 at Pittsburgh 1 (9th straight loss for Pittsburgh)

Detroit 4 at Colorado 3 (no scoring in 3rd)

San Jose 4 at Los Angeles 3 (Marleau 4:51 pp OT)

NY Rangers 3 at Boston 2 (Sykora 3rd sudden-death SO)

Toronto 0 at Ottawa 7 [Hasek] (fifth straight loss to Ottawa for Toronto)

Tampa Bay 2 at Atlanta 0 [Grahame]

Carolina 2 at Washington 5 (Washington led 3–0 after 1st)

Columbus 2 at Nashville 7 (Nashville scored four goals in 3rd)

Buffalo 4 at Calgary 4 (game tied 1–1 after 1st)

Edmonton 3 at Phoenix 4 (Nagy SO)

Montreal 2 at Vancouver 6 (Vancouver led 6–0 after 1st)

Florida 0 at Anaheim 1 (Kunitz 0:29 1st) [Giguere]

January 22, 2006

New Jersey 1 at NY Rangers 3 (New Jersey's first loss after nine wins)

Minnesota 3 at Chicago 2 (Minnesota led 3–0 after 2nd)

January 23, 2006

Pittsburgh 2 at Philadelphia 4 (Pittsburgh's 10th straight loss)

Boston 3 at Washington 2 (Boston led 3–0 late in 2nd)

Montreal 3 at Carolina 7 (Carolina led 6–1 early in 3rd)

Toronto 3 at Ottawa 4 (Ottawa's sixth straight win over Toronto this season)

Nashville 3 at Detroit 2 (completion of game started November 21, 2005, in which Detroit's Jiri Fischer suffered a heart seizure during the first period with Nashville leading 1–0. That game was postponed and this was played in full (60 minutes), but the Predators started with a 1–0 lead. The total playing time of this game was 72:30, the longest regular season game in NHL history.)

Vancouver 0 at St. Louis 4 [Sanford]

Phoenix 1 at Dallas 4 (Phoenix scored early in 1st for 1–0 lead)

Calgary 3 at Edmonton 1 (game tied 1–1 midway through 2nd)

Anaheim 2 at Los Angeles 3 (Corvo 2nd sudden-death SO)

January 24, 2006

New Jersey 4 at NY Islanders 0 [Brodeur]

Buffalo 2 at NY Rangers 1 (Buffalo scored only goal of 3rd)

Boston 3 at Atlanta 2 (Boston scored only goal of 3rd)

Vancouver 5 at Columbus 6 (Columbus blew leads of 2–0, 3–2, 4–3, 5–4 before scoring winning goal at 15:23 of 3rd)

Florida 3 at Tampa Bay 2 (Jokinen 3:15 OT)

Nashville 2 at Detroit 1 (Kariya 0:35 OT)

Phoenix 2 at Minnesota 3 (Minnesota scored only goal of 3rd)

Calgary 4 at Colorado 7 (game tied 2–2 early in 2nd; Colorado scored five goals in 2nd)

Los Angeles 1 at San Jose 4 (San Jose 2–9 on pp)

January 25, 2006

Montreal 5 at Philadelphia 3 (Philadelphia led 2–0, 3–2; Montreal scored only two goals of 3rd)

Carolina 4 at Florida 3 (Cole 1st sudden-death SO)

Washington 1 at Pittsburgh 8 (Crosby four points, Ovechkin one)

St. Louis 3 at Dallas 4 (Zubov SO)

Edmonton 6 at Anaheim 3 (Anaheim led 2–0, 3–1)

January 26, 2006

Washington 2 at Boston 3 (game tied 2–2 midway through 3rd)
Pittsburgh 3 at NY Islanders 4 (Satan SO) (Islanders led 3–1;
    Pittsburgh tied game sh at 19:33 of 3rd)
Carolina 5 at Atlanta 1
Buffalo 8 at Toronto 4 (seventh straight loss for Toronto)
Montreal 0 at Ottawa 3 [Hasek] (Montreal tied a team record with
    just 12 total shots)
New Jersey 0 at Tampa Bay 1 [Grahame] (Fedotenko 2:22 OT)
Vancouver 1 at Detroit 2 (Detroit scored only goal of 3rd)
Phoenix 5 at St. Louis 3 (Phoenix scored only three goals of 3rd to
    win on coach Gretzky's 45th birthday)
Nashville 1 at Minnesota 5 (teams combined 0–13 on pp)
Calgary 0 at Chicago 2 [Munro] (both goals in 3rd)
Dallas 3 at Colorado 2 [Jokinen] SO
Edmonton 5 at Los Angeles 3 (game tied 2–2 after 2nd)
Anaheim 2 at San Jose 0 [Bryzgalov]

January 27, 2006

Minnesota 3 at Columbus 4 (Columbus scored only three goals of
    3rd)
New Jersey 0 at Florida 4 [Luongo]

January 28, 2006

Pittsburgh 1 at NY Rangers 7 (Rangers scored only four goals of 3rd)
Tampa Bay 6 at Philadelphia 0 [Burke] (Modin hat trick)
Detroit 1 at Dallas 2 (Modano 1st sudden death SO)
Anaheim 6 at Los Angeles 2 (Anaheim scored six straight goals
    after trailing 1–0)
NY Islanders 4 at Boston 3 (game tied 1–1 after 2nd)
Montreal 4 at Toronto 3 (Koivu 1:04 pp OT) (Toronto led 1–0, 2–1,
    lost eighth straight game)
Atlanta 1 at Carolina 4 (Carolina retired Ron Francis's #10)

Nashville 3 at Columbus 4 (Columbus scored only goal of 3rd)
San Jose 2 at Phoenix 6 (Phoenix led 3–0 after 2nd)
Vancouver 4 at Colorado 3 (Ruutu SO)

January 29, 2006

Tampa Bay 1 at Washington 2 (game tied 1–1 after 2nd)
Calgary 5 at Chicago 3 (Chicago led 3–2 after 1st)
Edmonton 4 at Phoenix 3 (Dvorak 3rd sudden-death SO) (Pronger
    [EDM] tied game with 0.2 seconds left in 3rd after Pisani won
    a faceoff with 2.2 seconds left)

January 30, 2006

Philadelphia 3 at NY Rangers 2 (Pitkanen 1:28 OT)
Toronto 4 at Florida 2 (Toronto 3–9 on pp)
Boston 5 at Ottawa 0 [Thomas]
Calgary 2 at St. Louis 3 (Stempniak 2nd sudden-death SO) (all
    regulation goals in 2nd)
Detroit 5 at Minnesota 4 (Detroit led 4–0 after 1st)
San Jose 2 at Dallas 3 (Arnott 4:24 OT)
Los Angeles 3 at Anaheim 4 (S. Niedermayer 1:48 OT)

January 31, 2006

Washington 2 at NY Islanders 5 (game tied 3–3 midway through 3rd)
Buffalo 5 at Atlanta 2 (Atlanta led 2–1 after 1st)
Carolina 8 at Montreal 2 (Cole hat trick)
Toronto 2 at Tampa Bay 3 (Lecavalier SO)
Minnesota 2 at Colorado 3 (Colorado scored three straight goals
    after trailing 1–0)
Vancouver 7 at Phoenix 4 (H. Sedin goal, three assists)

February 1, 2006

Pittsburgh 1 at NY Rangers 3 (game tied 1–1 after 1st)
Ottawa 3 at New Jersey 5 (New Jersey led 3–0 late in 1st)

St. Louis 2 at Detroit 3 (St. Louis led 2–0 after 1st)
Nashville 1 at Dallas 2 (Dallas led 2–0 after 2nd)
Columbus 2 at Calgary 1 (Balastik SO)
San Jose 6 at Anaheim 4 (Cheechoo [SJ] hat trick)

February 2, 2006

Montreal 1 at Boston 3 (Montreal scored only goal of 1st)
Philadelphia 2 at Buffalo 4 (teams combined 0–10 on pp)
NY Rangers 5 at NY Islanders 2 (Rangers led 4–0 after 2nd)
Ottawa 7 at Pittsburgh 2 (Pittsburgh led 2–0 midway through 2nd)
Chicago 5 at St. Louis 6 (Stempniak SO) (Chicago scored only two goals of 3rd)
Colorado 3 at Nashville 4 (Sullivan 2:09 OT) (Colorado led 1–0, 2–1, 3–2)
Columbus 2 at Edmonton 1 (Chimera 5th sudden-death SO)
Los Angeles 1 at Phoenix 2 (Reinprecht SO)
Minnesota 3 at San Jose 2 (Rolston 2nd sudden-death SO)

February 3, 2006

Toronto 1 at Washington 4 (Toronto scored first goal)
Carolina 0 at New Jersey 3 [Brodeur] (New Jersey retired Scott Stevens's #4)
Atlanta 2 at Florida 5 (Atlanta led 2–1 late in 2nd)
Vancouver 3 at Calgary 1 (Calgary led 1–0 after 1st)

February 4, 2006

Boston 0 at Montreal 2 [Huet] (both goals in 3rd)
Dallas 3 at St. Louis 4 (Jackman 2:16 OT)
Detroit 3 at Colorado 0 [Legace] (all goals in 3rd)
NY Islanders 5 at Pittsburgh 4 (Satan SO)
NY Rangers 4 at Philadelphia 3 (Jagr 1:25 pp OT) (Rangers tied game at 19:18 of 3rd)
New Jersey 2 at Toronto 4 (Toronto led 3–0 after 1st & 2nd)

Chicago 0 at Nashville 6 [Vokoun] (Nashville led 4–0 after 1st & 2nd)

Florida 4 at Atlanta 6 (game tied 3–3 midway through 2nd)

Ottawa 1 at Buffalo 2 (Vanek SO)

Washington 0 at Tampa Bay 5 [Grahame]

Minnesota 6 at Phoenix 4 (Minnesota outscored Phoenix 4–2 in 2nd)

Vancouver 1 at Edmonton 3 (Edmonton 5–0–0 vs. Vancouver this year)

Anaheim 2 at San Jose 0 [Giguere]

February 5, 2006

Carolina 4 at Boston 3 (Weight 1st sudden-death SO)

Philadelphia 0 at Montreal 5 [Huet] (second straight shutout for Huet)

February 6, 2006

Tampa Bay 3 at NY Islanders 2 (Lecavalier 4:05 OT) (Lecavalier tied game at 18:48 of 3rd)

Pittsburgh 2 at Ottawa 5 (game tied 1–1 after 1st)

Nashville 2 at Dallas 4 (Nashville led 1–0 after 1st)

Anaheim 5 at Edmonton 6 (Pisani SO)

Columbus 4 at Vancouver 7 (Vancouver led 4–0 after 1st; teams combined for five pp goals in 3rd)

Calgary 4 at San Jose 3 (game tied 1–1 after 1st)

February 7, 2006

Florida 5 at Washington 0 (Sim hat trick) [Luongo]

Atlanta 1 at Toronto 4 (Toronto led 2–0 after 2nd)

Buffalo 3 at Montreal 2 (Afinogenov 0:30 pp OT)

Tampa Bay 4 at New Jersey 7 (New Jersey led 3–0 midway through 1st, 6–1 after 2nd)

Los Angeles 1 at Minnesota 5 (Minnesota 5–10 on pp)

Edmonton 2 at Colorado 5 (Colorado scored three goals in 2nd)
Chicago 3 at Phoenix 1 (Phoenix led 1–0 after 1st)

February 8, 2006

Ottawa 1 at NY Rangers 5 (Rangers led 3–0 late in 2nd)
NY Islanders 2 at Philadelphia 5 (Richards hat trick)
Los Angeles 4 at Columbus 7 (L.A. led 3–1 after 1st, lost 7th straight
  game)
Boston 3 at Pittsburgh 1 (Boston led 3–0 early in 3rd)
Nashville 0 at Detroit 6 [Legace] (second straight shutout for
  Legace)
Anaheim 1 at Calgary 3 (game tied 1–1 after 1st)
St. Louis 4 at Vancouver 2 (St. Louis led 3–1 after 1st)
Chicago 1 at San Jose 2 (San Jose led 2–0 after 1st)

February 9, 2006

New Jersey 3 at Boston 2 (Gionta 2:10 OT)
Montreal 2 at Buffalo 2 Kovalev 0:39 OT) (Pominville [BUF] tied
  game at 19:33 of 3rd)
Atlanta 2 at Ottawa 1 (Atlanta scored only goal of 3rd)
Carolina 3 at Tampa Bay 5 (Carolina led 2–0 early in 1st)
Detroit 3 at Nashville 2 (Detroit scored only goal of 3rd)
Colorado 2 at Minnesota 1 (game tied 1–1 midway through 3rd)
Dallas 5 at Phoenix 1 (Dallas led 4–0 after 2nd)

February 10, 2006

Toronto 2 at NY Rangers 4 (Toronto led 1–0, 2–1)
Washington 4 at Philadelphia 5 (Philadelphia scored only four
  goals of 2nd)
Pittsburgh 4 at Carolina 3 (game tied 2–2 late in 2nd)
Colorado 4 at Columbus 1 (Colorado led 1–1 after 1st & 2nd)
St. Louis 2 at Calgary 3 (Phaneuf 2:40 pp OT)
Minnesota 6 at Edmonton 3 (Minnesota led 3–0 after 1st)

Anaheim 3 at Vancouver 1 (all goals in 1st)

Dallas 3 at San Jose 6 (San Jose scored only four goals of 2nd)

February 11, 2006

NY Islanders 2 at New Jersey 1 (game tied 1–1 after 1st)

Chicago 4 at Los Angeles 5 (Corvo 0:40 pp OT) (L.A. led 1–0, 3–1, 4–2)

NY Rangers 4 at Toronto 2 (Rangers led 4–0 midway through 2nd)

Tampa Bay 6 at Boston 5 ((Tampa Bay led 1–0, trailed 3–1, 4–3, 5–4)

Atlanta 2 at Montreal 1 (Kozlov SO)

Philadelphia 2 at Ottawa 3 (Ottawa led 3–0 early in 2nd)

Pittsburgh 6 at Washington 3 (Pittsburgh led 5–0 after 2nd)

Florida 3 at Buffalo 5 (game tied 2–2 late in 2nd)

Columbus 2 at Nashville 5 (game tied 2–2 late in 1st)

February 12, 2006

St. Louis 5 at Edmonton 4 (Wideman SO) (St. Louis trailed 1–0, 2–1,
led 3–2, 4–3)

Dallas 5 at Los Angeles 6 (Dallas led 5–2 after 2nd; L.A. scored only
four goals of 3rd)

Buffalo 3 at Carolina 4 (Staal 3rd sudden-death SO)

Colorado 3 at Detroit 6 (Detroit scored only three goals of 3rd)

San Jose 5 at Phoenix 4 (Preissing 1:54 OT) (San Jose led 1–0, 2–1,
3–2, 4–3)

Chicago 1 at Anaheim 4 (game tied 1–1 after 2nd)

Minnesota 2 at Vancouver 3 (D. Sedin 1:26 OT)

BREAK FOR OLYMPICS

February 28, 2006

Montreal 5 at NY Islanders 3 (Montreal led 3–0 after 2nd)

Washington 5 at Toronto 3 (game tied 2–2 after 1st)

Florida 8 at Tampa Bay 2 (Florida led 7–0 after 2nd)

Minnesota 2 at Colorado 4 (Minnesota led 1–0 late in 1st)

Vancouver 2 at Calgary 1 (Vancouver scored both goals in 2nd after trailing 1–0)

Detroit 1 at San Jose 5 (Thornton goal, three assists)

March 1, 2006

Atlanta 4 at Buffalo 2 (Atlanta led 2–0 early in 2nd)

Boston 3 at Carolina 4 (Carolina trailed 1–0, 3–2)

Philadelphia 1 at New Jersey 2 (Kozlov SO)

Ottawa 4 at Pittsburgh 3 (Ottawa led 4–0 after 2nd)

Nashville 0 at Chicago 3 [Anderson] (Chicago scored in each period)

St. Louis 4 at Edmonton 2 (St. Louis led 3–0 late in 2nd)

Detroit 2 at Anaheim 0 [Osgood] (both goals in 1st)

March 2, 2006

Atlanta 2 at Boston 3 (Sturm scored game–winning goal at 17:19 of 3rd on pp)

New Jersey 2 at NY Islanders 3 (Satan SO)

NY Rangers 6 at Philadelphia 1 (Rangers scored four goals in 2nd)

Montreal 1 at Florida 0 (Kovalev 14:11 3rd) [Huet]

Washington 1 at Ottawa 7 (Ottawa led 6–0 after 2nd, seven different scorers in game for Ottawa)

Vancouver 1 at Nashville 3 (Vancouver led 1–0 early in 2nd)

Columbus 0 at Colorado 1 (Clark 15:51 pp 2nd) [Aebischer]

St. Louis 1 at Calgary 3 (Calgary led 2–0 after 2nd)

Dallas 2 at Phoenix 6 (Phoenix led 4–1 after 2nd)

Minnesota 2 at Los Angeles 3 (Visnovsky scored game winning goal at 17:24 of 3rd)

March 3, 2006

Florida 2 at Carolina 5 (Carolina led 2–1 after 2nd)

Toronto 2 at Buffalo 6 (game tied 1–1 midway through 1st; Pat LaFontaine's #16 retired by Sabres)

Vancouver 5 at Chicago 4 (Naslund SO)
San Jose 2 at Edmonton 3 (all goals in 3rd)
Minnesota 2 at Anaheim 4 (game tied 2–2 midway through 3rd)

March 4, 2006

Columbus 2 at Los Angeles 3 (LA led 2–0 after 2nd)
Buffalo 3 at Boston 2 (Buffalo trailed 2–0 late in 1st)
Ottawa 4 at Toronto 2 (Ottawa beat Toronto for seventh straight
    game this season; Toronto honours Tie Domi for 1,000th
    career game, played the previous night)
Philadelphia 2 at NY Islanders 4 (game tied 2–2 midway through
    3rd)
Washington 2 at Atlanta 3 (Hossa 1:49 OT)
NY Rangers 1 at New Jersey 2 (goalie Martin Brodeur won his 30th
    game, a record 10th straight season doing so)
Carolina 7 at Pittsburgh 5 (Carolina led 5–0 after 1st; Recchi [PIT]
    hat trick; Staal [CAR] one goal, three assists)
Montreal 6 at Tampa Bay 2 (game tied 2–2 early in 3rd)
Colorado 3 at Dallas 5 (Dallas led 5–1 after 2nd)
Detroit 7 at Phoenix 3 (Lidstrom one goal, three assists)
San Jose 0 at Calgary 2 [Kiprusoff]

March 5, 2006

Nashville 2 at Edmonton 3 (Pronger 4:17 pp OT) (Nashville led 1–0,
    2–1)
Columbus 3 at Anaheim 2 (Nash SO)
Dallas 7 at Chicago 2
Colorado 3 at Minnesota 5 (game tied 2–2 after 1st)
St. Louis 4 at Vancouver 1 (St. Louis led 3–0 midway through 2nd)

March 6, 2006

Carolina 2 at NY Rangers 1 (Carolina led 2–0 after 2nd)
Montreal 4 at Philadelphia 5 (Nedved 1st sudden-death SO)

NY Islanders 2 at Washington 5 (Ovechkin scored 40th, 41st goals)
Florida 3 at Atlanta 4 (Kozlov SO) (Atlanta led 1–0, 2–1, 3–2)
Ottawa 4 at Tampa Bay 0 [Emery] (Ottawa scored in every period)

March 7, 2006

Boston 2 at Buffalo 3 (Buffalo trailed 1–0, 2–1)
New Jersey 1 at NY Islanders 2 (Hunter SO)
Chicago 3 at Columbus 1 (Chicago scored only two goals of 2nd)
Montreal 3 at Toronto 5 (Toronto 4–11 on pp)
Tampa Bay 5 at Pittsburgh 4 (Prospal SO) (Tampa led 4–1 early in 3rd)
Phoenix 5 at Detroit 2 (Phoenix led 3–0 early in 1st)
Colorado 2 at St. Louis 1 (Hejduk SO)
Los Angeles 3 at Minnesota 2 (Visnovsky 1:53 OT) (LA trailed 2–0 early in 3rd)
Nashville 3 at Calgary 2
Dallas 4 at Edmonton 3 (Zubov SO)
San Jose 4 at Anaheim 5 (Ozolinsh 0:58 OT) (Anaheim led 1–0, trailed 2–1, led 3–2 and 4–3)

March 8, 2006

Carolina 2 at Philadelphia 3 (Gagne 1st sudden-death SO)
Pittsburgh 3 at Washington 6 (Washington 2–10 on pp)
NY Rangers 2 at Atlanta 3 (Hossa 1st sudden-death SO)
Ottawa 3 at Florida 6 (game tied 1–1 early in 2nd)

March 9, 2006

Montreal 3 at Boston 0 [Huet]
Tampa Bay 5 at Buffalo 8 (Roy [BUF] hat trick) (Buffalo led 1–0, trailed 2–1, led 3–2, led 4–3, led 5–4; Buffalo scored last three goals of the game)
Phoenix 4 at Columbus 5 (Columbus led 3–0 early in 2nd)
Los Angeles 3 at Detroit 7 (game tied 2–2 midway through game)

Colorado 2 at Chicago 1 (no scoring in 3rd)

Dallas 0 at Calgary 1 (Langkow 14:50 1st) [Kiprusoff]

Nashville 3 at Vancouver 2 (Legwand 0:06 OT)

Edmonton 2 at San Jose 5 (game tied 2–2 after 2nd)

March 10, 2006

Ottawa 3 at Atlanta 1 (Ottawa led 3–0 after 5:02 of 1st)

Toronto 1 at NY Islanders 2 (Satan SO)

New Jersey 4 at Washington 3 (Brylin 2nd sudden-death SO)
(Zubrus [Was] tied game at 19:26 of 3rd on pp)

Carolina 3 at Florida 5

Minnesota 1 at St. Louis 2 (Stempniak 0:25 OT)

March 11, 2006

Buffalo 6 at Philadelphia 5 (teams combined for seven goals in
2nd; Grier scored winning goal at 19:55 of 3rd)

Nashville 2 at San Jose 3 (Ehrhoff 2:56 pp OT) (Kariya [NAS] tied
game at 19:49 of 3rd)

NY Islanders 3 at Boston 1 (Boston led 1–0 midway through 2nd)

Tampa Bay 1 at Toronto 5 (Toronto scored three times in 3rd)

NY Rangers 0 at Montreal 1 (Rivet 17:15 pp 1st) [Huet] (Habs retired
#5 of Bernie Geoffrion on the same day he died)

Edmonton 3 at Columbus 4 (Klesla 4:06 OT) (Edmonton led 2–0,
3–1)

New Jersey 3 at Pittsburgh 6 (Pittsburgh chased Brodeur from NJ
net with five goals in first 26 minutes)

Carolina 3 at Florida 4 (Kwiatkowski SO)

Chicago 4 at Detroit 6 (Detroit led 3–2 after 1st)

Los Angeles 2 at St. Louis 1 (Robitaille SO) (both regulation goals
in 3rd)

Anaheim 5 at Phoenix 3 (game tied 2–2 after 1st)

Dallas 2 at Vancouver 1 (Modano scored both Dallas goals in 3rd to
overcome 1–0 deficit)

March 12, 2006

Ottawa 5 at Washington 2
Calgary 0 at Colorado 3 [Budaj]
Boston 2 at Buffalo 6 (Buffalo's sixth straight win)
Atlanta 3 at NY Rangers 2 (Savard 2:45 pp OT) (Rangers led 2–0 after 2nd)
Detroit 5 at Chicago 3 (Detroit led 3–0 midway through 1st)
Edmonton 3 at Minnesota 4 (Edmonton led 2–1, 3–2)
Philadelphia 0 at Pittsburgh 2 [Fleury] (Armstrong both Pittsburgh goals)
Phoenix 2 at Anaheim 5 (Phoenix led 2–0 midway through game)

March 13, 2006

Tampa Bay 2 at Montreal 1 (Tampa Bay led 2–0 after 2nd)
Columbus 2 at St. Louis 3 (Backman 3:49 OT)
Vancouver 2 at Dallas 4 (Dallas scored only two goals of 3rd)
Colorado 3 at Calgary 4 (Calgary led 3–0 after 2nd)
Los Angeles 3 at San Jose 4 (Cheechoo [SJ] hat trick)

March 14, 2006

Buffalo 6 at Washington 4 (Washington led 3–1 after 1st, 4–3 after 2nd)
NY Rangers 3 at Carolina 5
Boston 4 at Toronto 5 (Tucker SO)
Tampa Bay 3 at Ottawa 4 (Tampa Bay led 1–0, 3–1)
NY Islanders 6 at New Jersey 1 (Islanders led 6–0 midway through 3rd)
Vancouver 0 at Nashville 5 [Vokoun]
Edmonton 2 at Minnesota 1 (Edmonton led 2–0 after 2nd)
Phoenix 6 at Los Angeles 2 (Los Angeles scored first)

March 15, 2006

Philadelphia 4 at Florida 0 [Esche] (Philadelphia scored in every period)
Anaheim 1 at Detroit 3 (Detroit led 2–1 after 1st & 2nd)
Columbus 2 at Chicago 3 (Chicago led 2–0 after 1st)

March 16, 2006

Ottawa 2 at Boston 3 (Bergeron SO)

Toronto 1 at Buffalo 3 (game tied 1–1 early in 3rd)

Washington 4 at NY Rangers 5 (Rangers led 2–0, 3–2, trailed 4–3)

NY Islanders 2 at Atlanta 4

Carolina 5 at Montreal 1 (Carolina led 2–1 early in 3rd)

Pittsburgh 1 at New Jersey 2 (Pittsburgh led 1–0 after 1st)

Phoenix 0 at Nashville 2 [Vokoun] (Vokoun's second consecutive shutout)

Calgary 2 at Edmonton 3 (Horcoff 3:04 OT) (Calgary led 2–1 after 2nd)

Dallas 4 at Los Angeles 1 (Dallas led 4–0 after 2nd)

St. Louis 2 at San Jose 5 (St. Louis led 2–1 early in 2nd)

March 17, 2006

Vancouver 3 at Columbus 2 (Morrison broke 2–2 tie at 13:49 of 3rd)

Philadelphia 3 at Tampa Bay 6 (eighth consecutive win by Tampa over Philadelphia)

NY Islanders 2 at Florida 4 (game tied 2–2 midway through 3rd)

Anaheim 2 at Chicago 1 (Anaheim scored only goal of 3rd)

March 18, 2006

Carolina 2 at Boston 4 (Boyes hat trick)

Dallas 4 at San Jose 3 (Miettinen 1st sudden-death SO)

Pittsburgh 5 at Montreal 4 (Pittsburgh led 2–0, trailed 3–2 && 4–3, scored only goal of 3rd)

Buffalo 2 at Ottawa 4 (Ottawa led 3–0 early in 2nd)

Toronto 2 at NY Rangers 5 (Rangers led 4–0 after 2nd)

Florida 4 at Washington 3 (Nieuwendyk SO)

Philadelphia 4 at Atlanta 2 (Atlanta 1–9 on pp)

Calgary 4 at Nashville 9 (Boucher in Calgary net for all goals)

Detroit 4 at Edmonton 3 (Williams SO)

St. Louis 1 at Los Angeles 3 (Los Angeles scored only three goals of 3rd)

March 19, 2006

Phoenix 3 at Chicago 2 (Phoenix led 3–1 after 2nd)

NY Islanders 2 at Tampa Bay 5 (Tampa Bay scored only three goals of 3rd)

Anaheim 4 at Columbus 3 (Anaheim scored only goal of 3rd)

Calgary 3 at Minnesota 2 (Calgary led 1–0, 2–1; Huselius broke 2–2 tie at 14:52 of 3rd)

Ottawa 4 at New Jersey 0 [Emery]

Toronto 1 at Pittsburgh 0 (Kilger 13:09 3rd—penalty shot) [Tellqvist] (game twice delayed by lengthy power outages at Mellon Arena of 18 and 25 mins.)

Colorado 5 at San Jose 6 (San Jose led 1–0, 4–1, 5–3; McCauley broke 5–5 tie at 15:47 of 3rd)

Detroit 7 at Vancouver 3 (Detroit led 4–0 early in 2nd)

March 20, 2006

Boston 2 at NY Rangers 5 (Rangers led 3–0 early in 2nd)

Montreal 4 at Washington 2 (Montreal scored three goals in 2:06 midway through 2nd to break 1–1 tie)

Buffalo 0 at Atlanta 5 [Lehtonen]

Tampa Bay 5 at Florida 6 (Jokinen 3:16 OT) (Florida led 5–1 after 2nd)

St. Louis 2 at Nashville 4 (Nashville led 4–0 late in 2nd)

Anaheim 2 at Dallas 1 (Anaheim scored only two goals of 3rd)

Colorado 5 at Los Angeles 0 [Budaj] (Colorado scored in all periods)

March 21, 2006

Atlanta 5 at Boston 4 (Slater 4th sudden-death SO)

Pittsburgh 2 at Ottawa 5 (game tied 1–1 early in 2nd)

Montreal 1 at NY Islanders 3 (game tied 1–1 after 1st)

New Jersey 1 at Philadelphia 2 (Philadelphia led 2–0 after 2nd)

Phoenix 5 at Columbus 2 (Columbus led 2–0 late in 1st)

Carolina 2 at Toronto 3 (Allison scored game winner at 15:12 of 3rd on pp) (Toronto 3–5 on pp)

Nashville 3 at Detroit 2 (Erat 3rd sudden-death SO) (all regulation goals in 1st)

San Jose 6 at St. Louis 0 [Toskala] (San Jose scored in every period)

Calgary 1 at Minnesota 3 (Calgary led 1–0 early in 2nd)

Vancouver 4 at Edmonton 1 (Vancouver 1–10 on pp)

March 22, 2006

Carolina 4 at Buffalo 3 (Carolina scored four goals in 2nd, Buffalo scored all three in 3rd)

Philadelphia 6 at NY Rangers 3 (Jagr [NYR] hat trick)

Washington 2 at Florida 3 (Florida scored all three goals in 2nd)

Minnesota 2 at Dallas 4 (Dallas scored only three goals of 3rd)

Colorado 4 at Anaheim 5 (Hedstrom 3:22 penalty shot OT) (Colorado led 3–0, 4–1)

March 23, 2006

New Jersey 5 at Atlanta 6 (Bondra 1:03 OT) (New Jersey led 2–0, 4–1)

Toronto 1 at Montreal 5 (Montreal led 4–0 after 1st)

Washington 3 at Tampa Bay 4 (Kubina 0:37 pp OT) (Washington led 1–0, 2–1, 3–2)

San Jose 0 at Detroit 4 [Legace] (Detroit led 1–0 after 2nd)

Calgary 7 at St. Louis 2 (Calgary led 5–0 after 2nd)

Chicago 3 at Phoenix 4 (Phoenix led 3–2 after 2nd)

Edmonton 3 at Vancouver 4 (Bertuzzi SO) (Vancouver led 2–0, trailed 3–2)

March 24, 2006

Calgary 2 at Columbus 3 (Chimera [COL] scored only goal of 3rd at 17:13)

Boston 2 at New Jersey 4 (New Jersey led 3–0 midway through 2nd) (New Jersey retired Ken Daneyko's #3 sweater)

NY Islanders 3 at Pittsburgh 4 Crosby 3:28 OT)

NY Rangers 2 at Florida 3 (Jokinen SO)
Ottawa 3 at Buffalo 1 (Ottawa led 2–0 after 1st)
Chicago 2 at Dallas 3 (Morrow 5th sudden-death SO)
Nashville 2 at Anaheim 6 (Selanne two goals, two assists)

March 25, 2006

Buffalo 4 at Boston 5 (Sturm broke 4–4 tie at 15:11 of 3rd)
Toronto 2 at Montreal 6 (Toronto scored first goal early in 1st)
Atlanta 1 at NY Islanders 5 (Islanders led 5–0 early in 3rd)
Ottawa 3 at Philadelphia 6 (Philadelphia led 4–0 after 1st)
Washington 5 at Carolina 1 (Washington led 2–0 after 2nd)
NY Rangers 3 at Tampa Bay 4 (Richards SO)
Columbus 5 at Detroit 4 (Balastik SO)
Colorado 3 at St. Louis 2 (Sakic 0:57 pp OT) (St. Louis led 2–0 midway through 3rd)
San Jose 5 at Minnesota 1 (game tied 1–1 midway through 2nd)
Anaheim 5 at Phoenix 2 (game tied 2–2 early in 2nd)
Edmonton 3 at Vancouver 2 (Edmonton led 2–1 after 2nd)
Nashville 4 at Los Angeles 6 (Nashville led 2–0, 4–3; Los Angeles scored only three goals of 3rd)

March 26, 2006

Calgary 2 at Dallas 3 (no scoring in 3rd)
San Jose 5 at Chicago 4 (Preissing 1:24 OT)(game tied 2–2 after 1st, 3–3 after 2nd)
Toronto 4 at New Jersey 3 (Toronto did not have a single power play chance)
Montreal 6 at Pittsburgh 5
Edmonton 4 at Colorado 3 (Samsonov SO)

March 27, 2006

Florida 4 at Boston 3 (Jokinen SO) (Bergeron [BOS] tied game at 19:17 of 3rd on pp)

Buffalo 4 at NY Rangers 5 (Sykora SO) (Buffalo led 1–0, 4–2)
Tampa Bay 1 at Carolina 2 (no scoring in 3rd)
Detroit 4 at St. Louis 1 (Detroit led 4–0 late in 3rd)
Los Angeles 4 at Vancouver 7 (Los Angeles led 1–0, 3–1)

March 28, 2006

Toronto 3 at Philadelphia 2 (game tied 1–1 after 1st & 2nd)
San Jose 1 at Columbus 4 (Columbus scored only three goals of 3rd)
NY Islanders 0 at Montreal 2 [Huet]
New Jersey 3 at Ottawa 2 (Gomez SO) (Heatley [OTT] tied game at 19:29 of 3rd)
Anaheim 3 at Colorado 4 (Brunette broke 3–3 tie at 13:57 of 3rd)
Minnesota 3 at Edmonton 2 (Minnesota scored only two goals of 3rd)
Nashville 3 at Phoenix 5 (game tied 2–2 midway through 2nd)

March 29, 2006

Boston 3 at Buffalo 4 (Buffalo trailed 1–0, led 2–1, led 3–2)
NY Rangers 5 at NY Islanders 1 (Jagr four assists)
Washington 5 at Carolina 1 (Carolina outshot Washington 50–28)
Florida 5 at Pittsburgh 3 (Florida's 7th win in a row)
St. Louis 2 at Chicago 3 (Calder 3:49 OT) (Chicago led 2–0 after 1st & 2nd)
Los Angeles 1 at Calgary 2 (Calgary led 2–0 after 2nd)
Anaheim 1 at Dallas 2 (all goals in 2nd)
Minnesota 1 at Vancouver 2 (Carter scored winning goal at 19:53 of 3rd on pp)

March 30, 2006

Washington 2 at Montreal 3 (Koivu 4:02 OT) (Halpern [WAS] tied game at 19:57 pp of 3rd)
NY Rangers 1 at Ottawa 4 (Ottawa 3–9 on pp)
Buffalo 1 at New Jersey 3 (fifth straight road loss for Buffalo)
Atlanta 3 at Tampa Bay 4 (Tampa Bay led 4–0 midway through 3rd)
Detroit 4 at Nashville 2 (game tied 2–2 after 1st & 2nd)

Los Angeles 0 at Edmonton 4 [Roloson]
Phoenix 5 at San Jose 2 (Phoenix scored only three goals of 3rd)

March 31, 2006

Chicago 3 at Detroit 2 (Sharp 1:29 OT) (Datsyuk [DET] tied game at 19:14 of 3rd)
Pittsburgh 4 at NY Islanders 0 [Caron]
Florida 2 at Carolina 3 (Carolina scored only goal of 3rd)
Columbus 4 at St. Louis 2 (game tied 1–1 after 1st)
Colorado 3 at Calgary 6 (Calgary scored only three goals of 2nd to turn 2–1 deficit into 4–2 lead)
Minnesota 2 at Vancouver 1 (Koivu SO) (both regulation goals in 2nd)
Dallas 4 at Anaheim 5 (Rob Niedermayer SO)

April 1, 2006

New Jersey 4 at Philadelphia 1 (New Jersey led 3–0 after 2nd)
Buffalo 0 at Toronto 7 (Toronto led 4–0 less than seven minutes into the game) [Aubin]
Boston 0 at Montreal 2 [Huet]
Washington 1 at Ottawa 0 (Zubrus 19:07 pp 2nd) [Johnson]
Carolina 2 at Atlanta 5 (Atlanta led 3–0 early in 2nd)
Chicago 2 at Columbus 5 (Chicago led 2–1 early in 3rd)
Tampa Bay 2 at Florida 4 (game tied 1–1 late in 2nd)
St. Louis 1 at Nashville 2 (St. Louis led 1–0 after 1st & 2nd)
Calgary 4 at Edmonton 1 (Calgary led 3–0 early in 2nd)
Dallas 0 at Los Angeles 1 (Roenick 10:21 1st) [Garon]
Phoenix 4 at San Jose 3 (Reinprecht 3:55 pp OT) (Phoenix led 3–0 after 2nd)

April 2, 2006

Philadelphia 4 at NY Islanders 1 (Philadelphia led 3–0 after 1st & 2nd)
New Jersey 3 at Pittsburgh 2 (Gionta 2:22 OT) (Elias [NJ] tied game at 19:40 of 3rd on pp)

Detroit 3 at Minnesota 2 (no scoring in 3rd)

Vancouver 2 at Anaheim 6 (after giving up first goal, Anaheim scored five in a row over 1st & 2nd)

April 3, 2006

Washington 5 at Carolina 6 (Whitney 3:35 pp OT) (Carolina trailed 1–0, 2–1, led 4–2, 5–4)

Buffalo 3 at Toronto 2 (Afinogenov SO)

Atlanta 4 at Ottawa 6 (Ottawa scored five straight goals in middle of game)

Florida 1 at Tampa Bay 4

Columbus 3 at Nashville 1 (Nashville scored opening goal early in 1st)

San Jose 3 at Dallas 2 (Joe Thornton 4:39 pp OT)

Chicago 3 at Colorado 4 (Colorado led 1–0, trailed 2–1, 3–2, scored game winner at 19:48 of 3rd)

Detroit 2 at Calgary 1 (Datsyuk SO)

Phoenix 1 at Edmonton 7 (Edmonton scored final five goals of game)

Vancouver 0 at Los Angeles 1 (Demitra 13:13 pp 2nd) [Mathieu Garon]

April 4, 2006

Philadelphia 2 at NY Rangers 3 (Sykora SO)

Boston 3 at Montreal 5 (Boston led 3–2 early in 3rd)

St. Louis 4 at Minnesota 5 (Rolson SO)

Los Angeles 2 at Anaheim 6 (Los Angeles led 2–1 after 1st)

April 5, 2006

Ottawa 4 at Buffalo 5 (Briere 4:13 pp OT) (Buffalo led 1–0, trailed 3–1, 4–3, tied game at 19:20 of 3rd)

Carolina 4 at Washington 3 (Cullen SO) (Carolina led 2–0, trailed 3–2)

Atlanta 5 at Florida 2 (Florida led 2–1 midway through game)

NY Islanders 2 at Toronto 3 (Islanders led 1–0, 2–1)

Pittsburgh 4 at New Jersey 6 (game tied 2–2 after 1st; Elias hat trick and two assists)

Nashville 3 at Chicago 4 (Chicago led 4–1 after 1st)

San Jose 2 at Colorado 1 San Jose scored only goal of 3rd

Phoenix 2 at Calgary 5 (Calgary led 3–0 midway through game)

April 6, 2006

Toronto 2 at Boston 3 (Boyes SO) (Toronto tied game at 19:47 of 3rd)

NY Islanders 1 at NY Rangers 3 (Islanders led 1–0 after 1st)

Montreal 5 at Ottawa 3 (score tied 2–2 midway through game)

Atlanta 2 at Tampa Bay 3 (Richards SO)

Nashville 3 at St. Louis 0 [Mason]

Edmonton 1 at Minnesota 2 (Rolston SO)

Dallas 5 at Anaheim 3 (Anaheim led 2–1 after 1st)

San Jose 5 at Los Angeles 0 [Toskala]

April 7, 2006

Carolina 4 at Washington 3 (Washington led 1–0 after 1st; Carolina led 4–1 early in 3rd)

Pittsburgh 5 at Florida 1 (Crosby one goal, three assists)

Columbus 5 at Detroit 6 (Holmstrom 2nd sudden-death SO)

Philadelphia 4 at Buffalo 2 (Philadelphia led 2–0 after 1st)

Edmonton 4 at Chicago 3 (Smyth 3:18 pp OT) (Edmonton led 1–0, 3–1)

Minnesota 1 at Calgary 2 (Calgary led 1–0 after 1st & 2nd)

April 8, 2006

NY Rangers 4 at Boston 3 (Nylander 0:40 OT) (Rangers trailed 2–0, led 3–2)

St. Louis 2 at Colorado 4 (St. Louis led 1–0 after 1st)

Anaheim 4 at Los Angeles 2 (Los Angeles 1–9 on pp)

New Jersey 3 at Montreal 2 (New Jersey led 3–0 midway through 3rd)
Buffalo 6 at Ottawa 2 (game tied 1–1 midway through 1st)
Washington 0 at NY Islanders 5 [DiPietro]
Toronto 5 at Philadelphia 2 (Toronto led 3–0 midway through 2nd)
Carolina 2 at Atlanta 5 (Kovalchuk [ATL] scored 51st goal)
Detroit 4 at Columbus 2 (score tied 2–2 midway through 2nd)
Pittsburgh 0 at Tampa Bay 1 [Burke] (Lecavalier 0:51 2nd)
Chicago 1 at Nashville 2 (Erat SO)
Calgary 2 at Vancouver 3 (Jovanovski 2:27 OT) (Vancouver led 2–0
     after 1st & 2nd)
Dallas 3 at Phoenix 2 (Jokinen SO)

April 9, 2006

Tampa Bay 3 at Florida 6 (Tampa Bay led 2–1 after 2nd)
Edmonton 1 at St. Louis 2 (Edmonton scored in final minute)
NY Rangers 2 at New Jersey 3 (Rangers led 2–1 after 2nd)
Minnesota 5 at Colorado 2 (Jose Theodore made debut in goal for
     Colorado)
Dallas 1 at San Jose 4 (San Jose scored three goals in 2nd)

April 10, 2006

Washington 2 at Boston 1 (Ovechkin 3:30 OT)
Ottawa 2 at Montreal 3 (Montreal scored only goal of 3rd)
Anaheim 4 at Vancouver 2 (Aneheim led 4–0 midway through
     game)
San Jose 3 at Phoenix 2 (Cheechoo [SJ] scored 50th & 51st goals)

April 11, 2006

NY Islanders 3 at NY Rangers 2 (Islanders led 3–0 after 2nd)
Pittsburgh 3 at Philadelphia 4 (Philadelphia led 3–0; Pittsburgh
     tied game in 3rd)
New Jersey 4 at Carolina 3 (Gionta 0:28 pp OT) (Staal [CAR] tied
     game sh at 19:14 of 3rd)

Florida 5 at Toronto 6 (Kaberle 4:49 pp OT) (Sundin four goals, two assists)

Boston 3 at Ottawa 4 (Chara 0:40 OT) (B. Stuart [BOS] tied game at 19:42 of 3rd)

Atlanta 6 at Tampa Bay 2 (Tampa Bay scored first, then Atlanta scored six straight goals)

Edmonton 0 at Detroit 2 [Legace]

Nashville 2 at St. Louis 0 [Mason] (Nashville finished 8–0–0 vs. St. Louis this season)

Chicago 0 at Minnesota 2 [Harding] (both goals in 3rd)

Columbus 2 at Dallas 3 (Dallas led 3–0 after 2nd)

Phoenix 2 at Colorado 6 (Colorado led 6–0 late in 2nd)

Anaheim 0 at Calgary 3 [Kiprusoff]

April 12, 2006

Montreal 1 at Buffalo 3 (Buffalo led 2–0 after 1st)

San Jose 5 at Vancouver 4 (Joe Thornton [SJ] four assists)

April 13, 2006

Montreal 4 at Boston 3 (Montreal led 4–1 early in 3rd)

Toronto 4 at NY Islanders 3 (Stajan 3:52 OT)

Washington 3 at Atlanta 5 (game tied 3–3 midway through 2nd)

St. Louis 1 at Columbus 4

Florida 3 at Ottawa 4 (Nieuwendyk 3:30 OT) (Alfredsson [OTT] tied game at 19:58 of 3rd)

Philadelphia 1 at New Jersey 4 (New Jersey led 3–0 after 2nd)

NY Rangers 3 at Pittsburgh 5 (Crosby one goal, three assists)

Minnesota 2 at Nashville 4 (game tied 1–1 early in 2nd)

Detroit 7 at Chicago 3 (Detroit led 3–2 early in 3rd)

Colorado 0 at Calgary 2 [Kiprusoff]

Anaheim 1 at Edmonton 2 (Hemsky scored game winner at 19:26 of 3rd)

Los Angeles 0 at Phoenix 3 [Joseph] (all goals in 2nd)

Vancouver 3 at San Jose 5 (Vancouver led 3–2 after 2nd; Joe
Thornton [SJ] three assists to tie Jagr for scoring race)

April 14, 2006

Tampa Bay 4 at Carolina 5 (Cullen SO) (Carolina led 1–0, 2–1, trailed
3–2, 4–3)

April 15, 2006

Boston 3 at Atlanta 4 (Boston led 2–0, 3–2 after 2nd)
NY Rangers 1 at Philadelphia 4 (Philadelphia led 4–0 midway
through game)
Minnesota 3 at Dallas 4 (Daley 4:26 OT) (Dallas led 3–1 after 2nd)
Anaheim 3 at San Jose 6 (Cheechoo [SJ] hat trick)
Ottawa 1 at Toronto 5 (Toronto led 5–0 after 2nd)
Buffalo 4 at Montreal 2 (Montreal led 2–1 after 2nd)
Pittsburgh 4 at NY Islanders 5 (Nilsson 3rd sudden-death SO)
Chicago 2 at Columbus 5 (Columbus scored only three goals of
3rd)
Carolina 2 at Tampa Bay 3 (St. Louis 4:49 OT)
Washington 2 at Florida 1 (Pettinger 1st sudden-death SO)
Detroit 3 at St. Louis 2 (Zetterberg [DET] scored only goal of 3rd at
19:51)
Phoenix 1 at Nashville 5 (Nashville goalie Chris Mason credited
with a goal after Phoenix shot puck into own net on delayed
penalty midway through 3rd)
Colorado 3 at Vancouver 4 (Morrison 4:23 OT)
Calgary 1 at Los Angeles 2 (Demitra SO)

April 16, 2006

Philadelphia 1 at New Jersey 5 (tenth win in a row for New Jersey)
Toronto 0 at Buffalo 6 [Miller] (Buffalo scored two goals in each
period)
Columbus 3 at Chicago 4 (Chicago trailed 1–0, led 2–1, trailed 3–2)
Phoenix 3 at St. Louis 0 [Joseph]

April 17, 2006

Atlanta 4 at Washington 6 (Atlanta led 4–3 after 2nd)

NY Islanders 1 at Pittsburgh 6 (Crosby had three assists to reach 100 points, the youngest player in NHL history to do so)

Dallas 2 at Detroit 3 (Dallas led 1–0 after 1st & 2nd)

Colorado 2 at Edmonton 4 (game tied 2–2 midway through 3rd)

Calgary 3 at Anaheim 4

Los Angeles 4 at San Jose 0 [LaBarbera]

April 18, 2006

Atlanta 1 at Florida 2 (Van Ryn 1:34 pp OT)

Buffalo 4 at Carolina 0 [Biron]

Dallas 4 at Columbus 5 (Fedorov 0:35 pp OT) (Columbus tied game at 19:03 of 3rd on pp)

Ottawa 5 at NY Rangers 1 (Heatley [OTT] scored 50th of year)

Philadelphia 4 at NY Islanders 1 (Islanders led 1–0 after 1st & 2nd)

Pittsburgh 3 at Toronto 5 (Sundin four points)

New Jersey 4 at Montreal 3 (New Jersey scored only three goals of 3rd)

Washington 4 at Tampa Bay 1

Detroit 3 at Nashville 6 (Detroit led 1–0 after 1st but Nashville scored only four goals of 2nd)

St. Louis 2 at Chicago 3 (Calder 3:20 OT)

END OF REGULAR SEASON

NATIONALITY OF ALL PLAYERS, 2005–06

SUMMARY

(figure in parentheses shows league representation as a percentage)

TOTAL	**963**
CANADA	518 (53.8%)
Alberta	89
British Columbia	53
Manitoba	20
New Brunswick	1
Newfoundland	6
Northwest Territories	1
Nova Scotia	10
Ontario	200
Prince Edward Island	2
Quebec	91
Saskatchewan	44
USA	179 (18.6%)
CZECH REPUBLIC	65 (6.7%)
SWEDEN	45 (4.7%)
RUSSIA	41 (4.3%)
FINLAND	39 (4.0%)
SLOVAKIA	31 (3.2%)
GERMANY	8 (0.8%)
UKRAINE	7 (0.7%)
KAZAKHSTAN	6 (0.6%)
SWITZERLAND	4 (0.4%)
AUSTRIA	3 (0.3%)
BELARUS	3 (0.3%)
LATVIA	3 (0.3%)
POLAND	3 (0.3%)

LITHUANIA	2 (0.2%)
BRAZIL	1 (0.1%)
FRANCE	1 (0.1%)
MALAYSIA	1 (0.1%)
NORWAY	1 (0.1%)
SOUTH AFRICA	1 (0.1%)
SOUTH KOREA	1 (0.1%)

NATIONALITY BREAKDOWN

CANADA	**518**	
Alberta	**89**	
Banff	1	Ryan Smyth
Beaverlodge	1	Matt Walker
Blackie	1	Jeremy Colliton
Calgary	14	Nolan Baumgartner, Braydon Coburn, Rob DiMaio, Patrick Eaves, Mike Green, Connor James, Krys Kolanos, Robert Nilsson, Chris Phillips, Jason Smith, Brent Sopel, Jeff Tambellini, Wes Walz, Kyle Wanvig
Camrose	3	Tyler Bouck, Scott Ferguson, Josh Green
Caroline	1	Jim Vandermeer
Castor	1	Darcy Tucker
Cold Lake	1	Alexander Auld
Coleman	1	Rick Rypien
Daysland	2	Richard Petiot, Matthew Spiller
Edmonton	32	Blair Betts, Jay Bouwmeester, Gilbert Brule, Jason Chimera, Erik Christensen, Mike Comrie, Chris Dingman, Andrew Ference, Vernon Fiddler, Paul Healey, Cale Hulse, Jarome Iginla, Brad Isbister,

		Matt Keith, Daymond Langkow, Jamie Lundmark, Richard Matvichuk, Jamie McLennan, Derek Morris, Tyson Nash, Scott Nichol, Scott Niedermayer, Matt Pettinger, Dion Phaneuf, Fernando Pisani, Steve Regier, Steve Reinprecht, Mark Smith, Nathan Smith, Jason Strudwick, Brian Sutherby, Darryl Sydor
Elk Point	1	Sheldon Souray
Fort McMurray	2	Nolan Pratt, Scottie Upshall
Fort Saskatchewan	3	Mike Commodore, Ray Whitney, Jofferey Lupul
Grand Cache	1	Dean McAmmond
Halkirk	1	Shane Doan
Hinton	1	Dave Scatchard
Lac La Biche	2	Rene Bourque, Darren Reid
Lethbridge	1	Jamie Pushor
Lloydminster	1	Cory Cross
Mannville	2	Kyle Calder, Mike Rathje
Medicine Hat	1	Trevor Linden
Peace River	1	Chris Osgood
Red Deer	3	Trent Hunter, Chris Mason, Glen Wesley
Redwater	1	Todd Fedoruk
Rocky Mountain House	2	Brad Stuart, Nick Tarnasky
Sherwood Park	2	Ben Ondrus, Cam Ward
Spruce Grove	3	Stu Barnes, Nathan Dempsey, Grant Stevenson
Stony Plain	1	Steve Goertzen
St. Paul	1	Kyle Brodziak
Vermilion	1	Jeff Woywitka

British Columbia	53	
Abbotsford	1	Ryan Craig
Burnaby	5	Jason LaBarbera, Darren McCarty, Byron Ritchie, Joe Sakic, Greg Zanon
Campbell River	1	Carsen Germyn
Cassiar	1	Rob Niedermayer
Castlegar	1	Travis Green
Comox	1	Brett McLean
Cranbrook	4	Jon Klemm, Brad Lukowich, Jason Marshall, Steve Yzerman
Duncan	1	Matt Ellison
Fernie	2	David Leneveu, Dan Smith
Fort St. John	1	Mark Hartigan
Hope	1	Jeff Hoggan
Invermere	1	Wade Dubielewicz
Kamloops	1	Mark Recchi
Kelowna	1	Josh Gorges
Kimberley	1	Jason Wiemer
Maple Ridge	1	Andrew Ladd
Nakusp	1	Brad Larsen
New Westminster	2	Colin Forbes, Jordan Sigalet
North Vancouver	2	Mike Brown, Todd Simpson
Osoyoos	1	Chuck Kobasew
Penticton	1	Mark Rycroft
Pitt Meadows	1	Brendan Morrison
Port McNeill	1	Willie Mitchell
Prince George	1	Turner Stevenson
Princeton	1	Stephen Peat
Richmond	2	Scott Hannan, Brent Seabrook
Salmon Arm	1	Kris Beech
Sechelt	1	David Oliver
Sicamous	1	Shea Weber
Smithers	1	Dan Hamhuis

Surrey	1	Colin Hemingway
Trail	4	Dallas Drake, Shawn Horcoff, Barret Jackman, Steve McCarthy
Vancouver	4	Chris Holt, Paul Kariya, Steve Montador, Shaone Morrisonn
Vernon	3	Eric Brewer, Eric Godard, Jerred Smithson

Manitoba	**20**	
Brandon	2	Rob McVicar, Bryce Salvador
Carman	1	Ed Belfour
Churchill	1	Jordin Tootoo
Deloraine	1	Ryan Caldwell
Neepawa	1	Shane Hnidy
Notre Dame de Lourdes	1	J-P Vigier
Portage La Prairie	1	Arron Asham
Thompson	1	Jody Shelley
Winkler	2	Eric Fehr, Dustin Penner
Winnipeg	9	Cam Barker, Lee Goren, Duncan Keith, Mike Leclerc, Bryan Muir, Colton Orr, Alexander Steen, Duvie Westcott, Ian White

Ontario	**200**	
Ajax	1	Brent Burns
Barrie	2	Joe DiPenta, John Madden
Beaconsfield	1	Ben Walter
Belleville	4	Matt Cooke, Brett Hull, Andrew Raycroft, Brad Richardson
Bramalea	2	Andrew Cassels, Mike Weaver
Brampton	1	Rick Nash
Brantford	2	Chris Gratton, Josh Gratton
Brockville	1	Alyn McCauley
Burlington	1	Chad Wiseman

Cambridge	2	Trevor Gillies, Scott Walker
Carp	1	Kurtis Foster
Cayuga	1	Ray Emery
Chapleau	1	Jason Ward
Cobourg	1	Justin Williams
Collingwood	1	Jason Arnott
Cornwall	2	Chad Kilger, Steve Poapst
Dryden	1	Chris Pronger
Elliot Lake	1	Alex Henry
Grimsby	1	Kevin Bieksa
Guelph	2	Greg Jacina, Kirk Maltby
Hamilton	6	Dave Andreychuk, Todd Harvey, Adam Mair, Brian McGratton, Steve Staios, Joey Tenute
Hawkesbury	1	Dan McGillis
Huntsville	1	Ethan Moreau
Kanata	1	Todd White
Kenora	1	Mike Richards
Keswick	1	Curtis Joseph
Kingston	6	Bryan Allen, Kip Brennan, John Erskine, Jay McClement, Jay McKee, Andy Sutton
Kitchener	4	Rob Collins, Kevin Klein, Kyle Quincey, Dennis Wideman
LaSalle	1	Andy Delmore
Lindsay	1	Jamie Allison
London	9	Gregory Campbell, Jeff Carter, Eric Lindros, Cody McCormick, Joe Thornton, Scott Thornton, Mike Van Ryn, Jason Williams, Brian Willsie
Markdale	1	Chris Neil
Millgrove	1	Danny Syvret
Mimico	1	Brendan Shanahan

Mississauga	7	Brad Boyes, Manny Malhotra, Grant Marshall, Allan Rourke, Jason Spezza, Matt Stajan, Tom Kostopoulos
Moose Factory	1	Jonathan Cheechoo
Niagara Falls	2	Kevin Dallman, Mike Glumac
Niagara-on-the-Lake	1	Zenon Konopka
Nobleton	1	Nick Boynton
North Bay	1	Craig Rivet
Oakville	2	Eric Cairns, Matt Foy
Oshawa	5	Scott Barney, Sean Brown, Jay Harrison, Joe Nieuwendyk, Shawn Thornton
Ottawa	17	Derek Armstrong, Adrian Aucoin, Matthew Barnaby, Brendan Bell, Dan Boyle, Rod Brind'Amour, Ben Eager, Pat Kavanagh, Sean O'Donnell, Luke Richardson, Jamie Rivers, Randy Robitaille, Derek Roy, Marc Savard, Martin St. Pierre, Chris Therien, Stephane Yelle
Owen Sound	2	Nathan Perrott, Curtis Sanford
Peterborough	4	Mike Fisher, Corey Perry, Ryan Ready, Cory Stillman
Pickering	1	Sean Avery
Richmond Hill	2	Mike Cammalleri, Jeff O'Neill
Rockland	1	Serge Payer
Sault Ste. Marie	6	Ken Belanger, Rico Fata, Brian Finley, Cole Jarrett, Chris Thorburn, Marty Turco
Seaforth	1	Boyd Devereaux
Sharon	1	Matt Ryan
Shelburne	1	Aaron Downey
Simcoe	4	Rob Blake, Jassen Cullimore, Dwayne Roloson, Ryan Vandenbussche

St. Catharines	3	Rob Davison, Bryan McCabe, Andrew Peters
St. George	1	Adam Munro
Stittsville	1	Matt Bradley
Stoney Creek	1	Mark Popovic
St. Paul's	1	Mark Bell
Stratford	2	Rem Murray, Tim Taylor
Strathroy	2	Brian Campbell, Andy McDonald
Sudbury	5	Todd Bertuzzi, Andrew Brunette, Aaron Gavey, Derek MacKenzie, Brian Savage
Sundridge	1	Greg de Vries
Thornhill	1	Dominic Moore
Thunder Bay	7	Greg Johnson, Ryan Johnson, Trevor Letowski, Taylor Pyatt, Steve Rucchin, Patrick Sharp, Eric Staal
Timmins	2	Shean Donovan, Steve Sullivan
Toronto	35	Jason Allison, Chris Campoli, Anson Carter, Carlo Colaiacovo, Jeff Cowan, Trevor Daley, Kris Draper, Manny Fernandez, Adam Foote, Mark Giordano, Josh Gratton, Ric Jackman, Mike Johnson, Chris Kelly, Mike Knuble, Manny Legace, Bryan Marchment, Brad May, Jamal Mayers, Norm Milley, Michael Peca, Geoff Platt, Keith Primeau, Wayne Primeau, Mike Ricci, Gary Roberts, Nathan Robinson, Peter Sarno, Steve Shields, Karl Stewart, Raffi Torres, Kevin Weekes, Stephen Weiss, Jason Woolley, Mike Zigomanis
Wawa	1	Chris Simon
Welland	2	Nathan Horton, Daniel Paille
Whitby	1	Paul Ranger

Winchester	1	Matt Carkner
Windsor	8	Bob Boughner, Sean Burke, Tie Domi, Dan Jancevski, Ed Jovanovski, David Liffiton, Aaron Ward, Kyle Wellwood
Woodbridge	1	Steve Eminger
Quebec	**91**	.
Amos	1	Guillaume Lefebvre
Amqui	1	Sebastien Caron
Ancienne-Lorette	1	Patrice Bergeron
Beauport	1	Maxime Ouellet
Beaureville	1	Stephane Veilleux
Blainville	1	Pierre Dagenais
Chandler	1	Mathieu Garon
Charlesbourg	1	Marc Chouinard
Gatineau	3	Daniel Briere, Steve Martins, Alexandre Picard (b. Jul '85)
Ile Bizard	1	Vincent Lecavalier
Lac St. Charles	2	Martin Biron, Mathieu Biron
Lachute	1	Denis Hamel
Lafontaine	1	Jann Danis
La Salle	1	Anthony Stewart
Laval	3	Pascal Dupuis, Martin St. Louis, Jose Theodore
Lemoyne	1	Maxime Talbot
Les Saules	1	Alexandre Picard (b. Oct '85)
Longueuil	1	Bruno Gervais
Mont Laurier	1	Dan Cloutier
Montreal	30	Ramzi Abid, J-S Aubin, Joel Bouchard, Patrice Brisebois, Martin Brodeur, Corey Crawford, Alexandre Daigle, Eric Daze, Marc Denis, J-P Dumont, Steve Gainey, Denis Gauthier, J-S Giguere, Ben Guite, Ian Laperriere,

		Georges Laraque, Yanick Lehoux, Mario Lemieux, Francis Lessard, Matt Lombardi, Roberto Luongo, Scott Mellanby, Alain Nasreddine, Joel Perrault, Mike Ribeiro, Louis Robitaille, Luc Robitaille, Bruno St. Jacques, Jocelyn Thibault, Patrick Traverse
Pointe Claire	1	Alexandre Burrows
Quebec City	7	Steve Bernier, Jean-Philippe Cote, Jonathan Ferland, Alexandre Giroux, Marc-Antoine Pouliot, Pascal Rheaume, Yan Stastny
Repentigny	2	Pascal Leclaire, Jason Pominville
Rimouski	1	Michel Ouellet
Rouyn	2	Eric Desjardins, Pierre Turgeon
Shawinigan	1	Martin Gelinas
Sherbrooke	5	Eric Belanger, Pierre-Marc Bouchard, Mathieu Dandenault, Yanic Perreault, Stephane Robidas
Sorel	3	Francois Beauchemin, Frederic Cassivi, Marc-Andre Fleury
St. Agapit	1	Antoine Vermette
St. Bonaventure	1	Patrick Lalime
Ste. Apollinaire	1	Philippe Boucher
Ste. Foy	1	Simon Gagne
Ste. Justine	1	Alex Tanguay
St. Georges	1	Mathieu Roy
St. Joseph de Beauce	1	Junior Lessard
St. Leonard	1	Maxim Lapierre
St. Louis de France	1	Marc-Andre Bergeron
Terrebonne	1	J-F Jacques
Thetford Mines	1	Simon Gamache
Three Rivers	1	Steve Begin

| Val d'Or | 2 | Serge Aubin, Dany Sabourin |
| Ville St. Pierre | 1 | Martin Lapointe |

New Brunswick **1**
| Quispamsis | 1 | Randy Jones |

Newfoundland **6**
Bonavista	1	Michael Ryder
Carbonear	1	Daniel Cleary
Deer Lake	1	Darren Langdon
St. John's	3	Ryan Clowe, Jason Morgan, Doug O'Brien

Northwest Territories **1**
| Hay River | 1 | Geoff Sanderson |

Nova Scotia **10**
Antigonish	1	Craig MacDonald
Cole Harbour	1	Sidney Crosby
Glace Bay	1	Doug Doull
Halifax	3	Eric Boulton, Ryan Flinn, Glen Murray
New Glasgow	2	Jon Sim, Colin White
Port Hawkesbury	1	Aaron Johnson
Sydney	1	Don MacLean

Prince Edward Island **2**
| Murray Harbour | 1 | Brad Richards |
| Summerside | 1 | Steve Ott |

Saskatchewan **45**
Aneroid	1	Patrick Marleau
Arcola	1	Prestin Ryan
Canora	1	Cam Severson
Carlyle	1	Brenden Morrow

Central Butte	1	Clarke Wilm
Craik	1	Garnet Exelby
Estevan	1	Trent Whitfield
Humboldt	2	Kyle McLaren, Brendan Witt
Kamsack	2	Darcy Hordichuk, Tyler Wright
Kindersley	1	Joel Kwiatkowski
Lanigan	1	Wade Brookbank
Leroy	1	Nathan Paetsch
Lloydminster	2	Colby Armstrong, Wade Redden
Meadow Lake	1	Jeff Friesen
Melville	1	Jarret Stoll
Naicam	1	Lynn Loyns
Punnichy	1	Nolan Yonkman
Quill Lake	1	Lyle Odelein
Regina	8	Ryan Getzlaf, Josh Harding, Scott Hartnell, Jamie Heward, Chris Kunitz, Garth Murray, Mike Sillinger, Jeremy Williams
Rosthern	1	Richie Regehr (born Indonesia)
Saskatoon	5	Wade Belak, Derek Boogaard, Shane Endicott, Michael Garnett, Cory Sarich
Shaunavon	1	Rhett Warrener
Strasbourg	1	Nick Schultz
Swift Current	2	Boyd Kane, Travis Moen
Unity	2	Curtis Brown, Boyd Gordon
Wapella	1	Brett Clark
Wawota	1	Brooks Laich
Wynyard	1	Wade Skolney
Yellow Grass	2	Nolan Schaefer, Peter Schaefer
USA	**179**	
Alaska	4	Matt Carle, Ty Conklin, Scott Gomez, Jason Ryznar
California	5	Noah Clarke, Ryan Hollweg, Brooks Orpik, Scott Parker, Jeremy Stevenson

Colorado	2	John Grahame, David Hale
Connecticut	6	Eric Boguniecki, Chris Clark, Kevin Colley, Chris Drury, Ron Hainsey, Matt Hussey
Delaware	1	Mark Eaton
Florida	1	Dan Hinote
Georgia	1	Eric Chouinard
Illinois	10	Craig Anderson, Chris Chelios, Gerald Coleman, Joe Corvo, Andrew Hutchinson, Matt Jones, Brett Lebda, Danny Richmond, Mike Stuart, Andy Wosniewski
Indiana	3	Donald Brashear, Ken Klee, John-Michael Liles
Iowa	1	Scott Clemmensen
Maine	2	Jon Disalvatore, Mike Morrison
Maryland	2	Kevyn Adams, Jeff Halpern
Massachusetts	29	Tony Amonte, Keith Aucoin, Shawn Bates, Jim Campbell, Niko Dimitrakos, Rick DiPietro, Brian Eklund, Jim Fahey, Tom Fitzgerald, Hal Gill, David Gove, Bill Guerin, Eric Healey, Doug Janik, Dan LaCouture, Pat Leahy, Shawn McEachern, Eric Nickulas, Brad Norton, Jay Pandolfo, Brian Pothier, Tom Poti, Pat Rismiller, Jeremy Roenick, Garth Snow, Keith Tkachuk, Noah Welch, Ryan Whitney, Scott Young
Michigan	23	Jason Bacashihua, Tim Gleason, Rob Globke, Matt Greene, Mike Grier, Adam Hall, Derian Hatcher, Andy Hilbert, Brent Johnson, Ryan Kesler, Chad LaRose, David Legwand, Ryan

		Miller, Mike Modano, Brian Rafalski, Eric Reitz, Andy Roach, Brian Rolston, Jim Slater, Tim Thomas, Doug Weight, James Wisniewski, Mike York
Minnesota	31	Andrew Alberts, Keith Ballard, Adam Berkhoel, Jason Blake, Brandon Bochenski, Dustin Byfuglien, Ben Clymer, Mark Cullen, Matt Cullen, Adam Hauser, Bret Hedican, Sean Hill, Matt Koalska, Bryce Lampman, Jamie Langenbrunner, Josh Langfeld, Jordan Leopold, Paul Martin, Joe Motzko, Zach Parise, Mark Parrish, Toby Petersen, John Pohl, Tom Preissing, Erik Rasmussen, Kurt Sauer, Wyatt Smith, Mark Stuart, Jeff Taffe, David Tanabe, Erik Westrum
Missouri	1	Cam Janssen
Nebraska	1	Jed Ortmeyer
New Hampshire	2	Jeff Giuliano, Freddy Meyer
New Jersey	2	Jim Dowd, Paul Mara
New York	25	Francis Bouillon, Jesse Boulerice, Dustin Brown, Erik Cole, Tim Connolly, Craig Conroy, Mike Dunham, Robert Esche, Rory Fitzpatrick, Brian Gionta, Chris Higgins, James Howard, Mike Komisarek, Jay Leach, Todd Marchant, Aaron Miller, Mark Mowers, Matt Murley, Eric Nystrom, Marty Reasoner, Andre Roy, Philippe Sauve, Mathieu Schneider, Rob Scuderi, Lee Stempniak
North Dakota	4	Paul Gaustad, Tim Jackman, Ryan Potulny, Barry Tallackson

Ohio	6	Dan Fritsche, Jeff Hamilton, Ian Moran, Mike Rupp, Ben Simon, Brian Smolinski
Oklahoma	1	Tyler Arnason
Pennsylvania	4	Ryan Malone, George Parros, Bill Thomas, R.J. Umberger
Rhode Island	4	Bryan Berard, Brian Boucher, Keith Carney, Jeff Jillson
Texas	1	Brian Leetch
Utah	1	Steve Konowalchuk
Vermont	2	John LeClair, Graham Mink
Virginia	1	Eric Weinrich
Wisconsin	3	David Steckel, Ryan Suter, Brad Winchester
CZECH REPUBLIC	65	Jaroslav Balastik, Michal Barinka, Zdenek Blatny, Radek Bonk, Pavel Brendl, Jan Bulis, Petr Cajanek, Radek Dvorak, Patrik Elias, Martin Erat, Jiri Fischer, Tomas Fleischmann, Roman Hamrlik, Dominik Hasek, Martin Havlat, Milan Hejduk, Ales Hemsky, Bobby Holik, Jan Hrdina, Jiri Hudler, Jaromir Jagr, Frantisek Kaberle, Tomas Kaberle, Petr Kanko, Jakub Klepis, Rostislav Klesla, Tomas Kloucek, Ales Kotalik, Lukas Krajicek, Filip Kuba, Pavel Kubina, Robert Lang, Marek Malik, Radek Martinek, Josef Melichar, Milan Michalek, Zbynek Michalek, Jaroslav Modry, Tomas Mojzis, Petr Nedved, Filip Novak, Jiri Novotny, Rostislav Olesz, Tomas Plekanec, Vojtech Polak, Vaclav Prospal, Petr

Prucha, Martin Prusek, Michal Rozsival, Martin Rucinsky, Martin Skoula, Jiri Slegr, Jaroslav Spacek, Patrik Stefan, Martin Straka, Jaroslav Svoboda, Petr Sykora (b. 1976), Petr Sykora (b. 1978), Petr Taticek, Vaclav Varada, Josef Vasicek, Tomas Vokoun, Radim Vrbata, David Vyborny, Marek Zidlicky

SWEDEN   45   Tommy Albelin, Daniel Alfredsson, P-J Axelsson, Christian Backman, Nils Ekman, Peter Forsberg, Johan Franzen, Niclas Havelid, Johan Hedberg, Jonathan Hedstrom, Mikael Holmqvist, Tomas Holmstrom, Kristian Huselius, Jonas Johansson, Kim Johnsson, Niklas Kronvall, Staffan Kronvall, Nicklas Lidstrom, Andreas Lilja, Joakim Lindstrom, Henrik Lundqvist, Fredrik Modin, Doug Murray, Markus Naslund, Marcus Nilson, Niklas Nordgren, Mattias Norstrom, Michael Nylander, Mattias Ohlund, Samuel Pahlsson, David Printz, Mikael Samuelsson, Daniel Sedin, Henrik Sedin, Fredrik Sjostrom, Mats Sundin, Niklas Sundstrom, Henrik Tallinder, Dick Tarnstrom, Mikael Tellqvist, Daniel Tjarnqvist, Mathias Tjarnqvist, Niclas Wallin, Mattias Weinhandl, Henrik Zetterberg

RUSSIA

41 Dmitry Afanasenkov, Maxim Afinogenov, Evgeni Artyukhin, Sergei Brylin, Ilya Bryzgalov, Pavel Datsyuk, Fedor Fedorov, Sergei Fedorov, Alexander Frolov, Sergei Gonchar, Denis Grebeshkov, Dmitri Kalinin, Alexander Karpovtsev, Nikolai Khabibulin, Alexander Khavanov, Maxim Kondratiev, Ilya Kovalchuk, Alexei Kovalev, Viktor Kozlov, Vyacheslav Kozlov, Oleg Kvasha, Vladimir Malakhov, Andrei Markov, Danny Markov, Alexander Mogilny, Andrei Nazarov, Alexander Ovechkin, Sergei Samsonov, Oleg Saprykin, Alexei Semenov, Timofei Shishkanov, Aleksander Suglobov, Fedor Tyutin, Igor Ulanov, Anton Volchenkov, Mikhail Yakubov, Alexei Yashin, Alexei Zhamnov, Alexei Zhitnik, Sergei Zubov, Andrei Zyuzin

FINLAND

39 Aki Berg, Sean Bergenheim, Valtteri Filppula, Niklas Hagman, Jarkko Immonen, Jussi Jokinen, Olli Jokinen, Niko Kapanen, Sami Kapanen, Miikka Kiprusoff, Mikko Koivu, Saku Koivu, Antti Laaksonen, Jere Lehtinen, Kari Lehtonen, Toni Lydman, Masi Marjamaki, Jussi Markkanen, Antti Miettinen, Ville Nieminen, Janne Niinimaa, Antero Niittymaki, Petteri Nokelainen, Mika Noronen, Teppo

Numminen, Tomi Pettinen, Thomas
Pihlman, Lasse Pirjeta, Joni Pitkanen,
Pekka Rinne, Jani Rita, Jarkko Ruutu,
Tuomo Ruutu, Sami Salo, Teemu
Selanne, Kimmo Timonen, Hannu
Toivonen, Vesa Toskala, Ossi Vaananen

SLOVAKIA   31   Josef Balej, Milan Bartovic, Peter
Budaj, Zdeno Chara, Martin Cibak,
Pavol Demitra, Marian Gaborik,
Michal Handzus, Marcel Hossa,
Marian Hossa, Milan Jurcina, Juraj
Kolnik, Tomas Kopecky, Ivan Majesky,
Tomas Malec, Andrei Meszaros,
Branislav Mezei, Ladislav Nagy,
Vladimir Orszagh, Ziggy Palffy, Ronald
Petrovicky, Branko Radivojevic, Stefan
Ruzicka, Miroslav Satan, Peter Sejna,
Jozef Stumpel, Radoslav Suchy, Tomas
Surovy, Marek Svatos, Lubomir
Visnovsky, Richard Zednik

GERMANY   8   Sven Butenschon, Christian Ehrhoff,
Marcel Goc, Dany Heatley, Jochen
Hecht, Christoph Schubert, Dennis
Seidenberg, Marco Sturm

UKRAINE   7   Anton Babchuk, Peter Bondra, Ruslan
Fedotenko, Alexei Ponikarovsky, Oleg
Tverdovsky, Vitali Vishnevsky, Nikolai
Zherdev

KAZAKHSTAN	6	Nik Antropov, Vitaliy Kolesnik, Evgeny Nabokov, Alexander Perezhogin, Konstantin Pushkarev, Pavel Vorobiev
SWITZERLAND	4	David Aebischer, Martin Gerber, Timo Helbling, Mark Streit
AUSTRIA	3	Reinhard Divis, Thomas Pock, Thomas Vanek
BELARUS	3	Konstantin Koltsov, Andrei Kostitsyn, Ruslan Salei
LATVIA	3	Raitis Ivanins, Sandis Ozolinsh, Karlis Skrastins
POLAND	3	Mariusz Czerkawski, Krzysztof Oliwa, Wojtek Wolski
LITHUANIA	2	Darius Kasparaitis, Dainius Zubrus
BRAZIL	1	Robyn Regehr
FRANCE	1	Cristobal Huet
MALAYSIA	1	Craig Adams
NORWAY	1	Ole-Kristian Tollefsen
SOUTH AFRICA	1	Olaf Kolzig
SOUTH KOREA	1	Richard Park

FIRST GAMES PLAYED, 2005–06

SKATERS (Nationality) NHL TEAM (first game)	G	A	P	Pim
GOALIES (Nationality) NHL TEAM (first game)	Mins	GA	W-L-T	

* indicates player traded later in season

Regular Season

ND indicates No Decision

Andrew Alberts (USA)	BOS (Oct. 5)	0	0	0	0
Colby Armstrong (CAN)	PIT (Dec. 29)	0	0	0	0
Evgeny Artyukhin (RUS)	TB (Oct. 20)	0	0	0	0
Keith Aucoin (USA)	CAR (Jan. 23)	0	1	1	2
Jason Bacashihua (USA)	STL (Dec. 16)	34:19	2	ND	
Jaroslav Balastik (CZE)	CBJ (Oct. 5)	0	0	0	2
Keith Ballard (USA)	PHO (Oct. 5)	1	0	1	0
Cam Barker (CAN)	CHI (Oct. 5)	0	0	0	0
Brendan Bell (CAN)	TOR (Mar. 21)	0	0	0	0
Adam Berkhoel (USA)	ATL (Oct. 15)	60:00	5	L	
Steve Bernier (CAN)	SJ (Nov. 4)	0	0	0	0
Kevin Bieksa (CAN)	VAN (Dec. 19)	0	0	0	2
Brandon Bochenski (USA)	OTT (Oct. 5)	0	0	0	0
Derek Boogaard (CAN)	MIN (Oct. 5)	0	0	0	0
Rene Bourque (CAN)	CHI (Oct. 5)	1	0	1	0
Kyle Brodziak (CAN)	EDM (Oct. 15)	0	0	0	0
Gilbert Brule (CAN)	CBJ (Oct. 5)	0	1	1	0
Peter Budaj (SVK)	COL (Oct. 8)	60:00	2	W	
Alexandre Burrows (CAN)	VAN (Jan. 2)	0	0	0	5
Dustin Byfuglien (USA)	CHI (Mar. 1)	1	0	1	0
Ryan Caldwell (CAN)	NYI (Apr. 15)	0	0	0	0
Chris Campoli (CAN)	NYI (Oct. 5)	1	0	1	0
Matt Carkner (CAN)	SJ (Feb. 6)	0	1	1	2

Matthew Carle (USA)	SJ (Mar. 25)	1	0	1	4
Jeff Carter (CAN)	PHI (Oct. 5)	0	0	0	0
Erik Christensen (CAN)	PIT (Nov. 1)	0	0	0	4
Ryane Clowe (CAN)	SJ (Oct. 5)	0	0	0	2
Braydon Coburn (CAN)	ATL (Oct. 5)	0	0	0	0
Gerald Coleman (USA)	TB (Nov. 11)	20:00	1	ND	
Kevin Colley (USA)	NYI (Oct. 27)	0	0	0	0
Jeremy Colliton (CAN)	NYI (Nov. 23)	0	0	0	0
Rob Collins (CAN)	NYI (Dec. 17)	0	0	0	0
Jean-Philippe Cote (CAN)	MTL (Nov. 29)	0	0	0	2
Ryan Craig (CAN)	TB (Dec. 17)	1	0	1	0
Corey Crawford (CAN)	CHI (Jan. 22)	21:27	0	ND	
Sidney Crosby (CAN)	PIT (Oct. 5)	0	1	1	0
Mark Cullen (USA)	CHI (Nov. 10)	1	0	1	0
Kevin Dallman (CAN)	BOS (Oct. 5)	0	0	0	0
Yann Danis (CAN)	MTL (Oct. 12)	59:50	0	W	
Jon Disalvatore (USA)	STL (Jan. 19)	0	0	0	0
Ben Eager (CAN)	PHI (Nov. 30)	0	1	1	0
Patrick Eaves (CAN)	OTT (Nov. 11)	0	0	0	0
Brian Eklund (USA)	TB (Nov. 8)	58:13	3	L	
Eric Fehr (CAN)	WAS (Dec. 18)	0	0	0	2
Jonathan Ferland (CAN)	MTL (Jan. 3)	1	0	1	0
Valtteri Filppula (FIN)	DET (Dec. 15)	0	1	1	2
Tomas Fleischmann (CZE)	WAS (Nov. 3)	0	0	0	0
Matt Foy (CAN)	MIN (Oct. 5)	0	1	1	2
Johan Franzen (SWE)	DET (Oct. 5)	0	0	0	0
Michael Garnett (CAN)	ATL (Oct. 12)	51:44	1	ND	
Carsen Germyn (CAN)	CAL (Apr. 1)	0	0	0	0
Bruno Gervais (CAN)	NYI (Dec. 4)	0	0	0	0
Ryan Getzlaf (CAN)	ANA (Oct. 5)	0	0	0	0
Trevor Gillies (CAN)	ANA (Nov. 6)	0	0	0	21
Mark Giordano (CAN)	CAL (Jan. 30)	0	0	0	2
Alexandre Giroux (CAN)	NYR (Mar. 25)	0	0	0	0
Jeff Giuliano (USA)	LA (Nov. 5)	0	0	0	0

Rob Globke (USA)	FLO (Dec. 28)	0	0	0	0
Mike Glumac (CAN)	STL (Jan. 30)	0	1	1	0
Steve Goertzen (CAN)	CBJ (Oct. 21)	0	0	0	0
Josh Gorges (CAN)	SJ (Oct. 7)	0	0	0	0
David Gove (USA)	CAR (Jan. 31)	0	1	1	0
Josh Gratton (CAN)	PHI (Dec. 15)	0	0	0	4
Matt Greene (USA)	EDM (Dec. 30)	0	0	0	4
Ben Guite (CAN)	BOS (Jan. 30)	0	0	0	0
Josh Harding (CAN)	MIN (Apr. 4)	65:00	4	W	
Jay Harrison (CAN)	TOR (Jan. 28)	0	0	0	0
Adam Hauser (USA)	LA (Jan. 14)	50:49	6	ND	
Eric Healey (USA)	BOS (Nov. 25)	0	0	0	2
Timo Helbling (SUI)	TB (Oct. 5)	0	0	0	2
Colin Hemingway (CAN)	STL (Oct. 19)	0	0	0	0
Jeff Hoggan (CAN)	STL (Oct. 5)	0	0	0	0
Ryan Hollweg (USA)	NYR (Oct. 5)	0	1	1	2
Chris Holt (CAN)	NYR (Dec. 3)	10:24	0	ND	
James Howard (USA)	DET (Nov. 28)	59:55	2	W	
Jarkko Immonen (FIN)	NYR (Apr. 6)	1	0	1	0
Raitis Ivanins (LAT)	MON (Oct. 8)	0	0	0	0
Greg Jacina (CAN)	FLO (Nov. 12)	0	0	0	0
Jean-Francois Jacques (CAN)	EDM (Feb. 2)	0	0	0	0
Connor James (CAN)	LA (Jan. 7)	0	0	0	0
Dan Jancevski (CAN)	DAL (Feb. 4)	0	0	0	0
Cam Janssen (USA)	NJ (Nov. 5)	0	0	0	0
Cole Jarrett (CAN)	NYI (Apr. 18)	0	0	0	0
Jonas Johansson (SWE)	WAS (Apr. 18)	0	0	0	2
Jussi Jokinen (FIN)	DAL (Oct. 5)	0	0	0	0
Matt Jones (USA)	PHO (Nov. 25)	0	0	0	0
Milan Jurcina (SVK)	BOS (Oct. 8)	0	0	0	4
Petr Kanko (CZE)	LA (Dec. 16)	1	0	1	0
Duncan Keith (CAN)	CHI (Oct. 5)	0	0	0	0
Kevin Klein (CAN)	NAS (Dec. 3)	0	0	0	0
Jakub Klepis (CZE)	WAS (Nov. 4)	1	0	1	0

Matt Koalska (USA)	NYI (Apr. 13)	0	0	0	2
Mikko Koivu (FIN)	MIN (Nov. 5)	0	0	0	2
Vitaliy Kolesnik (KAZ)	COL (Dec. 20)	58:28	3	L	
Zenon Konopka (CAN)	ANA (Oct. 30)	0	0	0	0
Tomas Kopecky (SVK)	DET (Feb. 28)	0	0	0	2
Andrei Kostitsyn (RUS)	MTL (Dec. 1)	0	0	0	0
Staffan Kronvall (SWE)	TOR (Oct. 29)	0	0	0	0
Andrew Ladd (CAN)	CAR (Nov. 20)	0	0	0	0
Maxim Lapierre (CAN)	MTL (Nov. 15)	0	0	0	0
Chad LaRose (USA)	CAR (Dec. 6)	0	0	0	0
Jay Leach (USA)	BOS (Nov. 5)	0	0	0	7
Brett Lebda (USA)	DET (Oct. 5)	1	0	1	0
Yanick Lehoux (CAN)	LA (Nov. 8)	1	0	1	2
David Leneveu (CAN)	PHO (Oct. 6)	58:40	3	L	
Junior Lessard (CAN)	DAL (Oct. 22)	0	0	0	0
David Liffiton (CAN)	NYR (Apr. 11)	0	0	0	2
Joakim Lindstrom (SWE)	CBJ (Feb. 8)	0	0	0	0
Henrik Lundqvist (SWE)	NYR (Oct. 8)	63:10	3	OTL	
Masi Marjamaki (FIN)	NYI (Apr. 18)	0	0	0	0
Jay McClement (CAN)	STL (Oct. 5)	0	0	0	0
Brian McGrattan (CAN)	OTT (Oct. 5)	0	0	0	2
Rob McVicar (CAN)	VAN (Dec. 1)	2:44	0	ND	
Andrej Meszaros (SVK)	OTT (Oct. 5)	0	0	0	0
Tomas Mojzis (CZE)	VAN (Feb. 4)	0	1	1	2
Mike Morrison (USA)	EDM (Nov. 7)	18:12	0	ND	
Doug Murray (SWE)	SJ (Dec. 2)	0	0	0	4
Robert Nilsson (SWE)	NYI (Oct. 5)	0	0	0	0
Petteri Nokelainen (FIN)	NYI (Oct. 5)	0	0	0	2
Niklas Nordgren (SWE)	CAR (Oct. 5)	0	0	0	0
Filip Novak (CZE)	OTT (Mar. 24)	0	0	0	2
Jiri Novotny (CZE)	BUF (Jan. 12)	0	0	0	0
Eric Nystrom (USA)	CAL (Oct. 10)	0	0	0	0
Doug O'Brien (CAN)	TB (Jan. 29)	0	0	0	0
Rostislav Olesz (CZE)	FLO (Oct. 5)	0	0	0	0

Ben Ondrus (CAN)	TOR (Mar. 7)	0	0	0	2
Michel Ouellet (CAN)	PIT (Nov. 22)	0	0	0	0
Alexander Ovechkin (RUS)	WAS (Oct. 5)	2	0	2	2
Nathan Paetsch (CAN)	BUF (Jan. 7)	0	1	1	0
Daniel Paille (CAN)	BUF (Dec. 22)	0	0	0	2
Zach Parise (USA)	NJ (Oct. 5)	1	1	2	4
George Parros (USA)	LA (Oct. 5)	0	0	0	5
Dustin Penner (CAN)	ANA (Nov. 23)	0	0	0	2
Alexander Perezhogin (KAZ)	MTL (Oct. 6)	1	0	1	0
Joel Perrault (CAN)	PHO (Apr. 8)	0	0	0	0
Corey Perry (CAN)	ANA (Oct. 5)	0	1	1	0
Richard Petiot (CAN	LA (Jan. 17)	0	0	0	2
Dion Phaneuf (CAN)	CAL (Oct. 5)	0	0	0	0
Alexandre Picard (CAN)	CBJ (Nov. 18)	0	0	0	2
Alexandre Picard (CAN)	PHI (Jan. 2)	0	0	0	0
Geoff Platt (CAN)	CBJ (Dec. 1)	0	0	0	2
Vojtech Polak (CZE)	DAL (Oct. 22)	0	0	0	0
Ryan Potulny (USA)	PHI (Apr. 7)	0	0	0	0
Marc-Antoine Pouliot (CAN)	EDM (Mar. 30)	0	0	0	0
David Printz (SWE)	PHI (Apr. 11)	0	0	0	0
Petr Prucha (CZE)	NYR (Oct. 8)	0	0	0	0
Konstantin Pushkarev (KAZ)	LA (Mar. 27)	0	1	1	0
Kyle Quincey (CAN)	DET (Nov. 25)	0	0	0	0
Paul Ranger (CAN)	TB (Oct. 15)	0	0	0	0
Ryan Ready (CAN)	PHI (Nov. 29)	0	0	0	0
Richie Regehr (CAN)	CAL (Dec. 29)	0	1	1	0
Steve Regier (CAN)	NYI (Apr. 2)	0	0	0	0
Darren Reid (CAN)	TB (Dec. 17)	0	0	0	0
Erik Reitz (USA)	MIN (Apr. 7)	0	0	0	2
Mike Richards (CAN)	PHI (Oct. 5)	1	0	1	0
Brad Richardson (CAN)	COL (Nov. 27)	0	0	0	0
Danny Richmond (USA)	CAR (Nov. 11)	0	0	0	0
Pekka Rinne (FIN)	NAS (Dec. 15)	60:00	3	W	
Andy Roach (USA)	STL (Oct. 5)	0	0	0	6

Louis Robitaille (CAN)	WAS (Feb. 7)	0	0	0	5
Mathieu Roy (CAN)	EDM (Feb. 12)	0	0	0	0
Stefan Ruzicka (SVK)	PHI (Feb. 8)	0	0	0	2
Matt Ryan (CAN)	LA (Dec. 31)	0	0	0	0
Prestin Ryan (CAN)	VAN (Feb. 8)	0	0	0	2
Rick Rypien (CAN)	VAN (Dec. 21)	1	0	1	0
Jason Ryznar (USA)	NJ (Jan. 24)	0	0	0	0
Nolan Schaefer (CAN)	SJ (Oct. 26)	35:29	1	W	
Christoph Schubert (GER)	OTT (Oct. 29)	0	0	0	2
Brent Seabrook (CAN)	CHI (Oct. 5)	0	1	1	2
Jordan Sigalet (CAN)	BOS (Jan. 7)	0:43	0	ND	
Wade Skolney (CAN)	PHI (Oct. 11)	0	0	0	2
Jim Slater (USA)	ATL (Oct. 5)	0	0	0	0
Yan Stastny (CAN)	BOS (Mar. 1)	0	0	0	0
David Steckel (USA)	WAS (Dec. 31)	0	0	0	0
Alexander Steen (SWE)	TOR (Oct. 5)	0	0	0	2
Lee Stempniak (USA)	STL (Oct. 6)	0	0	0	0
Grant Stevenson (CAN)	SJ (Nov. 23)	1	0	1	0
Anthony Stewart (CAN)	FLO (Oct. 18)	0	1	1	0
Martin St. Pierre (CAN)	CHI (Nov. 4)	0	0	0	0
Mark Streit (SUI)	MTL (Oct. 8)	0	1	1	0
Mark Stuart (USA)	BOS (Mar. 11)	0	0	0	0
Ryan Suter (USA)	NAS (Oct. 5)	0	1	1	4
Danny Syvret (CAN)	EDM (Nov. 4)	0	0	0	0
Maxime Talbot (CAN)	PIT (Oct. 5)	0	0	0	0
Barry Tallackson (USA)	NJ (Nov. 12)	0	0	0	0
Jeff Tambellini (CAN)	LA (Nov. 30)	0	0	0	0
Nick Tarnasky (CAN)	TB (Oct. 20)	0	0	0	2
Peter Taticek (CZE)	FLO (Jan. 21)	0	0	0	0
Joey Tenute (CAN)	WAS (Feb. 7)	0	0	0	0
Bill Thomas (USA)	PHO (Mar. 28)	0	0	0	2
Chris Thorburn (CAN)	BUF (Dec. 2)	0	0	0	2
Hannu Toivonen (FIN)	BOS (Oct. 8)	60:55	6	W	
Ole-Kristian Tollefsen (NOR)	CBJ (Nov. 23)	0	0	0	2

R. J. Umberger (USA)	PHI (Oct. 30)	0	0	0	0
Thomas Vanek (AUT)	BUF (Oct. 5)	0	1	1	0
Ben Walter (CAN)	BOS (Jan. 12)	0	0	0	0
Cam Ward (CAN)	CAR (Oct. 5)	20:00	1	ND	
Shea Weber (CAN)	NAS (Jan. 6)	0	0	0	2
Noah Welch (USA)	PIT (Mar. 24)	0	1	1	0
Ian White (CAN)	TOR (Mar. 26)	0	1	1	2
Ryan Whitney (USA)	PIT (Nov. 1)	0	1	1	0
Dennis Wideman (CAN)	STL (Nov. 9)	0	0	0	2
Jeremy Williams (CAN)	TOR (Apr. 18)	1	0	1	0
Brad Winchester (USA)	EDM (Oct. 10)	0	0	0	0
James Wisniewski (USA)	CHI (Feb. 2)	0	0	0	4
Wojtek Wolski (POL)	COL (Oct. 5)	0	0	0	0
Jeff Woywitka (CAN)	STL (Oct. 6)	0	0	0	2
Andrew Wozniewski (USA)	TOR (Oct. 5)	0	0	0	0
Greg Zanon (CAN)	NAS (Dec. 1)	0	1	1	6

BY NATIONALITY

TOTAL	209
CANADA	114
USA	49
CZECH REPUBLIC	11
SWEDEN	9
FINLAND	8
SLOVAKIA	5
KAZAKHSTAN	3
RUSSIA	3
SWITZERLAND	2
AUSTRIA	1
GERMANY	1
LATVIA	1
NORWAY	1
POLAND	1

PLAYER REGISTER, REGULAR SEASON, 2005–06

Player						
YEAR	**GP**	**G**	**A**	**P**	**Pim**	
Goalie						
YEAR	**GP**	**W-L-OT**	**Mins**	**GA**	**SO**	**GAA**

NOTE: As a result of the introduction of the shootout for 2005–06, the NHL has changed how it keeps goaltenders' records. Formerly, a goalie was credited with a win or loss if his team won or lost a game that went to overtime. Of course, a tie meant both goalies were credited with a tie. Now, however, all games have a winner and a loser. If a game is won in overtime, the winning goalie gets credit for a win. If his team wins a shootout, he also gets credit for a win. But the losing goalie (in either overtime or a shootout) is credited with a tie. But, so as not to confuse this with what we formerly knew as ties, the NHL has created a new column called "OT," meaning, essentially, an overtime or shootout loss. So, in the statistics below, the 2005–06 number that follows wins and losses for goalies refers to "OT" games, and the career number after wins and losses refers to actual ties.

Abid, Ramzi b. Montreal, Quebec, March 24, 1980

	GP	G	A	P	Pim
2005–06 ATL	6	0	2	2	6
NHL Totals	55	13	12	25	65

Adams, Craig b. Seria, Brunei (Malaysia), April 26, 1977

	GP	G	A	P	Pim
2005–06 CAR	67	10	11	21	51
NHL Totals	305	24	34	58	249

Adams, Kevyn b. Washington, D.C., October 8, 1974

	GP	G	A	P	Pim
2005–06 CAR	82	15	8	23	36
NHL Totals	445	56	66	122	279

Aebischer, David b. Fribourg, Switzerland, February 7, 1978

2005–06 COL/MON*	50	29-17-2	2,895	149	3	3.09
NHL Totals	181	93-61-12	10,409	417	13	2.40

* traded March 8, 2006 by Colorado to Montreal for Jose Theodore

Afanasenkov, Dmitry b. Arkhangelsk, Soviet Union (Russia), May 12, 1980

2005–06 TB	68	9	6	15	16
NHL Totals	153	16	17	33	32

Afinogenov, Maxim b. Moscow, Soviet Union (Russia), September 4, 1979

2005–06 BUF	77	22	51	73	84
NHL Totals	409	95	130	225	312

Albelin, Tommy b. Stockholm, Sweden, May 21, 1964

2005–06 NJ	36	0	6	6	2
NHL Totals	952	44	211	255	417

Alberts, Andrew b. Minneapolis, Minnesota, June 30, 1981

2005–06 BOS	73	1	6	7	68
NHL Totals	73	1	6	7	68

Alfredsson, Daniel b. Goteborg, Sweden, December 11, 1972

2005–06 OTT	77	43	60	103	50
NHL Totals	706	262	409	671	309

Allen, Bryan b. Kingston, Ontario, August 21, 1980

2005–06 VAN	77	7	10	17	115
NHL Totals	216	14	18	32	288

Allison, Jamie b. Lindsay, Ontario, May 13, 1975

2005–06 FLO	27	0	1	1	56
NHL Totals	372	7	23	30	639

Allison, Jason b. North York (Toronto), Ontario, May 29, 1975

2005–06 TOR	66	17	43	60	76
NHL Totals	552	154	331	485	441

Amonte, Tony b. Hingham, Massachusetts, August 2, 1970

2005–06 CAL	80	14	28	42	43
NHL Totals	1,093	406	464	870	712

Anderson, Craig b. Park Ridge, Illinois, May 21, 1981

2005–06 CHI	29	6-12-4	1,553	86	1	3.32
NHL Totals	56	12-29-2	3,028	161	2	3.19

Andreychuk, Dave b. Hamilton, Ontario, September 29, 1963

2005–06 TB	42	6	12	18	16
NHL Totals	1,639	640	698	1,338	1,125

* placed on waivers on January 10, 2006, and retired

Antropov, Nik b. Ust-Kamenogorsk, Soviet Union, (Kazakhstan) February 18, 1980

2005–06 TOR	57	12	19	31	56
NHL Totals	320	60	96	156	317

Armstrong, Colby b. Lloydminster, Saskatchewan, November 23, 1982

2005–06 PIT	47	16	24	40	58
NHL Totals	47	16	24	40	58

Armstrong, Derek b. Ottawa, Ontario, April 23, 1973

2005–06 LA	62	13	28	41	46
NHL Totals	271	48	85	133	165

Arnason, Tyler b. Oklahoma City, Oklahoma, March 16, 1979

2005–06 CHI/OTT*	79	13	32	45	44
NHL Totals	264	57	86	143	84

* traded March 9, 2006 from Chicago to Ottawa for Brandon Bochenski and a 2nd-round draft choice in 2006

Arnott, Jason b. Collingwood, Ontario, October 11, 1974

2005–06 DAL	81	32	44	76	102
NHL Totals	824	276	368	644	999

Artyukhin, Evgeni b. Moscow, Soviet Union (Russia), April 4, 1983

2005–06 TB	72	4	13	17	90
NHL Totals	72	4	13	17	90

Asham, Arron b. Portage La Prairie, Manitoba, April 13, 1978

2005–06 NYI	63	9	15	24	103
NHL Totals	341	47	55	102	390

Aubin, Jean-Sebastien b. Montreal, Quebec, July 19, 1977

2005–06 TOR	11	9-0-2	677	25	1	2.22
NHL Totals	179	72-72-11	9,566	457	7	2.87

Aubin, Serge b. Val d'Or, Quebec, February 15, 1975

2005–06 ATL	74	7	17	24	79
NHL Totals	374	44	64	108	361

Aucoin, Adrian b. Ottawa, Ontario, July 3, 1973

2005–06 CHI	33	1	5	6	38
NHL Totals	635	84	167	251	494

Aucoin, Keith b. Waltham, Massachusetts, November 6, 1978

2005–06 CAR	7	0	1	1	4
NHL Totals	7	0	1	1	4

Auld, Alexander b. Cold Lake, Alberta, January 7, 1981

2005–06 VAN	67	33-26-6	3,858	189	0	2.94
NHL Totals	81	39-31-2	4,650	213	1	2.75

Avery, Sean b. Pickering, Ontario, April 10, 1980

2005–06 LA	75	15	24	39	257
NHL Totals	238	32	54	86	739

released April 13, 2006

Axelsson, P-J b. Kungalv, Sweden, February 26, 1975

2005–06 BOS	59	10	18	28	4
NHL Totals	592	73	128	201	193

Babchuk, Anton b. Kiev, Soviet Union (Ukraine), May 6, 1984

2005–06 CHI/CAR	39	5	5	10	22
NHL Totals	44	5	7	12	24

traded January 18, 2006, by Chicago to Carolina with a 4th-round draft choice in 2007 for Danny Richmond and a 4th-round draft choice in 2006

Bacashihua, Jason b. Garden City, Michigan, September 20, 1982

2005–06 STL	19	4-10-1	966	52	0	3.23
NHL Totals	19	4-10-1	966	52	0	3.23

Backman, Christian b. Alingsas, Sweden, April 28, 1980

2005–06 STL	52	6	12	18	48
NHL Totals	122	11	25	36	64

Balastik, Jaroslav b. Gottwaldov (Zlin), Czechoslovakia (Czech Republic), November 28, 1979

2005–06 CBJ	66	12	10	22	26
NHL Totals	66	12	10	22	26

Balej, Josef b. Myjava, Czechoslovakia (Slovakia), February 22, 1982

2005–06 VAN	1	0	1	1	0
NHL Totals	18	1	5	6	4

traded October 7, 2005, by the New York Rangers to Vancouver with a conditional draft choice for Fedor Fedorov

Ballard, Keith b. Baudette, Minnesota, November 26, 1982

2005–06 PHO	82	8	31	39	99
NHL Totals	82	8	31	39	99

Barinka, Michal b. Vyskov, Czechoslovakia (Czech Republic), June 12, 1984

2005–06 CHI	25	0	1	1	20
NHL Totals	34	0	2	2	26

Barker, Cam b. Winnipeg, Manitoba, April 4, 1986

2005–06 CHI	1	0	0	0	0
NHL Totals	1	0	0	0	0

Barnaby, Matthew b. Ottawa, Ontario, May 4, 1973

2005–06 CHI	82	8	20	28	178
NHL Totals	795	112	181	293	2,435

Barnes, Stu b. Spruce Grove, Alberta, December 25, 1970

2005–06 DAL	78	15	21	36	44
NHL Totals	975	236	313	549	372

Barney, Scott b. Oshawa, Ontario, March 27, 1979

2005–06 ATL	3	0	0	0	0
NHL Totals	27	5	6	11	4

Bartovic, Milan b. Trencin, Czechoslovakia (Slovakia), April 9, 198

2005–06 CHI	24	1	6	7	8
NHL Totals	50	3	14	17	26

Bates, Shawn b. Melrose, Massachusetts, April 3, 1975

2005–06 NYI	66	15	19	34	60
NHL Totals	415	68	120	188	232

Baumgartner, Nolan b. Calgary, Alberta, March 23, 1976

2005–06 VAN	70	5	29	34	30
NHL Totals	118	6	36	42	46

Beauchemin, Francois b. Sorel, Quebec, June 4, 1980

2005–06 CBJ/ANA	72	8	28	36	52
NHL Totals	73	8	28	36	52

* traded November 15, 2005, by Columbus to Anaheim with Tyler Wright
  for Sergei Fedorov and a 5th-round draft choice in 2005

Beech, Kris b. Salmon Arm, British Columbia, February 5, 1981

2005–06 NAS/WAS	10	1	2	3	4
NHL Totals	109	11	19	30	63

* traded March 9, 2006, from Nashville to Washington with a 1st-round draft
  choice in 2006 for Brendan Witt

Begin, Steve b. Trois-Rivieres, Quebec, June 14, 1978

2005–06 MON	76	11	12	23	113
NHL Totals	251	32	24	56	346

Belak, Wade b. Saskatoon, Saskatchewan, July 3, 1976

2005–06 TOR	55	0	3	3	109
NHL Totals	330	7	18	25	920

Belanger, Eric b. Sherbrooke, Quebec, December 16, 1977

2005–06 LA	65	17	20	37	62
NHL Totals	323	63	87	150	169

Belanger, Ken b. Sault Ste. Marie, Ontario, May 14, 1974

2005–06 LA	5	0	0	0	7
NHL Totals	248	11	12	23	695

Belfour, Ed b. Carman, Manitoba, April 21, 1965

2005–06 TOR	49	22-22-4	2,896	159	0	3.29
NHL Totals	905	457-303-111	52,406	2,165	75	2.48

* missed last part of season with back injury

Bell, Brendan b. Ottawa, Ontario, March 31, 1983

2005–06 TOR	1	0	0	0	0
NHL Totals	1	0	0	0	0

Bell, Mark b. St. Paul's, Ontario, August 5, 1980

2005–06 CHI	82	25	23	48	107
NHL Totals	339	72	79	151	454

Berard, Bryan b. Woonsocket, Rhode Island, March 5, 1977

2005–06 CBJ	44	12	20	32	32
NHL Totals	554	71	227	298	444

* tested positive for banned substance during pre-Olympic drug testing
  by NHL

Berg, Aki b. Turku, Finland, July 28, 1977

2005–06 TOR	75	0	8	8	56
NHL Totals	606	15	70	85	374

Bergenheim, Sean b. Helsinki, Finland, February 8, 1984

2005–06 NYI	28	4	5	9	20
NHL Totals	46	5	6	11	24

Bergeron, Marc-Andre b. St. Louis de France, Quebec,
October 13, 1980

2005–06 EDM	75	15	20	35	38
NHL Totals	134	25	38	63	73

Bergeron, Patrice b. Ancienne-Lorette, Quebec, July 24, 1985

2005–06 BOS	81	31	42	73	22
NHL Totals	152	47	65	112	44

Berkhoel, Adam b. St. Paul, Minnesota, May 16, 1981

2005–06 ATL	9	2-4-1	473	30	0	3.81
NHL Totals	9	2-4-1	473	30	0	3.81

Bernier, Steve b. Quebec City, Quebec, March 31, 1985

2005–06 SJ	39	14	13	27	35
NHL Totals	39	14	13	27	35

Bertuzzi, Todd b. Sudbury, Ontario, February 2, 1975

2005–06 VAN	82	25	46	71	120
NHL Totals	710	223	306	529	1,031

Betts, Blair b. Edmonton, Alberta, February 16, 1980

2005–06 NYR	66	8	2	10	24
NHL Totals	101	11	7	18	38

Bieksa, Kevin b. Grimsby, Ontario, June 16, 1981

2005–06 VAN	39	0	6	6	77
NHL Totals	39	0	6	6	77

Biron, Martin b. Lac St. Charles, Quebec, August 15, 1977

2005–06 BUF	35	21-8-3	1,934	93	1	2.89
NHL Totals	281	122-111-25	15,706	653	18	2.49

Biron, Mathieu b. Lac St. Charles, Quebec, April 29, 1980

2005–06 WAS	52	4	9	13	50
NHL Totals	253	12	32	44	177

Blake, Jason b. Moorhead, Minnesota, September 2, 1973

2005–06 NYI	76	28	29	57	60
NHL Totals	426	94	123	217	270

Blake, Rob b. Simcoe, Ontario, December 10, 1969

2005–06 COL	81	14	37	51	94
NHL Totals	984	200	437	637	1,329

Blatny, Zdenek b. Brno, Czechoslovakia (Czech Republic), January 14, 1981

2005–06 BOS/TB	5	0	0	0	2
NHL Totals	25	3	0	3	8

* traded February 8, 2006, by Boston to Tampa Bay for Brian Eklund

Bochenski, Brandon b. Blaine, Minnesota, April 4, 1982

2005–06 OTT/CHI	40	8	9	17	22
NHL Totals	40	8	9	17	22

* traded March 9, 2006, from Ottawa to Chicago with a 2nd-round draft choice in 2006 for Tyler Arnason

Boguniecki, Eric b. New Haven, Connecticut, May 6, 1975

2005–06 STL/PIT	47	6	10	16	33
NHL Totals	167	34	42	76	97

* traded December 9, 2005, by St. Louis to Pittsburgh for Steve Poapst

Bondra, Peter b. Luck, Soviet Union (Ukraine), February 7, 1968

2005–06 ATL	60	21	18	39	40
NHL Totals	1,044	498	380	878	735

Bonk, Radek b. Krnov, Czechoslovakia (Czech Republic), January 9, 1976

2005–06 MON	61	6	15	21	52
NHL Totals	750	158	262	420	453

Boogaard, Derek b. Saskatoon, Saskatchewan, June 23, 1982

2005–06 MIN	65	2	4	6	158
NHL Totals	65	2	4	6	158

Bouchard, Joel b. Montreal, Quebec, January 23, 1974

2005–06 NYI	25	1	8	9	23
NHL Totals	364	22	53	75	264

Bouchard, Pierre-Marc b. Sherbrooke, Quebec, April 27, 1984

2005–06 MIN	80	17	42	59	28
NHL Totals	191	28	73	101	68

Boucher, Brian b. Woonsocket, Rhode Island, January 2, 1977

2005–06 PHO/CAL	14	4-8-0	693	48	0	4.15
NHL Totals	202	75-85-30	11,403	521	12	2.74

* traded February 1, 2006, by Phoenix to Calgary with Mike Leclerc for Steve Reinprecht and Philippe Sauve

Boucher, Philippe b. St. Apollinaire, Quebec, March 24, 1973

2005–06 DAL	66	16	27	43	77
NHL Totals	593	70	156	226	533

Bouck, Tyler b. Camrose, Alberta, January 13, 1980

2005–06 VAN	12	1	1	2	21
NHL Totals	85	4	8	12	77

Boughner, Bob b. Windsor, Ontario, March 8, 1971

2005–06 COL	41	1	6	7	54
NHL Totals	630	15	57	72	1,382

Bouillon, Francis b. New York, New York, October 17, 1975

2005–06 MON	67	3	19	22	34
NHL Totals	295	11	60	71	205

Boulerice, Jesse b. Plattsburgh, New York, August 10, 1978

2005–06 CAR/STL	38	0	0	0	64
NHL Totals	165	8	2	10	304

* traded January 30, 2006, by Carolina to St. Louis with Mike Zigomanis, the rights to Magnus Kahnberg, and a 1st- and 4th-round draft choice in 2006 for Doug Weight and Erkki Rajamaki

Boulton, Eric b. Halifax, Nova Scotia, August 17, 1976

2005–06 ATL	51	4	5	9	87
NHL Totals	223	9	17	26	598

Bourque, Rene b. Lac la Biche, Alberta, December 10, 1981

2005–06 CHI	77	16	18	34	56
NHL Totals	77	16	18	34	56

Bouwmeester, Jay b. Edmonton, Alberta, September 27, 1983

2005–06 FLO	82	5	41	46	79
NHL Totals	225	11	71	82	123

Boyes, Brad b. Mississauga, Ontario, April 17, 1982

2005–06 BOS	82	26	43	69	30
NHL Totals	83	26	43	69	32

Boyle, Dan b. Ottawa, Ontario, July 12, 1976

2005–06 TB	79	15	38	53	38
NHL Totals	404	52	152	204	219

Boynton, Nick b. Nobleton, Ontario, January 14, 1979

2005–06 BOS	54	5	7	12	93
NHL Totals	299	22	62	84	397

Bradley, Matt b. Stittsville, Ontario, June 13, 1978

2005–06 WAS	74	7	12	19	72
NHL Totals	277	26	38	64	236

Brashear, Donald b. Bedford, Indiana, January 7, 1972

2005–06 PHI	76	4	5	9	166
NHL Totals	769	75	104	179	2,165

Brendl, Pavel b. Opocno, Czechoslovakia (Czech Republic), March 23, 1981

2005–06 CAR/PHO	2	0	0	0	0
NHL Totals	78	11	11	22	16

* traded December 28, 2005, by Carolina to Phoenix for Krys Kolanos

Brennan, Kip b. Kingston, Ontario, August 27, 1980

2005–06 ANA	12	0	1	1	35
NHL Totals	58	1	1	2	210

Brewer, Eric b. Vernon, British Columbia, April 17, 1979

2005–06 STL	32	6	3	9	45
NHL Totals	436	40	82	122	307

Briere, Daniel b. Gatineau, Quebec, October 6, 1977

2005–06 BUF	48	25	33	58	48
NHL Totals	402	130	151	281	276

Brind'Amour, Rod b. Ottawa, Ontario, August 9, 1970

2005–06 CAR	78	31	39	70	68
NHL Totals	1,187	382	599	981	944

Brisebois, Patrice b. Montreal, Quebec, January 27, 1971

2005–06 COL	80	10	28	38	55
NHL Totals	871	89	291	380	556

Brodeur, Martin b. Montreal, Quebec, May 6, 1972

2005–06 NJ	73	43-23-7	4,364	187	5	2.57
NHL Totals	813	446-240-105	47,875	1,760	80	2.21

Brodziak, Kyle b. St. Paul, Alberta, May 25, 1984

2005–06 EDM	10	0	0	0	4
NHL Totals	10	0	0	0	4

Brookbank, Wade b. Lanigan, Saskatchewan, September 29, 1977

2005–06 VAN	32	1	2	3	81
NHL Totals	61	3	2	5	214

Brown, Curtis b. Unity, Saskatchewan, February 12, 1976

2005–06 CHI	71	5	10	15	38
NHL Totals	625	116	155	271	332

Brown, Dustin b. Ithaca, New York, November 4, 1984

2005–06 LA	79	14	14	28	80
NHL Totals	110	15	18	33	96

Brown, Mike b. North Vancouver, British Columbia, April 27, 1979

2005–06 CHI	2	0	1	1	9
NHL Totals	34	1	2	3	130

Brown, Sean b. Oshawa, Ontario, November 5, 1976

2005–06 NJ/VAN	47	1	11	12	35
NHL Totals	436	14	43	57	907

* traded March 9, 2006, by New Jersey to Vancouver for a 4th-round draft choice in 2006

Brule, Gilbert b. Edmonton, Alberta, January 1, 1987

2005–06 CBJ	7	2	2	4	0
NHL Totals	7	2	2	4	0

Brunette, Andrew b. Sudbury, Ontario, August 24, 1973

2005–06 COL	82	24	39	63	48
NHL Totals	624	145	262	407	214

Brylin, Sergei b. Moscow, Soviet Union (Russia), January 13, 1974

2005–06 NJ	82	15	22	37	46	
NHL Totals	601	107	145	252	218	

Bryzgalov, Ilya b. Togliatti, Soviet Union (Russia), June 22, 1980

2005–06 ANA	31	13-12-1	1,575	66	1	2.51
NHL Totals	33	14-12-0	1,667	69	1	2.48

Budaj, Peter b. Banska Bystrica, Czechoslovakia (Slovakia), September 18, 1982

2005–06 COL	34	14-10-6	1,802	86	2	2.86
NHL Totals	34	14-10-6	1,802	86	2	2.86

Bulis, Jan b. Pardubice, Czechoslovakia (Czech Republic), March 18, 1978

2005–06 MON	73	20	20	40	50	
NHL Totals	473	84	138	222	198	

Burke, Sean b. Windsor, Ontario, January 29, 1967

2005–06 TB	35	14-10-4	1,713	80	2	2.80
NHL Totals	797	318-331-201	45,130	2,222	37	2.95

Burns, Brent b. Ajax, Ontario, March 9, 1985

2005–06 MIN	72	4	12	16	32	
NHL Totals	108	5	17	22	44	

Burrows, Alexandre b. Pointe Claire, Quebec, April 11, 1981

2005–06 VAN	43	7	5	12	61	
NHL Totals	43	7	5	12	61	

Butenschon, Sven b. Itzehoe, West Germany (Germany), March 22, 1976

2005–06 VAN	8	0	0	0	10	
NHL Totals	140	2	12	14	86	

Byfuglien, Dustin b. Minneapolis, Minnesota, March 27, 1985

2005–06 CHI	25	3	2	5	24
NHL Totals	25	3	2	5	24

Cairns, Eric b. Oakville, Ontario, June 27, 1974

2005–06 FLO/PIT	50	1	1	2	124
NHL Totals	456	10	32	42	1,177

* traded January 18, 2006, from Florida to Pittsburgh for a 6th-round draft
  choice in 2006

Cajanek, Petr b. Gottwaldov (Zlin), Czechoslovakia (Czech
Republic), August 18, 1975

2005–06 STL	71	10	31	41	54
NHL Totals	192	31	74	105	90

Calder, Kyle b. Mannville, Alberta, January 5, 1979

2005–06 CHI	79	26	33	59	52
NHL Totals	359	85	125	210	184

Caldwell, Ryan b. Deloraine, Manitoba, June 15, 1981

2005–06 NYI	2	0	0	0	2
NHL Totals	2	0	0	0	2

Cammalleri, Mike b. Richmond Hill, Ontario, June 8, 1982

2005–06 LA	80	26	29	55	50
NHL Totals	139	40	38	78	92

Campbell, Brian b. Strathroy, Ontario, May 23, 1979

2005–06 BUF	79	12	32	44	16
NHL Totals	246	21	64	85	66

Campbell, Gregory b. London, Ontario, December 17, 1983

2005–06 FLO	64	3	6	9	40
NHL Totals	66	3	6	9	45

Campbell, Jim b. Worcester, Massachusetts, February 3, 1973

2005–06 TB	1	0	0	0	2
NHL Totals	285	61	75	136	268

Campoli, Chris b. North York (Toronto), Ontario, July 9, 1984

2005–06 NYI	80	9	25	34	46
NHL Totals	80	9	25	34	46

Carkner, Matt b. Winchester, Ontario, November 3, 1980

2005–06	1	0	1	1	2
NHL Totals	1	0	1	1	2

Carle, Matt b. Anchorage, Alaska, September 25, 1984

2005–06 SJ	12	3	3	6	14
NHL Totals	12	3	3	6	14

Carney, Keith b. Providence, Rhode Island, February 3, 1970

2005–06 ANA/VAN	79	2	18	20	62
NHL Totals	877	40	160	200	804

* traded March 9, 2006, from Anaheim to Vancouver with Juha Alen for
  Brett Skinner and a 2nd-round draft choice in 2006

Caron, Sebastian b. Amqui, Quebec, June 25, 1980

2005–06 PIT	26	8-9-5	1,312	87	1	3.98
NHL Totals	90	24-47-7	4,933	287	4	3.49

Carter, Anson b. Toronto, Ontario, June 6, 1974

2005–06 VAN	81	33	22	55	41
NHL Totals	610	191	202	393	211

Carter, Jeff b. London, Ontario, January 1, 1985

2005–06 PHI	81	23	19	42	40
NHL Totals	81	23	19	42	40

Cassels, Andrew b. Bramalea, Ontario, July 23, 1969

2005–06 WAS	31	4	8	12	14
NHL Totals	1,015	204	528	732	410

Cassivi, Frederic b. Sorel, Quebec, June 12, 1975

2005–06 WAS	1	0-1-0	58	4	0	4.07
NHL Totals	8	3-5-0	488	32	0	3.93

Chara, Zdeno b. Trencin, Czechoslovakia (Slovakia), March 18, 1977

2005–06 OTT	71	16	27	43	135
NHL Totals	530	57	118	175	901

Cheechoo, Jonathan b. Moose Factory, Ontario, July 15, 1980

2005–06 SJ	82	56	38	93	58
NHL Totals	229	93	63	156	130

Chelios, Chris b. Chicago, Illinois, January 25, 1962

2005–06 DET	81	4	7	11	108
NHL Totals	1,476	182	743	925	2,803

Chimera, Jason b. Edmonton, Alberta, May 2, 1979

2005–06 CBJ	80	17	13	30	95
NHL Totals	210	36	30	66	188

* traded October 8, 2005, by Phoenix to Columbus with Michael Rupp and
  Cale Hulse for Geoff Sanderson and Tim Jackman

Chouinard, Eric b. Atlanta, Georgia, July 8, 1980

2005–06 PHI	1	0	0	0	2
NHL Totals	90	11	11	22	16

Chouinard, Marc b. Charlesbourg, Quebec, May 6, 1977

2005–06 MIN	74	14	16	30	34
NHL Totals	278	35	39	74	113

Christensen, Erik b. Edmonton, Alberta, December 17, 1983

2005–06 PIT	33	6	7	13	34
NHL Totals	33	6	7	13	34

Cibak, Martin b. Liptovsky Mikulas, Czechoslovakia (Slovakia), May 17, 1980

2005–06 TB	65	2	6	8	22
NHL Totals	154	5	18	23	60

Clark, Brett b. Wapella, Saskatchewan, December 23, 1976

2005–06 COL	80	9	27	36	56
NHL Totals	238	14	33	47	116

Clark, Chris b. South Windsor, Connecticut, March 8, 1976

2005–06 WAS	78	20	19	39	110
NHL Totals	356	55	55	110	473

Clarke, Noah b. La Verne, California, June 11, 1979

2005–06 LA	5	0	0	0	0
NHL Totals	7	0	1	1	0

Cleary, Daniel b. Carbonear, Newfoundland, December 18, 1978

2005–06 DET	77	3	12	15	40
NHL Totals	406	44	83	127	233

Clemmensen, Scott b. Des Moines, Iowa, July 23, 1977

2005–06 NJ	13	3-4-2	626	35	0	3.35
NHL Totals	19	6-5-0	884	40	2	2.71

Cloutier, Dan b. Mont Laurier, Quebec, April 22, 1976

2005–06 VAN	13	8-3-1	680	36	0	3.17
NHL Totals	318	131-124-33	17,158	761	15	2.66

Clowe, Ryane b. St. John's, Newfoundland, September 30, 1982

2005–06 SJ	18	0	2	2	9
NHL Totals	18	0	2	2	9

Clymer, Ben b. Bloomington, Minnesota, April 11, 1978

2005–06 WAS	77	16	17	33	72
NHL Totals	372	45	64	109	323

Coburn, Braydon b. Calgary, Alberta, February 27, 1985

2005–06 ATL	9	0	1	1	4
NHL Totals	9	0	1	1	4

Colaiacovo, Carlo b. Toronto, Ontario, January 27, 1983

2005–06 TOR	21	2	5	7	17
NHL Totals	25	2	7	9	19

* missed majority of season suffering from post-concussion syndrome

Cole, Erik b. Oswego, New York, November 6, 1978

2005–06 CAR	60	30	29	59	54
NHL Totals	274	78	90	168	254

Coleman, Gerald b. Romeoville, Illinois, April 3, 1985

2005–06 TB	2	0-0-1	43	2	0	2.79
NHL Totals	2	0-0-1	43	2	0	2.79

Colley, Kevin b. New Haven, Connecticut, January 4, 1979

2005–06 NYI	16	0	0	0	52
NHL Totals	16	0	0	0	52

Collins, Rob b. Kitchener, Ontario, March 15, 1974

2005–06 NYI	8	1	1	2	0
NHL Totals	8	1	1	2	0

Colliton, Jeremy b. Blackie, Alberta, January 13, 1985

2005–06 NYI	19	1	1	2	6
NHL Totals	19	1	1	2	6

Commodore, Mike b. Fort Saskatchewan, Alberta, November 7, 1979

2005–06 CAR	72	3	10	13	138
NHL Totals	147	4	16	20	226

Comrie, Mike b. Edmonton, Alberta, September 11, 1980

2005–06 PHO	80	30	30	60	55
NHL Totals	321	103	114	217	232

Conklin, Ty b. Anchorage, Alaska, March 30, 1976

2005–06 EDM	18	8-5-1	922	43	1	2.80
NHL Totals	60	27-19-4	3,155	131	2	2.49

Connolly, Tim b. Syracuse, New York, May 7, 1981

2005–06 BUF	63	16	39	55	28
NHL Totals	388	62	138	200	180

Conroy, Craig b. Potsdam, New York, September 4, 1971

2005–06 LA	78	22	44	66	78
NHL Totals	687	140	266	406	415

Cooke, Matt b. Belleville, Ontario, September 7, 1978

2005–06 VAN	45	8	10	18	71
NHL Totals	424	66	91	157	497

Corvo, Joe b. Oak Park, Illinois, June 20, 1977

2005–06 LA	81	14	26	40	38
NHL Totals	203	27	50	77	88

Cote, Jean-Philippe b. Quebec City, Quebec, April 22, 1982

2005–06 MON	8	0	0	0	4
NHL Totals	8	0	0	0	4

Cowan, Jeff b. Scarborough (Toronto), Ontario, September 27, 1976

2005–06 LA	46	8	1	9	73
NHL Totals	304	40	28	68	460

Craig, Ryan b. Abbotsford, British Columbia, January 6, 1982

2005–06 TB	48	15	13	28	6
NHL Totals	48	15	13	28	6

Crawford, Corey b. Montreal, Quebec, December 31, 1984

2005–06 CHI	2	0-0-1	86	5	0	3.49
NHL Totals	2	0-0-1	86	5	0	3.49

Crosby, Sidney b. Cole Harbour, Nova Scotia, August 7, 1987

2005–06 PIT	81	39	63	102	110
NHL Totals	81	39	63	102	110

Cross, Cory b. Lloydminster, Alberta, January 3, 1971

2005–06 EDM/PIT/DET	56	3	5	8	59
NHL Totals	659	34	97	131	684

* traded January 26, 2006, by Edmonton to Pittsburgh with Jani Rita for Dick Tarnstrom
* traded March 9, 2006, from Pittsburgh to Detroit for a 4th-round draft choice in 2007

Cullen, Mark b. Moorhead, Minnesota, October 28, 1978

2005–06 CHI	29	7	9	16	2
NHL Totals	29	7	9	16	2

Cullen, Matt b. Virginia, Minnesota, November 2, 1976

2005–06 CAR	78	25	24	49	40
NHL Totals	591	102	178	280	254

Cullimore, Jassen b. Simcoe, Ontario, December 4, 1972

2005–06 CHI	54	1	6	7	53
NHL Totals	578	20	53	73	557

Czerkawski, Mariusz b. Radomsko, Poland, April 13, 1972

2005–06 TOR/BOS*	35	8	2	10	10
NHL Totals	745	215	220	435	274

* claimed off waivers from Toronto on March 8, 2006

Dagenais, Pierre b. Blainville, Quebec, March 4, 1978

2005–06 MON	32	5	7	12	16
NHL Totals	142	35	23	58	58

Daigle, Alexandre b. Montreal, Quebec, February 7, 1975

2005–06 MIN	46	5	23	28	12
NHL Totals	616	129	198	327	186

Daley, Trevor b. Toronto, Ontario, October 9, 1983

2005–06 DAL	81	3	11	14	87
NHL Totals	108	4	16	20	101

Dallman, Kevin b. Niagara Falls, Ontario, February 26, 1981

2005–06 BOS/STL	67	4	10	14	29
NHL Totals	67	4	10	14	29

* claimed off waivers from Boston on December 3, 2005

Dandenault, Mathieu b. Sherbrooke, Quebec, February 3, 1976

2005–06 MON	82	5	15	20	83
NHL Totals	698	53	116	169	425

Danis, Yann b. Lafontaine, Quebec, June 21, 1981

| 2005–06 MON | 6 | 3-2-0 | 312 | 14 | 1 | 2.69 |
| NHL Totals | 6 | 3-2-0 | 312 | 14 | 1 | 2.69 |

* recorded shutout in his first NHL game

Datsyuk, Pavel b. Sverdlovsk, Soviet Union (Russia), July 20, 1978

| 2005–06 DET | 75 | 28 | 59 | 87 | 22 |
| NHL Totals | 284 | 81 | 160 | 241 | 77 |

Davison, Rob b. St. Catharines, Ontario, May 1, 1980

| 2005–06 SJ | 69 | 1 | 5 | 6 | 76 |
| NHL Totals | 139 | 2 | 10 | 12 | 190 |

Daze, Eric b. Montreal, Quebec, July 2, 1975

| 2005–06 CHI | 1 | 0 | 0 | 0 | 2 |
| NHL Totals | 601 | 226 | 172 | 398 | 176 |

* missed most of season with back injury

Delmore, Andy b. LaSalle, Ontario, December 26, 1976

| 2005–06 CBJ | 7 | 0 | 0 | 0 | 2 |
| NHL Totals | 283 | 43 | 58 | 101 | 105 |

Demitra, Pavol b. Dubnica, Czechoslovakia (Slovakia), November 29, 1974

| 2005–06 LA | 58 | 25 | 37 | 62 | 42 |
| NHL Totals | 611 | 241 | 340 | 581 | 212 |

Dempsey, Nathan b. Spruce Grove, Alberta, July 14, 1974

| 2005–06 LA | 53 | 2 | 11 | 13 | 48 |
| NHL Totals | 243 | 21 | 66 | 87 | 114 |

Denis, Marc b. Montreal, Quebec, August 1, 1977

| 2005–06 CBJ | 49 | 21-25-1 | 2,786 | 151 | 1 | 3.25 |
| NHL Totals | 294 | 94-156-28 | 16,738 | 828 | 15 | 2.97 |

Desjardins, Eric b. Rouyn, Quebec, June 14, 1969

2005–06 PHI	45	4	20	24	56
NHL Totals	1,143	136	439	575	757

Devereaux, Boyd b. Seaforth, Ontario, April 16, 1978

2005–06 PHO	78	8	14	22	44
NHL Totals	509	46	85	131	167

de Vries, Greg b. Sundridge, Ontario, January 4, 1973

2005–06 ATL	82	7	28	35	76
NHL Totals	648	40	110	150	578

DiMaio, Rob b. Calgary, Alberta, February 19, 1968

2005–06 TB	61	4	13	17	30
NHL Totals	894	106	171	277	840

Dimitrakos, Niko b. Boston, Massachusetts, May 21, 1979

2005–06 SJ/PHI	64	9	16	25	32
NHL Totals	153	24	38	62	89

* traded March 9, 2006, from San Jose to Philadelphia for a 3rd-round draft choice in 2006

Dingman, Chris b. Edmonton, Alberta, July 6, 1976

2005–06 TB	34	0	1	1	22
NHL Totals	385	15	19	34	769

DiPenta, Joe b. Barrie, Ontario, February 25, 1979

2005–06 ANA	72	2	6	8	46
NHL Totals	75	3	7	10	46

DiPietro, Rick b. Winthrop, Massachusetts, September 19, 1981

2005–06 NYI	63	30-24-5	3,571	180	1	3.02
NHL Totals	143	58-62-8	8,083	384	6	2.85

Disalvatore, Jon b. Bangor, Maine, March 30, 1981

2005–06 STL	5	0	0	0	2
NHL Totals	5	0	0	0	2

Divis, Reinhard b. Vienna, Austria, July 4, 1975

2005–06 STL	12	0-5-1	475	37	0	4.67
NHL Totals	28	6-9-2	1,212	67	0	3.32

Doan, Shane b. Halkirk, Alberta, October 10, 1976

2005–06 PHO	82	30	36	66	123
NHL Totals	730	172	245	417	711

Domi, Tie b. Windsor, Ontario, November 1, 1969

2005–06 TOR	77	5	11	16	109
NHL Totals	1,020	104	141	245	3,515

Donovan, Shean b. Timmins, Ontario, January 22, 1975

2005–06 CAL	80	9	11	20	82
NHL Totals	698	94	103	197	502

Doull, Doug b. Glace Bay, Nova Scotia, May 31, 1974

2005–06 WAS	2	0	0	0	19
NHL Totals	37	0	1	1	151

Dowd, Jim b. Brick, New Jersey, December 25, 1968

2005–06 CHI/COL	78	5	13	18	40
NHL Totals	589	62	159	221	329

* traded March 9, 2006, by Chicago to Colorado for a 4th-round draft choice in 2006

Downey, Aaron b. Shelburne, Ontario, August 27, 1974

2005–06 MON	42	3	4	7	95
NHL Totals	162	6	6	12	323

Drake, Dallas b. Trail, British Columbia, February 4, 1969

2005–06 STL	62	2	24	26	59
NHL Totals	884	168	291	459	806

Draper, Kris b. Toronto, Ontario, May 24, 1971

2005–06 DET	80	10	22	32	58
NHL Totals	804	118	150	268	584

Drury, Chris b. Trumbull, Connecticut, August 20, 1976

2005–06 BUF	81	30	37	67	32
NHL Totals	551	156239	395	322	

Dubielewicz, Wade b. Invermere, British Columbia, January 30, 1978

2005–06 NYI	7	2-3-0	310	15	0	2.90
NHL Totals	9	3-3-1	415	18	0	2.60

Dumont, J-P b. Montreal, Quebec, April 1, 1978

2005–06 BUF	54	20	20	40	38
NHL Totals	434	121	135	256	246

Dunham, Mike b. Johnson City, New York, June 1, 1972

2005–06 ATL	17	8-5-2	779	36	1	2.77
NHL Totals	375	137-168-39	20,674	929	19	2.69

Dupuis, Pascal b. Laval, Quebec, April 7, 1979

2005–06 MIN	67	10	16	26	40
NHL Totals	286	57	71	128	124

Dvorak, Radek b. Tabor, Czechoslovakia (Czech Republic), March 9, 1977

2005–06 EDM	64	8	20	28	26
NHL Totals	746	161	251	412	244

Eager, Ben b. Ottawa, Ontario, January 22, 1984

2005–06 PHI	25	3	5	8	18
NHL Totals	25	3	5	8	18

Eaton, Mark b. Wilmington, Delaware, May 6, 1977

2005–06 NAS	69	3	1	4	44
NHL Totals	313	16	31	47	138

Eaves, Patrick b. Calgary, Alberta, May 1, 1984

2005–06 OTT	58	20	9	29	22
NHL Totals	58	20	9	29	22

Ehrhoff, Christian b. Moers, West Germany (Germany), July 6, 1982

2005–06 SJ	64	5	18	23	32
NHL Totals	105	6	29	35	46

Eklund, Brian b. Braintree, Massachusetts, May 24, 1980

2005–06 TB	1	0-1-0	58	3	0	3.10
NHL Totals	1	0-1-0	58	3	0	3.10

Ekman, Nils b. Stockholm, Sweden, March 11, 1976

2005–06 SJ	77	21	36	57	54
NHL Totals	230	54	82	136	164

Elias, Patrik b. Trebic, Czechoslovakia (Czech Republic), April 13, 1976

2005–06 NJ	38	16	29	45	20
NHL Totals	596	223	281	504	295

Ellison, Matt b. Duncan, British Columbia, December 8, 1983

2005–06 CHI/PHI	31	3	10	13	19
NHL Totals	41	3	11	14	19

* traded December 5, 2005, by Chicago to Philadelphia with a 3rd-round draft choice in 2006 for Patrick Sharp and Eric Meloche

Emery, Ray b. Cayuga, Ontario, September 28, 1982

2005–06 OTT	39	23-11-4	2,167	102	3	2.82
NHL Totals	45	26-11-0	2,378	109	3	2.75

Eminger, Steve b. Woodbridge, Ontario, October 31, 1983

2005–06 WAS	66	5	13	18	81
NHL Totals	124	5	19	23	150

Endicott, Shane b. Saskatoon, Saskatchewan, December 21, 1981

2005–06 PIT	41	1	1	2	43
NHL Totals	45	1	2	3	47

Erat, Martin b. Trebic, Czechoslovakia (Czech Republic), August 28, 1981

2005–06 NAS	80	20	29	49	76
NHL Totals	263	46	93	139	160

Erskine, John b. Kingston, Ontario, June 26, 1980

2005–06 DAL/NYI	60	1	0	1	161
NHL Totals	141	3	2	5	336

* traded January 10, 2006, by Dallas to the New York Islanders with a 2nd-round draft choice in 2006 for Janne Niinimaa and a 5th-round draft choice in 2007

Esche, Robert b. Whitesboro, New York, January 22, 1978

2005–06 PHI	40	22-11-5	2,286	113	1	2.97
NHL Totals	168	73-55-16	9,279	402	9	2.60

Exelby, Garnet b. Craik, Saskatchewan, August 16, 1981

2005–06 ATL	75	1	9	10	175
NHL Totals	161	2	20	22	250

Fahey, Jim b. Boston, Massachusetts, May 11, 1979

2005–06 SJ	21	0	2	2	14
NHL Totals	79	1	23	24	65

Fata, Rico b. Sault Ste. Marie, Ontario, February 12, 1980

2005–06 WAS	47	3	4	7	22
NHL Totals	220	26	35	61	102

Fedorov, Fedor b. Moscow, Soviet Union (Russia), June 11, 1981

2005–06 NYR	3	0	0	0	6
NHL Totals	18	0	2	2	14

* traded October 7, 2005, by Vancouver to the New York Rangers for Jozef
  Balej and a conditional draft choice

Fedorov, Sergei b. Pskov, Soviet Union (Russia), December 13, 1969

2005–06 ANA/CBJ	67	12	32	44	66
NHL Totals	1,055	443	620	1,063	695

* traded November 15, 2005, by Anaheim to Columbus with a 5th-round
  draft choice in 2006 for Tyler Wright and Francois Beauchemin

Fedoruk, Todd b. Redwater, Alberta, February 13, 1979

2005–06 ANA	76	4	19	23	174
NHL Totals	296	14	37	51	665

Fedotenko, Ruslan b. Kiev, Soviet Union (Ukraine), January 18, 1979

2005–06 TB	80	26	15	41	44
NHL Totals	385	95	79	174	233

Fehr, Eric b. Winkler, Manitoba, September 7, 1985

2005–06 WAS	11	0	0	0	2
NHL Totals	11	0	0	0	2

Ference, Andrew b. Edmonton, Alberta, March 17, 1979

2005–06 CAL	82	4	27	31	85
NHL Totals	333	19	68	87	301

Ferguson, Scott b. Camrose, Alberta, January 6, 1973

2005–06 MIN	15	0	0	0	22
NHL Totals	218	7	14	21	310

Ferland, Jonathan b. Quebec City, Quebec, February 9, 1983

2005–06 MON	7	1	0	1	2
NHL Totals	7	1	0	1	2

Fernandez, Manny b. Etobicoke (Toronto), Ontario, August 26, 1974

2005–06 MIN	58	30-18-7	3,411	130	1	2.29
NHL Totals	249	103-97-24	14,270	585	11	2.46

Fiddler, Vernon b. Edmonton, Alberta, May 9, 1980

2005–06 NAS	40	8	4	12	42
NHL Totals	76	12	6	18	79

Filppula, Valtteri b. Vantaa, Finland, March 20, 1984

2005–06 DET	4	0	1	1	2
NHL Totals	4	0	1	1	2

Finley, Brian b. Sault Ste. Marie, Ontario, July 3, 1981

2005–06 NAS	1	0-1-0	60	7	0	7.00
NHL Totals	2	0-1-0	106	10	0	5.62

Fischer, Jiri b. Horovice, Czechoslovakia (Czech Republic), July 31, 1980

2005–06 DET	22	3	5	8	33
NHL Totals	305	11	49	60	295

Fisher, Mike b. Peterborough, Ontario, June 5, 1980

2005–06 OTT	68	22	22	44	64
NHL Totals	316	70	74	144	273

Fitzgerald, Tom b. Billerica, Massachusetts, August 28, 1968

2005–06 BOS	71	4	6	10	40
NHL Totals	1,097	139	190	329	776

Fitzpatrick, Rory b. Rochester, New York, January 11, 1975

2005–06 BUF	56	4	5	9	50
NHL Totals	210	9	18	27	144

Fleischmann, Tomas b. Koprivnice, Czechoslovakia (Czech Republic), May 16, 1984

2005–06 WAS	14	0	2	2	0
NHL Totals	14	0	2	2	0

Fleury, Marc-Andre b. Sorel, Quebec, November 28, 1984

2005–06 PIT	50	13-27-6	2,809	152	1	3.25
NHL Totals	71	17-41-2	3,963	222	2	3.36

Flinn, Ryan b. Halifax, Nova Scotia, April 20, 1980

2005–06 LA	2	0	0	0	5
NHL Totals	31	1	0	1	84

Foote, Adam b. Toronto, Ontario, July 10, 1971

2005–06 CBJ	65	6	16	22	89
NHL Totals	864	61	195	256	1,229

Forbes, Colin b. New Westminster, British Columbia, February 16, 1976

2005–06 WAS	9	0	0	0	2
NHL Totals	311	33	28	61	213

* traded December 28, 2005, by Carolina to Washington for Stephen Peat

Forsberg, Peter b. Ornskoldsvik, Sweden, July 20, 1973

2005–06 PHI	60	19	56	75	46
NHL Totals	640	235	581	816	590

Foster, Kurtis b. Carp, Ontario, November 24, 1981

2005–06 MIN	58	10	18	28	60
NHL Totals	63	10	19	29	60

Foy, Matt b. Oakville, Ontario, May 18, 1983

2005–06 MIN	19	2	3	5	16
NHL Totals	19	2	3	5	16

Franzen, Johan b. Landsbro, Sweden, December 23, 1979

2005–06 DET	80	12	4	16	36
NHL Totals	80	12	4	16	36

Friesen, Jeff b. Meadow Lake, Saskatchewan, August 5, 1976

2005–06 WAS/ANA	51	4	7	11	32
NHL Totals	821	212	292	504	454

* traded March 9, 2006, by Washington to Anaheim for a 2nd-round draft choice in 2006

Fritsche, Dan b. Parma, Ohio, July 13, 1985

2005–06 CBJ	59	6	7	13	22
NHL Totals	78	7	7	14	34

Frolov, Alexander b. Moscow, Soviet Union (Russia), June 19, 1982

2005–06 LA	69	21	33	54	40
NHL Totals	225	59	74	133	98

Gaborik, Marian b. Trencin, Czechoslovakia (Slovakia), February 14, 1982

2005–06 MIN	65	38	28	66	64
NHL Totals	360	134	140	274	196

Gagne, Simon b. Ste. Foy, Quebec, February 29, 1980

2005–06 PHI	72	47	32	79	38
NHL Totals	426	160	164	324	155

Gainey, Steve b. Montreal, Quebec, January 26, 1979

| 2005–06 PHO | 20 | 0 | 1 | 1 | 20 |
| NHL Totals | 33 | 0 | 2 | 2 | 34 |

Gamache, Simon b. Thetford Mines, Quebec, January 3, 1981

| 2005–06 STL | 26 | 3 | 4 | 7 | 10 |
| NHL Totals | 37 | 4 | 5 | 9 | 12 |

Garnett, Michael b. Saskatoon, Saskatchewan, November 25, 1982

| 2005–06 ATL | 24 | 10-7-4 | 1,271 | 73 | 2 | 3.45 |
| NHL Totals | 24 | 10-7-4 | 1,271 | 73 | 2 | 3.45 |

Garon, Mathieu b. Chandler, Quebec, January 9, 1978

| 2005–06 LA | 63 | 31-26-3 | 3,446 | 185 | 4 | 3.22 |
| NHL Totals | 106 | 47-46-3 | 5,781 | 282 | 8 | 2.93 |

Gaustad, Paul b. Fargo, North Dakota, February 3, 1982

| 2005–06 BUF | 78 | 9 | 15 | 24 | 65 |
| NHL Totals | 79 | 9 | 15 | 24 | 65 |

Gauthier, Denis b. Montreal, Quebec, October 1, 1976

| 2005–06 PHO/PHI | 62 | 2 | 9 | 11 | 98 |
| NHL Totals | 446 | 15 | 54 | 69 | 613 |

* traded March 9, 2006, by Phoenix to Philadelphia for Josh Gratton and two 2nd-round draft choices in 2006

Gavey, Aaron b. Sudbury, Ontario, February 22, 1974

| 2005–06 ANA | 5 | 0 | 0 | 0 | 2 |
| NHL Totals | 360 | 41 | 50 | 91 | 272 |

Gelinas, Martin b. Shawinigan, Quebec, June 5, 1970

| 2005–06 FLO | 82 | 17 | 24 | 41 | 80 |
| NHL Totals | 1,134 | 286 | 310 | 596 | 764 |

Gerber, Martin b. Burgdorf, Switzerland, September 3, 1974

2005–06 CAR	60	38-14-6	3,492	162	3	2.78
NHL Totals	114	55-37-7	6,394	265	6	2.49

Germyn, Carsen b. Campbell River, British Columbia, February 22, 1985

2005–06 CAL	2	0	0	0	0
NHL Totals	2	0	0	0	0

Gervais, Bruno b. Longueuil, Quebec, October 3, 1984

2005–06 NYI	27	3	4	7	8
NHL Totals	27	3	4	7	8

Getzlaf, Ryan b. Regina, Saskatchewan, May 10, 1985

2005–06 ANA	57	14	25	39	22
NHL Totals	57	14	25	39	22

Giguere, Jean-Sebastien b. Montreal, Quebec, May 16, 1977

2005–06 ANA	60	30-15-11	3,381	150	2	2.66
NHL Totals	297	120-124-25	17,109	718	21	2.52

Gill, Hal b. Concord, Massachusetts, April 6, 1975

2005–06 BOS	80	1	9	10	124
NHL Totals	626	20	77	97	588

Gillies, Trevor b. Cambridge, Ontario, January 30, 1979

2005–06 ANA	1	0	0	0	21
NHL Totals	1	0	0	0	21

Gionta, Brian b. Rochester, New York, January 18, 1979

2005–06 NJ	82	48	41	89	46
NHL Totals	248	85	69	154	113

Giordano, Mark b. Toronto, Ontario, October 3, 1983

2005–06 CAL	7	0	1	1	8
NHL Totals	7	0	1	1	8

Giroux, Alexandre b. Quebec City, Quebec, June 16, 1981

2005–06 NYR	1	0	0	0	0
NHL Totals	1	0	0	0	0

Giuliano, Jeff b. Nashua, New Hampshire, June 20, 1979

2005–06 LA	48	3	4	7	26
NHL Totals	48	3	4	7	26

Gleason, Tim b. Southfield, Michigan, January 29, 1983

2005–06 LA	78	2	19	21	77
NHL Totals	125	2	26	28	98

Globke, Rob b. Farmington, Michigan, October 24, 1982

2005–06 FLO	18	1	0	1	6
NHL Totals	18	1	0	1	6

Glumac, Mike b. Niagara Falls, Ontario, April 5, 1980

2005–06 STL	33	7	5	12	33
NHL Totals	33	7	5	12	33

Goc, Marcel b. Calw, West Germany (Germany), August 24, 1983

2005–06 SJ	81	8	14	22	22
NHL Totals	81	8	14	22	22

Godard, Eric b. Vernon, British Columbia, March 7, 1980

2005–06 NYI	57	2	2	4	115
NHL Totals	107	2	3	5	260

Goertzen, Steve b. Stony Plain, Alberta, May 26, 1984

2005–06 CBJ	39	0	0	0	44
NHL Totals	39	0	0	0	44

Gomez, Scott b. Anchorage, Alaska, December 23, 1979

2005–06 NJ	82	33	51	84	42
NHL Totals	476	103	287	390	320

Gonchar, Sergei b. Chelyabinsk, Soviet Union (Russia), April 13, 1974

2005–06 PIT	75	12	46	58	100
NHL Totals	744	160	323	483	629

Gordon, Boyd b. Unity, Saskatchewan, October 19, 1983

2005–06 WAS	25	0	1	1	4
NHL Totals	66	1	6	7	12

Goren, Lee b. Winnipeg, Manitoba, December 26, 1977

2005–06 VAN	28	1	2	3	30
NHL Totals	65	5	4	9	44

Gorges, Josh b. Kelowna, British Columbia, August 14, 1984

2005–06 SJ	49	0	6	6	31
NHL Totals	49	0	6	6	31

Gove, David b. Centerville, Massachusetts, May 4, 1978

2005–06 CAR	1	0	1	1	0
NHL Totals	1	0	1	1	0

Grahame, John b. Denver, Colorado, August 31, 1975

2005–06 TB	57	29-22-1	3,152	161	5	3.06
NHL Totals	179	82-66-14	10,000	449	12	2.69

Gratton, Chris b. Brantford, Ontario, July 5, 1975

| 2005–06 FLO | 76 | 17 | 22 | 39 | 104 |
| NHL Totals | 927 | 191 | 318 | 509 | 1,455 |

Gratton, Josh b. Brantford (Toronto), Ontario, September 9, 1982

| 2005–06 PHI/PHO | 14 | 1 | 0 | 1 | 44 |
| NHL Totals | 14 | 1 | 0 | 1 | 44 |

* traded March 9, 2006, by Philadelphia to Phoenix with two 2nd-round draft choices in 2006 for Denis Gauthier

Grebeshkov, Denis b. Yaroslavl, Soviet Union (Russia), October 11, 1983

| 2005–06 LA/NYI | 29 | 0 | 5 | 5 | 20 |
| NHL Totals | 33 | 0 | 6 | 6 | 20 |

* traded March 8, 2006, by Los Angeles to the Islanders with Jeff Tambellini and a conditional 3rd-round draft choice for Mark Parrish and Brent Sopel

Green, Josh b. Camrose, Alberta, November 16, 1977

| 2005–06 VAN | 33 | 4 | 2 | 6 | 14 |
| NHL Totals | 265 | 33 | 34 | 67 | 168 |

Green, Mike b. Calgary, Alberta, October 12, 1985

| 2005–06 WAS | 22 | 1 | 2 | 3 | 18 |
| NHL Totals | 22 | 1 | 2 | 3 | 18 |

Green, Travis b. Castlegar, British Columbia, December 20, 1970

| 2005–06 BOS | 82 | 10 | 12 | 22 | 79 |
| NHL Totals | 939 | 192 | 261 | 453 | 737 |

Greene, Matt b. Grand Ledge, Michigan, May 13, 1983

| 2005–06 EDM | 27 | 0 | 2 | 2 | 43 |
| NHL Totals | 27 | 0 | 2 | 2 | 43 |

Grier, Mike b. Detroit, Michigan, January 5, 1975

2005–06 BUF	81	7	16	23	28
NHL Totals	693	112	155	267	392

Guerin, Bill b. Worcester, Massachusetts, November 9, 1970

2005–06 DAL	70	13	27	40	115
NHL Totals	949	328	335	663	1,373

Guite, Ben b. Montreal, Quebec, July 17, 1978

2005–06 BOS	1	0	0	0	0
NHL Totals	1	0	0	0	0

Hagman, Niklas b. Espoo, Finland, December 5, 1979

2005–06 FLO/DAL	84	8	13	21	18
NHL Totals	317	36	59	95	68

* traded December 12, 2005, by Florida to Dallas for a 7th-round draft choice in 2007

Hainsey, Ron b. Bolton, Connecticut, March 24, 1981

2005–06 CBJ	55	2	15	17	43
NHL Totals	87	3	16	19	49

Hale, David b. Colorado Springs, Colorado, June 18, 1981

2005–06 NJ	38	0	4	4	21
NHL Totals	103	0	8	8	93

Hall, Adam b. Kalamazoo, Michigan, August 14, 1980

2005–06 NAS	75	14	15	29	40
NHL Totals	234	43	42	85	108

Halpern, Jeff b. Potomac, Maryland, May 3, 1976

2005–06 WAS	70	11	33	44	79
NHL Totals	438	87	127	214	351

Hamel, Denis b. Lachute, Quebec, May 10, 1977

2005–06 OTT	4	1	0	1	0
NHL Totals	139	14	9	23	67

Hamhuis, Dan b. Smithers, British Columbia, December 13, 1982

2005–06 NAS	82	7	31	38	70
NHL Totals	162	14	50	64	127

Hamilton, Jeff b. Englewood, Ohio, September 4, 1977

2005–06 NYI	13	2	6	8	8
NHL Totals	14	2	6	8	8

Hamrlik, Roman b. Gottwaldov (Zlin), Czechoslovakia (Czech Republic), April 12, 1974

2005–06 CAL	51	7	19	26	56
NHL Totals	924	124	343	467	1,041

Handzus, Michal b. Banska Bystrica, Czechoslovakia (Slovakia), March 11, 1977

2005–06 PHI	73	11	33	44	38
NHL Totals	509	112	180	292	307

Hannan, Scott b. Richmond, British Columbia, January 23, 1979

2005–06 SJ	81	6	18	24	58
NHL Totals	429	21	82	103	291

Harding, Josh b. Regina, Saskatchewan, June 18, 1984

2005–06 MIN	3	2-1-0	185	8	1	2.59
NHL Totals	3	2-1-0	185	8	1	2.59

Harrison, Jay b. Oshawa, Ontario, November 3, 1982

2005–06 TOR	8	0	1	1	2
NHL Totals	8	0	1	1	2

Hartigan, Mark b. Fort St. John, British Columbia, October 15, 1977

2005–06 CBJ	33	9	3	12	22
NHL Totals	67	15	8	23	36

Hartnell, Scott b. Regina, Saskatchewan, April 18, 1982

2005–06 NAS	81	25	23	48	101
NHL Totals	372	71	101	172	448

Harvey, Todd b. Hamilton, Ontario, February 17, 1975

2005–06 EDM	63	5	2	7	32
NHL Totals	671	91	132	223	950

Hasek, Dominik b. Pardubice, Czechoslovakia (Czech Republic), January 29, 1965

2005–06 OTT	43	28-10-4	2,583	90	5	2.09
NHL Totals	638	324-202-82	37,145	1,374	68	2.22

Hatcher, Derian b. Sterling Heights, Michigan, June 4, 1972

2005–06 PHI	77	4	13	17	93
NHL Totals	919	75	240	315	1,481

Hauser, Adam b. Bovey, Minnesota, May 27, 1980

2005–06 LA	1	0-0-0	50	6	0	7.06
NHL Totals	1	0-0-0	50	6	0	7.06

Havelid, Niclas b. Stockholm, Sweden, April 12, 1973

2005–06 ATL	82	4	28	32	48
NHL Totals	392	28	89	117	200

Havlat, Martin b. Mlada Boleslav, Czechoslovakia (Czech Republic), April 19, 1981

2005–06 OTT	18	9	7	16	4
NHL Totals	298	105	130	235	166

* missed most of regular season with a shoulder injury

Healey, Eric b. Hull, Massachusetts, January 20, 1975

2005–06 BOS	2	0	0	0	2
NHL Totals	2	0	0	0	2

Healey, Paul b. Edmonton, Alberta, March 20, 1975

2005–06 COL	2	0	0	0	14
NHL Totals	77	6	14	20	44

Heatley, Dany b. Freiburg, West Germany (Germany), January 21, 1981

2005–06 OTT	82	50	53	103	86
NHL Totals	272	130	154	284	218

Hecht, Jochen b. Mannheim, West Germany (Germany), June 21, 1977

2005–06 BUF	64	18	24	42	34
NHL Totals	397	91	147	238	249

Hedberg, Johan b. Leksand, Sweden, May 3, 1973

2005–06 DAL	19	12-4-1	1,078	48	0	2.67
NHL Totals	156	66-67-14	9,008	422	10	2.81

Hedican, Bret b. St. Paul, Minnesota, August 10, 1970

2005–06 CAR	74	5	22	27	58
NHL Totals	872	52	209	261	751

Hedstrom, Jonathan b. Skelleftea, Sweden, December 27, 1977

2005–06 ANA	79	13	14	27	48
NHL Totals	83	13	14	27	48

Hejduk, Milan b. Usti-nad-Labem, Czechoslovakia (Czech Republic), February 14, 1976

2005–06 COL	74	24	34	58	24
NHL Totals	544	221	253	474	178

Helbling, Timo b. Basel, Switzerland, July 21, 1981

2005–06 TB	9	0	1	1	6
NHL Totals	9	0	1	1	6

Hemingway, Colin b. Surrey, British Columbia, August 12, 1980

2005–06 STL	3	0	0	0	0
NHL Totals	3	0	0	0	0

Hemsky, Ales b. Pardubice, Czechoslovakia (Czech Republic), August 13, 1983

2005–06 EDM	81	19	58	77	64
NHL Totals	211	37	104	141	92

Henry, Alex b. Elliot Lake, Ontario, October 18, 1979

2005–06 MIN	63	0	5	5	73
NHL Totals	175	2	9	11	259

Heward, Jamie b. Regina, Saskatchewan, March 30, 1971

2005–06 WAS	71	7	21	28	54
NHL Totals	310	32	66	98	170

Higgins, Chris b. Smithtown, New York, June 2, 1983

2005–06 MON	80	23	15	38	26
NHL Totals	82	23	15	38	26

Hilbert, Andy b. Lansing, Michigan, February 6, 1981

2005–06 CHI/PIT	47	12	15	27	38
NHL Totals	85	15	18	33	56

* traded November 6, 2005, by Boston to Chicago for a 5th-round draft choice in 2006
* claimed off waivers by Pittsburgh on March 9, 2006

Hill, Sean b. Duluth, Minnesota, February 14, 1970

| 2005–06 FLO | 78 | 2 | 18 | 20 | 80 |
| NHL Totals | 760 | 59 | 205 | 264 | 866 |

Hinote, Dan b. Leesburg, Florida, January 30, 1977

| 2005–06 COL | 73 | 5 | 8 | 13 | 48 |
| NHL Totals | 353 | 27 | 38 | 65 | 254 |

Hnidy, Shane b. Neepawa, Manitoba, November 8, 1975

| 2005–06 ATL | 66 | 0 | 3 | 3 | 33 |
| NHL Totals | 264 | 4 | 21 | 25 | 386 |

Hoggan, Jeff b. Hope, British Columbia, February 1, 1978

| 2005–06 STL | 52 | 2 | 6 | 8 | 34 |
| NHL Totals | 52 | 2 | 6 | 8 | 34 |

Holik, Bobby b. Jihlava, Czechoslovakia (Czech Republic), January 1, 1971

| 2005–06 ATL | 64 | 15 | 18 | 33 | 79 |
| NHL Totals | 1,088 | 296 | 379 | 675 | 1,181 |

Hollweg, Ryan b. Downey, California, April 23, 1983

| 2005–06 NYR | 52 | 2 | 3 | 5 | 84 |
| NHL Totals | 52 | 2 | 3 | 5 | 84 |

Holmqvist, Mikael b. Stockholm, Sweden, June 8, 1979

| 2005–06 CHI | 72 | 10 | 10 | 20 | 16 |
| NHL Totals | 93 | 12 | 10 | 22 | 41 |

Holmstrom, Tomas b. Pitea, Sweden, January 23, 1973

| 2005–06 DET | 81 | 29 | 30 | 59 | 66 |
| NHL Totals | 622 | 125 | 170 | 295 | 453 |

Holt, Chris b. Vancouver, British Columbia, June 5, 1985

2005–06 NYR	1	0-0-0	10	0	0	0.00
NHL Totals	1	0-0-0	10	0	0	0.00

Horcoff, Shawn b. Trail, British Columbia, September 17, 1978

2005–06 EDM	79	22	51	73	85
NHL Totals	347	66	118	184	241

Hordichuk, Darcy b. Kamsack, Saskatchewan, August 10, 1980

2005–06 NAS	74	7	6	13	163
NHL Totals	204	11	8	19	597

Horton, Nathan b. Welland, Ontario, May 29, 1985

2005–06 FLO	71	28	19	47	89
NHL Totals	126	42	27	69	146

Hossa, Marcel b. Ilava, Czechoslovakia (Slovakia), October 12, 1981

2005–06 NYR	64	10	6	16	28
NHL Totals	123	20	15	35	52

Hossa, Marian b. Stara Lubovna, Czechoslovakia (Slovakia), January 12, 1979

2005–06 ATL	80	39	53	92	67
NHL Totals	547	227	255	482	310

Howard, James b. Syracuse, New York, March 26, 1984

2005–06 DET	4	1-2-0	200	10	0	2.99
NHL Totals	4	1-2-0	200	10	0	2.99

Hrdina, Jan b. Hradec Kralove, Czechoslovakia (Czech Republic), February 5, 1976

2005–06 CBJ	75	10	23	33	78
NHL Totals	513	101	196	297	341

Hudler, Jiri b. Olomouc, Czechoslovakia (Czech Republic),
January 4, 1984

2005–06 DET	4	0	0	0	2
NHL Totals	16	1	2	3	12

Huet, Cristobal b. St. Martin d'Heres, France, September 3, 1975

2005–06 MON	36	18-11-4	2,103	77	7	2.20
NHL Totals	89	32-31-11	4,843	187	11	2.32

Hull, Brett b. Belleville, Ontario, August 9, 1964

2005–06 PHO	5	0	1	1	0
NHL Totals	1,269	741	650	1,391	458

* retired October 16, 2005

Hulse, Cale b. Edmonton, Alberta, November 10, 1973

2005–06 CBJ/CAL	39	0	4	4	63
NHL Totals	619	16	79	95	1,000

* traded October 8, 2005, by Phoenix to Columbus with Jason Chimera and
  Michael Rupp for Geoff Sanderson and Tim Jackman
* traded February 28, 2006, by Columbus to Calgary for Cam Severson

Hunter, Trent b. Red Deer, Alberta, July 5, 1980

2005–06 NYI	82	16	19	35	34
NHL Totals	167	41	49	90	54

Huselius, Kristian b. Osterhaninge, Sweden, November 10, 1978

2005–06 FLO/CAL	78	20	27	47	40
NHL Totals	311	73	93	166	98

* traded December 2, 2005, by Florida to Calgary for Steve Montador and
  Dustin Johner

Hussey, Matt b. New Haven, Connecticut, May 28, 1979

2005–06 PIT	13	0	1	1	0
NHL Totals	16	2	2	4	0

Hutchinson, Andrew b. Evanston, Illinois, March 24, 1980

2005–06 CAR	36	3	8	11	18
NHL Totals	54	7	12	19	22

Iginla, Jarome b. Edmonton, Alberta, July 1, 1977

2005–06 CAL	82	35	32	67	86
NHL Totals	708	285	285	570	508

Immonen, Jarkko b. Rantasalmi, Finland, April 19, 1982

2005–06 NYR	6	2	0	2	0
NHL Totals	6	2	0	2	0

Isbister, Brad b. Edmonton, Alberta, May 7, 1977

2005–06 BOS	58	6	17	23	46
NHL Totals	467	99	107	206	563

Ivanans, Raitis b. Riga, Soviet Union (Latvia), January 1, 1979

2005–06 MON	4	0	0	0	9
NHL Totals	4	0	0	0	9

Jacina, Greg b. Guelph, Ontario, May 22, 1982

2005–06 FLO	11	0	1	1	4
NHL Totals	11	0	1	1	4

Jackman, Barret b. Trail, British Columbia, March 5, 1981

2005–06 STL	63	4	6	10	156
NHL Totals	161	8	24	32	387

Jackman, Ric b. Toronto, Ontario, June 28, 1978

2005–06 PIT/FLO	64	7	23	30	52
NHL Totals	200	17	48	65	146

* traded March 9, 2006, by Pittsburgh to Florida for Petr Taticek

Jackman, Tim b. Minot, North Dakota, November 14, 1981

2005–06 PHO	8	0	0	0	21
NHL Totals	27	1	2	3	37

* traded October 8, 2005, by Columbus to Phoenix with Geoff Sanderson for Jason Chimera, Michael Rupp, and Cale Hulse
* traded March 9, 2006, by Phoenix to Los Angeles for Yannick Lehoux

Jacques, Jean-Francois b. Terrebonne, Quebec, April 29, 1985

2005–06 EDM	7	0	0	0	0
NHL Totals	7	0	0	0	0

Jagr, Jaromir b. Kladno, Czechoslovakia (Czech Republic), February 15, 1972

2005–06 NYR	82	54	69	123	72
NHL Totals	1,109	591	841	1,432	771

James, Connor b. Calgary, Alberta, August 25, 1982

2005–06 LA	2	0	0	0	0
NHL Totals	2	0	0	0	0

Jancevski, Dan b. Windsor, Ontario, June 15, 1981

2005–06 DAL	2	0	0	0	0
NHL Totals	2	0	0	0	0

Janik, Doug b. Agawam, Massachusetts, March 26, 1980

2005–06 BUF	—	—	—	—	—
NHL Totals	10	0	0	0	21

* appeared only in the playoffs this year

Janssen, Cam b. St. Louis, Missouri, April 15, 1984

2005–06 NJ	47	0	0	0	91
NHL Totals	47	0	0	0	91

Jarrett, Cole b. Sault Ste. Marie, Ontario, January 4, 1983

2005–06 NYI	1	0	0	0	0
NHL Totals	1	0	0	0	0

Jillson, Jeff b. North Smithfield, Rhode Island, July 24, 1980

2005–06 BUF	2	0	0	0	4
NHL Totals	140	9	32	41	96

Johansson, Jonas b. Jonkoping, Sweden, March 18, 1984

2005–06 WAS	1	0	0	0	2
NHL Totals	1	0	0	0	2

Johnson, Aaron b. Port Hawkesbury, Nova Scotia, April 30, 1983

2005–06 CBJ	26	2	6	8	23
NHL Totals	55	4	12	16	55

Johnson, Brent b. Farmington, Michigan, March 12, 1977

2005–06 WAS	26	9-12-1	1,412	81	1	3.44
NHL Totals	177	86-65-13	9,954	406	13	2.45

Johnson, Greg b. Thunder Bay, Ontario, March 16, 1971

2005–06 NAS	68	11	8	19	10
NHL Totals	785	145	224	369	345

Johnson, Mike b. Scarborough (Toronto), Ontario, October 3, 1974

2005–06 PHO	80	16	38	54	50
NHL Totals	560	116	223	339	267

Johnson, Ryan b. Thunder Bay, Ontario, June 14, 1976

2005–06 STL	65	3	6	9	33
NHL Totals	409	22	51	73	149

Johnsson, Kim b. Malmo, Sweden, March 16, 1976

| 2005–06 PHI | 47 | 6 | 19 | 25 | 34 |
| NHL Totals | 442 | 51 | 143 | 194 | 226 |

Jokinen, Jussi b. Kalajoki, Finland, April 1, 1983

| 2005–06 DAL | 81 | 17 | 38 | 55 | 30 |
| NHL Totals | 81 | 17 | 38 | 55 | 30 |

Jokinen, Olli b. Kuopio, Finland, December 5, 1978

| 2005–06 FLO | 82 | 38 | 51 | 89 | 88 |
| NHL Totals | 559 | 135 | 164 | 299 | 582 |

Jones, Matt b. Downers Grove, Illinois, August 8, 1983

| 2005–06 PHO | 16 | 0 | 2 | 2 | 14 |
| NHL Totals | 16 | 0 | 2 | 2 | 14 |

Jones, Randy b. Quispamsis, New Brunswick, July 23, 1981

| 2005–06 PHI | 28 | 0 | 8 | 8 | 16 |
| NHL Totals | 33 | 0 | 8 | 8 | 16 |

Joseph, Curtis b. Keswick, Ontario, April 29, 1967

| 2005–06 PHO | 60 | 32-21-3 | 3,424 | 166 | 4 | 2.91 |
| NHL Totals | 858 | 428-310-90 | 49,820 | 2,290 | 47 | 2.76 |

Jovanovski, Ed b. Windsor, Ontario, June 26, 1976

| 2005–06 VAN | 44 | 8 | 25 | 33 | 58 |
| NHL Totals | 687 | 86 | 231 | 317 | 1,085 |

Jurcina, Milan b. Liptovsky Mikulas, Czechoslovakia (Slovakia), June 7, 1983

| 2005–06 BOS | 51 | 6 | 5 | 11 | 54 |
| NHL Totals | 51 | 6 | 5 | 11 | 54 |

Kaberle, Frantisek b. Kladno, Czechoslovakia (Czech Republic), November 8, 1973

2005–06 CAR	77	6	38	44	46
NHL Totals	386	26	129	155	160

Kaberle, Tomas b. Rakovnik, Czechoslovakia (Czech Republic), March 2, 1978

2005–06 TOR	82	9	58	67	46
NHL Totals	525	50	241	291	156

Kalinin, Dmitri b. Chelyabinsk, Soviet Union (Russia), July 22, 1980

2005–06 BUF	55	2	16	18	54
NHL Totals	338	26	82	108	221

Kane, Boyd b. Swift Current, Saskatchewan, April 18, 1978

2005–06 WAS	5	0	1	1	2
NHL Totals	12	0	1	1	9

Kanko, Petr b. Pribram, Czechoslovakia (Czech Republic), February 7, 1984

2005–06 LA	10	1	0	1	0
NHL Totals	10	1	0	1	0

Kapanen, Niko b. Hattula, Finland, April 29, 1978

2005–06 DAL	81	14	21	35	36
NHL Totals	239	20	56	76	98

Kapanen, Sami b. Vantaa, Finland, June 14, 1973

2005–06 PHI	58	12	22	34	12
NHL Totals	680	173	252	425	137

Kariya, Paul b. Vancouver, British Columbia, October 16, 1974

2005–06 NAS	82	31	54	85	40
NHL Totals	739	342	448	790	275

Karpovtsev, Alexander b. Moscow, Soviet Union (Russia), April 7, 1970

2005–06 FLO	6	0	0	0	4
NHL Totals	596	34	154	188	430

Kasparaitis, Darius b. Elektrenai, Soviet Union (Lithuania), October 16, 1972

2005–06 NYR	67	0	6	6	97
NHL Totals	839	25	134	159	1,349

Kavanagh, Pat b. Ottawa, Ontario, March 14, 1979

2005–06 PHI	8	0	0	0	2
NHL Totals	14	2	0	2	4

Keith, Duncan b. Winnipeg, Manitoba, July 16, 1983

2005–06 CHI	81	9	12	21	79
NHL Totals	81	9	12	21	79

Keith, Matt b. Edmonton, Alberta, April 11, 1983

2005–06 CHI	2	0	0	0	0
NHL Totals	22	2	3	5	10

Kelly, Chris b. Toronto, Ontario, November 11, 1980

2005–06 OTT	82	10	20	30	76
NHL Totals	86	10	20	30	76

Kesler, Ryan b. Detroit, Michigan, August 31, 1984

2005–06 VAN	82	10	13	23	79
NHL Totals	110	12	16	28	95

Khabibulin, Nikolai b. Sverdlovsk, Soviet Union (Russia), January 13, 1973

2005–06 CHI	50	17-26-6	2,814	157	0	3.35
NHL Totals	526	226-213-58	29,920	1,334	35	2.68

Khavanov, Alexander b. Moscow, Soviet Union (Russia), January 30, 1972

2005–06 TOR	64	6	6	12	60
NHL Totals	348	27	75	102	233

Kilger, Chad b. Cornwall, Ontario, November 27, 1976

2005–06 TOR	79	17	11	28	63
NHL Totals	579	83	90	173	287

Kiprusoff, Miikka b. Turku, Finland, October 26, 1976

2005–06 CAL	74	42-20-11	4,379	151	10	2.07
NHL Totals	159	80-51-7	9,070	329	17	2.18

Klee, Ken b. Indianapolis, Indiana, April 24, 1971

2005–06 TOR/NJ	74	3	12	15	80
NHL Totals	710	50	105	155	724

* traded March 8, 2006, by Toronto to New Jersey for Alexander Suglobov

Klein, Kevin b. Kitchener, Ontario, December 13, 1984

2005–06 NAS	2	0	0	0	0
NHL Totals	2	0	0	0	0

Klemm, Jon b. Cranbrook, British Columbia, January 8, 1970

2005–06 DAL	76	4	7	11	60
NHL Totals	713	41	98	139	402

Klepis, Jakub b. Prague, Czechoslovakia (Czech Republic), June 5, 1984

2005–06 WAS	25	1	3	4	8
NHL Totals	25	1	3	4	8

Klesla, Rostislav b. Novy Jicin, Czechoslovakia (Czech Republic), March 21, 1982

2005–06 CBJ	51	6	13	19	75
NHL Totals	253	20	46	66	253

Kloucek, Tomas b. Prague, Czechoslovakia (Czech Republic), March 7, 1980

2005–06 ATL	1	0	0	0	2
NHL Totals	141	2	8	10	250

Knuble, Mike b. Toronto, Ontario, July 4, 1972

2005–06 PHI	82	34	31	65	80
NHL Totals	592	135	138	273	304

Koalska, Matt b. St. Paul, Minnesota, May 16, 1980

2005–06 NYI	3	0	0	0	2
NHL Totals	3	0	0	0	2

Kobasew, Chuck b. Osoyoos, British Columbia, April 17, 1982

2005–06 CAL	77	20	11	31	64
NHL Totals	170	30	24	54	123

Koivu, Mikko b. Turku, Finland, March 12, 1983

2005–06 MIN	64	6	15	21	40
NHL Totals	64	6	15	21	40

Koivu, Saku b. Turku, Finland, November 23, 1974

2005–06 MON	72	17	45	62	70
NHL Totals	569	137	323	460	412

Kolanos, Krys b. Calgary, Alberta, July 27, 1981

2005–06 PHO/CAR/PIT	15	2	1	3	4
NHL Totals	115	17	18	35	76

* traded December 28, 2005, by Phoenix to Carolina for Pavel Brendl
* traded March 9, 2006, by Carolina to Pittsburgh with Niklas Nordgren and a 2nd-round draft choice in 2007 for Mark Recchi

Kolesnik, Vitaly b. Ust-Kamenogorsk, Soviet Union (Kazakhstan), August 20, 1979

2005–06 COL	8	3-3-0	370	20	0	3.24
NHL Totals	8	3-3-0	370	20	0	3.24

Kolnik, Juraj b. Nitra, Czechoslovakia (Slovakia), November 13, 1980

2005–06 FLO	77	15	20	35	40
NHL Totals	176	35	35	70	66

Koltsov, Konstantin b. Minsk, Soviet Union (Belarus), April 17, 1981

2005–06 PIT	60	3	6	9	20
NHL Totals	144	12	26	38	50

Kolzig, Olaf b. Johannesburg, South Africa, April 9, 1970

2005–06 WAS	59	20-28-11	3,506	206	0	3.53
NHL Totals	603	254-248-63	34,921	1,548	33	2.66

Komisarek, Mike b. Islip Terrace, New York, January 19, 1982

2005–06 MON	71	2	4	6	116
NHL Totals	138	2	9	11	178

Kondratiev, Maxim b. Togliatti, Soviet Union (Russia), January 20, 1983

2005–06 NYR	29	1	2	3	22
NHL Totals	36	1	2	3	24

* traded January 8, 2006, by the New York Rangers to Anaheim for Petr Sykora and a 4th-round draft choice

Konopka, Zenon b. Niagara-on-the-Lake, Ontario, January 2, 1981

2005–06 ANA	23	4	3	7	48
NHL Totals	23	4	3	7	48

Konowalchuk, Steve b. Salt Lake City, Utah, November 11, 1972

2005–06 COL	21	6	9	15	14
NHL Totals	790	171	225	396	703

Kopecky, Tomas b. Ilava, Czechoslovakia (Slovakia), February 5, 1982

2005–06 DET	1	0	0	0	2
NHL Totals	1	0	0	0	2

Kostitsyn, Andrei b. Novopolosk, Soviet Union (Belarus), February 3, 1985

2005–06 MON	12	2	1	3	2
NHL Totals	12	2	1	3	2

Kostopoulos, Tom b. Mississauga, Ontario, January 24, 1979

2005–06 LA	76	8	14	22	100
NHL Totals	155	18	30	48	176

Kotalik, Ales b. Jindrichuv Hradec, Czechoslovakia (Czech Republic), December 23, 1978

2005–06 BUF	82	25	37	62	62
NHL Totals	225	62	65	127	135

Kovalchuk, Ilya b. Tver, Soviet Union (Russia), April 15, 1983

2005–06 ATL	78	52	46	98	68
NHL Totals	305	160	143	303	216

Kovalev, Alexei b. Togliatti, Soviet Union (Russia), February 24, 1973

2005–06 MON	69	23	42	65	76
NHL Totals	918	315	430	745	978

Kozlov, Viktor b. Togliatti, Soviet Union (Russia), February 14, 1975

2005–06 NJ	69	12	13	25	16
NHL Totals	668	144	247	391	186

Kozlov, Vyacheslav b. Voskresensk, Soviet Union (Russia), May 3, 1972

2005–06 ATL	82	25	46	71	33
NHL Totals	882	277	353	630	565

Krajicek, Lukas b. Prostejov, Czechoslovakia (Czech Republic), March 11, 1983

2005–06 FLO	67	2	14	16	50
NHL Totals	90	3	20	23	62

Kronvall, Niklas b. Stockholm, Sweden, January 12, 1981

2005–06 DET	27	1	8	9	28
NHL Totals	47	2	12	14	44

Kronvall, Staffan b. Jarfalla, Sweden, September 10, 1982

2005–06 TOR	34	0	1	1	14
NHL Totals	34	0	1	1	14

Kuba, Filip b. Ostrava, Czechoslovakia (Czech Republic), December 29, 1976

2005–06 MIN	65	9	16	25	44
NHL Totals	375	34	105	139	163

Kubina, Pavel b. Celadna, Czechoslovakia (Czech Republic), April 15, 1977

2005–06 TB	76	5	33	38	96
NHL Totals	531	65	144	209	663

Kunitz, Chris b. Regina, Saskatchewan, September 26, 1979

2005–06 ANA	69	19	22	41	71
NHL Totals	90	19	28	47	83

Kvasha, Oleg b. Moscow, Soviet Union (Russia), July 26, 1978

2005–06 NYI/PHO	64	13	19	32	38
NHL Totals	493	81	136	217	335

* traded March 9, 2006, by Islanders to Phoenix with a 5th-round draft choice in 2006 for a 3rd-round and 7th-round draft choice in 2007

Kwiatkowski, Joel b. Kindersley, Saskatchewan, March 22, 1977

2005–06 FLO	73	4	8	12	86
NHL Totals	222	11	19	30	205

Laaksonen, Antti b. Tammela, Finland, October 3, 1973

2005–06 COL	81	16	18	34	40
NHL Totals	442	78	86	164	136

LaBarbera, Jason b. Burnaby, British Columbia, January 18, 1980

2005–06 LA	29	11-9-2	1,432	69	1	2.89
NHL Totals	34	12-11-0	1,640	85	1	3.11

LaCouture, Dan b. Hyannis, Massachusetts, April 18, 1977

2005–06 BOS	55	2	2	4	53
NHL Totals	320	18	25	43	331

Ladd, Andrew b. Maple Ridge, British Columbia, December 12, 1985

2005–06 CAR	29	6	5	11	4
NHL Totals	29	6	5	11	4

Laich, Brooks b. Wawota, Alberta, June 23, 1983

2005–06 WAS	73	7	14	21	26
NHL Totals	78	7	15	22	28

Lalime, Patrick b. St. Bonaventure, Quebec, July 7, 1974

2005–06 STL	31	4-18-8	1,699	103	0	3.64
NHL Totals	353	171-130-32	20,252	841	33	2.49

Lampman, Bryce b. Rochester, Minnesota, August 31, 1982

2005–06 NYR	1	0	0	0	2
NHL Totals	9	0	0	0	2

Lang, Robert b. Teplice, Czechoslovakia (Czech Republic), December 19, 1970

2005–06 DET	72	20	42	62	72
NHL Totals	718	194	335	529	242

Langdon, Darren b. Deer Lake, Newfoundland, January 8, 1971

2005–06 NJ	14	0	1	1	22
NHL Totals	521	16	23	391	251

Langenbrunner, Jamie b. Duluth, Minnesota, July 24, 1975

2005–06 NJ	80	19	34	53	74
NHL Totals	657	144	231	375	566

Langfeld, Josh b. Fridley, Minnesota, July 17, 1977

2005–06 BOS	57	2	10	12	26
NHL Totals	108	9	21	30	48

Langkow, Daymond b. Edmonton, Alberta, September 27, 1976

2005–06 CAL	82	25	34	59	46
NHL Totals	707	161	252	413	420

Laperriere, Ian b. Montreal, Quebec, January 19, 1974

2005–06 COL	82	21	24	45	116
NHL Totals	776	99	150	249	1,358

Lapierre, Maxim b. St. Leonard, Quebec, March 29, 1985

2005–06 MON	1	0	0	0	0
NHL Totals	1	0	0	0	0

Lapointe, Martin b. Ville St. Pierre, Quebec, September 12, 1973

2005–06 CHI	82	14	17	31	106
NHL Totals	839	162	182	344	1,249

Laraque, Georges b. Montreal, Quebec, December 7, 1976

2005–06 EDM	72	2	10	12	73
NHL Totals	490	43	68	111	826

LaRose, Chad b. Fraser, Michigan, March 27, 1982

2005–06 CAR	49	1	12	13	35
NHL Totals	49	1	12	13	35

Larsen, Brad b. Nakusp, British Columbia, June 28, 1977

2005–06 ATL	62	7	8	15	21
NHL Totals	160	11	20	31	83

Leach, Jay b. Syracuse, New York, September 2, 1979

2005–06 BOS	2	0	0	0	7
NHL Totals	2	0	0	0	7

Leahy, Pat b. Boston, Massachusetts, June 9, 1979

2005–06 BOS	43	4	4	8	19
NHL Totals	49	4	4	8	19

Lebda, Brett b. Buffalo Grove, Illinois, January 15, 1982

2005–06 DET	46	3	9	12	20
NHL Totals	46	3	9	12	20

Lecavalier, Vincent b. Ile Bizard, Quebec, April 21, 1980

2005–06 TB	80	35	40	75	90
NHL Totals	547	181	221	402	374

LeClair, John b. St. Albans, Vermont, July 5, 1969

2005–06 PIT	73	22	29	51	61
NHL Totals	946	404	408	812	489

Leclaire, Pascal b. Repentigny, Quebec, November 7, 1982

2005–06 CBJ	33	11-15-3	1,803	97	0	3.23
NHL Totals	35	11-17-0	1,922	104	0	3.25

Leclerc, Mike b. Winnipeg, Manitoba, November 10, 1976

2005–06 PHO/CAL	50	10	16	26	37
NHL Totals	341	64	94	158	288

* traded February 1, 2006, by Phoenix to Calgary with Brian Boucher for Steve Reinprecht and Philippe Sauve

Leetch, Brian b. Corpus Christi, Texas, March 3, 1968

2005–06 BOS	61	5	27	32	36
NHL Totals	1,205	247	781	1,028	571

Lefebvre, Guillaume b. Amos, Quebec, May 7, 1981

2005–06 PIT	9	0	0	0	9
NHL Totals	38	2	4	6	13

Legace, Manny b. Toronto, Ontario, February 4, 1973

2005–06 DET	51	37-8-3	2,905	106	7	2.19
NHL Totals	197	114-43-18	11,028	407	13	2.21

Legwand, David b. Detroit, Michigan, August 17, 1980

2005–06 NAS	44	7	19	26	34
NHL Totals	406	79	141	220	236

Lehoux, Yanick b. Montreal, Quebec, April 8, 1982

2005–06 PHO	3	1	0	1	2
NHL Totals	3	1	0	1	2

Lehtinen, Jere b. Espoo, Finland, June 24, 1973

2005–06 DAL	80	33	19	52	30
NHL Totals	648	190	203	393	164

Lehtonen, Kari b. Helsinki, Finland, November 16, 1983

2005–06 ATL	38	20-15-0	2,165	106	2	2.94
NHL Totals	42	24-15-0	2,405	111	3	2.77

Lemieux, Mario b. Montreal, Quebec, October 5, 1965

2005–06	26	7	15	22	16
NHL Totals	915	690	1,033	1,723	834

* retired on January 24, 2006

Leneveu, David b. Fernie, British Columbia, May 23, 1983

2005–06 PHO	15	3-8-2	814	44	0	3.24
NHL Totals	15	3-8-2	814	44	0	3.24

Leopold, Jordan b. Golden Valley, Minnesota, August 3, 1980

2005–06 CAL	74	2	18	20	68
NHL Totals	214	15	52	67	104

Lessard, Francis b. Montreal, Quebec, May 30, 1979

2005–06 ATL	6	0	0	0	0
NHL Totals	91	1	3	4	268

Lessard, Junior b. St. Joseph de Beauce, Quebec, May 26, 1980

2005–06 DAL	5	1	0	1	12
NHL Totals	5	1	0	1	12

Letowski, Trevor b. Thunder Bay, Ontario, April 5, 1977

2005–06 CBJ	81	10	18	28	36
NHL Totals	480	73	102	175	161

Lidstrom, Nicklas b. Vasteras, Sweden, April 28, 1970

2005–06 DET	80	16	64	80	50
NHL Totals	1,096	189	617	806	326

Liffiton, David b. Windsor, Ontario, October 18, 1984

2005–06 NYR	1	0	0	0	2
NHL Totals	1	0	0	0	2

Liles, John-Michael b. Zionsville, Indiana, November 25, 1980

2005–06 COL	82	14	35	49	44
NHL Totals	161	24	59	83	72

Lilja, Andreas b. Landskrona, Sweden, July 13, 1975

2005–06 DET	82	2	13	15	98
NHL Totals	262	10	32	42	284

Linden, Trevor b. Medicine Hat, Alberta, April 11, 1970

2005–06 VAN	82	7	9	16	15
NHL Totals	1,243	356	474	830	846

Lindros, Eric b. London, Ontario, February 28, 1973

2005–06 TOR	33	11	11	22	43
NHL Totals	711	367	472	839	1,328

* missed much of the season with injured wrist

Lindstrom, Joakim b. Skelleftea, Sweden, December 5, 1983

2005–06 CBJ	3	0	0	0	0
NHL Totals	3	0	0	0	0

Lombardi, Matt b. Montreal, Quebec, March 18, 1982

2005–06 CAL	55	6	20	26	48
NHL Totals	134	22	33	55	80

Loyns, Lynn b. Naicam, Saskatchewan, February 22, 1981

2005–06 CAL	1	0	0	0	0
NHL Totals	34	3	2	5	21

Lukowich, Brad b. Cranbrook, British Columbia, August 12, 1976

2005–06 NYI/NJ	75	2	19	21	40
NHL Totals	448	17	67	84	297

* traded March 9, 2006, by the Islanders to New Jersey for a 3rd-round draft
  choice in 2006

Lundmark, Jamie b. Edmonton, Alberta, January 16, 1981

2005–06 NYR/PHO/CAL	53	10	19	29	62
NHL Totals	164	20	38	58	111

* traded October 18, 2005, by the New York Rangers to Phoenix for Jeff Taffe
* traded March 9, 2006, from Phoenix to Calgary for a 4th-round draft
  choice in 2006

Lundqvist, Henrik b. Are, Sweden, March 2, 1982

2005–06 NYR	53	30-12-9	3,111	116	2	2.24
NHL Totals	53	30-12-9	3,111	116	2	2.24

Luongo, Roberto b. Montreal, Quebec, April 4, 1979

2005–06 FLO	75	35-30-9	4,304	213	4	2.97
NHL Totals	341	115-68-33	19,134	866	27	2.72

Lupul, Joffrey b. Fort Saskatchewan, Alberta, September 23, 1983

2005–06 ANA	81	28	25	53	48
NHL Totals	156	41	46	87	76

Lydman, Toni b. Lahti, Finland, September 25, 1977

2005–06 BUF	75	1	16	17	82
NHL Totals	364	20	90	110	222

MacDonald, Craig b. Antigonish, Nova Scotia, April 7, 1977

2005–06 CAL	25	3	2	5	8
NHL Totals	135	5	12	17	61

MacKenzie, Derek b. Sudbury, Ontario, June 11, 1981

2005–06 ATL	11	0	1	1	8
NHL Totals	24	0	2	2	20

MacLean, Don b. Sydney, Nova Scotia, January 14, 1977

2005–06 DET	3	1	1	2	0
NHL Totals	32	7	4	11	6

Madden, John b. Barrie, Ontario, May 4, 1973

2005–06 NJ	82	16	20	36	36
NHL Totals	482	101	98	199	127

Mair, Adam b. Hamilton, Ontario, February 15, 1979

2005–06 BUF	40	2	5	7	47
NHL Totals	252	16	33	49	422

* missed much of season suffering from post-concussion syndrome

Majesky, Ivan b. Banska Bystrica, Czechoslovakia (Slovakia), September 2, 1976

2005–06 WAS	57	1	8	9	66
NHL Totals	202	8	23	31	234

Malakhov, Vladimir b. Sverdlovsk, Soviet Union (Russia), August 30, 1968

2005–06 NJ	29	4	5	9	26
NHL Totals	712	86	260	346	697

Malec, Tomas b. Skalica, Czechoslovakia (Slovakia), May 13, 1982

2005–06 OTT	2	0	0	0	2
NHL Totals	45	0	2	2	47

Malhotra, Manny b. Mississauga, Ontario, May 18, 1980

2005–06 CBJ	58	10	21	31	41
NHL Totals	404	45	63	108	206

Malik, Marek b. Ostrava, Czechoslovakia (Czech Republic), June 24, 1975

2005–06 NYR	74	2	16	18	78
NHL Totals	538	29	103	132	466

Malone, Ryan b. Pittsburgh, Pennsylvania, December 1, 1979

2005–06 PIT	77	22	22	44	63
NHL Totals	158	44	43	87	127

Maltby, Kirk b. Guelph, Ontario, December 22, 1972

2005–06 DET	82	5	6	11	80
NHL Totals	799	107	115	222	725

Mara, Paul b. Ridgewood, New Jersey, September 7, 1979

2005–06 PHO	78	15	32	47	70
NHL Totals	424	52	126	178	381

Marchant, Todd b. Buffalo, New York, August 12, 1973

2005–06 CBJ/ANA	79	9	25	34	66
NHL Totals	835	154	257	411	590

* claimed off waivers by Anaheim on November 21, 2005

Marchment, Bryan b. Scarborough (Toronto), Ontario, May 1, 1969

2005–06 CAL	37	1	2	3	75
NHL Totals	926	40	142	182	2,307

Marjamaki, Masi b. Pori Satakunta, Finland, January 16, 1985

2005–06 NYI	1	0	0	0	0
NHL Totals	1	0	0	0	0

Markkanen, Jussi b. Imatra, Finland, May 8, 1975

2005–06 EDM	37	15-12-6	2,015	105	0	3.13
NHL Totals	106	38-38-8	5,618	245	7	2.62

Markov, Andrei b. Voskresensk, Soviet Union (Russia), December 20, 1978

2005–06 MON	67	10	36	46	74
NHL Totals	334	40	118	158	170

Markov, Danny b. Moscow, Soviet Union (Russia), July 30, 1976

2005–06 NAS	58	0	11	11	62
NHL Totals	472	25	106	131	397

Marleau, Patrick b. Aneroid, Saskatchewan, September 15, 1979

2005–06 SJ	82	34	52	86	26
NHL Totals	640	187	226	413	219

Marshall, Grant b. Mississauga, Ontario, June 9, 1973

2005–06 NJ	76	8	17	25	70
NHL Totals	700	92	147	239	793

Marshall, Jason b. Cranbrook, British Columbia, February 22, 1971

2005–06 ANA	23	0	4	4	34
NHL Totals	526	16	51	67	1,004

Martin, Paul b. Minneapolis, Minnesota, March 5, 1981

2005–06 NJ	80	5	32	37	32
NHL Totals	150	11	50	61	36

Martinek, Radek b. Havlickuv Brod, Czechoslovakia (Czech Republic), August 31, 1976

2005–06 NYI	74	1	16	17	32
NHL Totals	210	8	34	42	117

Martins, Steve b. Gatineau, Quebec, April 13, 1972

2005–06 OTT	4	1	1	2	0
NHL Totals	267	21	25	46	142

Mason, Chris b. Red Deer, Alberta, April 20, 1976

2005–06 NAS	23	12-5-1	1,226	52	2	2.54
NHL Totals	44	16-10-1	2,098	87	3	2.49

Matvichuk, Richard b. Edmonton, Alberta, February 5, 1973

2005–06 NJ	62	1	10	11	40
NHL Totals	795	39	139	178	624

May, Brad b. Toronto, Ontario, November 29, 1971

2005–06 COL	54	3	3	6	82
NHL Totals	858	123	149	272	2,019

Mayers, Jamal b. Toronto, Ontario, October 24, 1974

2005–06 STL	67	15	11	26	129
NHL Totals	435	51	58	109	576

McAmmond, Dean b. Grand Cache, Alberta, June 15, 1973

2005–06 STL	78	15	22	37	32
NHL Totals	723	150	214	364	386

McCabe, Bryan b. St. Catharines, Ontario, June 8, 1975

2005–06 TOR	73	19	49	68	116
NHL Totals	781	95	243	338	1,378

McCarthy, Steve b. Trail, British Columbia, February 3, 1981

2005–06 VAN/ATL	67	9	7	16	51
NHL Totals	201	12	20	32	96

* traded March 9, 2006, from Vancouver to Atlanta for a conditional draft choice in 2007

McCarty, Darren b. Burnaby, British Columbia, April 1, 1972

2005–06 CAL	67	7	6	13	117
NHL Totals	710	126	160	286	1,392

McCauley, Alyn b. Brockville, Ontario, May 29, 1977

2005–06 SJ	76	12	14	26	30
NHL Totals	478	68	97	165	114

McClement, Jay b. Kingston, Ontario, March 2, 1983

2005–06 STL	67	6	21	27	30
NHL Totals	67	6	21	27	30

McCormick, Cody b. London, Ontario, April 18, 1983

2005–06 COL	45	4	4	8	29
NHL Totals	89	6	7	13	102

McDonald, Andy b. Strathroy, Ontario, August 25, 1977

2005–06 ANA	82	34	51	85	32
NHL Totals	276	61	104	165	86

McEachern, Shawn b. Waltham, Massachusetts, February 28, 1969

2005–06 BOS	28	2	6	8	28
NHL Totals	911	256	323	579	506

McGillis, Dan b. Hawkesbury, Ontario, July 1, 1972

2005–06 NJ	27	0	6	6	36
NHL Totals	634	56	182	238	570

McGrattan, Brian b. Hamilton, Ontario, September 2, 1981

2005–06 OTT	60	2	3	5	141
NHL Totals	60	2	3	5	141

McKee, Jay b. Kingston, Ontario, September 8, 1977

2005–06 BUF	75	5	11	16	57
NHL Totals	582	17	81	98	470

McLaren, Kyle b. Humboldt, Saskatchewan, June 18, 1977

2005–06 SJ	77	2	21	23	66
NHL Totals	591	38	141	179	526

McLean, Brett b. Comox, British Columbia, August 14, 1978

2005–06 COL	82	9	31	40	51
NHL Totals	160	20	51	71	105

McLennan, Jamie b. Edmonton, Alberta, June 30, 1971

2005–06 FLO	17	2-4-2	677	34	0	3.01
NHL Totals	245	77-104-33	13,302	585	13	2.64

McVicar, Rob b. Brandon, Manitoba, January 15, 1982

2005–06 VAN	1	0-0-0	2	0	0	0.00
NHL Totals	1	0-0-0	2	0	0	0.00

Melichar, Josef b. Ceske Budejovice, Czechoslovakia (Czech Republic), January 20, 1979

2005–06 PIT	72	3	12	15	66
NHL Totals	240	6	22	28	219

Mellanby, Scott b. Montreal, Quebec, June 11, 1966

2005–06 ATL	71	12	22	34	56
NHL Totals	1,362	352	452	804	2,416

Meszaros, Andrej b. Povazska Bystrica, Czechoslovakia (Slovakia), October 13, 1985

2005–06 OTT	82	10	29	39	61
NHL Totals	82	10	29	39	61

Meyer, Freddy b. Sanbornville, New Hampshire, January 4, 1981

2005–06 PHI	57	6	21	27	33
NHL Totals	58	6	21	27	33

Mezei, Branislav b. Nitra, Czechoslovakia (Slovakia), October 8, 1980

2005–06 FLO	16	0	1	1	37
NHL Totals	138	3	14	17	192

Michalek, Milan b. Jindrichuv Hradec, Czechoslovakia (Czech Republic), December 7, 1984

2005–06 SJ	81	17	18	35	45
NHL Totals	83	18	18	36	49

Michalek, Zbynek b. Jindrichuv Hradec, Czechoslovakia (Czech Republic), December 23, 1982

2005–06 PHO	82	9	15	24	62
NHL Totals	104	10	16	26	66

Miettinen, Antti b. Hameenlinna, Finland, July 3, 1980

2005–06 DAL	79	11	20	31	46
NHL Totals	95	12	20	32	46

Miller, Aaron b. Buffalo, New York, August 11, 1971

2005–06 LA	56	0	8	8	27
NHL Totals	538	24	78	102	330

Miller, Ryan b. East Lansing, Michigan, July 17, 1980

2005–06 BUF	48	30-14-3	2,861	124	1	2.60
NHL Totals	66	36-25-1	3,952	179	2	2.72

Milley, Norm b. Toronto, Ontario, February 14, 1980

2005–06 TB	14	2	1	3	4
NHL Totals	29	2	4	6	12

Mink, Graham b. Stowe, Vermont, May 21, 1979

2005–06 WAS	3	0	0	0	0
NHL Totals	5	0	0	0	2

Mitchell, Willie b. Port McNeill, British Columbia, April 23, 1977

2005–06 MIN/DAL	80	2	8	10	113
NHL Totals	322	9	52	61	388

* traded March 9, 2006, by Minnesota to Dallas with a 2nd-round draft
 choice in 2007 for Martin Skoula and Shawn Belle

Modano, Mike b. Livonia, Michigan, June 7, 1970

2005–06 DAL	78	27	50	77	58
NHL Totals	1,179	485	698	1,183	768

Modin, Fredrik b. Sundsvall, Sweden, October 8, 1974

2005–06 TB	77	31	23	54	56
NHL Totals	662	183	179	362	315

Modry, Jaroslav b. Ceske Budejovice, Czechoslovakia (Czech
Republic), February 27, 1971

2005–06 ATL	79	7	31	38	76
NHL Totals	569	47	176	223	406

Moen, Travis b. Stewart Valley, Saskatchewan, April 6, 1982

2005–06 ANA	39	4	1	5	72
NHL Totals	121	8	3	11	214

Mogilny, Alexander b. Khabarovsk, Soviet Union (Russia),
February 18, 1969

2005–06 NJ	34	12	13	25	6
NHL Totals	990	473	559	1,032	432

* spent the last half of the season in the minors

Mojzis, Tomas b. Kolin, Czechoslovakia (Czech Republic),
May 2, 1982

2005–06 VAN	7	0	1	1	12
NHL Totals	7	0	1	1	12

Montador, Steve b. Vancouver, British Columbia, December 21, 1979

2005–06 CAL/FLO	58	2	5	7	79
NHL Totals	145	5	10	15	269

* traded December 2, 2005, by Calgary to Florida with Dustin Johner for
  Kristian Huselius

Moore, Dominic b. Thornhill, Ontario, August 3, 1980

2005–06 NYR	82	9	9	18	28
NHL Totals	87	9	12	21	28

Moran, Ian b. Cleveland, Ohio, August 24, 1972

2005–06 BOS	12	1	1	2	10
NHL Totals	488	21	50	71	321

Moreau, Ethan b. Huntsville, Ontario, September 22, 1975

2005–06 EDM	74	11	16	27	87
NHL Totals	678	106	117	223	820

Morgan, Jason b. St. John's, Newfoundland, October 9, 1976

2005–06 CHI	7	1	1	2	6
NHL Totals	40	2	5	7	14

Morris, Derek　b. Edmonton, Alberta, August 24, 1978

2005–06 PHO	53	6	21	27	54
NHL Totals	554	57	213	270	556

Morrison, Brendan　b. Pitt Meadows, British Columbia, August 15, 1975

2005–06 VAN	82	19	37	56	84
NHL Totals	553	130	268	398	274

Morrison, Mike　b. Medford, Maine, July 11, 1979

2005–06 EDM/OTT	25	11-4-3	1,098	54	0	2.95
NHL Totals	25	11-4-3	1,098	54	0	2.95

* claimed off waivers by Ottawa on March 9, 2006

Morrisonn, Shaone　b. Vancouver, British Columbia, December 23, 1982

2005–06 WAS	80	1	13	14	91
NHL Totals	124	2	20	22	109

Morrow, Brenden　b. Carlyle, Saskatchewan, January 16, 1979

2005–06 DAL	81	23	42	65	183
NHL Totals	451	120	149	269	756

Motzko, Joe　b. Bemidji, Minnesota, March 14, 1980

2005–06 CBJ	2	0	0	0	0
NHL Totals	4	0	0	0	0

Mowers, Mark　b. Whitesboro, New York, February 16, 1974

2005–06 DET	46	4	11	15	16
NHL Totals	183	12	32	44	36

Muir, Bryan　b. Winnipeg, Manitoba, June 8, 1973

2005–06 WAS	72	8	18	26	72
NHL Totals	253	13	33	46	239

Munro, Adam b. St. George, Ontario, November 12, 1982

2005–06 CHI	10	3-5-2	500	25	1	2.99
NHL Totals	17	4-10-1	926	51	1	3.30

Murley, Matt b. Troy, New York, December 17, 1979

2005–06 PIT	41	1	5	6	24
NHL Totals	59	2	6	8	38

Murray, Doug b. Bromma, Sweden, March 12, 1980

2005–06 SJ	34	0	1	1	27
NHL Totals	34	0	1	1	27

Murray, Garth b. Regina, Saskatchewan, September 17, 1982

2005–06 MON	36	5	1	6	44
NHL Totals	56	6	1	7	68

Murray, Glen b. Halifax, Nova Scotia, November 1, 1972

2005–06 BOS	64	24	29	53	52
NHL Totals	887	292	284	576	585

Murray, Rem b. Stratford, Ontario, October 9, 1972

2005–06 EDM	9	1	1	2	2
NHL Totals	560	94	121	215	161

Nabokov, Evgeni b. Ust-Kamenogorsk, Soviet Union (Kazakhstan), July 25, 1975

2005–06 SJ	45	16-19-7	2,574	133	1	3.10
NHL Totals	303	137-113-29	17,271	705	27	2.45

Nagy, Ladislav b. Saca, Czechoslovakia (Slovakia), June 1, 1979

2005–06 PHO	51	15	41	56	74
NHL Totals	317	94	136	230	286

Nash, Rick b. Brampton, Ontario, June 16, 1984

2005–06 CBJ	54	31	23	54	51
NHL Totals	208	89	61	150	216

Nash, Tyson b. Edmonton, Alberta, March 11, 1975

2005–06 PHO	50	0	6	6	84
NHL Totals	374	27	37	64	673

Naslund, Markus b. Ornskoldsvik, Sweden, July 30, 1973

2005–06 VAN	81	32	47	79	66
NHL Totals	871	322	386	708	579

Nasreddine, Alain b. Montreal, Quebec, July 10, 1975

2005–06 PIT	6	0	0	0	8
NHL Totals	24	0	0	0	62

Nazarov, Andrei b. Chelyabinsk, Soviet Union (Russia), May 22, 1974

2005–06 MIN	2	0	0	0	6
NHL Totals	571	53	71	124	1,409

Nedved, Petr b. Liberec, Czechoslovakia (Czech Republic), December 9, 1971

2005–06 PHO/PHI	53	7	18	25	70
NHL Totals	942	308	397	705	680

* traded January 18, 2006, by Phoenix to Philadelphia for Dennis Seidenberg

Neil, Chris b. Markdale, Ontario, June 18, 1979

2005–06 OTT	79	16	17	33	204
NHL Totals	301	40	36	76	776

Nichol, Scott b. Edmonton, Alberta, December 31, 1974

2005–06 NAS	34	3	3	6	79
NHL Totals	242	23	28	51	494

Nickulas, Eric b. Hyannis, Massachusetts, March 25, 1975

2005–06 BOS	16	2	4	6	8
NHL Totals	118	15	23	38	82

Niedermayer, Rob b. Cassiar, British Columbia, December 28, 1974

2005–06 ANA	76	15	24	39	89
NHL Totals	772	144	231	375	664

Niedermayer, Scott b. Edmonton, Alberta, August 31, 1973

2005–06 ANA	82	13	50	63	96
NHL Totals	974	125	414	539	574

Nieminen, Ville b. Tampere, Finland, April 6, 1977

2005–06 NYR/SJ	70	8	16	24	63
NHL Totals	341	47	68	115	290

* traded March 8, 2006, by the Rangers to San Jose for a 3rd-round draft choice in 2006

Nieuwendyk, Joe b. Oshawa, Ontario, September 10, 1966

2005–06 FLO	65	26	30	56	46
NHL Totals	1,242	559	559	1,118	673

Niinimaa, Janne b. Raahe, Finland, May 22, 1975

2005–06 NYI/DAL	63	3	13	16	86
NHL Totals	700	54	262	316	697

* traded January 10, 2006, by the New York Islanders to Dallas with a 5th-round draft choice in 2007 for John Erskine and a 2nd-round draft choice in 2006

Niittymaki, Antero b. Turku, Finland, June 18, 1980

2005–06 PHI	46	23-15-6	2,690	133	2	2.97
NHL Totals	49	26-15-0	2,870	136	2	2.84

Nilson, Marcus b. Balsta, Sweden, March 1, 1978

2005–06 CAL	70	6	11	17	32
NHL Totals	411	59	89	149	239

Nilsson, Robert b. Calgary, Alberta, January 10, 1985

2005–06 NYI	53	6	14	20	26
NHL Totals	53	6	14	20	26

Nokelainen, Petteri b. Imatra, Finland, January 16, 1986

2005–06 NYI	15	1	1	2	4
NHL Totals	15	1	1	2	4

Nordgren, Niklas b. Ornskoldsvik, Sweden, June 28, 1979

2005–06 CAR/PIT	58	4	2	6	34
NHL Totals	58	4	2	6	34

* traded March 9, 2006, by Carolina to Pittsburgh with Krys Kolanos and a 2nd-round draft choice in 2007 for Mark Recchi

Noronen, Mika b. Tampere, Finland, June 17, 1979

2005–06 BUF/VAN	8	2-3-0	338	22	0	3.89
NHL Totals	71	23-32-6	3,652	163	3	2.68

* traded March 9, 2006, from Buffalo to Vancouver for a 2nd-round draft choice in 2006

Norstrom, Mattias b. Stockholm, Sweden, January 2, 1972

2005–06 LA	77	4	23	27	58
NHL Totals	761	14	127	141	573

Norton, Brad b. Cambridge, Massachusetts, February 13, 1975

2005–06 OTT	7	0	0	0	31
NHL Totals	118	3	7	10	267

Novak, Filip b. Ceske Budejovice, Czechoslovakia (Czech Republic), May 7, 1982

2005–06 OTT	11	0	0	0	4
NHL Totals	11	0	0	0	4

* traded October 5, 2005, by Florida to Ottawa for a 6th-round draft choice in 2007

Novotny, Jiri b. Pelhrimov, Czechoslovakia (Czech Republic), August 12, 1983

2005–06 BUF	14	2	1	3	0
NHL Totals	14	2	1	3	0

Numminen, Teppo b. Tampere, Finland, July 3, 1968

2005–06 BUF	75	2	38	40	36
NHL Totals	1,235	113	478	591	459

Nylander, Michael b. Stockholm, Sweden, October 3, 1972

2005–06 NYR	81	23	56	79	76
NHL Totals	729	163	363	526	370

Nystrom, Eric b. Syosset, New York, February 14, 1983

2005–06 CAL	2	0	0	0	0
NHL Totals	2	0	0	0	0

O'Brien, Doug b. St. John's, Newfoundland, February 16, 1984

2005–06 TB	5	0	0	0	2
NHL Totals	5	0	0	0	2

Odelein, Lyle b. Quill Lake, Saskatchewan, July 21, 1968

2005–06 PIT	27	0	1	1	50
NHL Totals	1,056	50	202	252	2,316

O'Donnell, Sean b. Ottawa, Ontario, October 13, 1971

2005–06 PHO/ANA	78	2	9	11	147
NHL Totals	771	23	128	151	1,382

* traded March 9, 2006, by Phoenix to Anaheim for Joel Perrault

Ohlund, Mattias b. Pitea, Sweden, September 9, 1976

2005–06 VAN	78	13	20	33	92
NHL Totals	558	67	178	245	492

Olesz, Rostislav b. Bilovec, Czechoslovakia (Czech Republic), October 10, 1985

2005–06 FLO	59	8	13	21	24
NHL Totals	59	8	13	21	24

Oliver, David b. Sechelt, British Columbia, April 17, 1971

2005–06 DAL	3	0	0	0	0
NHL Totals	233	49	49	98	84

Oliwa, Krzysztof b. Tychy, Poland, April 12, 1973

2005–06 NJ	3	0	0	0	0
NHL Totals	410	17	28	45	1,447

* released by New Jersey and retired during season

Ondrus, Ben b. Sherwood Park, Alberta, June 25, 1982

2005–06 TOR	22	0	0	0	18
NHL Totals	22	0	0	0	18

O'Neill, Jeff b. Richmond Hill, Ontario, February 23, 1976

2005–06 TOR	74	19	19	38	64
NHL Totals	747	217	237	454	616

Orpik, Brooks b. San Francisco, California, September 26, 1980

2005–06 PIT	64	2	7	9	124
NHL Totals	149	3	16	19	253

Orr, Colton b. Winnipeg, Manitoba, March 3, 1982

2005–06 NYR	35	0	1	1	71
NHL Totals	36	0	1	1	71

Orszagh, Vladimir b. Banska Bystrica, Czechoslovakia (Slovakia), May 24, 1977

2005–06 STL	16	4	5	9	14
NHL Totals	289	54	65	119	194

Ortmeyer, Jed b. Omaha, Nebraska, September 3, 1978

2005–06 NYR	78	5	2	7	38
NHL Totals	136	7	6	13	54

Osgood, Chris b. Peace River, Alberta, November 26, 1972

2005–06 DET	32	20-6-5	1,846	85	2	2.76
NHL Totals	600	325-183-66	34,448	1,409	43	2.45

Ott, Steve b. Summerside, Prince Edward Island, August 19, 1982

2005–06 DAL	82	5	17	22	178
NHL Totals	181	10	31	41	361

Ouellet, Maxime b. Beauport, Quebec, June 17, 1981

2005–06 VAN	4	0-2-1	221	12	0	3.24
NHL Totals	12	2-6-1	662	34	1	3.08

Ouellet, Michel b. Rimouski, Quebec, March 5, 1982

2005–06 PIT	50	16	16	32	16
NHL Totals	50	16	16	32	16

Ovechkin, Alexander b. Moscow, Soviet Union (Russia), September 17, 1985

2005–06 WAS	81	52	54	106	52
NHL Totals	81	52	54	106	52

Ozolinsh, Sandis b. Riga, Soviet Union (Latvia), August 3, 1972

2005–06 ANA/NYR	36	6	14	20	28
NHL Totals	815	164	381	545	606

* traded March 9, 2006, from Anaheim to the Rangers for a 3rd-round draft choice in 2006

Paetsch, Nathan b. Leroy, Saskatchewan, March 30, 1983

2005–06 BUF	1	0	1	1	0
NHL Totals	1	0	1	1	0

Pahlsson, Samuel b. Ornskoldsvik, Sweden, December 17, 1977

2005–06 ANA	82	11	10	21	34
NHL Totals	354	33	54	87	150

Paille, Daniel b. Welland, Ontario, April 15, 1984

2005–06 BUF	14	1	2	3	2
NHL Totals	14	1	2	3	2

Palffy, Ziggy b. Skalica, Czechoslovakia (Slovakia), May 5, 1972

2005–06 PIT	42	11	31	42	12
NHL Totals	684	329	384	713	322

Pandolfo, Jay b. Winchester, Massachusetts, December 27, 1974

2005–06 NJ	82	10	10	20	16
NHL Totals	570	65	88	153	108

Parise, Zach b. Minneapolis, Minnesota, July 28, 1984

2005–06 NJ	81	14	18	32	28
NHL Totals	81	14	18	32	28

Park, Richard b. Seoul, South Korea, May 27, 1976

2005–06 VAN	60	8	10	18	29
NHL Totals	368	50	57	107	139

Parker, Scott b. Hanford, California, January 29, 1978

2005–06 SJ	10	1	0	1	38
NHL Totals	262	6	13	19	601

Parrish, Mark b. Edina, Minnesota, February 2, 1977

2005–06 NYI/LA	76	29	20	49	20
NHL Totals	518	173	130	303	190

* traded March 8, 2006, by the Islanders to Los Angeles with Brent Sopel
  for Denis Grebeshkov, Jeff Tambellini and a conditional 3rd-round draft
  choice

Parros, George b. Washington, Pennsylvania, December 29, 1979

2005–06 LA	55	2	3	5	138
NHL Totals	55	2	3	5	138

Payer, Serge b. Rockland, Ontario, May 7, 1979

2005–06 FLO	71	2	4	6	26
NHL Totals	119	7	6	13	49

Peat, Stephen b. Princeton, British Columbia, March 10, 1980

2005–06 WAS	1	0	0	0	2
NHL Totals	130	8	2	10	234

* traded December 28, 2005, by Washington to Carolina for Colin Forbes

Peca, Michael b. Toronto, Ontario, March 26, 1974

2005–06 EDM	71	9	14	23	56
NHL Totals	693	160	234	394	616

Penner, Dustin b. Winkler, Manitoba, September 28, 1982

2005–06 ANA	19	4	3	7	14
NHL Totals	19	4	3	7	14

Perezhogin, Alexander b. Ust-Kamenogorsk, Soviet Union (Kazakhstan), August 10, 1983

2005–06 MON	67	9	10	19	38
NHL Totals	67	9	10	19	38

Perrault, Joel b. Montreal, Quebec, April 6, 1983

2005–06 PHO	5	1	1	2	2
NHL Totals	5	1	1	2	2

Perreault, Yanic b. Sherbrooke, Quebec, April 4, 1971

2005–06 NAS	69	22	35	57	30
NHL Totals	740	217	247	464	344

Perrott, Nathan b. Owen Sound, Ontario, December 8, 1976

2005–06 DAL	26	2	1	3	56
NHL Totals	89	4	5	9	251

* traded November 6, 2005, by Toronto to Dallas for a 6th-round draft choice in 2006

Perry, Corey b. Peterborough, Ontario, May 16, 1985

2005–06 ANA	56	13	12	25	50
NHL Totals	56	13	12	25	50

Peters, Andrew b. St. Catharines, Ontario, May 5, 1980

2005–06 BUF	28	0	0	0	100
NHL Totals	70	2	0	2	251

Petersen, Toby b. Minneapolis, Minnesota, October 27, 1978

2005–06 EDM	—	—	—	—	—
NHL Totals	91	10	16	26	8

* appeared only in the playoffs this season

Petiot, Richard b. Daysland, Alberta, August 20, 1982

2005–06 LA	2	0	0	0	2
NHL Totals	2	0	0	0	2

Petrovicky, Ronald b. Zilina, Czechoslovakia (Slovakia), February 15, 1977

2005–06 ATL	60	8	12	20	62
NHL Totals	311	38	48	86	401

Pettinen, Tomi b. Ylojarvi, Finland, June 17, 1977

2005–06 NYI	18	0	0	0	16
NHL Totals	24	0	0	0	18

Pettinger, Matt b. Edmonton, Alberta, October 22, 1980

2005–06 WAS	71	20	18	38	39
NHL Totals	214	34	26	60	122

Phaneuf, Dion b. Edmonton, Alberta, April 10, 1985

2005–06 CAL	82	20	29	49	93
NHL Totals	82	20	29	49	93

Phillips, Chris b. Calgary, Alberta, March 9, 1978

2005–06 OTT	69	1	18	19	90
NHL Totals	536	32	106	138	376

Picard, Alexandre b. Les Saules, Quebec, October 9, 1985

2005–06 CBJ	17	0	0	0	14
NHL Totals	17	0	0	0	14

Picard, Alexandre b. Gatineau, Quebec, July 5, 1985

2005–06 PHI	6	0	0	0	4
NHL Totals	6	0	0	0	4

Pihlman, Thomas b. Espoo, Finland, November 13, 1982

2005–06 NJ	11	1	1	2	10
NHL Totals	13	1	1	2	12

Pirjeta, Lasse b. Oulu, Finland, April 4, 1974

2005–06 PIT	25	4	3	7	18
NHL Totals	146	23	27	50	50

Pisani, Fernando b. Edmonton, Alberta, December 27, 1976

2005–06 EDM	80	18	19	37	42
NHL Totals	191	42	38	80	98

Pitkanen, Joni b. Oulu, Finland, September 19, 1983

2005–06 PHI	58	13	33	46	78
NHL Totals	129	21	52	73	122

Platt, Geoff b. Toronto, Ontario, July 10, 1985

2005–06 CBJ	15	0	5	5	16
NHL Totals	15	0	5	5	16

Plekanec, Tomas b. Kladno, Czechoslovakia (Czech Republic), October 31, 1982

2005–06 MON	67	9	20	29	32
NHL Totals	69	9	20	29	32

Poapst, Steve b. Cornwall, Ontario, January 3, 1969

2005–06 STL	62	0	5	5	47
NHL Totals	307	8	28	36	173

* traded December 9, 2005, by Pittsburgh to St. Louis for Eric Boguniecki

Pock, Thomas b. Klagenfurt, Austria, December 2, 1981

2005–06 NYR	8	1	1	2	4
NHL Totals	14	3	3	6	4

Pohl, John b. Rochester, Minnesota, June 29, 1979

2005–06 TOR	7	3	1	4	4
NHL Totals	8	3	1	4	4

Polak, Vojtech b. Ostrov nad Ohri, Czechoslovakia (Czech Republic), June 27, 1985

2005–06 DAL	3	0	0	0	0
NHL Totals	3	0	0	0	0

Pominville, Jason b. Repentigny, Quebec, November 30, 1982

2005–06 BUF	57	18	12	30	22
NHL Totals	58	18	12	30	22

Ponikarovsky, Alexei b. Kiev, Soviet Union (Ukraine), April 9, 1980

2005–06 TOR	81	21	17	38	68
NHL Totals	197	33	42	75	137

Popovic, Mark b. Stoney Creek, Ontario, October 11, 1982

2005–06 ATL	7	0	0	0	0
NHL Totals	8	0	0	0	0

Pothier, Brian b. New Bedford, Massachusetts, April 15, 1977

2005–06 OTT	77	5	30	35	59
NHL Totals	182	12	46	58	113

Poti, Tom b. Worcester, Massachusetts, March 22, 1977

2005–06 NYR	73	3	20	23	70
NHL Totals	516	52	156	208	386

Potulny, Ryan b. Grand Forks, North Dakota, September 5, 1984

2005–06 PHI	2	0	1	1	0
NHL Totals	2	0	1	1	0

Pouliot, Marc-Antoine b. Quebec City, Quebec, May 22, 1985

2005–06 EDM	8	1	0	1	0
NHL Totals	8	1	0	1	0

Pratt, Nolan b. Fort McMurray, Alberta, August 14, 1975

2005–06 TB	82	0	9	9	60
NHL Totals	456	7	43	50	463

Preissing, Tom b. Rosemount, Minnesota, December 3, 1978

2005–06 SJ	74	11	32	43	26
NHL Totals	143	13	49	62	38

Primeau, Keith b. Toronto, Ontario, November 24, 1971

2005–06 PHI	9	1	6	7	6
NHL Totals	909	266	353	619	1,541

* missed most of season suffering from post-concussion syndrome

Primeau, Wayne b. Scarborough (Toronto), Ontario, June 4, 1976

2005–06 SJ/BOS	71	11	11	22	57
NHL Totals	570	53	97	150	603

* traded November 30, 2005, by San Jose to Boston with Marco Sturm and
  Brad Stuart for Joe Thornton

Printz, David b. Stockholm, Sweden, July 24, 1980

2005–06 PHI	1	0	0	0	0
NHL Totals	1	0	0	0	0

Pronger, Chris b. Dryden, Ontario, October 10, 1974

2005–06 EDM	80	12	44	56	74
NHL Totals	802	106	350	456	1,172

Prospal, Vaclav b. Ceske Budejovice, Czechoslovakia (Czech Republic), February 17, 1975

2005–06 TB	81	25	55	80	50
NHL Totals	630	132	296	428	340

Prucha, Petr b. Chrudim, Czechoslovakia (Czech Republic), September 14, 1982

2005–06 NYR	68	30	17	47	32
NHL Totals	68	30	17	47	32

Prusek, Martin b. Ostrava, Czechoslovakia (Czech Republic), December 11, 1975

2005–06 CBJ	9	3-3-0	373	20	0	3.22
NHL Totals	57	31-12-4	2,897	114	3	2.36

Pushkarev, Konstantin b. Ust-Kamenogorsk, Soviet Union (Kazakhstan), February 12, 1985

2005–06 LA	1	0	1	1	0
NHL Totals	1	0	1	1	0

Pushor, Jamie b. Lethbridge, Alberta, February 11, 1973

2005–06 CBJ	4	1	2	3	0
NHL Totals	521	14	46	60	648

Pyatt, Taylor b. Thunder Bay, Ontario, August 19, 1981

2005–06 BUF	41	6	6	12	33
NHL Totals	308	42	56	98	170

Quincey, Kyle b. Kitchener, Ontario, August 12, 1985

2005–06 DET	1	0	0	0	0
NHL Totals	1	0	0	0	0

Radivojevic, Branko b. Piestany, Czechoslovakia (Slovakia), November 24, 1980

2005–06 PHI	64	8	6	14	44
NHL Totals	238	34	45	79	183

Rafalski, Brian b. Dearborn, Michigan, September 28, 1973

2005–06 NJ	82	6	43	49	36
NHL Totals	459	36	220	256	146

Ranger, Paul b. Whitby, Ontario, September 12, 1984

2005–06 TB	76	1	17	18	58
NHL Totals	76	1	17	18	58

Rasmussen, Erik b. Minneapolis, Minnesota, March 28, 1977

2005–06 NJ	67	5	5	10	32
NHL Totals	474	49	69	118	280

Rathje, Mike b. Mannville, Alberta, May 11, 1974

2005–06 PHI	79	3	21	24	46
NHL Totals	750	30	149	179	485

Raycroft, Andrew b. Belleville, Ontario, May 4, 1980

2005–06 BOS	30	8-19-2	1,618	100	0	3.71
NHL Totals	108	43-46-10	6,052	264	3	2.62

Ready, Ryan b. Peterborough, Ontario, November 7, 1978

2005–06 PHI	7	0	1	1	0
NHL Totals	7	0	1	1	0

Reasoner, Marty b. Honeoye Falls, New York, February 26, 1977

2005–06 EDM/BOS	77	11	23	34	28
NHL Totals	311	47	84	131	149

* traded March 9, 2006, by Edmonton to Boston with Yan Stastny and a 2nd-round draft choice in 2006 for Sergei Samsonov

Recchi, Mark b. Kamloops, British Columbia, February 1, 1968

2005–06 PIT/CAR	83	28	36	64	68
NHL Totals	1,256	484	781	1,265	848

* traded March 9, 2006, by Pittsburgh to Carolina for Niklas Nordgren, Krys Kolanos, and a 2nd-round draft choice in 2007

Redden, Wade b. Lloydminster, Saskatchewan, June 12, 1977

2005–06 OTT	65	10	40	50	63
NHL Totals	694	88	248	336	466

Regehr, Richie b. Bandung, Indonesia, January 17, 1983

2005–06 CAL	14	0	2	2	6
NHL Totals	14	0	2	2	6

Regehr, Robyn b. Recife, Brazil, April 19, 1980

2005–06 CAL	68	6	20	26	67
NHL Totals	431	18	62	80	437

Regier, Steve b. Edmonton, Alberta, August 31, 1984

2005–06 NYI	9	0	0	0	0
NHL Totals	9	0	0	0	0

Reid, Darren b. Lac la Biche, Alberta, May 8, 1983

2005–06 TB	7	0	1	1	0
NHL Totals	7	0	1	1	0

Reinprecht, Steve b. Edmonton, Alberta, May 7, 1976

2005–06 CAL/PHO	80	22	30	52	32
NHL Totals	349	81	133	214	88

* traded February 1, 2006, by Calgary to Phoenix with Philippe Sauve for Brian Boucher and Mike Leclerc

Reitz, Eric b. Detroit, Michigan, July 29, 1982

2005–06 MIN	5	0	0	0	4
NHL Totals	5	0	0	0	4

Rheaume, Pascal b. Quebec City, Quebec, June 21, 1973

2005–06 NJ/PHO	13	0	0	0	4
NHL Totals	318	39	52	91	144

* traded November 25, 2005, by New Jersey to Phoenix with Ray Schultz and Steven Spencer for Brad Ference

Ribeiro, Mike b. Montreal, Quebec, February 10, 1980

2005–06 MON	79	16	35	51	36
NHL Totals	276	50	103	153	92

Ricci, Mike b. Scarborough (Toronto), Ontario, October 27, 1971

2005–06 PHO	78	10	6	16	69
NHL Totals	1,092	243	361	604	970

Richards, Brad b. Murray Harbour, Prince Edward Island, May 2, 1980

2005–06 TB	82	23	68	91	32
NHL Totals	408	107	261	368	95

Richards, Mike b. Kenora, Ontario, February 11, 1985

2005–06 PHI	79	11	23	34	65
NHL Totals	79	11	23	34	65

Richardson, Brad b. Belleville, Ontario, February 4, 1985

2005–06 COL	41	3	10	13	12
NHL Totals	41	3	10	13	12

Richardson, Luke b. Ottawa, Ontario, March 26, 1969

2005–06 CBJ/TOR	65	1	9	10	71
NHL Totals	1,312	33	156	189	1,996

* traded March 8, 2006, by Columbus to Toronto for a conditional draft choice

Richmond, Danny b. Chicago, Illinois, August 1, 1984

2005–06 CAR/CHI	20	0	1	1	25
NHL Totals	20	0	1	1	25

* traded January 20, 2006, by Carolina to Chicago with a 4th-round draft choice in 2006 for Anton Babchuk and a 4th-4round draft choice in 2007

Rinne, Pekka b. Kempele, Finland, November 3, 1982

2005–06 NAS	2	1-1-0	63	4	0	3.81
NHL Totals	2	1-1-0	63	4	0	3.81

Rissmiller, Pat b. Belmont, Massachusetts, October 26, 1978

2005–06 SJ	18	3	3	6	8
NHL Totals	22	3	3	6	8

Rita, Jani b. Helsinki, Finland, July 25, 1981

2005–06 EDM/PIT	51	6	4	10	10
NHL Totals	66	9	5	14	10

* traded January 26, 2006, by Edmonton to Pittsburgh with Cory Cross for Dick Tarnstrom

Ritchie, Byron b. Burnaby, British Columbia, April 24, 1977

2005–06 CAL	45	4	2	6	69
NHL Totals	189	14	19	33	225

Rivers, Jamie b. Ottawa, Ontario, March 16, 1975

2005–06 DET/PHO	33	0	6	6	38
NHL Totals	423	16	46	62	349

* traded March 9, 2006, by Detroit to Phoenix for a 7th-round draft choice in 2006

Rivet, Craig b. North Bay, Ontario, September 13, 1974

2005–06 MON	82	7	27	34	109
NHL Totals	599	33	102	135	738

Roach, Andy b. Mattawan, Michigan, August 22, 1973

2005–06 STL	5	1	2	3	10
NHL Totals	5	1	2	3	10

Roberts, Gary b. North York (Toronto), Ontario, May 23, 1966

2005–06 FLO	58	14	26	40	51
NHL Totals	1,087	411	435	846	2,396

Robidas, Stephane b. Sherbrooke, Quebec, March 3, 1977

2005–06 DAL	75	5	15	20	67
NHL Totals	332	18	48	66	171

Robinson, Nathan b. Scarborough (Toronto), Ontario, December 31, 1981

2005–06 BOS	2	0	0	0	0
NHL Totals	7	0	0	0	2

Robitaille, Louis b. Montreal, Quebec, March 16, 1982

2005–06 WAS	2	0	0	0	5
NHL Totals	2	0	0	0	5

Robitaille, Luc b. Montreal, Quebec, February 17, 1966

2005–06 LA	65	15	9	24	52
NHL Totals	1,431	668	726	1,394	1,177

Robitaille, Randy b. Ottawa, Ontario, October 12, 1975

2005–06 MIN	67	12	28	40	54
NHL Totals	385	63	124	187	139

Roenick, Jeremy b. Boston, Massachusetts, January 17, 1970

2005–06 LA	58	9	13	22	36
NHL Totals	1,182	484	658	1,142	1,381

Roloson, Dwayne b. Simcoe, Ontario, October 12, 1969

2005–06 MIN/EDM	43	14-24-5	2,523	115	2	2.73
NHL Totals	288	97-123-42	16,233	676	18	2.50

* traded March 8, 2006, by Minnesota to Edmonton for a 1st-round draft
  choice and a conditional draft choice in 2006

Rolston, Brian b. Flint, Michigan, February 21, 1973

2005–06 MIN	82	34	45	79	50
NHL Totals	818	224	287	511	273

Rourke, Allan b. Mississauga, Ontario, March 6, 1980

2005–06 NYI	6	0	1	1	0
NHL Totals	25	1	3	4	22

Roy, Andre b. Port Chester, New York, February 8, 1975

2005–06 PIT	42	2	1	3	116
NHL Totals	352	27	28	55	850

Roy, Derek b. Ottawa, Ontario, May 4, 1983

2005–06 BUF	70	18	28	46	57
NHL Totals	119	27	38	65	69

Roy, Mathieu b. St. Georges, Quebec, August 10, 1983

2005–06 EDM	1	0	0	0	0
NHL Totals	1	0	0	0	0

Rozsival, Michal b. Vlasim, Czechoslovakia (Czech Republic),
September 3, 1978

2005–06 NYR	82	5	25	30	90
NHL Totals	319	23	72	95	251

Rucchin, Steve b. Thunder Bay, Ontario, July 4, 1971

2005–06 NYR	72	13	23	36	10
NHL Totals	688	166	302	468	150

Rucinsky, Martin b. Most, Czechoslovakia (Czech Republic), March 11, 1971

2005–06 NYR	52	16	39	55	56
NHL Totals	869	224	339	563	733

Rupp, Mike b. Cleveland, Ohio, January 13, 1980

2005–06 CBJ	40	4	2	6	58
NHL Totals	123	15	11	26	126

* traded October 8, 2005, by Phoenix to Columbus with Jason Chimera and Cale Hulse for Geoff Sanderson and Tim Jackman

Ruutu, Jarkko b. Vantaa, Finland, August 23, 1975

2005–06 VAN	82	10	7	17	142
NHL Totals	267	23	28	51	453

Ruutu, Tuomo b. Vantaa, Finland, February 16, 1983

2005–06 CHI	15	2	3	5	31
NHL Totals	97	25	24	49	89

Ruzicka, Stefan b. Nitra, Czechoslovakia (Slovakia), February 17, 1985

2005–06 PHI	1	0	0	0	2
NHL Totals	1	0	0	0	2

Ryan, Matt b. Sharon, Ontario, November 12, 1983

2005–06 LA	12	0	1	1	2
NHL Totals	12	0	1	1	2

Ryan, Prestin b. Arcola, Saskatchewan, June 29, 1980

2005–06 VAN	1	0	0	0	2
NHL Totals	1	0	0	0	2

Rycroft, Mark b. Penticton, British Columbia, July 12, 1978

2005–06 STL	80	6	4	10	46
NHL Totals	160	15	19	34	82

Ryder, Michael b. Bonavista, Newfoundland, March 31, 1980

2005–06 MON	81	30	25	55	40
NHL Totals	162	55	63	118	66

Rypien, Rick b. Coleman, Alberta, May 16, 1984

2005–06 VAN	5	1	0	1	4
NHL Totals	5	1	0	1	4

Ryznar, Jason b. Anchorage, Alaska, February 19, 1983

2005–06 NJ	8	0	0	0	2
NHL Totals	8	0	0	0	2

Sabourin, Dany b. Val d'Or, Quebec, September 2, 1980

2005–06 PIT	1	0-1-0	20	4	0	11.43
NHL Totals	5	0-4-0	189	14	0	4.44

St. Jacques, Bruno b. Montreal, Quebec, August 22, 1980

2005–06 ANA	1	1	0	1	0
NHL Totals	67	3	7	10	47

St. Louis, Martin b. Laval, Quebec, June 18, 1975

2005–06 TB	80	31	30	61	38
NHL Totals	444	140	180	320	158

St. Pierre, Martin b. Ottawa, Ontario, August 11, 1983

2005–06 CHI	2	0	0	0	0
NHL Totals	2	0	0	0	0

Sakic, Joe b. Burnaby, British Columbia, July 7, 1969

2005–06 COL	82	32	55	87	60
NHL Totals	1,237	574	915	1,489	542

Salei, Ruslan b. Minsk, Soviet Union (Belarus), November 2, 1974

2005–06 ANA	78	1	18	19	114
NHL Totals	594	26	79	105	735

Salo, Sami b. Turku, Finland, September 2, 1974

2005–06 VAN	59	10	23	33	38
NHL Totals	407	45	113	158	120

Salvador, Bryce b. Brandon, Manitoba, February 11, 1976

2005–06 STL	46	1	4	5	26
NHL Totals	327	13	32	45	315

Samsonov, Sergei b. Moscow, Soviet Union (Russia), October 27, 1978

2005–06 BOS/EDM	74	23	30	53	28
NHL Totals	533	169	223	392	109

* traded March 9, 2006, by Boston to Edmonton for Marty Reasoner, Yan Stastny, and a 2nd-round draft choice in 2006

Samuelsson, Mikael b. Mariefred, Sweden, December 23, 1976

2005–06 DET	71	23	22	45	42
NHL Totals	259	42	52	94	140

Sanderson, Geoff b. Hay River, Northwest Territories, February 1, 1972

2005–06 CBJ/PHO	77	25	21	46	58
NHL Totals	1,005	341	317	658	451

* traded October 8, 2005, by Columbus to Phoenix with Tim Jackman for Jason Chimera, Michael Rupp, and Cale Hulse

Sanford, Curtis b. Owen Sound, Ontario, October 5, 1979

2005–06 STL	34	13-13-5	1,830	81	3	2.66
NHL Totals	42	18-14-0	2,227	94	4	2.53

Saprykin, Oleg b. Moscow, Soviet Union (Russia), February 12, 1981

2005–06 PHO	67	11	14	25	50
NHL Totals	254	40	61	101	182

Sarich, Cory b. Saskatoon, Saskatchewan, August 16, 1978

2005–06 TB	82	1	14	15	79
NHL Totals	454	10	64	74	519

Sarno, Peter b. Toronto, Ontario, July 26, 1979

2005–06 CBJ	1	0	0	0	0
NHL Totals	7	1	0	1	2

Satan, Miroslav b. Topolcany, Czechoslovakia (Slovakia), October 22, 1974

2005–06 NYI	82	35	31	66	54
NHL Totals	786	294	291	585	331

Sauer, Kurt b. St. Cloud, Minnesota, January 16, 1981

2005–06 COL	37	1	4	5	24
NHL Totals	186	3	11	13	149

Sauve, Philippe b. Buffalo, New York, February 27, 1980

2005–06 CAL/PHO	13	3-7-0	589	39	0	3.97
NHL Totals	30	10-14-3	1,575	89	0	3.39

* traded February 1, 2006, by Calgary to Phoenix with Steve Reinprecht for Brian Boucher and Mike Leclerc

Savage, Brian b. Sudbury, Ontario, February 24, 1971

2005–06 PHI	66	9	5	14	28
NHL Totals	674	192	167	359	321

Savard, Marc b. Ottawa, Ontario, July 17, 1977

2005–06 ATL	82	28	69	97	100
NHL Totals	503	133	268	401	462

Scatchard, Dave b. Hinton, Alberta, February 20, 1976

2005–06 BOS/PHO	63	15	18	33	112
NHL Totals	589	122	133	255	945

* traded November 15, 2005, by Boston to Phoenix for David Tanabe

Schaefer, Nolan b. Yellow Grass, Saskatchewan, January 15, 1980

2005–06 SJ	7	5-1-0	352	11	1	1.88
NHL Totals	7	5-1-0	352	11	1	1.88

Schaefer, Peter b. Yellow Grass, Saskatchewan, July 12, 1977

2005–06 OTT	82	20	30	50	40
NHL Totals	416	77	110	187	148

Schneider, Mathieu b. New York, New York, June 12, 1969

2005–06 DET	72	21	38	59	86
NHL Totals	1,064	189	422	611	1,049

Schubert, Christoph b. Munich, (West) Germany, February 5, 1982

2005–06 OTT	56	4	6	10	48
NHL Totals	56	4	6	10	48

Schultz, Nick b. Strasbourg, Saskatchewan, August 25, 1982

2005–06 MIN	79	2	12	14	43
NHL Totals	285	15	35	50	96

Scuderi, Rob b. Syosset, New York, December 30, 1978

2005–06 PIT	57	0	4	4	36
NHL Totals	70	1	6	7	40

Seabrook, Brent b. Richmond, British Columbia, April 20, 1985

2005–06 CHI	69	5	27	32	60
NHL Totals	69	5	27	32	60

Sedin, Daniel b. Ornskoldsvik, Sweden, September 26, 1980

2005–06 VAN	82	22	49	71	34
NHL Totals	397	83	139	222	142

Sedin, Henrik b. Ornskoldsvik, Sweden, September 26, 1980

2005–06 VAN	82	18	57	75	56
NHL Totals	400	62	159	221	200

Seidenberg, Dennis b. Schwenningen, West Germany (Germany), July 18, 1981

2005–06 PHI/PHO	63	3	15	18	18
NHL Totals	126	7	24	31	40

* traded January 18, 2006, by Philadelphia to Phoenix for Petr Nedved

Sejna, Peter b. Liptovski Mikulas, Czechoslovakia (Slovakia), October 5, 1979

2005–06 STL	6	1	1	2	4
NHL Totals	27	4	3	7	8

Selanne, Teemu b. Helsinki, Finland, July 3, 1970

2005–06 ANA	80	40	50	90	44
NHL Totals	959	492	549	1,041	379

Semenov, Alexei b. Murmansk, Soviet Union (Russia), April 10, 1981

2005–06 EDM/FLO	27	2	2	4	38
NHL Totals	119	5	11	16	128

* traded November 19, 2005, by Edmonton to Florida for a conditional draft choice in 2006

Severson, Cam b. Canora, Saskatchewan, January 15, 1978

2005–06 CAL/CBJ	4	0	0	0	5
NHL Totals	37	3	0	3	63

* traded February 28, 2006, by Calgary to Columbus for Cale Hulse

Shanahan, Brendan b. Mimico, Ontario, January 23, 1969

2005–06 DET	82	40	41	81	105
NHL Totals	1,350	598	634	1,232	2,378

Sharp, Patrick b. Thunder Bay, Ontario, December 27, 1981

2005–06 CHI	72	14	17	31	46
NHL Totals	116	19	19	38	103

* traded December 5, 2005, by Philadelphia to Chicago with Eric Meloche for Matt Ellison and a 3rd-round draft choice in 2006

Shelley, Jody b. Thompson, Manitoba, February 7, 1976

2005–06 CBJ	80	3	7	10	163
NHL Totals	277	10	17	27	856

Shields, Steve b. Toronto, Ontario, July 19, 1972

2005–06 ATL	5	1-2-1	266	19	0	4.29
NHL Totals	246	80-104-39	13,631	606	10	2.67

Shishkanov, Timofei b. Moscow, Soviet Union (Russia), June 10, 1983

2005–06 NAS/STL	22	3	2	5	6
NHL Totals	24	3	2	5	6

* traded January 29, 2006, by Nashville to St. Louis for Mike Sillinger

Sigalet, Jordan b. New Westminster, British Columbia, February 19, 1981

2005–06 BOS	1	0-0-0	1	0	0	0.00
NHL Totals	1	0-0-0	1	0	0	0.00

Sillinger, Mike b. Regina, Saskatchewan, June 29, 1971

2005–06 STL/NAS	79	32	31	63	63
NHL Totals	908	198	263	461	570

* traded January 29, 2006, by St. Louis to Nashville for Timofei Shishkanov

Sim, Jon b. New Glasgow, Nova Scotia, September 29, 1977

2005–06 PHI/FLO	72	17	15	32	54
NHL Totals	230	35	33	68	144

* traded January 23, 2006, by Philadelphia to Florida for a 6th-round draft choice in 2007

Simon, Ben b. Shaker Heights, Ohio, June 14, 1978

2005–06 CBJ	13	0	0	0	4
NHL Totals	81	3	1	4	47

Simon, Chris b. Wawa, Ontario, January 30, 1972

2005–06 CAL	72	8	14	22	94
NHL Totals	677	133	142	275	1,690

Simpson, Todd b. North Vancouver, British Columbia, May 28, 1973

2005–06 CHI/MON	51	0	3	3	130
NHL Totals	580	14	63	77	1,357

* traded March 9, 2006, by Chicago to Montreal for a 6th-round draft choice in 2006

Sjostrom, Fredrik b. Fargelanda, Sweden, May 6, 1983

2005–06 PHO	75	6	17	23	42
NHL Totals	132	13	23	36	64

Skolney, Wade b. Wynyard, Saskatchewan, June 24, 1981

2005–06 PHI	1	0	0	0	2
NHL Totals	1	0	0	0	2

Skoula, Martin b. Litomerice, Czechoslovakia (Czech Republic), October 28, 1979

2005–06 DAL/MIN	78	5	16	21	46
NHL Totals	482	34	109	143	246

* traded March 9, 2006, from Dallas to Minnesota with Shawn Belle for Willie Mitchell and a 2nd-round draft choice in 2007

Skrastins, Karlis b. Riga, Soviet Union (Latvia), July 9, 1974

| 2005–06 COL | 82 | 3 | 11 | 14 | 65 |
| NHL Totals | 471 | 21 | 60 | 81 | 221 |

Slater, Jim b. Petoskey, Michigan, December 9, 1982

| 2005–06 ATL | 71 | 10 | 10 | 20 | 46 |
| NHL Totals | 71 | 10 | 10 | 20 | 46 |

Slegr, Jiri b. Jihlava, Czechoslovakia (Czech Republic), May 29, 1971

| 2005–06 BOS | 32 | 5 | 11 | 16 | 56 |
| NHL Totals | 622 | 56 | 193 | 249 | 838 |

Smith, Dan b. Fernie, British Columbia, October 19, 1976

| 2005–06 EDM | 7 | 0 | 0 | 0 | 7 |
| NHL Totals | 22 | 0 | 0 | 0 | 16 |

Smith, Jason b. Calgary, Alberta, November 2, 1973

| 2005–06 EDM | 76 | 4 | 13 | 17 | 84 |
| NHL Totals | 786 | 37 | 110 | 147 | 863 |

Smith, Mark b. Edmonton, Alberta, October 24, 1977

| 2005–06 SJ | 80 | 9 | 15 | 24 | 97 |
| NHL Totals | 282 | 19 | 34 | 53 | 356 |

Smith, Nathan b. Edmonton, Alberta, February 9, 1982

| 2005–06 VAN | 1 | 0 | 0 | 0 | 0 |
| NHL Totals | 3 | 0 | 0 | 0 | 0 |

Smith, Wyatt b. Thief River Falls, Minnesota, February 13, 1977

| 2005–06 NYI | 48 | 0 | 8 | 8 | 26 |
| NHL Totals | 125 | 7 | 16 | 23 | 41 |

Smithson, Jerred b. Vernon, British Columbia, February 4, 1979

2005–06 NAS	66	5	9	14	54
NHL Totals	96	5	12	17	79

Smolinski, Bryan b. Toledo, Ohio, December 27, 1971

2005–06 OTT	81	17	31	48	46
NHL Totals	910	248	334	582	549

Smyth, Ryan b. Banff, Alberta, February 21, 1976

2005–06 EDM	75	36	30	66	58
NHL Totals	717	234	262	496	569

Snow, Garth b. Wrentham, Massachusetts, July 28, 1969

2005–06 NYI	20	4-13-1	1,096	68	0	3.72
NHL Totals	368	135-147-43	19,837	925	16	2.80

Sopel, Brent b. Calgary, Alberta, January 7, 1977

2005–06 NYI/LA	68	2	26	28	70
NHL Totals	370	34	119	153	199

* traded March 8, 2006, by the Islanders to Los Angeles with Mark Parrish for Denis Grebeshkov, Jeff Tambellini, and a conditional 3rd-round draft choice

Souray, Sheldon b. Elk Point, Alberta, July 13, 1976

2005–06 MON	75	12	27	39	116
NHL Totals	425	40	82	122	686

Spacek, Jaroslav b. Rokycany, Czechoslovakia (Czech Republic), February 11, 1974

2005–06 CHI/EDM	76	12	31	43	96
NHL Totals	496	51	154	205	373

* traded January 26, 2006, from Chicago to Edmonton for Tony Salmelainen

Spezza, Jason b. Mississauga, Ontario, June 13, 1983

2005–06 OTT	68	19	71	90	33
NHL Totals	179	48	118	166	112

Spiller, Matthew b. Daysland, Alberta, February 7, 1983

2005–06 PHO	8	0	1	1	13
NHL Totals	59	0	1	1	67

Staal, Eric b. Thunder Bay, Ontario, October 29, 1984

2005–06 CAR	82	45	55	100	81
NHL Totals	163	56	75	131	121

Staios, Steve b. Hamilton, Ontario, July 28, 1973

2005–06 EDM	82	8	20	28	84
NHL Totals	619	41	104	145	860

Stajan, Matt b. Mississauga, Ontario, December 19, 1983

2005–06 TOR	80	15	12	27	50
NHL Totals	150	30	25	55	72

Stastny, Yan b. Quebec City, Quebec, September 30, 1982

2005–06 EDM/BOS	20	1	3	4	10
NHL Totals	20	1	3	4	10

* traded March 9, 2006, from Edmonton to Boston with Marty Reasoner and a 2nd-round draft choice in 2006 for Sergei Samsonov

Steckel, David b. Milwaukee, Wisconsin, March 15, 1982

2005–06 WAS	7	0	0	0	0
NHL Totals	7	0	0	0	0

Steen, Alexander b. Winnipeg, Manitoba, March 1, 1984

2005–06 TOR	75	18	27	45	42
NHL Totals	75	18	27	45	42

Stefan, Patrik b. Pribram, Czechoslovakia (Czech Republic), September 16, 1980

2005–06 ATL	64	10	14	24	36

NHL Totals	414	59	118	177	148

Stempniak, Lee b. Buffalo, New York, February 4, 1983

2005–06 STL	57	14	13	27	22
NHL Totals	57	14	13	27	22

Stevenson, Grant b. Spruce Grove, Alberta, October 15, 1981

2005–06 SJ	47	10	12	22	14
NHL Totals	47	10	12	22	14

* grandson of Hall of Fame goalie Glenn Hall

Stevenson, Jeremy b. San Bernardino, California, July 28, 1974

2005–06 DAL	51	5	3	8	95
NHL Totals	207	19	19	38	451

Stevenson, Turner b. Prince George, British Columbia, May 18, 1972

2005–06 PHI	31	1	3	4	45
NHL Totals	644	75	115	190	969

Stewart, Anthony b. La Salle, Quebec, January 5, 1985

2005–06 FLO	10	2	1	3	2
NHL Totals	10	2	1	3	2

Stewart, Karl b. Scarborough (Toronto), Ontario, June 30, 1983

2005–06 FLO	8	0	0	0	15
NHL Totals	13	0	1	1	19

Stillman, Cory b. Peterborough, Ontario, December 20, 1973

2005–06 CAR	72	21	55	76	32
NHL Totals	717	205	305	510	358

Stoll, Jarret b. Melville, Saskatchewan, June 25, 1982

2005–06 EDM	82	22	46	68	74
NHL Totals	154	32	58	90	116

Straka, Martin b. Plzen, Czechoslovakia (Czech Republic), September 3, 1972

2005–06 NYR	82	22	54	76	42
NHL Totals	812	214	392	606	314

Streit, Mark b. Englisberg, Switzerland, December 11, 1977

2005–06 MON	48	2	9	11	28
NHL Totals	48	2	9	11	28

Strudwick, Jason b. Edmonton, Alberta, July 17, 1975

2005–06 NYR	65	3	4	7	66
NHL Totals	428	10	26	36	636

Stuart, Brad b. Rocky Mountain House, Alberta, November 6, 1979

2005–06 SJ/BOS	78	12	31	43	52
NHL Totals	432	46	138	184	259

* traded November 30, 2005, by San Jose to Boston with Marco Sturm and Wayne Primeau for Joe Thornton

Stuart, Mark b. Rochester, Minnesota, April 27, 1984

2005–06 BOS	17	1	1	2	10
NHL Totals	17	1	1	2	10

Stuart, Mike b. Chicago, Illinois, August 31, 1980

2005–06 STL	1	0	0	0	0
NHL Totals	3	0	0	0	0

Stumpel, Jozef b. Nitra, Czechoslovakia (Slovakia), July 20, 1972

2005–06 FLO	74	15	37	52	26
NHL Totals	832	166	434	600	213

Sturm, Marco b. Dingolfing, West Germany (Germany),
September 8, 1978

2005–06 SJ/BOS	74	29	30	59	48
NHL Totals	604	151	165	316	274

* traded November 30, 2005, by San Jose to Boston with Brad Stuart and
  Wayne Primeau for Joe Thornton

Suchy, Radoslav b. Kezmarok, Czechoslovakia (Slovakia),
April 7, 1976

2005–06 CBJ	79	1	7	8	30
NHL Totals	451	13	58	71	104

Suglobov, Aleksander b. Elektrostal, Soviet Union (Russia),
January 15, 1982

2005–06 NJ/TOR	3	1	0	1	0
NHL Totals	4	1	0	1	0

* traded March 8, 2006, by New Jersey to Toronto for Ken Klee

Sullivan, Steve b. Timmins, Ontario, July 6, 1974

2005–06 NAS	69	31	37	68	50
NHL Totals	606	206	311	517	430

Sundin, Mats b. Bromma, Sweden, February 13, 1971

2005–06 TOR	70	31	47	78	58
NHL Totals	1,156	496	671	1,167	927

Sundstrom, Niklas b. Ornskoldsvik, Sweden, June 6, 1975

2005–06 MON	55	6	9	15	30
NHL Totals	750	117	232	349	256

Surovy, Tomas b. Banska Bystrica, Czechoslovakia (Slovakia),
September 24, 1981

2005–06 PIT	53	12	13	25	45
NHL Totals	126	27	32	59	71

Suter, Ryan b. Madison, Wisconsin, January 21, 1985

2005–06 NAS	71	1	15	16	66
NHL Totals	71	1	15	16	66

Sutherby, Brian b. Edmonton, Alberta, March 1, 1982

2005–06 WAS	76	14	16	30	73
NHL Totals	185	18	25	43	196

Sutton, Andy b. Kingston, Ontario, March 10, 1975

2005–06 ATL	76	8	17	25	144
NHL Totals	377	25	64	89	709

Svatos, Marek b. Kosice, Czechoslovakia (Slovakia), July 17, 1982

2005–06 COL	61	32	18	50	60
NHL Totals	65	34	18	52	60

Svoboda, Jaroslav b. Cervenka, Czechoslovakia (Czech Republic), June 1, 1980

2005–06 DAL	43	4	3	7	22
NHL Totals	134	12	17	29	62

Sydor, Darryl b. Edmonton, Alberta, May 13, 1972

2005–06 TB	80	4	19	23	30
NHL Totals	1,023	89	361	450	660

Sykora, Petr b. Plzen, Czechoslovakia (Czech Republic), November 19, 1976

2005–06 ANA/NYR	74	23	28	51	50
NHL Totals	682	225	287	512	290

* traded January 8, 2006, by Anaheim to the New York Rangers with a 4th-round draft choice for Maxim Kondratiev

Sykora, Petr b. Pardubice, Czechoslovakia (Czech Republic), December 21, 1978

2005–06 WAS	10	2	2	4	6
NHL Totals	12	2	2	4	6

Syvret, Danny b. Millgrove, Ontario, June 13, 1985

2005–06 EDM	10	0	0	0	6
NHL Totals	10	0	0	0	6

Taffe, Jeff b. Hastings, Minnesota, February 19, 1981

2005–06 NYR/PHO	4	0	0	0	0
NHL Totals	83	11	11	22	24

* traded October 18, 2005, by Phoenix to the New York Rangers for Jamie Lundmark
* traded January 24, 2006, by the New York Rangers back to Phoenix for Martin Sonnenberg

Talbot, Maxime b. Lemoyne, Quebec, February 11, 1984

2005–06 PIT	48	5	3	8	59
NHL Totals	48	5	3	8	59

Tallackson, Barry b. Grafton, North Dakota, April 14, 1983

2005–06 NJ	10	1	1	2	2
NHL Totals	10	1	1	2	2

Tallinder, Henrik b. Stockholm, Sweden, January 10, 1979

2005–06 BUF	82	6	15	21	74
NHL Totals	202	10	34	44	128

Tambellini, Jeff b. Calgary, Alberta, April 13, 1984

2005–06 LA/NYI	25	1	3	4	10
NHL Totals	25	1	3	4	10

* traded March 8, 2006, by Los Angeles to the Islanders with Denis Grebeshkov and a conditional 3rd-round draft choice for Mark Parrish and Brent Sopel

Tanabe, David b. White Bear Lake, Minnesota, July 19, 1980

2005–06 PHO/BOS	75	4	16	20	56
NHL Totals	371	24	70	94	193

* traded November 15, 2005, by Phoenix to Boston for Dave Sctachard

Tanguay, Alex b. Ste. Justine, Quebec, November 21, 1979

2005–06 COL	71	29	49	78	46
NHL Totals	450	137	263	400	219

Tarnasky, Nick b. Rocky Mountain House, Alberta, November 25, 1984

2005–06 TB	12	0	1	1	4
NHL Totals	12	0	1	1	4

Tarnstrom, Dick b. Sundbyberg, Sweden, January 20, 1975

2005–06 PIT/EDM	55	6	8	14	76
NHL Totals	258	32	94	126	202

* traded January 26, 2006, by Pittsburgh to Edmonton for Jani Rita and Cory Cross

Taticek, Petr b. Rakovnik, Czechoslovakia (Czech Republic), September 22, 1983

2005–06 FLO	3	0	0	0	0
NHL Totals	3	0	0	0	0

Taylor, Tim b. Stratford, Ontario, February 6, 1969

2005–06 TB	82	7	6	13	22
NHL Totals	675	72	89	161	417

Tellqvist, Mikael b. Sundbyberg, Sweden, September 19, 1979

2005–06 TOR	25	10-11-2	1,398	73	2	3.13
NHL Totals	39	16-15-2	2,131	108	2	3.04

Tenute, Joey b. Hamilton, Ontario, April 2, 1983

2005–06 WAS	1	0	0	0	0
NHL Totals	1	0	0	0	0

Theodore, Jose b. Laval, Quebec, September 13, 1976

2005–06 MON/COL	43	18-18-6	2,410	137	0	3.41
NHL Totals	358	142-161-30	20,348	891	23	2.63

* traded March 8, 2006, by Montreal to Colorado for David Aebischer

Therien, Chris b. Ottawa, Ontario, December 14, 1971

2005–06 PHI	47	0	4	4	34
NHL Totals	764	29	130	159	585

Thibault, Jocelyn b. Montreal, Quebec, January 12, 1975

2005–06 PIT	16	1-9-3	806	60	0	4.46
NHL Totals	552	228-226-68	31,284	1,428	36	2.74

Thomas, Bill b. Pittsburgh, Pennsylvania, June 20, 1983

2005–06 PHO	9	1	2	3	8
NHL Totals	9	1	2	3	8

Thomas, Tim b. Flint, Michigan, April 15, 1974

2005–06 BOS	38	12-13-10	2,186	101	1	2.77
NHL Totals	42	15-14-0	2,406	112	1	2.79

Thorburn, Chris b. Sault Ste. Marie, Ontario, June 3, 1983

2005–06 BUF	2	0	1	1	7
NHL Totals	2	0	1	1	7

Thornton, Joe b. London, Ontario, July 2, 1979

2005–06 BOS/SJ	81	29	96	125	61
NHL Totals	590	189	357	546	672

* traded November 30, 2005, by Boston to San Jose for Marco Sturm,
Brad Stuart, and Wayne Primeau

Thornton, Scott b. London, Ontario, January 9, 1971

2005–06 SJ	71	10	11	21	84
NHL Totals	838	132	132	264	1,335

Thornton, Shawn b. Oshawa, Ontario, July 23, 1977

2005–06 CHI	10	0	0	0	16
NHL Totals	31	2	1	3	70

Timonen, Kimmo b. Kuopio, Finland, March 18, 1975

2005–06 NAS	79	11	39	50	74
NHL Totals	493	66	180	246	306

Tjarnqvist, Daniel b. Umea, Sweden, October 14, 1976

2005–06 MIN	60	3	15	18	32
NHL Totals	278	13	58	71	92

Tjarnqvist, Mathias b. Umea, Sweden, April 15, 1979

2005–06 DAL	33	2	4	6	18
NHL Totals	51	3	5	8	20

Tkachuk, Keith b. Melrose, Massachusetts, March 28, 1972

2005–06 STL	41	15	21	36	46
NHL Totals	897	446	422	868	1,907

Toivonen, Hannu b. Kalvola, Finland, May 18, 1984

2005–06 BOS	20	9-5-4	1,162	51	1	2.63
NHL Totals	20	9-5-4	1,162	51	1	2.63

Tollefsen, Ole-Kristian b. Oslo, Norway, March 29, 1984

2005–06 CBJ		5	0	0	0	2
NHL Totals	5	0	0	0	2

Tootoo, Jordin b. Churchill, Manitoba, February 2, 1983

2005–06 NAS	34	4	6	10	55
NHL Totals	104	8	10	18	192

Torres, Raffi b. Toronto, Ontario, October 8, 1981

2005–06 EDM	82	27	14	41	50
NHL Totals	193	47	34	81	131

Toskala, Vesa b. Tampere, Finland, May 20, 1977

2005–06 SJ	37	23-7-4	2,039	87	2	2.56
NHL Totals	77	39-18-5	4,126	161	4	2.34

Traverse, Patrick b. Montreal, Quebec, March 14, 1974

2005–06 DAL	1	0	0	0	0
NHL Totals	279	14	51	65	113

Tucker, Darcy b. Castor, Alberta, March 15, 1975

2005–06 TOR	74	28	33	61	100
NHL Totals	683	155	204	359	1,115

Turco, Marty b. Sault Ste. Marie, Ontario, August 13, 1975

2005–06 DAL	68	41-19-5	3,910	166	3	2.55
NHL Totals	253	137-62-26	14,256	495	24	2.08

Turgeon, Pierre b. Rouyn, Quebec, August 28, 1969

2005–06 COL	62	16	30	46	32
NHL Totals	1,277	511	809	1,320	442

Tverdovsky, Oleg b. Donetsk, Soviet Union (Ukraine), May 18, 1976

2005–06 CAR	72	3	20	23	37
NHL Totals	687	77	236	313	281

Tyutin, Fedor b. Izhevsk, Soviet Union (Russia), July 19, 1983

2005–06 NYR	77	6	19	25	58
NHL Totals	102	8	24	32	72

Ulanov, Igor b. Krasnokamsk, Soviet Union (Russia), October 1, 1969

2005–06 EDM	37	3	6	9	29
NHL Totals	739	27	135	162	1,151

Umberger, R.J. b. Pittsburgh, Pennsylvania, May 3, 1982

2005–06 PHI	73	20	18	38	18
NHL Totals	73	20	18	38	18

Upshall, Scottie b. Fort McMurray, Alberta, October 7, 1983

2005–06 NAS	48	8	16	24	34
NHL Totals	63	9	17	26	34

Vaananen, Ossi b. Vantaa, Finland, August 18, 1980

2005–06 COL	53	0	4	4	56
NHL Totals	356	10	39	49	391

Vandenbussche, Ryan b. Simcoe, Ontario, February 28, 1973

2005–06 PIT	20	1	0	1	42
NHL Totals	310	10	10	20	702

Vandermeer, Jim b. Caroline, Alberta, February 21, 1980

2005–06 CHI	76	6	18	24	116
NHL Totals	146	13	31	44	226

Vanek, Thomas b. Vienna, Austria, January 19, 1984

2005–06 BUF	81	25	23	48	72
NHL Totals	81	25	23	48	72

Van Ryn, Mike b. London, Ontario, May 14, 1979

2005–06 FLO	80	8	29	37	90
NHL Totals	228	23	64	87	168

Varada, Vaclav b. Vsetin, Czechoslovakia (Czech Republic), April 26, 1976

2005–06 OTT	76	5	16	21	50
NHL Totals	493	58	125	183	410

Vasicek, Josef b. Havlickuv Brod, Czechoslovakia (Czech Republic), September 12, 1980

2005–06 CAR	23	4	5	9	8
NHL Totals	316	55	71	126	207

Veilleux, Stephane b. Beauceville, Quebec, November 16, 1981

2005–06 MIN	71	7	9	16	63
NHL Totals	128	12	19	31	106

Vermette, Antoine b. St. Agapit, Quebec, July 20, 1982

2005–06 OTT	82	21	12	33	44
NHL Totals	139	28	19	47	60

Vigier, J-P b. Notre Dame de Lourdes, Manitoba, September 11, 1976

2005–06 ATL	41	4	6	10	40
NHL Totals	141	18	15	33	70

Vishnevski, Vitali b. Kharkov, Soviet Union (Ukraine), March 18, 1980

2005–06 ANA	82	1	7	8	91
NHL Totals	416	11	37	48	403

Visnovsky, Lubomir b. Topolcany, Czechoslovakia (Slovakia), August 11, 1976

2005–06 LA	80	17	50	67	50
NHL Totals	348	44	136	180	154

Vokoun, Tomas b. Karlovy Vary, Czechoslovakia (Czech Republic), July 2, 1976

2005–06 NAS	61	36-18-7	3,600	160	4	2.67
NHL Totals	340	134-147-35	19,207	822	16	2.57

Volchenkov, Anton b. Moscow, Soviet Union (Russia), February 25, 1982

2005–06 OTT	75	4	13	17	53
NHL Totals	151	8	28	36	101

Vorobiev, Pavel b. Karaganda, Soviet Union (Kazakhstan), May 5, 1982

2005–06 CHI	39	9	12	21	34
NHL Totals	57	10	15	25	38

Vrbata, Radim b. Mlada Boleslav, Czechoslovakia (Czech Republic), June 13, 1981

2005–06 CHI	61	15	24	39	22
NHL Totals	269	61	68	129	78

* traded December 30, 2005, by Carolina to Chicago for future considerations

Vyborny, David b. Jihlava, Czechoslovakia (Czech Republic), June 2, 1975

2005–06 CBJ	80	22	43	65	50
NHL Totals	395	90	137	227	134

Walker, Matt b. Beaverlodge, Alberta, April 7, 1980

2005–06 STL	54	0	2	2	79
NHL Totals	84	0	4	4	142

Walker, Scott b. Cambridge, Ontario, July 19, 1973

2005–06 NAS	33	5	11	16	36
NHL Totals	607	106	185	291	931

Wallin, Niclas b. Boden, Sweden, February 20, 1975

2005–06 CAR	50	4	4	8	42	
NHL Totals	273	12	24	36	221	

Walter, Ben b. Beaconsfield, Quebec, May 11, 1984

2005–06 BOS	6	0	0	0	4	
NHL Totals	6	0	0	0	4	

Walz, Wes b. Calgary, Alberta, May 15, 1970

2005–06 MIN	82	19	18	37	61	
NHL Totals	534	99	133	232	307	

Wanvig, Kyle b. Calgary Alberta, January 29, 1981

2005–06 MIN	51	4	8	12	64	
NHL Totals	64	5	9	14	87	

Ward, Aaron b. Windsor, Ontario, January 17, 1973

2005–06 CAR	71	6	19	25	62	
NHL Totals	552	31	68	99	501	

Ward, Cam b. Sherwood Park, Alberta, February 29, 1984

2005–06 CAR	28	14-8-2	1,484	91	0	3.68
NHL Totals	28	14-8-2	1,484	91	0	3.68

Ward, Jason b. Chapleau, Ontario, January 16, 1979

2005–06 NYR	81	10	18	28	44	
NHL Totals	186	20	28	48	87	

Warrener, Rhett b. Shaunavon, Saskatchewan, January 27, 1976

2005–06 CAL	61	3	3	6	54	
NHL Totals	621	19	73	92	811	

Weaver, Mike b. Bramalea, Ontario, May 2, 1978

2005–06 LA	53	0	9	9	14
NHL Totals	110	0	15	15	44

Weber, Shea b. Sicamous, British Columbia, August 14, 1985

2005–06 NAS	28	2	8	10	42
NHL Totals	28	2	8	10	42

Weekes, Kevin b. Toronto, Ontario, April 4, 1975

2005–06 NYR	32	14-14-3	1,850	91	0	2.95
NHL Totals	309	92-150-33	16,937	811	19	2.87

Weight, Doug b. Warren, Michigan, January 21, 1971

2005–06 STL/CAR	70	15	42	57	75
NHL Totals	982	239	646	885	809

* traded January 30, 2006, by St. Louis to Carolina with Erkki Rajamaki for Jesse Boulerice, Mike Zigomanis, the rights to Magnus Kahnberg, and a 1st- and 4th-round draft choice in 2006

Weinhandl, Mattias b. Ljungby, Sweden, June 1, 1980

2005–06 MIN	68	4	7	11	24
NHL Totals	170	18	36	54	60

Weinrich, Eric b. Roanoke, Virginia, December 19, 1966

2005–06 STL/VAN	75	1	16	17	52
NHL Totals	1,157	70	318	388	825

* traded March 9, 2006, from St. Louis to Vancouver for Tomas Mojzis and a 3rd-round draft choice in 2006

Weiss, Stephen b. Toronto, Ontario, April 3, 1983

2005–06 FLO	41	9	12	21	22
NHL Totals	175	28	45	73	49

Welch, Noah b. Brighton, Massachusetts, August 26, 1982

2005–06 PIT	5	1	3	4	2
NHL Totals	5	1	3	4	2

Wellwood, Kyle b. Windsor, Ontario, May 16, 1983

2005–06 TOR	81	11	34	45	14
NHL Totals	82	11	34	45	14

Wesley, Glen b. Red Deer, Alberta, October 2, 1968

2005–06 CAR	64	2	8	10	46
NHL Totals	1,311	126	390	516	937

Westcott, Duvie b. Winnipeg, Manitoba, October 30, 1977

2005–06 CBJ	78	6	22	28	133
NHL Totals	155	6	36	42	251

Westrum, Erik b. Minneapolis, Minnesota, July 26, 1979

2005–06 MIN	10	0	1	1	2
NHL Totals	25	1	2	3	22

White, Colin b. New Glasgow, Nova Scotia, December 12, 1977

2005–06 NJ	73	3	14	17	91
NHL Totals	396	15	56	71	613

White, Ian b. Winnipeg, Manitoba, June 4, 1984

2005–06 TOR	12	1	5	6	10
NHL Totals	12	1	5	6	10

White, Todd b. Kanata, Ontario, May 21, 1975

2005–06 MIN	61	19	21	40	18
NHL Totals	337	84	115	199	118

Whitfield, Trent b. Estevan, Saskatchewan, June 17, 1977

2005–06 STL	30	2	5	7	14
NHL Totals	174	11	16	27	97

Whitney, Ray b. Fort Saskatchewan, Alberta, May 8, 1972

2005–06 CAR	63	17	38	55	42
NHL Totals	763	222	368	590	261

Whitney, Ryan b. Boston, Massachusetts, February 19, 1983

2005–06 PIT	68	6	32	38	85
NHL Totals	68	6	32	38	85

Wideman, Dennis b. Kitchener, Ontario, March 20, 1983

2005–06 STL	67	8	16	24	83
NHL Totals	67	8	16	24	83

Wiemer, Jason b. Kimberley, British Columbia, April 14, 1976

2005–06 CAL/NJ	49	2	2	4	103
NHL Totals	726	90	112	202	1,420

* traded March 9, 2006, by Calgary to New Jersey for a 4th-round draft
choice in 2006

Williams, Jason b. London, Ontario, August 11, 1980

2005–06 DET	80	21	37	58	26
NHL Totals	175	38	52	90	49

Williams, Jeremy b. Regina, Saskatchewan, January 26, 1984

2005–06 TOR	1	1	0	1	0
NHL Totals	1	1	0	1	0

Williams, Justin b. Cobourg, Ontario, October 4, 1981

2005–06 CAR	82	31	45	76	60
NHL Totals	340	79	130	209	200

Willsie, Brian b. London, Ontario, March 16, 1978

2005–06 WAS	82	19	22	41	77
NHL Totals	200	36	35	71	124

Wilm, Clarke b. Central Butte, Saskatchewan, October 24, 1976

2005–06 TOR	60	1	7	8	43
NHL Totals	455	37	60	97	336

Winchester, Brad b. Madison, Wisconsin, March 1, 1981

2005–06 EDM	19	0	1	1	21
NHL Totals	19	0	1	1	21

Wiseman, Chad b. Burlington, Ontario, March 25, 1981

2005–06 NYR	1	0	1	1	4
NHL Totals	9	1	1	2	8

Wisniewski, James b. Canton, Michigan, February 21, 1984

2005–06 CHI	19	2	5	7	36
NHL Totals	19	2	5	7	36

Witt, Brendan b. Humboldt, Saskatchewan, February 20, 1975

2005–06 WAS/NAS	75	1	13	14	209
NHL Totals	643	20	66	86	1,103

* traded March 9, 2006, from Washington to Nashville for Kris Beech and a 1st-round draft choice in 2006

Wolski, Wojtek b. Zabrze, Poland, February 24, 1986

2005–06 COL	9	2	4	6	4
NHL Totals	9	2	4	6	4

Woolley, Jason b. Toronto, Ontario, July 27, 1969

2005–06 DET	53	1	18	19	28
NHL Totals	718	68	246	314	430

Woywitka, Jeff b. Vermilion, Alberta, September 1, 1983

2005–06 STL	26	0	2	2	25
NHL Totals	26	0	2	2	25

Wozniewski, Andy b. Buffalo Grove, Illinois, May 25, 1980

2005–06 TOR	13	0	1	1	13
NHL Totals	13	0	1	1	13

Wright, Tyler b. Kamsack, Saskatchewan, April 6, 1973

2005–06 CBJ/ANA	43	2	6	8	51
NHL Totals	613	79	70	149	854

* traded November 15, 2005, by Columbus to Anaheim with
Francois Beauchemin for Sergei Fedorov and a 5ᵗʰ-round draft choice
in 2006

Yakubov, Mikhail b. Barnaul, Soviet Union (Russia),
February 16, 1982

2005–06 FLO	23	1	3	4	12
NHL Totals	53	2	10	12	20

Yashin, Alexei b. Sverdlovsk, Soviet Union (Russia),
November 5, 1973

2005–06 NYI	82	28	38	66	68
NHL Totals	792	319	412	731	357

Yelle, Stephane b. Ottawa, Ontario, May 9, 1974

2005–06 CAL	74	4	14	18	48
NHL Totals	714	72	131	203	374

Yonkman, Nolan b. Punnichy, Saskatchewan, April 1, 1981

2005–06 WAS	38	0	7	7	86
NHL Totals	50	1	7	8	90

York, Mike b. Waterford, Michigan, January 3, 1978

2005–06 NYI	75	13	39	52	30
NHL Totals	449	111	176	287	109

Young, Scott b. Clinton, Massachusetts, October 1, 1967

2005–06 STL	79	18	31	49	52
NHL Totals	1,181	342	415	757	448

Yzerman, Steve b. Cranbrook, British Columbia, May 9, 1965

2005–06 DET	61	14	20	34	18
NHL Totals	1,514	692	1,063	1,755	924

Zanon, Greg b. Burnaby, British Columbia, June 5, 1980

2005–06 NAS	4	0	2	2	6
NHL Totals	4	0	2	2	6

Zednik, Richard b. Bystrica, Czechoslovakia (Slovakia), January 6, 1976

2005–06 MON	67	16	14	30	48
NHL Totals	579	161	138	299	456

Zetterberg, Henrik b. Njurunda, Sweden, October 9, 1980

2005–06 DET	77	39	46	85	30
NHL Totals	217	76	96	172	52

Zhamnov, Alexei b. Moscow, Soviet Union (Russia), October 1, 1970

2005–06 BOS	24	1	9	10	30
NHL Totals	807	249	470	719	668

Zherdev, Nikolai b. Kiev, Soviet Union (Ukraine), November 5, 1984

2005–06 CBJ	73	27	27	54	50
NHL Totals	130	40	48	88	104

Zhitnik, Alexei b. Kiev, Soviet Union (Ukraine), October 10, 1972

2005–06 NYI	59	5	24	29	88
NHL Totals	941	86	339	425	1,118

Zidlicky, Marek b. Most, Czechoslovakia (Czech Republic), February 3, 1977

2005–06 NAS	67	12	37	49	82
NHL Totals	149	26	76	102	164

Zigomanis, Mike b. North York (Toronto), Ontario, January 17, 1981

2005–06 CAR/STL	23	1	0	1	4
NHL Totals	59	3	4	7	6

* traded January 30, 2006, by Carolina to St. Louis with Jesse Boulerice, the rights to Magnus Kahnberg, and a 1st- and 4th-round draft choice in 2006 for Doug Weight and Erkki Rajamaki

Zubov, Sergei b. Moscow, Soviet Union (Russia), July 22, 1970

2005–06 DAL	78	13	58	71	46
NHL Totals	934	136	542	678	299

Zubrus, Dainius b. Eelektrenai, Soviet Union (Lithuania), June 16, 1978

2005–06 WAS	71	23	34	57	84
NHL Totals	610	114	186	300	387

Zyuzin, Andrei b. Ufa, Soviet Union (Russia), January 21, 1978

2005–06 MIN	57	7	11	18	50
NHL Totals	415	35	74	109	378

COACHES REGISTER, REGULAR SEASON, 2005–06

G/W/L/T (OTL are listed in L column)

Babcock, Mike b. Manitouwadge, Ontario, April 29, 1963

2005–06 DET	82	58	16	8
NHL Totals	246	127	92	27

* hired July 14, 2005

Carlyle, Randy b. Sudbury, Ontario, April 19, 1956

2005–06 ANA	82	43	27	12
NHL Totals	82	43	27	12

* hired August 1, 2005

Crawford, Marc b. Belleville, Ontario, February 13, 1961

2005–06 VAN	82	42	32	8
NHL Totals	823	411	301	111

* hired January 24, 1999; fired April 25, 2006

Gainey, Bob b. Peterborough, Ontario, December 13, 1953

2005–06 MON	41	23	15	3
NHL Totals	456	188	205	63

* fired Claude Julien on January 14, 2006, and took over as head coach for remainder of season
* hired Guy Carbonneau as coach for 2006–07 after end of season

Gallant, Gerard b. Summerside, Prince Edward Island, September 2, 1963

2005–06 CBJ	82	35	43	4
NHL Totals	127	51	68	8

* hired January 1, 2004

Gretzky, Wayne b. Brantford, Ontario, January 26, 1961

2005–06 PHO	82	38	39	5
NHL Totals	82	38	39	5

* assumed coaching duties on August 8, 2005

Hanlon, Glen b. Brandon, Manitoba, February 20, 1957

2005–06 WAS	82	29	41	12
NHL Totals	136	44	71	21

* hired December 10, 2003 to replace Bruce Cassidy

Hartley, Bob b. Hawkesbury, Ontario, September 7, 1960

2005–06 ATL	82	41	33	8
NHL Totals	562	286	207	69

* hired January 14, 2003

Hitchcock, Ken b. Edmonton, Alberta, December 17, 1951

2005–06 PHI	82	45	26	11
NHL Totals	749	407	243	99

* hired May 14, 2002

Julien, Claude b. Blind River, Ontario, April 23, 1960

2005–06 MON	41	19	16	6
NHL Totals	159	72	71	16

* hired January 17, 2003; fired January 14, 2006

Kitchen, Mike b. Newmarket, Ontario, February 1, 1956

2005–06 STL	82	21	46	15
NHL Totals	103	31	53	19

* hired February 24, 2004, to replace Joel Quenneville on an interim basis

Lamoriello, Lou b. Providence, Rhode Island, October 21, 1942

2005–06 NJ	50	32	14	4
NHL Totals	50	32	14	4

* took over for Larry Robinson on December 18, 2005

Laviolette, Peter b. Norwood, Massachusetts, December 7, 1964

2005–06 CAR	82	52	22	8
NHL Totals	298	149	116	33

* hired December 15, 2003, to replace Paul Maurice

Lemaire, Jacques b. La Salle, Quebec, September 7, 1945

2005–06 MIN	82	38	36	8
NHL Totals	885	408	345	132

* hired June 19, 2000

MacTavish, Craig b. London, Ontario, August 15, 1958

2005–06 EDM	82	41	28	13
NHL Totals	410	190	160	60

* hired June 22, 2000

Martin, Jacques b. Bowmanville, Ontario, October 21, 1949

2005–06 FLO	82	37	34	11
NHL Totals	934	444	360	130

* hired May 26, 2004

Murray, Andy b. Gladstone, Manitoba, March 3, 1951

2005–06 LA	70	37	28	5
NHL Totals	480	215	202	63

* hired June 14, 1999; fired March 21, 2006

Murray, Bryan b. Shawville, Quebec, December 5, 1942

2005–06 OTT	82	52	21	9
NHL Totals	1,139	565	434	140

* hired June 8, 2004

Olczyk, Ed b. Chicago, Illinois, August 16, 1966

2005–06 PIT	31	8	19	4
NHL Totals	113	31	70	12

* hired June 11, 2003; fired December 15, 2005

Quenneville, Joel b. Windsor, Ontario, September 15, 1958

2005–06 COL	82	43	30	9
NHL Totals	675	350	239	86

* hired July 7, 2004

Quinn, Pat b. Hamilton, Ontario, January 29, 1943

2005–06 TOR	82	41	33	8
NHL Totals	1,318	657	499	162

* hired June 26, 1998; fired April 20, 2006

Renney, Tom b. Cranbrook, British Columbia, January 3, 1955

2005–06 NYR	82	44	26	12
NHL Totals	203	88	94	21

* hired February 25, 2004, to replace Glen Sather on an interim basis

Robinson, Larry b. Winchester, Ontario, June 2, 1951

2005–06 NJ	32	14	13	5
NHL Totals	501	209	223	69

* hired July 14, 2005; stepped down December 18, 2005

Ruff, Lindy b. Warburg, Alberta, February 17, 1960

2005–06 BUF	82	52	24	6
NHL Totals	656	305	267	84

* hired July 21, 1997

Shaw, Brad b. Cambridge, Ontario, April 28, 1964

2005–06 NYI	40	18	18	4
NHL Totals	40	18	18	4

* hired January 13, 2006

Stirling, Steve b. Clarkson, Ontario, November 19, 1949

2005–06 NYI	42	18	22	2
NHL Totals	124	56	55	13

* hired June 3, 2003; fired January 12, 2006

Sullivan, Mike b. Marshfield, Massachusetts, February 27, 1968

2005–06 BOS	82	29	37	16
NHL Totals	164	70	63	31

* hired June 23, 2003

Sutter, Darryl b. Viking, Alberta, August 19, 1958

2005–06 CAL	82	46	25	11
NHL Totals	860	409	339	112

* hired December 28, 2002

Therrien, Michel b. Montreal, Quebec, November 4, 1963

2005–06 PIT	51	14	27	10
NHL Totals	241	91	118	32

* named head coach on December 15, 2005

Tippett, Dave b. Moosomin, Saskatchewan, August 25, 1961

2005–06 DAL	82	53	23	6
NHL Totals	246	140	72	34

* hired May 16, 2002

Torchetti, John b. Boston, Massachusetts, 1964

2005–06 LA	12	5	7	0
NHL Totals	12	5	7	0

* hired March 22, 2006

Tortorella, John b. Boston, Massachusetts, June 24, 1958

2005–06 TB	82	43	33	6
NHL Totals	375	164	168	43

* hired January 6, 2001

Trotz, Barry b. Winnipeg, Manitoba, July 15, 1962

2003–04 NAS	82	49	25	8
NHL Totals	574	232	274	68

* hired August 6, 1997, a year before the Predators played their first NHL game

Wilson, Ron b. Windsor, Ontario, May 28, 1955

2005–06 SJ	82	44	27	11
NHL Totals	927	418	397	112

* hired December 4, 2003

Yawney, Trent b. Hudson Bay, Saskatchewan, September 29, 1965

2005–06 CHI	82	26	43	13
NHL Totals	82	26	43	13

* hired July 7, 2005

2006 NHL ENTRY DRAFT

Vancouver, June 24, 2006

Draft Day Trades

* Atlanta trades Patrik Stefan and Jaroslav Modry to Dallas for Niko Kapanen and a 7th-round draft choice (Will O'Neill)
* Atlanta trades 3rd-round draft choice (Theo Peckham) to Edmonton for a 3rd-round (Michael Forney) and 7th-round draft choice (Arturs Kulda)
* Boston trades 4th-round draft choice (James Delory) and 5th-round draft choice (Shane Sims) to NY Islanders for 3rd-round draft choice (Brad Marchand)
* Calgary trades Jordan Leopold, a 2nd-round draft choice in 2006 (Codey Burki), and a 2nd-round draft choice in 2007 or 2008 to Colorado for Alex Tanguay
* Chicago trades two 4th-round draft choices to Toronto (99th overall, James Reimer and 111th overall, Korbinian Holzer) for a 3rd-round draft choice (Tony Lagerstrom)
* Colorado trades 5th-round draft choice (Kim Johansson) and 6th-round draft choice (Brian Day) to NY Islanders for 4th-round draft choice (Kevin Montgomery)
* Columbus trades 2nd-round draft choice to San Jose (Jamie McGinn) for a 3rd-round (Tommy Sestito) and 4th-round draft choice (Ben Wright) in 2006 and a 2nd-round draft choice in 2007
* Florida trades Roberto Luongo, Lukas Krajicek, and a 6th-round draft choice in 2006 (Sergei Shirokov) to Vancouver for Alex Auld, Todd Bertuzzi, and Bryan Allen (June 23)
* Los Angeles trades Pavol Demitra to Minnesota for Patrick O'Sullivan and a 1st-round draft choice in 2006 (Trevor Lewis)
* New Jersey trades 1st-round draft choice (Patrik Berglund) to St. Louis for 1st-round draft choice (Matthew Corrente) and 3rd-round draft choice (Vladimir Zharkov)

* NY Rangers trade 4th-round (Niclas Andersen) and 5th-round draft choice (Martin Nolet) to Los Angeles for 4th-round draft choice (David Kveton)
* Phoenix trades two 2nd-round draft choices (41st overall, Cory Emmerton and 47th overall, Shawn Matthias) selection to Detroit for 1st-round draft choice (Chris Summers) and 5th-round draft choice (Jordan Bendfeld)
* Phoenix trades two 4th-round draft choices (115th overall, Tomas Marcinko and 119th overall, Doug Rogers), to NY Islanders for a 3rd-round draft choice (88th overall, Jonas Ahnelov)
* Phoenix trades 6th-round draft choice (161st overall, Viktor Stahlberg) to Toronto for two 7th-round draft choices (188th overall, Chris Frank and 196th overall, Benn Ferriero)
* San Jose trades 4th-round draft choice (Jase Weslosky) and 6th-round draft choice (Stefan Ridderwal) to NY Islanders for a 4th-round draft choice (James Delory)
* San Jose trades 1st-round draft choice (David Fischer) and 2nd-round draft choice (Mathieu Carle) to Montreal for 1st-round draft choice (Ty Wishart)
* St. Louis trades 1st-round draft choice (Matthew Corrente) and 3rd-round draft choice (Vladimir Zharkov) to New Jersey for 1st-round draft choice (Patrik Berglund)
* Toronto trades Tuukka Rask to Boston for Andrew Raycroft
* Washington trades 5th-round draft choice in 2006 to Vancouver for 4th-round draft choice in 2007; Vancouver trades 5th-round draft choice in 2006 (Tomas Zaborsky) to NY Rangers for 4th-round draft choice in 2007

The Draft

First Round

1. Erik Johnson (USA)—St. Louis
2. Jordan Staal (CAN)—Pittsburgh
3. Jonathan Toews (CAN)—Chicago
4. Nicklas Backstrom (SWE)—Washington
5. Phil Kessel (USA)—Boston
6. Derrick Brassard (CAN)—Columbus
7. Kyle Okposo (USA)—NY Islanders
8. Peter Mueller (USA)—Phoenix
9. James Sheppard (CAN)—Minnesota
10. Michael Frolik (CZE)—Florida
11. Jonathan Bernier (CAN)—Los Angeles
12. Bryan Little (CAN)—Atlanta
13. Jiri Tlusty (CZE)—Toronto
14. Michael Grabner (AUT)—Vancouver
15. Riku Helenius (FIN)—Tampa Bay
16. Ty Wishart (CAN)—San Jose (from Montreal)
17. Trevor Lewis (USA)—Los Angeles (from Edmonton-Minnesota)
18. Chris Stewart (CAN)—Colorado
19. Mark Mitera (USA)—Anaheim
20. David Fischer (USA)—Montreal (from San Jose)
21. Bobby Sanguinetti (USA)—NY Rangers
22. Claude Giroux (CAN)—Philadelphia
23. Semen Varlamov (RUS)—Washington (from Nashville)
24. Dennis Person (SWE)—Buffalo
25. Patrik Berglund (SWE)—St. Louis (from New Jersey)
26. Leland Irving (CAN)—Calgary
27. Ivan Vishnevsky (RUS)—Dallas
28. Nick Foligno (USA)—Ottawa
29. Chris Summers (USA)—Phoenix (from Detroit)
30. Matthew Corrente (CAN)—New Jersey (from Carolina-St. Louis)

Second Round

31. Tomas Kana (CZE)—St. Louis
32. Carl Sneep (USA)—Pittsburgh
33. Igor Makarov (RUS)—Chicago
34. Michal Neuvirth (CZE)—Washington
35. Francois Bouchard (CAN)—Washington (from Boston)
36. Jamie McGinn (CAN)—San Jose (from Columbus)
37. Yuri Alexandrov (RUS)—Boston
38. Bryce Swan (CAN)—Anaheim (from NY Islanders)
39. Andreas Nodl (AUT)—Philadelphia (from Phoenix)
40. Ondrej Fiala (CZE)—Minnesota
41. Cory Emmerton (CAN)—Detroit (from Philadelphia-Florida)
42. Michael Ratchuk (USA)—Philadelphia (from Los Angeles)
43. Riley Holzapfel (CAN)—Atlanta
44. Nikolai Kulemin (RUS)—Toronto
45. Jeff Petry (USA)—Edmonton
46. Jhonas Enroth (SWE)—Buffalo (from Vancouver)
47. Shawn Matthias (CAN)—Detroit (from Philadelphia-Tampa Bay-Phoenix)
48. Joe Ryan (USA)—Los Angeles
49. Ben Maxwell (CAN)—Montreal
50. Milan Lucic (CAN)—Boston (from Edmonton)
51. Nigel Williams (USA)—Colorado
52. Keith Seabrook (CAN)—Washington (from Anaheim)
53. Mathieu Carle (CAN)—Montreal (from San Jose)
54. Artem Anisimov (RUS)—NY Rangers
55. Denis Bodrov (RUS)—Philadelphia
56. Blake Geoffrion (USA)—Nashville
57. Mike Weber (USA)—Buffalo
58. Alexander Vasyunov (RUS)—New Jersey
59. Codey Burki (CAN)—Colorado (from Calgary)
60. Jesse Joensuu (FIN)—NY Islanders (from Dallas)
61. Simon Danis-Pepin (CAN)—Chicago (from Ottawa)

62. Dick Axelsson (SWE)—Detroit
63. Jamie McBain (USA)—Carolina

Third Round

64. Jonas Junland (SWE)—St. Louis
65. Brian Strait (USA)—Pittsburgh
66. Ryan White (CAN)—Montreal (from Chicago-Philadelphia)
67. Kirill Tulupov (RUS)—New Jersey (from Washington)
68. Eric Gryba (CAN)—Ottawa (from Boston)
69. Steve Mason (CAN)—Columbus
70. Robin Figren (SWE)—NY Islanders
71. Brad Marchand (CAN)—Boston (from Phoenix-NY Islanders)
72. Cal Clutterbuck (CAN)—Minnesota
73. Brady Calla (CAN)—Florida
74. Jeff Zatkoff (USA)—Los Angeles
75. Theo Peckham (CAN)—Edmonton (from Atlanta)
76. Tony Lagerstrom (SWE)—Chicago (from Toronto)
77. Vladimir Zharkov (RUS)—New Jersey (from Vancouver-St. Louis)
78. Kevin Quick (USA)—Tampa Bay
79. Jonathan Matsumoto (CAN)—Philadelphia (from Montreal)
80. Michael Forney (USA)—Atlanta (from Edmonton)
81. Michael Carman (USA)—Colorado
82. Daniel Rahimi (SWE)—Vancouver (from Anaheim)
83. John DeGray (CAN)—Anaheim (from NY Rangers-San Jose)
84. Ryan Hillier (CAN)—NY Rangers
85. Tommy Sestito (USA)—Columbus (from Philadelphia-San Jose)
86. Bud Holloway (CAN)—Los Angeles (from Philadelphia-Nashville)
87. John Armstrong (CAN)—Calgary (from Buffalo)
88. Jonas Ahnelov (SWE)—Phoenix (from New Jersey-NY Islanders)

89. Aaron Marvin (USA)—Calgary
90. Aaron Snow (CAN)—Dallas
91. Kaspars Daugavins (LAT)—Ottawa
92. Daniel Larsson (SWE)—Detroit
93. Harrison Reed (CAN)—Carolina

Fourth Round

94. Ryan Turek (USA)—St. Louis
95. Ben Shutron (CAN)—Chicago (from Pittsburgh)
96. Joseph Palmer (USA)—Chicago
97. Oskar Osala (FIN)—Washington
98. James Delory (CAN)—San Jose (from Boston)
99. James Reimer (CAN)—Toronto (from Carolina-Columbus-Chicago)
100. Rhett Rakhshani (USA)—NY Islanders
101. Joonas Lehtivuori (FIN)—Philadelphia
102. Kyle Medvec (USA)—Minnesota
103. Michael Caruso (CAN)—Florida
104. David Kveton (CZE)—NY Rangers (from Los Angeles)
105. Niko Snellman (FIN)—Nashville (from Atlanta)
106. Reto Berra (SUI)—St. Louis (from Carolina-Toronto)
107. T.J. Miller (USA)—New Jersey (from Vancouver)
108. Jase Weslosky (CAN)—NY Islanders (from Tampa Bay-San Jose)
109. Jakub Kovar (CZE)—Philadelphia (from Montreal)
110. Kevin Montgomery (USA)—Colorado (from Edmonton)
111. Korbinian Holzer (GER)—Toronto (from Colorado)
112. Matt Beleskey (CAN)—Anaheim
113. Ben Wright (CAN)—Columbus (from San Jose)
114. Niclas Andersen (SWE)—Los Angeles (from NY Rangers)
115. Tomas Marcinko (SVK)—NY Islanders (from Philadelphia-Phoenix)
116. Derrick Lapoint (USA)—Florida (from Nashville-Pittsburgh)
117. Felix Schutz (GER)—Buffalo

118. Hugo Carpenter (CAN)—Calgary (from New Jersey)
119. Doug Rogers (USA)—NY Islanders (from Calgary-Phoenix)
120. Richard Bachman (USA)—Dallas
121. Pierre-Luc Lessard (CAN)—Ottawa
122. Luke Lynes (USA)—Washington (from Detroit)
123. Bobby Hughes (CAN)—Carolina

Fifth Round

124. Andy Sackrison (USA)—St. Louis
125. Chad Johnson (CAN)—Pittsburgh
126. Shane Sims (USA)—NY Islanders (from Chicago-Boston)
127. Maxime Lacroix (CAN)—Washington
128. Andrew Bodnarchuk (CAN)—Boston
129. Robert Nyholm (FIN)—Columbus
130. Brett Bennett (USA)—Phoenix (from NY Islanders)
131. Martin Latal (CZE)—Phoenix
132. Niko Hovinen (FIN)—Minnesota
133. Bryan Pitton (CAN)—Edmonton (from Florida)
134. David Meckler (USA)—Los Angeles
135. Alex Kangas (USA)—Atlanta
136. Nick Sucharski (CAN)—Columbus (from Toronto)
137. Tomas Zaborsky (SVK)—NY Rangers (from Vancouver)
138. David McIntyre (CAN)—Dallas (from Tampa Bay)
139. Pavel Valentenko (RUS)—Montreal
140. Cody Wild (USA)—Edmonton
141. Kim Johansson (SWE)—NY Islanders (from Colorado)
142. Maxime Frechette (CAN)—Columbus (from Anaheim)
143. Ashton Rome (CAN)—San Jose
144. Martin Nolet (CAN)—Los Angeles (from NY Rangers)
145. Jonathan Rheault (USA)—Philadelphia
146. Mark Dekanich (CAN)—Nashville
147. Alex Biega (CAN)—Buffalo
148. Olivier Magnan (CAN)—New Jersey

149. Juuso Puustinen (FIN)—Calgary
150. Max Warn (FIN)—Dallas
151. Ryan Daniels (CAN)—Ottawa
152. Jordan Bendfeld (CAN)—Phoenix (from Detroit)
153. Stefan Chaput (CAN)—Carolina

Sixth Round

154. Matthew McCollem (USA)—St. Louis
155. Peter Aston (CAN)—Florida (from Pittsburgh)
156. Jan-Mikael Juutilainen (FIN)—Chicago
157. Brent Gwidt (USA)—Washington
158. Levi Nelson (CAN)—Boston
159. Jesse Dudas (CAN)—Columbus
160. Andrew MacDonald (CAN)—NY Islanders
161. Viktor Stahlberg (SWE)—Toronto (from Phoenix)
162. Julian Walker (SUI)—Minnesota
163. Sergei Shirokov (RUS)—Vancouver (from Florida)
164. Constantin Braun (GER)—Los Angeles
165. Jonas Enlund (FIN)—Atlanta
166. Tyler Ruegsegger (USA)—Toronto
167. Juraj Simek (SVK)—Vancouver
168. Dane Crowley (CAN)—Tampa Bay
169. Chris Auger (CAN)—Chicago (from Montreal)
170. Alexander Bumagin (RUS)—Edmonton
171. Brian Day (USA)—NY Islanders (from San Jose-Colorado)
172. Petteri Wirtanen (FIN)—Anaheim
173. Stefan Ridderwall (SWE)—NY Islanders (from San Jose)
174. Eric Hunter (CAN)—NY Rangers
175. Michael Dupont (SUI)—Philadelphia
176. Ryan Flynn (USA)—Nashville
177. Mathieu Perreault (CAN)—Washington (from Buffalo)
178. Tony Romano (USA)—New Jersey
179. Jordan Fulton (USA)—Calgary

180. Leo Komarov (EST)—Toronto (from Dallas)
181. Kevin Koopman (CAN)—Ottawa
182. Jan Mursak (SLO)—Detroit
183. Nick Dodge (CAN)—Carolina

Seventh Round

184. Alexander Hellstrom (SWE)—St. Louis
185. Timo Seppanen (FIN)—Pittsburgh
186. Peter LeBlanc (CAN)—Chicago
187. Devin Didiomete (CAN)—Calgary (from Washington)
188. Chris Frank (USA)—Phoenix (from Boston-Toronto)
189. Derek Dorsett (CAN)—Columbus
190. Troy Mattila (USA)—NY Islanders
191. Nick Oslund (USA)—Detroit (from Phoenix)
192. Chris Hickey (USA)—Minnesota
193. Marc Cheverie (CAN)—Florida
194. Matt Marquardt (CAN)—Columbus (from Los Angeles)
195. Jesse Martin (CAN)—Atlanta
196. Benn Ferriero (USA)—Phoenix (from Toronto)
197. Evan Fuller (CAN)—Vancouver
198. Denis Kazionov (RUS)—Tampa Bay
199. Cameron Cepek (USA)—Montreal
200. Arturs Kulda (LAT)—Atlanta (from Edmonton)
201. Billy Sauer (USA)—Colorado
202. John McCarthy (USA)—San Jose (from Anaheim)
203. Jay Barriball (USA)—San Jose
204. Lukas Zeliska (SVK)—NY Rangers
205. Andrei Popov (RUS)—Philadelphia
206. Viktor Sjodin (SWE)—Nashville
207. Benjamin Breault (CAN)—Buffalo
208. Kyle Henegan (USA)—New Jersey
209. Per Jonsson (SWE)—Calgary
210. Will O'Neill (USA)—Atlanta (from Dallas)

211. Erik Condra (USA)—Ottawa
212. Logan Pyett (CAN)—Detroit
213. Justin Krueger (CAN)—Carolina

NOTES

2nd overall—Jordan Staal, brother of Eric (Carolina Hurricanes) and Marc (12th overall, NY Rangers, 2005)

18th overall—Chris Stewart, brother of Anthony (Florida Panthers)

28th overall—Nick Foligno, son of former NHLer Mike

33rd overall—Igor Makarov, son of Soviet great Sergei

35th overall—Francois Bouchard, brother of Pierre-Marc Bouchard (Minnesota Wild)

52nd overall—Keith Seabrook, brother of Brent (Chicago Blackhawks)

56th overall—Blake Geoffrion, grandson of Hall of Famer Bernie Geoffrion

83rd overall—John DeGray, son of former NHLer Dale

213th overall (last selection)—Justin Krueger, son of Canadian-born coach of Swiss National Team Ralph

YEAR-BY-YEAR STANDINGS AND
STANLEY CUP FINALS RESULTS

After playoff scores, goalies who have registered a shutout will appear in square brackets (i.e., [Broda] means Turk Broda registered a shutout). All overtime goals are also recorded.

1917–1918

First Half

	GP	W	L	GF	GA	PTS
Canadiens	14	10	4	81	47	20
Arenas	14	8	6	71	75	16
Ottawa	14	5	9	67	79	10
Wanderers+	6	1	5	17	35	2

Second Half

	GP	W	L	GF	GA	PTS
Arenas	8	5	3	37	34	10
Ottawa	8	4	4	35	35	8
Canadiens	8	3	5	34	37	6

+ Wanderers' rink burned down on January 2, 1918, and team withdrew from league. Arenas and Canadiens each counted a win for defaulted games with the Wanderers.

* winner of first half played winner of second half in a two-game total-goals series for a place in the Stanley Cup finals against the winner of the Pacific Coast Hockey Association and the Western Canada Hockey League. If one team won both halves, it went to the best-of-five Stanley Cup finals automatically.

* from 1917–21 games were played until a winner decided.

NHL Finals

March 11   Canadiens 3 at Arenas 7
March 13   Arenas 3 at Canadiens 4
Arenas won two-game total-goals series 10–7

Stanley Cup Finals
March 20   Vancouver 3 at Toronto 5
March 23   Vancouver 6 at Toronto 4
March 26   Vancouver 3 at Toronto 6
March 28   Vancouver 8 at Toronto 1
March 30   Vancouver 1 at Toronto 2
Toronto won Stanley Cup best-of-five 3–2

1918–1919

First Half

	GP	W	L	GF	GA	PTS
Canadiens	10	7	3	57	50	14
Ottawa	10	5	5	39	39	10
Arenas	10	3	7	42	49	6

Second Half

Ottawa	8	7	1	32	14	14
Canadiens	8	3	5	31	28	6
Arenas	8	2	6	22	43	4

* Spanish influenza epidemic caused the cancellation of the Stanley Cup finals
* the 1918–19 season was supposed to be, like the ones before and after it, a 24-game schedule. However, when Canadiens and Ottawa clinched first place in both halves early, Arenas manager Charlie Querrie refused to play the remaining games, fearing a lack of fan interest. The league almost sued the Arenas, but instead Canadiens and Ottawa played a best-of-seven, rather than a two-game total-goals series, to create extra home dates for the clubs.

NHL Finals
February 22   Ottawa 4 at Canadiens 8
February 27   Canadiens 5 at Ottawa 3
March 1   Ottawa 3 at Canadiens 6
March 3   Canadiens 3 at Ottawa 6
March 6   Ottawa 2 at Canadiens 4
Canadiens won best-of-seven 4–1

Stanley Cup Finals

March 19   Canadiens 0 at Seattle 7 [Holmes]
March 22   Canadiens 4 at Seattle 2
March 24   Canadiens 2 at Seattle 7
March 26   Canadiens 0 at Seattle 0 (20:00 OT) [Vezina/Holmes]
March 30   Canadiens 4 at Seattle 3 (Odie Cleghorn 15:57 OT)

Finals cancelled after five games because of Spanish influenza
and the death of Canadiens player Joe Hall

1919–1920

First Half

	GP	W	L	GP	GA	PTS
Ottawa	12	9	3	59	23	18
Canadiens	12	8	4	62	51	16
St. Pats	12	5	7	52	62	10
Bulldogs	12	2	10	44	81	4

Second Half

	GP	W	L	GP	GA	PTS
Ottawa	12	10	2	62	41	20
St. Pats	12	7	5	67	44	14
Canadiens	12	5	7	67	62	10
Bulldogs	12	2	10	47	96	4

No NHL finals because Ottawa won both halves

Stanley Cup Finals

March 22   Seattle 2 at Ottawa 3
March 24   Seattle 0 at Ottawa 3 [Benedict]
March 27   Seattle 3 at Ottawa 1
March 30   Seattle 5 Ottawa 2*
April 1   Ottawa 6 Seattle 1*
Ottawa won Stanley Cup best-of-five 3–2

* played in Toronto because of poor ice conditions in Ottawa

1920–1921

First Half

	GP	W	L	GP	GA	PTS
Ottawa	10	8	2	49	23	16
St. Pats	10	5	5	39	47	10
Canadiens	10	4	6	37	51	8
Hamilton	10	3	7	34	38	6

Second Half

	GP	W	L	GP	GA	PTS
St. Pats	14	10	4	66	53	20
Canadiens	14	9	5	75	48	18
Ottawa	14	6	8	48	52	12
Hamilton	14	3	11	58	94	6

NHL Finals

March 10   St. Pats 0 at Ottawa 5 [Benedict]
March 15   Ottawa 2 at St. Pats 0 [Benedict]
Ottawa won two-game total-goals series 7–0

Stanley Cup Finals

March 21   Ottawa 1 at Vancouver 3
March 24   Ottawa 4 at Vancouver 3
March 28   Ottawa 3 at Vancouver 2
March 31   Ottawa 2 at Vancouver 3
April 4   Ottawa 2 at Vancouver 1
Ottawa won Stanley Cup best-of-five 3–2

1921–1922

	GP	W	L	T	GF	GA	PTS
Ottawa	24	14	8	2	106	84	30
St. Pats	24	13	10	1	98	97	27
Canadiens	24	12	11	1	88	94	25
Hamilton	24	7	17	0	88	105	14

* overtime limited to 20 minutes (not sudden-death); minor penalties reduced from three to two minutes
* top two teams advance to playoffs; winner met the Pacific Coast Hockey Association–Western Canadian Hockey League Champion for the Stanley Cup

NHL Finals

March 11   Ottawa 4 at St. Pats 5
March 13   St. Pats 0 at Ottawa 0 [Roach/Benedict]
St. Pats won two-game total-goals series 5–4

Stanley Cup Finals

March 17   Vancouver 4 at St. Pats 3
March 21   Vancouver 1 at St. Pats 2   (Dye 4:50 OT)
March 23   Vancouver 3 at St. Pats 0 [Lehman]
March 25   Vancouver 0 at St. Pats 6 [Roach]
March 28   Vancouver 1 at St. Pats 5
St. Pats won Stanley Cup best-of-five 3–2

1922–1923

	GP	W	L	T	GF	GA	PTS
Ottawa	24	14	9	1	77	54	29
Canadiens	24	13	9	2	73	61	28
St. Pats	24	13	10	1	82	88	27
Hamilton	24	6	18	0	81	110	12

NHL Finals
March 7   Ottawa 2 at Canadiens 0 [Benedict]
March 9   Canadiens 2 at Ottawa 1
Ottawa won two-game total-goals series 3–2

Stanley Cup Playoffs
March 16   Ottawa 1 at Vancouver 0 [Benedict]
March 19   Ottawa 1 at Vancouver 4
March 23   Ottawa 3 at Vancouver 2
March 26   Ottawa 5 at Vancouver 1
Ottawa won best-of-five semifinals 3–1

Stanley Cup Finals
March 29   Ottawa 2 Edmonton 1 (Cy Denneny 2:08 OT)*
March 31   Ottawa 1 Edmonton 0 [Benedict]*
Ottawa won Stanley Cup best-of-three 2–0

* games played at Vancouver

1923–1924

	GP	W	L	T	GF	GA	PTS
Ottawa	24	16	8	0	74	54	32
Canadiens	24	13	11	0	59	48	26
St. Pats	24	10	14	0	59	85	20
Hamilton	24	9	15	0	63	68	18

NHL Finals
March 8   Ottawa 0 at Canadiens 1 [Vezina]
March 11   Canadiens 4 at Ottawa 2
Canadiens won two-game total-goals series 5–2

Stanley Cup Playoffs
March 18   Vancouver 2 at Canadiens 3
March 20   Vancouver 1 at Canadiens 2
Canadiens won best-of-three semi-finals 2–0

Stanley Cup Finals
March 22   Calgary 1 at Canadiens 6
March 25   Canadiens 3 Calgary 0 [Vezina]*
Canadiens won Stanley Cup best-of-three 2–0

* played at Ottawa

1924–1925

	GP	W	L	T	GF	GA	PTS
Hamilton	30	19	10	1	90	60	39
St. Pats	30	19	11	0	90	84	38
Canadiens	30	17	11	2	93	56	36
Ottawa	30	17	12	1	83	66	35
Maroons	30	9	19	2	45	65	20
Boston	30	6	24	0	49	119	12

* the top two teams (Hamilton and Toronto) were supposed to compete for the NHL championship and the right to advance to the Stanley Cup Finals against the WCHL winners. However, the Tigers' players demanded more money for these extra games and the NHL simply disqualified the team. Thus, the St. Pats played the Canadiens.

NHL Finals

March 19   St. Pats 2 at Canadiens 3
March 13   Canadiens 2 at St. Pats 0
Canadiens won 2 -game tota;-oals series 5–2

Stanley Cup Finals

March 21   Canadiens 2 at Victoria 5
March 23   Canadiens 1 at Victoria 3*
March 27   Canadiens 4 at Victoria 2
March 30   Canadiens 1 at Victoria 6
Victoria won Stanley Cup best-of-five finals 3–1

* played at Vancouver

1925–1926

	GP	W	L	T	GF	GA	PTS
Ottawa	36	24	8	4	77	42	52
Maroons	36	20	11	5	91	73	45
Pirates	36	19	16	1	82	70	39
Boston	36	17	15	4	92	85	38
Americans	36	12	20	4	68	89	28
St. Pats	36	12	21	3	92	114	27
Canadiens	36	11	24	1	79	108	23

NHL Finals

March 25   Ottawa 1 at Maroons 1
March 27   Maroons 1 at Ottawa 0 [Benedict]
Maroons win two-game total-goals finals 2–1

Stanley Cup Finals

March 30   Victoria 0 at Maroons 3 [Benedict]
April 1   Victoria 0 at Maroons 3 [Benedict]
April 3   Victoria 3 at Maroons 2
April 6   Victoria 0 at Maroons 2 [Benedict]
Maroons won Stanley Cup best-of-five finals 3–1

1926–1927

Canadian Division

	GP	W	L	T	GF	GA	PTS
Ottawa	44	30	10	4	86	69	64
Canadiens	44	28	14	2	99	67	58
Maroons	44	20	20	4	71	68	44
Americans	44	17	25	2	82	91	36
Toronto*	44	15	24	5	79	94	35

American Division

	GP	W	L	T	GF	GA	PTS
Rangers	44	25	13	6	95	72	56
Boston	44	21	20	3	97	89	45
Chicago	44	19	22	3	115	116	41
Pirates	44	15	26	3	79	108	33
Cougars	44	12	28	4	76	105	28

* on February 14, 1927, the St. Pats changed their name to Maple Leafs

Finals

April 7   Ottawa 0 at Boston 0* [Connell/Winkler]
April 9   Ottawa 3 at Boston 1
April 11   Boston 1 at Ottawa 1**
April 13   Boston 1 at Ottawa 3
Ottawa won Stanley Cup best-of-five 2–0–2

* two 10-minute overtime periods
** one 20-minute overtime period

1927–1928

Canadian Division

	GP	W	L	T	GF	GA	PTS
Canadiens	44	26	11	7	116	48	59
Maroons	44	24	14	6	96	77	54
Ottawa	44	20	14	10	78	57	50
Toronto	44	18	18	8	89	88	44
Americans	44	11	27	6	63	128	28

American Division

	GP	W	L	T	GF	GA	PTS
Boston	44	20	13	11	77	70	51
Rangers	44	19	16	9	94	79	47
Pirates	44	19	17	8	67	76	46
Cougars	44	19	19	6	88	79	44
Chicago	44	7	34	3	68	134	17

* overtime limited to 10 minutes of sudden-death; forward passing now allowed in defending zone

Finals

April 5	Rangers 0 at Maroons 2 [Benedict]
April 7	Rangers 2 at Maroons 1 (Frank Boucher 7:05 OT)
April 10	Rangers 0 at Maroons 2 [Benedict]
April 12	Rangers 1 at Maroons 0 [Miller]
April 14	Rangers 2 at Maroons 1

Rangers won Stanley Cup best-of-five 3–2

1928–1929

Canadian Division

	GP	W	L	T	GF	GA	PTS
Canadiens	44	22	7	15	71	43	59
Americans	44	19	13	12	53	53	50
Toronto	44	21	18	5	85	69	47
Ottawa	44	14	17	13	54	67	41
Maroons	44	15	20	9	67	65	39

American Division

Boston	44	26	13	5	89	52	57
Rangers	44	21	13	10	72	65	52
Cougars	44	19	16	9	72	63	47
Pirates	44	9	27	8	46	80	26
Chicago	44	7	29	8	33	85	22

* overtime set at 10 minutes without sudden-death; passing allowed into, but not within, the offensive zone
* the two division winners played a best-of-five and the two second place teams and third-place teams played two-game total-goals series. Those two winners then played to see who would play the winner of the two division champions' series.

Finals

March 28   Rangers 0 at Boston 2 [Thompson]
March 29   Boston 2 at Rangers 1
Boston won Stanley Cup best-of-three 2–0

1929–1930

Canadian Division

	GP	W	L	T	GF	GA	PTS
Maroons	44	23	16	5	141	114	51
Canadiens	44	21	14	9	142	114	51
Ottawa	44	21	15	8	138	118	50
Toronto	44	17	21	6	116	124	40
Americans	44	14	25	5	113	161	33

American Division

Boston	44	38	5	1	179	98	77
Chicago	44	21	18	5	117	111	47
Rangers	44	17	17	10	136	143	44
Falcons	44	14	24	6	117	133	34
Pirates	44	5	36	3	102	185	13

* forward passing allowed in all three zones, producing twice the number of goals this season over last

Finals

| April 1 | Canadiens 3 at Boston 0 [Hainsworth] |
| April 3 | Boston 3 at Canadiens 4 |

Canadiens won Stanley Cup best-of-three 2–0

1930–1931

Canadian Division

	GP	W	L	T	GF	GA	PTS
Canadiens	44	26	10	8	129	89	60
Toronto	44	22	13	9	118	99	53
Maroons	44	20	18	6	105	106	46
Americans	44	18	16	10	76	74	46
Ottawa	44	10	30	4	91	142	24

American Division

	GP	W	L	T	GF	GA	PTS
Boston	44	28	10	6	143	90	62
Chicago	44	24	17	3	108	78	51
Rangers	44	19	16	9	106	87	47
Falcons	44	16	21	7	102	105	39
Quakers	44	4	36	4	76	184	12

Finals

April 3	Canadiens 2 at Chicago 1
April 5	Canadiens 1 at Chicago 2 (24:50 OT)
April 9	Chicago 3 at Canadiens 2 (53:50 OT)
April 11	Chicago 2 at Canadiens 4
April 14	Chicago 0 at Canadiens 2 [Hainsworth]

Canadiens won Stanley Cup best-of-five 3–2

1931–1932

Canadian Division

	GP	W	L	T	GF	GA	PTS
Canadiens	48	25	16	7	128	111	57
Toronto	48	23	18	7	155	127	53
Maroons	48	19	22	7	142	139	45
Americans	48	16	24	8	95	142	40

American Division

	GP	W	L	T	GF	GA	PTS
Rangers	48	23	17	8	134	112	54
Chicago	48	18	19	11	86	101	47
Falcons	48	18	20	10	95	108	46
Boston	48	15	21	12	122	117	42

Finals

April 5	Toronto 6 at Rangers 4
April 7	Toronto 6 at Rangers 2*
April 9	Rangers 4 at Toronto 6

Toronto won Stanley Cup best-of-five 3–0

* played at Boston because Madison Square Garden unavailable April 7
  because of circus. Because of the scores in the finals (6–4, 6–2, 6–4) this series
  has long been dubbed the "Tennis Series"

* all members of this Toronto team were given gold coins by Conn Smythe as
  lifetime passes to the Gardens

1932–1933

Canadian Division

	GP	W	L	T	GF	GA	PTS
Toronto	48	24	18	6	119	111	54
Maroons	48	22	20	6	135	119	50
Canadiens	48	18	25	5	92	115	41
Americans	48	15	22	11	91	118	41
Ottawa	48	11	27	10	88	131	32

American Division

Boston	48	25	15	8	124	88	58
Detroit	48	25	15	8	111	93	58
Rangers	48	23	17	8	135	107	54
Chicago	48	16	20	12	88	101	44

Finals

April 4   Toronto 1 at Rangers 5
April 8   Rangers 3 at Toronto 1
April 11   Rangers 2 at Toronto 3
April 13   Rangers 1 at Toronto 0 (Bill Cook 7:33 OT) [Aitkenhead]
Rangers won Stanley Cup best-of-five 3–1

1933–1934

Canadian Division

	GP	W	L	T	GF	GA	PTS
Toronto	48	26	13	9	174	119	61
Canadiens	48	22	20	6	99	101	50
Maroons	48	19	18	11	117	122	49
Americans	48	15	23	10	104	132	40
Ottawa	48	13	29	6	115	143	32

American Division

Detroit	48	24	14	10	113	98	58
Chicago	48	20	17	11	88	83	51
Rangers	48	21	19	8	120	113	50
Boston	48	18	25	5	111	130	41

Finals

April 3   Chicago 2 at Detroit 1 (Paul Thompson 21:10 OT)
April 5   Chicago 4 at Detroit 1
April 8   Detroit 5 at Chicago 2
April 10   Detroit 0 at Chicago 1 (Mush March 30:05 OT) [Gardiner]
Chicago won Stanley Cup best-of-five 3–1

1934–1935

Canadian Division

	GP	W	L	T	GF	GA	PTS
Toronto	48	30	14	4	157	111	64
Maroons	48	24	19	5	123	92	53
Canadiens	48	19	23	6	110	145	44
Americans	48	12	27	9	100	142	33
Eagles	48	11	31	6	86	144	28

American Division

	GP	W	L	T	GF	GA	PTS
Boston	48	26	16	6	129	112	58
Chicago	48	26	17	5	118	88	57
Rangers	48	22	20	6	137	139	50
Detroit	48	19	22	7	127	114	45

Finals

April 4   Maroons 3 at Toronto 2 (Dave Trottier 5:28 OT)
April 6   Maroons 3 at Toronto 1
April 9   Toronto 1 at Maroons 4
Maroons won Stanley Cup best-of-five 3–0

1935–1936

Canadian Division

	GP	W	L	T	GF	GA	PTS
Maroons	48	22	16	10	114	106	54
Toronto	48	23	19	6	126	106	52
Americans	48	16	25	7	109	122	39
Canadiens	48	11	26	11	82	123	33

American Division

Detroit	48	24	16	8	124	103	56
Boston	48	22	20	6	92	83	50
Chicago	48	21	19	8	93	92	50
Rangers	48	19	17	12	91	96	50

Finals

April 5   Toronto 1 at Detroit 3
April 7   Toronto 4 at Detroit 9
April 9   Detroit 3 at Toronto 4 (Buzz Boll 0:31 OT)
April 11   Detroit 3 at Toronto 2
Detroit won Stanley Cup best-of-five 3–1

1936–1937

Canadian Division

	GP	W	L	T	GF	GA	PTS
Canadiens	48	24	18	6	115	111	54
Maroons	48	22	17	9	126	110	53
Toronto	48	22	21	5	119	115	49
Americans	48	15	29	4	122	161	34

American Division

Detroit	48	25	14	9	128	102	59
Boston	48	23	18	7	120	110	53
Rangers	48	19	20	9	117	106	47
Chicago	48	14	27	7	99	131	35

Finals

April 6   Detroit 1 at Rangers 5
April 8   Rangers 2 at Detroit 4
April 11   Rangers 1 at Detroit 0 [Kerr]
April 13   Rangers 0 at Detroit 1 [Robertson]
April 15   Rangers 0 at Detroit 3 [Robertson]
Detroit won Stanley Cup best-of-five 3–2

1937–1938

Canadian Division

	GP	W	L	T	GF	GA	PTS
Toronto	48	24	15	9	151	127	57
Americans	48	19	18	11	110	111	49
Canadiens	48	18	17	13	123	128	49
Maroons	48	12	30	6	101	149	30

American Division

	GP	W	L	T	GF	GA	PTS
Boston	48	30	11	7	142	89	67
Rangers	48	27	15	6	149	96	60
Chicago	48	14	25	9	97	139	37
Detroit	48	12	25	11	99	133	35

Finals

April 5   Chicago 3 at Toronto 1
April 7   Chicago 1 at Toronto 5
April 10   Toronto 1 at Chicago 2
April 12   Toronto 1 at Chicago 4
Chicago won Stanley Cup best-of-five 3–1

1938–1939

	GP	W	L	T	GF	GA	PTS
Boston	48	36	10	2	156	76	74
Rangers	48	26	16	6	149	105	58
Toronto	48	19	20	9	114	107	47
Americans	48	17	21	10	119	157	44
Detroit	48	18	24	6	107	128	42
Canadiens	48	15	24	9	115	146	39
Chicago	48	12	28	8	91	132	32

* only the last-place team did not qualify for the playoffs with the new one-division, 7-team format. The first- and second-place team played a best-of-seven to advance to the finals. The second played third and fourth played fifth in best-of-three, the two winners playing another best-of-three to advance to the finals.

Finals

April 6	Toronto 1 at Boston 2
April 9	Toronto 3 at Boston 2 (Doc Romnes 10:38 OT)
April 11	Boston 3 at Toronto 1
April 13	Boston 2 at Toronto 0 [Brimsek]
April 16	Toronto 1 at Boston 3

Boston won Stanley Cup best-of-seven 4–1

1939–1940

	GP	W	L	T	GF	GA	PTS
Boston	48	31	12	5	170	98	67
Rangers	48	27	11	10	136	77	64
Toronto	48	25	17	6	134	110	56
Chicago	48	23	19	6	112	120	52
Detroit	48	16	26	6	90	126	38
Americans	48	15	29	4	106	140	34
Canadiens	48	10	33	5	90	167	25

Finals

April 2	Toronto 1 at Rangers 2 (Alf Pike 15:30 OT)
April 3	Toronto 2 at Rangers 6
April 6	Rangers 1 at Toronto 2
April 9	Rangers 0 at Toronto 3 [Broda]
April 11	Rangers 2 at Toronto 1 (Muzz Patrick 31:43 OT)*
April 13	Rangers 3 at Toronto 2 (Bryan Hextall 2:07 OT)

Rangers won Stanley Cup best-of-seven 4–2

* game could not be played at Madison Square Garden as it was previously
 booked for the circus

1940–1941

	GP	W	L	T	GF	GA	PTS
Boston	48	27	8	13	168	102	67
Toronto	48	28	14	6	145	99	62
Detroit	48	21	16	11	112	102	53
Rangers	48	21	19	8	143	125	50
Chicago	48	16	25	7	112	139	39
Canadiens	48	16	26	6	121	147	38
Americans	48	8	29	11	99	186	27

Finals

April 6	Detroit 2 at Boston 3
April 8	Detroit 1 at Boston 2
April 10	Boston 4 at Detroit 2
April 12	Boston 3 at Detroit 1

Boston won Stanley Cup best-of-seven 4–0

1941–1942

	GP	W	L	T	GF	GA	PTS
Rangers	48	29	17	2	177	143	60
Toronto	48	27	18	3	158	136	57
Boston	48	25	17	6	160	118	56
Chicago	48	22	23	3	145	155	47
Detroit	48	19	25	4	140	147	42
Canadiens	48	18	27	3	134	173	39
Brooklyn	48	16	29	3	133	175	35

Finals

April 4	Detroit 3 at Toronto 2
April 7	Detroit 4 at Toronto 2
April 9	Toronto 2 at Detroit 5
April 12	Toronto 4 at Detroit 3
April 14	Detroit 3 at Toronto 9

April 16   Toronto 3 at Detroit 0 [Broda]
April 18   Detroit 1 at Toronto 3
Toronto won Stanley Cup best-of-seven 4–3

* first and only time in NHL history that a team has trailed 3–0 in the finals
  and won the Stanley Cup

1942–1943

	GP	W	L	T	GF	GA	PTS
Detroit	50	25	14	11	169	124	61
Boston	50	24	17	9	195	176	57
Toronto	50	22	19	9	198	159	53
Canadiens	50	19	19	12	181	191	50
Chicago	50	17	18	15	179	180	49
Rangers	50	11	31	8	161	253	30

* because of wartime restrictions on train schedules overtime was eliminated
  as of November 21, 1942
* the top four teams qualified for the playoffs in the six-team league, and both
  rounds were best-of-seven

Finals
April 1   Boston 2 at Detroit 6
April 4   Boston 3 at Detroit 4
April 7   Detroit 4 at Boston 0 [Mowers]
April 8   Detroit 2 at Boston 0 [Mowers]
Detroit won Stanley Cup best-of-seven 4–0

1943–1944

	GP	W	L	T	GF	GA	PTS
Canadiens	50	38	5	7	234	109	83
Detroit	50	26	18	6	214	177	58
Toronto	50	23	23	4	214	174	50
Chicago	50	22	23	5	178	187	49
Boston	50	19	26	5	223	268	43
Rangers	50	6	39	5	162	310	17

Finals

April 4	Chicago 1 at Canadiens 5
April 6	Chicago 1 at Canadiens 3
April 9	Chicago 2 at Canadiens 3
April 13	Chicago 4 at Canadiens 5 (Toe Blake 9:12 OT)

Canadiens won Stanley Cup best-of-seven 4–0

1944–1945

	GP	W	L	T	GF	GA	PTS
Canadiens	50	38	8	4	228	121	80
Detroit	50	31	14	5	218	161	67
Toronto	50	24	22	4	183	161	52
Boston	50	16	30	4	179	219	36
Chicago	50	13	30	7	141	194	33
Rangers	50	11	29	10	154	247	32

Finals

April 6	Toronto 1 at Detroit 0 [McCool]
April 8	Toronto 2 at Detroit 0 [McCool]
April 12	Detroit 0 at Toronto 1 [McCool]
April 14	Detroit 5 at Toronto 3
April 19	Toronto 0 at Detroit 2 [Lumley]
April 21	Detroit 1 at Toronto 0 (Ed Bruneteau 14:16 OT) [Lumley]
April 22	Toronto 2 at Detroit 1

Toronto won Stanley Cup best-of-seven 4–3

1945–1946

	GP	W	L	T	GF	GA	PTS
Canadiens	50	28	17	5	172	134	61
Boston	50	24	18	8	167	156	56
Chicago	50	23	20	7	200	178	53
Detroit	50	20	20	10	146	159	50
Toronto	50	19	24	7	174	185	45
Rangers	50	13	28	9	144	191	35

Finals

March 30   Boston 3 at Canadiens 4 (Maurice Richard 9:08 OT)
April 2   Boston 2 at Canadiens 3 (Jimmy Peters 16:55 OT)
April 4   Canadiens 4 at Boston 2
April 7   Canadiens 2 at Boston 3 (Terry Reardon 15:13 OT)
April 9   Boston 3 at Canadiens 6
Canadiens won Stanley Cup best-of-seven 4–1

1946–1947

	GP	W	L	T	GF	GA	PTS
Canadiens	60	34	16	10	189	138	78
Toronto	60	31	19	10	209	172	72
Boston	60	26	23	11	190	175	63
Detroit	60	22	27	11	190	193	55
Rangers	60	22	32	6	167	186	50
Chicago	60	19	37	4	193	274	42

Finals

April 8   Toronto 0 at Canadiens 6 [Durnan]
April 10   Toronto 4 at Canadiens 0 [Broda]
April 12   Canadiens 2 at Toronto 4
April 15   Canadiens 1 at Toronto 2 (Syl Apps 16:36 OT)
April 17   Toronto 1 at Canadiens 3
April 19   Canadiens 1 at Toronto 2
Toronto won Stanley Cup best-of-seven 4–2

1947–1948

	GP	W	L	T	GF	GA	PTS
Toronto	60	32	15	13	182	143	77
Detroit	60	30	18	12	187	148	72
Boston	60	23	24	13	167	168	59
Rangers	60	21	26	13	176	201	55
Canadiens	60	20	29	11	147	169	51
Chicago	60	20	34	6	195	225	46

Finals

April 7	Detroit 3 at Toronto 5
April 10	Detroit 2 at Toronto 4
April 11	Toronto 2 at Detroit 0 [Broda]
April 14	Toronto 7 at Detroit 2

Toronto won Stanley Cup best-of-seven 4–0

1948–1949

	GP	W	L	T	GF	GA	PTS
Detroit	60	34	19	7	195	145	75
Boston	60	29	23	8	178	163	66
Canadiens	60	28	23	9	152	126	65
Toronto	60	22	25	13	147	161	57
Chicago	60	21	31	8	173	211	50
Rangers	60	18	31	11	133	172	47

Finals

April 8	Toronto 3 at Detroit 2 (Joe Klukay 17:31 OT)
April 10	Toronto 3 at Detroit 1
April 13	Detroit 1 at Toronto 3
April 16	Detroit 1 at Toronto 3

Toronto won Stanley Cup best-of-seven 4–0

1949–1950

	GP	W	L	T	GF	GA	PTS
Detroit	70	37	19	14	229	164	88
Canadiens	70	29	22	19	172	150	77
Toronto	70	31	27	12	176	173	74
Rangers	70	28	31	11	170	189	67
Boston	70	22	32	16	198	228	60
Chicago	70	22	38	10	203	244	54

Finals

April 11	Rangers 1 at Detroit 4	
April 13	Detroit 1 Rangers 3*	
April 15	Detroit 4 Rangers 0*[Lumley]	
April 18	Rangers 4 at Detroit 3 (Don Raleigh 8:34 OT)	
April 20	Rangers 2 at Detroit 1 (Don Raleigh 1:38 OT)	
April 22	Rangers 4 at Detroit 5	
April 23	Rangers 3 at Detroit 4	(Pete Babando 28:31 OT)**

Detroit won Stanley Cup best-of-seven 4–3

* played at Toronto because Madison Square Garden was previously booke‹ for the circus. Games 6 and 7 played in Detroit because league by-laws stip‹ ulated a Stanley Cup-winning game cannot be played on neutral ice.

** first time in history the Cup was won on an OT goal in game 7

1950–1951

	GP	W	L	T	GF	GA	PTS
Detroit	70	44	13	13	236	139	101
Toronto	70	41	16	13	212	138	95
Canadiens	70	25	30	15	173	184	65
Boston	70	22	30	18	178	197	62
Rangers	70	20	29	21	169	201	61
Chicago	70	13	47	10	171	280	36

Finals

April 11	Canadiens 2 at Toronto 3 (Sid Smith 5:51 OT)
April 14	Canadiens 3 at Toronto 2 (Maurice Richard 2:55 OT)
April 17	Toronto 2 at Canadiens 1 (Ted Kennedy 4:47 OT)
April 19	Toronto 3 at Canadiens 2 (Harry Watson 5:15 OT)
April 21	Canadiens 2 at Toronto 3 (Bill Barilko 2:53 OT)

Toronto won Stanley Cup best-of-seven 4–1

1951–1952

	GP	W	L	T	GF	GA	PTS
Detroit	70	44	14	12	215	133	100
Canadiens	70	34	26	10	195	164	78
Toronto	70	29	25	16	168	157	74
Boston	70	25	29	16	162	176	66
Rangers	70	23	34	13	192	219	59
Chicago	70	17	44	9	158	241	43

Finals

April 10	Detroit 3 at Canadiens 1
April 12	Detroit 2 at Canadiens 1
April 13	Canadiens 0 at Detroit 3 [Sawchuk]
April 15	Canadiens 0 at Detroit 3 [Sawchuk]

Detroit won Stanley Cup best-of-seven 4–0

1952–1953

	GP	W	L	T	GF	GA	PTS
Detroit	70	36	16	18	222	133	90
Canadiens	70	28	23	19	155	148	75
Boston	70	28	29	13	152	172	69
Chicago	70	27	28	15	169	175	69
Toronto	70	27	30	13	156	167	67
Rangers	70	17	37	16	152	211	50

Finals

April 9	Boston 2 at Canadiens 4
April 11	Boston 4 at Canadiens 1
April 12	Canadiens 3 at Boston 0 [McNeil]
April 14	Canadiens 7 at Boston 3
April 16	Boston 0 at Canadiens 1 (Elmer Lach 1:22 OT) [McNeil]

Canadiens won Stanley Cup best-of-seven 4–1

1953–1954

	GP	W	L	T	GF	GA	PTS
Detroit	70	37	19	14	191	132	88
Canadiens	70	35	24	11	195	141	81
Toronto	70	32	24	14	152	131	78
Boston	70	32	28	10	177	181	74
Rangers	70	29	31	10	161	182	68
Chicago	70	12	51	7	133	242	31

Finals

April 4	Canadiens 1 at Detroit 3
April 6	Canadiens 3 at Detroit 1
April 8	Detroit 5 at Canadiens 2
April 10	Detroit 2 at Canadiens 0 [Sawchuk]
April 11	Canadiens 1 at Detroit 0 (Ken Mosdell 5:45 OT) [McNeil]
April 13	Detroit 1 at Canadiens 4
April 16	Canadiens 1 at Detroit 2 (Tony Leswick 4:29 OT)

Detroit won Stanley Cup best-of-seven 4–3

1954–1955

	GP	W	L	T	GF	GA	PTS
Detroit	70	42	17	11	204	134	95
Canadiens	70	41	18	11	228	157	93
Toronto	70	24	24	22	147	135	70
Boston	70	23	26	21	169	188	67
Rangers	70	17	35	18	150	210	52
Chicago	70	13	40	17	161	235	43

Finals

April 3   Canadiens 2 at Detroit 4
April 5   Canadiens 1 at Detroit 7
April 7   Detroit 2 at Canadiens 4
April 9   Detroit 3 at Canadiens 5
April 10 Canadiens 1 at Detroit 5
April 12 Detroit 3 at Canadiens 6
April 14 Canadiens 1 at Detroit 3
Detroit won Stanley Cup best-of-seven 4–3

1955–1956

	GP	W	L	T	GF	GA	PTS
Canadiens	70	45	15	10	222	131	100
Detroit	70	30	24	16	183	148	76
Rangers	70	32	28	10	204	203	74
Toronto	70	24	33	13	153	181	61
Boston	70	23	34	13	147	185	59
Chicago	70	19	39	12	155	216	50

Finals

March 31 Detroit 4 at Canadiens 6
April 3   Detroit 1 at Canadiens 5
April 5   Canadiens 1 at Detroit 3
April 8   Canadiens 3 at Detroit 0 [Plante]
April 10 Detroit 1 at Canadiens 3
Canadiens won Stanley Cup best-of-seven 4–1

1956–1957

	GP	W	L	T	GF	GA	PTS
Detroit	70	38	20	12	198	157	88
Canadiens	70	35	23	12	210	155	82
Boston	70	34	24	12	195	174	80
Rangers	70	26	30	14	184	227	66
Toronto	70	21	34	15	174	192	57
Chicago	70	16	39	15	169	225	47

* penalized player allowed to return to the ice after a power-play goal has been
  scored by the opposition

Finals

April 6	Boston 1 at Canadiens 5
April 9	Boston 0 at Canadiens 1 [Plante]
April 11	Canadiens 4 at Boston 2
April 14	Canadiens 0 at Boston 2 [Simmons]
April 16	Boston 1 at Canadiens 5

Canadiens won Stanley Cup best-of-seven 4–1

1957–1958

	GP	W	L	T	GF	GA	PTS
Canadiens	70	43	17	10	250	158	96
Rangers	70	32	25	13	195	188	77
Detroit	70	29	29	12	176	207	70
Boston	70	27	28	15	199	194	69
Chicago	70	24	39	7	163	202	55
Toronto	70	21	38	11	192	226	53

Finals

April 8	Boston 1 at Canadiens 2
April 10	Boston 5 at Canadiens 2
April 13	Canadiens 3 at Boston 0 [Plante]
April 15	Canadiens 1 at Boston 3

April 17   Boston 2 at Canadiens 3 (Maurice Richard 5:45 OT)
April 20   Canadiens 5 at Boston 3
Canadiens won Stanley Cup best-of-seven 4–2

1958–1959

	GP	W	L	T	GF	GA	PTS
Canadiens	70	39	18	13	258	158	91
Boston	70	32	29	9	205	215	73
Chicago	70	28	29	13	197	208	69
Toronto	70	27	32	11	189	201	65
Rangers	70	26	32	12	201	217	64
Detroit	70	25	37	8	167	218	58

Finals

April 9   Toronto 3 at Canadiens 5
April 11   Toronto 1 at Canadiens 3
April 14   Canadiens 2 at Toronto 3 (Dick Duff 10:06 OT)
April 16   Canadiens 3 at Toronto 2
April 18   Toronto 3 at Canadiens 5
Canadiens won Stanley Cup best-of-seven 4–1

1959–1960

	GP	W	L	T	GF	GA	PTS
Canadiens	70	40	18	12	255	178	92
Toronto	70	35	26	9	199	195	79
Chicago	70	28	29	13	191	180	69
Detroit	70	26	29	15	186	197	67
Boston	70	28	34	8	220	241	64
Rangers	70	17	38	15	187	247	49

Finals

April 7	Toronto 2 at Canadiens 4
April 9	Toronto 1 at Canadiens 2
April 12	Canadiens 5 at Toronto 2
April 14	Canadiens 4 at Toronto 0 [Plante]

Canadiens won Stanley Cup best-of-seven 4–0

1960–1961

	GP	W	L	T	GF	GA	PTS
Canadiens	70	41	19	10	254	188	92
Toronto	70	39	19	12	234	176	90
Chicago	70	29	24	17	198	180	75
Detroit	70	25	29	16	195	215	66
Rangers	70	22	38	10	204	248	54
Boston	70	15	42	13	176	254	43

Finals

April 6	Detroit 2 at Chicago 3
April 8	Chicago 1 at Detroit 3
April 10	Detroit 1 at Chicago 3
April 12	Chicago 1 at Detroit 2
April 14	Detroit 3 at Chicago 6
April 16	Chicago 5 at Detroit 1

Chicago won Stanley Cup best-of-seven 4–2

1961–1962

	GP	W	L	T	GF	GA	PTS
Canadiens	70	42	14	14	259	166	98
Toronto	70	37	22	11	232	180	85
Chicago	70	31	26	13	217	186	75
Rangers	70	26	32	12	195	207	64
Detroit	70	23	33	14	184	219	60
Boston	70	15	47	8	177	306	38

Finals

April 10	Chicago 1 at Toronto 4	
April 12	Chicago 2 at Toronto 3	
April 15	Toronto 0 at Chicago 3 [Hall]	
April 17	Toronto 1 at Chicago 4	
April 19	Chicago 4 at Toronto 8	
April 22	Toronto 2 at Chicago 1	

Toronto won Stanley Cup best-of-seven 4–2

1962–1963

	GP	W	L	T	GF	GA	PTS
Toronto	70	35	23	12	221	180	82
Chicago	70	32	21	17	194	178	81
Canadiens	70	28	19	23	225	183	79
Detroit	70	32	25	13	200	194	77
Rangers	70	22	36	12	211	233	56
Boston	70	14	39	17	198	281	45

Finals

April 9	Detroit 2 at Toronto 4
April 11	Detroit 2 at Toronto 4
April 14	Toronto 2 at Detroit 3
April 16	Toronto 4 at Detroit 2
April 18	Detroit 1 at Toronto 3

Toronto won Stanley Cup best-of-seven 4–1

1963–1964

	GP	W	L	T	GF	GA	PTS
Canadiens	70	36	21	13	209	167	85
Chicago	70	36	22	12	218	169	84
Toronto	70	33	25	12	192	172	78
Detroit	70	30	29	11	191	204	71
Rangers	70	22	38	10	186	242	54
Boston	70	18	40	12	170	212	48

Finals

April 11	Detroit 2 at Toronto 3
April 14	Detroit 4 at Toronto 3 (Larry Jeffrey 7:52 OT)
April 16	Toronto 3 at Detroit 4
April 18	Toronto 4 at Detroit 2
April 21	Detroit 2 at Toronto 1
April 23	Toronto 4 at Detroit 3 (Bobby Baun 1:43 OT)
April 25	Detroit 0 at Toronto 4 [Bower]

Toronto won Stanley Cup best-of-seven 4–3

1964–1965

	GP	W	L	T	GF	GA	PTS
Detroit	70	40	23	7	224	175	87
Canadiens	70	36	23	11	211	185	83
Chicago	70	34	28	8	224	176	76
Toronto	70	30	26	14	204	173	74
Rangers	70	20	38	12	179	246	52
Boston	70	21	43	6	166	253	48

Finals

April 17	Chicago 2 at Canadiens 3
April 20	Chicago 0 at Canadiens 2 [Worsley]
April 22	Canadiens 1 at Chicago 3
April 25	Canadiens 1 at Chicago 5
April 27	Chicago 0 at Canadiens 6 [Hodge]
April 29	Canadiens 1 at Chicago 2
May 1	Chicago 0 at Canadiens 4 [Worsley]

Canadiens won Stanley Cup best-of-seven 4–3

1965–1966

	GP	W	L	T	GF	GA	PTS
Canadiens	70	41	21	8	239	173	90
Chicago	70	37	25	8	240	187	82
Toronto	70	34	25	11	208	187	79
Detroit	70	31	27	12	221	194	74
Boston	70	21	43	6	174	275	48
Rangers	70	18	41	11	195	261	47

Finals

April 24   Detroit 3 at Canadiens 2
April 26   Detroit 5 at Canadiens 2
April 28   Canadiens 4 at Detroit 2
May 1   Canadiens 2 at Detroit 1
May 3   Detroit 1 at Canadiens 5
May 5   Canadiens 3 at Detroit 2 (Henri Richard 2:20 OT)
Canadiens won Stanley Cup best-of-seven 4–2

1966–1967

	GP	W	L	T	GF	GA	PTS
Chicago	70	41	17	12	264	170	94
Canadiens	70	32	25	13	202	188	77
Toronto	70	32	27	11	204	211	75
Rangers	70	30	28	12	188	189	72
Detroit	70	27	39	4	212	241	58
Boston	70	17	43	10	182	253	44

Finals

April 20   Toronto 2 at Canadiens 6
April 22   Toronto 3 at Canadiens 0 [Bower]
April 25   Canadiens 2 at Toronto 3 (Bob Pulford 28:26 OT)
April 27   Canadiens 6 at Toronto 2
April 29   Toronto 4 at Canadiens 1
May 2   Canadiens 1 at Toronto 3
Toronto won Stanley Cup best-of-seven 4–2

1967–1968

East Division

	GP	W	L	T	GF	GA	PTS
Canadiens	74	42	22	10	236	167	94
Rangers	74	39	23	12	226	183	90
Boston	74	37	27	10	259	216	84
Chicago	74	32	26	16	212	222	80
Toronto	74	33	31	10	209	176	76
Detroit	74	27	35	12	245	257	66

West Division

	GP	W	L	T	GF	GA	PTS
Philadelphia	74	31	32	11	173	179	73
Los Angeles	74	31	33	10	200	224	72
St. Louis	74	27	31	16	177	191	70
North Stars	74	27	32	15	191	226	69
Pittsburgh	74	27	34	13	195	216	67
Oakland	74	15	42	17	153	219	47

* top four teams in each division qualified for the playoffs

Finals

May 5   Canadiens 3 at St. Louis 2 (Jacques Lemaire 1:41 OT)
May 7   Canadiens 1 at St. Louis 0 [Worsley]
May 9   St. Louis 3 at Canadiens 4 (Bobby Rousseau 1:13 OT)
May 11 St. Louis 2 at Canadiens 3
Canadiens won Stanley Cup best-of-seven 4–0

1968–1969

East Division

	GP	W	L	T	GF	GA	PTS
Canadiens	76	46	19	11	271	202	103
Boston	76	42	18	16	303	221	100
Rangers	76	41	26	9	231	196	91
Toronto	76	35	26	15	234	217	85
Detroit	76	33	31	12	239	221	78
Chicago	76	34	33	9	280	246	77

West Division

	GP	W	L	T	GF	GA	PTS
St. Louis	76	37	25	14	204	157	88
Oakland	76	29	36	11	219	251	69
Philadelphia	76	20	35	21	174	225	61
Los Angeles	76	24	42	10	185	260	58
Pittsburgh	76	20	45	11	189	252	51
North Stars	76	18	43	15	189	270	51

Finals

April 27   St. Louis 1 at Canadiens 3
April 29   St. Louis 1 at Canadiens 3
May 1   Canadiens 4 at St. Louis 0 [Vachon]
May 4   Canadiens 2 at St. Louis 1
Canadiens won Stanley Cup best-of-seven 4–0

1969–1970

East Division

	GP	W	L	T	GF	GA	PTS
Chicago	76	45	22	9	250	170	99
Boston	76	40	17	19	277	216	99
Detroit	76	40	21	15	246	199	95
Rangers	76	38	22	16	246	189	92
Canadiens	76	38	22	16	244	201	92
Toronto	76	29	34	13	222	242	71

West Division

St. Louis	76	37	27	12	224	179	86
Pittsburgh	76	26	38	12	182	238	64
North Stars	76	19	35	22	224	257	60
Oakland	76	22	40	14	169	243	58
Philadelphia	76	17	35	24	197	225	58
Los Angeles	76	14	52	10	168	290	38

Finals

May 3	Boston 6 at St. Louis 1
May 5	Boston 6 at St. Louis 2
May 7	St. Louis 1 at Boston 4
May 10	St. Louis 3 at Boston 4 (Bobby Orr 0:40 OT)

Boston won Stanley Cup best-of-seven 4–0

1970–1971

East Division

	GP	W	L	T	GF	GA	PTS
Boston	78	57	14	7	399	207	121
Rangers	78	49	18	11	259	177	109
Canadiens	78	42	23	13	291	216	97
Toronto	78	37	33	8	248	211	82
Buffalo	78	24	39	15	217	291	63
Vancouver	78	24	46	8	229	296	56
Detroit	78	22	45	11	209	308	55

West Division

	GP	W	L	T	GF	GA	PTS
Chicago	78	49	20	9	277	184	107
St. Louis	78	34	25	19	223	208	87
Philadelphia	78	28	33	17	207	225	73
North Stars	78	28	34	16	191	223	72
Los Angeles	78	25	40	13	239	303	63
Pittsburgh	78	21	37	20	221	240	62
California	78	20	53	5	199	320	45

Finals

May 4	Canadiens 1 at Chicago 2 (Jim Pappin 1:11 2OT)
May 6	Canadiens 3 at Chicago 5
May 9	Chicago 2 at Canadiens 4
May 11	Chicago 2 at Canadiens 5
May 13	Canadiens 0 at Chicago 2 [Esposito]
May 16	Chicago 3 at Canadiens 4
May 18	Canadiens 3 at Chicago 2

Canadiens won Stanley Cup best-of-seven 4–3

1971–1972

East Division

	GP	W	L	T	GF	GA	PTS
Boston	78	54	13	11	330	204	119
Rangers	78	48	17	13	317	192	109
Canadiens	78	46	16	16	307	205	108
Toronto	78	33	31	14	209	208	80
Detroit	78	33	35	10	261	262	76
Buffalo	78	16	43	19	203	289	51
Vancouver	78	20	50	8	203	297	48

West Division

	GP	W	L	T	GF	GA	PTS
Chicago	78	46	17	15	256	166	107
North Stars	78	37	29	12	212	191	86
St. Louis	78	28	39	11	208	247	67
Pittsburgh	78	26	38	14	220	258	66
Philadelphia	78	26	38	14	200	236	66
California	78	21	39	18	216	288	60
Los Angeles	78	20	49	9	206	305	49

Finals

April 30	Rangers 5 at Boston 6
May 2	Rangers 1 at Boston 2
May 4	Boston 2 at Rangers 5
May 7	Boston 3 at Rangers 2
May 9	Rangers 3 at Boston 2
May 11	Boston 3 at Rangers 0 [Johnston]

Boston won Stanley Cup best-of-seven 4–2

1972–1973

East Division

	GP	W	L	T	GF	GA	PIM	PTS
Canadiens	78	52	10	16	329	184	783	120
Boston	78	51	22	5	330	235	1097	107
Rangers	78	47	23	8	297	208	765	102
Buffalo	78	37	27	14	257	219	940	88
Detroit	78	37	29	12	265	243	893	86
Toronto	78	27	41	10	247	279	716	64
Vancouver	78	22	47	9	233	339	943	53
Islanders	78	12	60	6	170	347	881	30

West Division

	GP	W	L	T	GF	GA	PIM	PTS
Chicago	78	42	27	9	284	225	864	93
Philadelphia	78	37	30	11	296	256	1756	85
North Stars	78	37	30	11	254	230	881	85
St. Louis	78	32	34	12	233	251	1195	76
Pittsburgh	78	32	37	9	257	265	866	73
Los Angeles	78	31	36	11	232	245	888	73
Flames	78	25	38	15	191	239	852	65
California	78	16	46	16	213	323	840	48

Finals

April 29	Chicago 3 at Canadiens 8
May 1	Chicago 1 at Canadiens 4
May 3	Canadiens 4 at Chicago 7
May 6	Canadiens 4 at Chicago 0 [Dryden]
May 8	Chicago 8 at Canadiens 7
May 10	Canadiens 6 at Chicago 4

Canadiens won Stanley Cup best-of-seven 4–2

1973–1974

East Division

	GP	W	L	T	GF	GA	PTS
Boston	78	52	17	9	349	221	113
Canadiens	78	45	24	9	293	240	99
Rangers	78	40	24	14	300	251	94
Toronto	78	35	27	16	274	230	86
Buffalo	78	32	34	12	242	250	76
Detroit	78	29	39	10	255	319	68
Vancouver	78	24	43	11	224	296	59
Islanders	78	19	41	18	182	247	56

West Division

Philadelphia	78	50	16	12	273	164	112
Chicago	78	41	14	23	272	164	105
Los Angeles	78	33	33	12	233	231	78
Flames	78	30	34	14	214	238	74
Pittsburgh	78	28	41	9	242	273	65
St. Louis	78	26	40	12	206	248	64
North Stars	78	23	38	17	235	275	63
California	78	13	55	10	195	342	36

Finals

May 7	Philadelphia 2 at Boston 3
May 9	Philadelphia 3 at Boston 2 (Bobby Clarke 12:01 OT)
May 12	Boston 1 at Philadelphia 4
May 14	Boston 2 at Philadelphia 4
May 16	Philadelphia 1 at Boston 5
May 19	Boston 0 at Philadelphia 1 [Parent]

Philadelphia won Stanley Cup best-of-seven 4–2

1974–1975

PRINCE OF WALES CONFERENCE
Adams Division

	GP	W	L	T	GF	GA	PTS
Buffalo	80	49	16	15	354	240	113
Boston	80	40	26	14	345	245	94
Toronto	80	31	33	16	280	309	78
California	80	19	48	13	212	316	51

Norris Division

	GP	W	L	T	GF	GA	PTS
Canadiens	80	47	14	19	374	225	113
Los Angeles	80	42	17	21	269	185	105
Pittsburgh	80	37	28	15	326	289	89
Detroit	80	23	45	12	259	335	58
Washington	80	8	67	5	181	446	21

CLARENCE CAMPBELL CONFERENCE
Patrick Division

	GP	W	L	T	GF	GA	PTS
Philadelphia	80	51	18	11	293	181	113
Rangers	80	37	29	14	319	276	88
Islanders	80	33	25	22	264	221	88
Flames	80	34	31	15	243	233	83

Smythe Division

	GP	W	L	T	GF	GA	PTS
Vancouver	80	38	32	10	271	254	86
St. Louis	80	35	31	14	269	267	84
Chicago	80	37	35	8	268	241	82
North Stars	80	23	50	7	221	341	53
Kansas City	80	15	54	11	184	328	41

* the top three teams in each division qualified for the playoffs. The four division champions received byes to the second round and all second- and third-place clubs were seeded 1–8 by points, #1 playing # 8, #2 and #7, etc. The first round was best-of-three, the subsequent rounds best-of-seven.

Finals

May 15	Buffalo 1 at Philadelphia 4
May 18	Buffalo 1 at Philadelphia 2
May 20	Philadelphia 4 at Buffalo 5 (Rene Robert 18:29 OT)
May 22	Philadelphia 2 at Buffalo 4
May 25	Buffalo 1 at Philadelphia 5
May 27	Philadelphia 2 at Buffalo 0 [Parent]

Philadelphia won Stanley Cup best-of-seven 4–2

1975–1976

PRINCE OF WALES CONFERENCE

Adams Division

	GP	W	L	T	GF	GA	PTS
Boston	80	48	15	17	313	237	113
Buffalo	80	46	21	13	339	240	105
Toronto	80	34	31	15	294	276	83
California	80	27	42	11	250	278	65

Norris Division

	GP	W	L	T	GF	GA	PTS
Canadiens	80	58	11	11	337	174	127
Los Angeles	80	38	33	9	263	265	85
Pittsburgh	80	35	33	12	339	303	82
Detroit	80	26	44	10	226	300	62
Washington	80	11	59	10	224	394	32

CLARENCE CAMPBELL CONFERENCE

Patrick Division

	GP	W	L	T	GF	GA	PTS
Philadelphia	80	51	13	16	348	209	118
Islanders	80	42	21	17	297	190	101
Flames	80	35	33	12	262	237	82
Rangers	80	29	42	9	262	333	67

Smythe Division

Chicago	80	32	30	18	254	261	82
Vancouver	80	33	32	15	271	272	81
St. Louis	80	29	37	14	249	290	72
North Stars	80	20	53	7	195	303	47
Kansas City	80	12	56	12	190	351	36

Finals

May 9	Philadelphia 3 at Canadiens 4
May 11	Philadelphia 1 at Canadiens 2
May 13	Canadiens 3 at Philadelphia 2
May 16	Canadiens 5 at Philadelphia 3

Canadiens won best-of-seven 4–0

1976–1977

PRINCE OF WALES CONFERENCE

Adams Division

	GP	W	L	T	GF	GA	PTS
Boston	80	49	23	8	312	240	106
Buffalo	80	48	24	8	301	220	104
Toronto	80	33	32	15	301	285	81
Cleveland	80	25	42	13	240	292	63

Norris Division

	GP	W	L	T	GF	GA	PTS
Canadiens	80	60	8	12	387	171	132
Los Angeles	80	34	31	15	271	241	83
Pittsburgh	80	34	33	13	240	252	81
Washington	80	24	42	14	221	307	62
Detroit	80	16	55	9	183	309	41

CLARENCE CAMPBELL CONFERENCE

Patrick Division

Philadelphia	80	48	16	16	323	213	112
Islanders	80	47	21	12	288	193	106
Flames	80	34	34	12	264	265	80
Rangers	80	29	37	14	272	310	64

Smythe Division

St. Louis	80	32	39	9	239	276	73
North Stars	80	23	39	18	240	310	64
Chicago	80	26	43	11	240	298	63
Vancouver	80	25	42	13	235	294	63
Rockies	80	20	46	14	226	307	54

Finals

May 7	Boston 3 at Canadiens 7
May 10	Boston 0 at Canadiens 3 [Dryden]
May 12	Canadiens 4 at Boston 2
May 14	Canadiens 2 at Boston 1

Canadiens won Stanley Cup best-of-seven 4–0

1977–1978

PRINCE OF WALES CONFERENCE

Adams Division

	GP	W	L	T	GF	GA	PTS
Boston	80	51	18	11	333	218	113
Buffalo	80	44	19	17	288	215	105
Toronto	80	41	29	10	271	237	92
Cleveland	80	22	45	13	230	325	57

Norris Division

Canadiens	80	59	10	11	359	183	129
Detroit	80	32	34	14	252	266	78
Los Angeles	80	31	34	15	243	245	77
Pittsburgh	80	25	37	18	254	321	68
Washington	80	17	49	14	195	321	48

CLARENCE CAMPBELL CONFERENCE

Patrick Division

Islanders	80	48	17	15	334	210	111
Philadelphia	80	45	20	15	296	200	105
Flames	80	34	27	19	274	252	87
Rangers	80	30	37	13	279	280	73

Smythe Division

Chicago	80	32	29	19	230	220	83
Rockies	80	19	40	21	257	305	59
Vancouver	80	20	43	17	239	320	57
St. Louis	80	20	47	13	195	304	53
North Stars	80	18	53	9	218	325	45

* all 1st- and 2nd-place teams qualified for playoffs and the next best four regardless of division also qualified

Finals

May 13	Boston 1 at Canadiens 4
May 16	Boston 2 at Canadiens 3 (Guy Lafleur 13:09 OT)
May 18	Canadiens 0 at Boston 4 [Cheevers]
May 21	Canadiens 3 at Boston 4 (Bobby Schmautz 6:22 OT)
May 23	Boston 1 at Canadiens 4
May 25	Canadiens 4 at Boston 1

Canadiens won Stanley Cup best-of-seven 4–2

1978–1979

PRINCE OF WALES CONFERENCE
Adams Division

	GP	W	L	T	GF	GA	PTS
Boston	80	43	23	14	316	270	100
Buffalo	80	36	28	16	280	263	88
Toronto	80	34	33	13	267	252	81
North Stars	80	28	40	12	257	289	68

Norris Division

	GP	W	L	T	GF	GA	PTS
Canadiens	80	52	17	11	337	204	115
Pittsburgh	80	36	31	13	281	279	85
Los Angeles	80	34	34	12	292	286	80
Washington	80	24	41	15	273	338	63
Detroit	80	23	41	16	252	295	62

CLARENCE CAMPBELL CONFERENCE
PATRICK DIVISION

	GP	W	L	T	GF	GA	PTS
Islanders	80	51	15	14	358	214	116
Philadelphia	80	40	25	15	281	248	95
Rangers	80	40	29	11	316	292	91
Flames	80	41	31	8	327	280	90

Smythe Division

	GP	W	L	T	GF	GA	PTS
Chicago	80	29	36	15	244	277	73
Vancouver	80	25	42	13	217	291	63
St. Louis	80	18	50	12	249	348	48
Rockies	80	15	53	12	210	331	42

Finals

May 13	Rangers 4 at Canadiens 1
May 15	Rangers 2 at Canadiens 6
May 17	Canadiens 4 at Rangers 1
May 19	Canadiens 4 at Rangers 3 (Serge Savard 7:25 OT)
May 21	Rangers 1 at Canadiens 4

Canadiens won Stanley Cup best-of-seven 4–1

1979–1980

PRINCE OF WALES CONFERENCE

Adams Division

	GP	W	L	T	GF	GA	PTS
Buffalo	80	47	17	16	318	201	110
Boston	80	46	21	13	310	234	105
North Stars	80	36	28	16	311	253	88
Toronto	80	35	40	5	304	327	75
Quebec	80	25	44	11	248	313	61

Norris Division

	GP	W	L	T	GF	GA	PTS
Canadiens	80	47	20	13	328	240	107
Los Angeles	80	30	36	14	290	313	74
Pittsburgh	80	30	37	13	251	303	73
Hartford	80	27	34	19	303	312	73
Detroit	80	26	43	11	268	306	63

CLARENCE CAMPBELL CONFERENCE
PATRICK DIVISION

	GP	W	L	T	GF	GA	PTS
Philadelphia	80	48	12	20	327	254	116
Islanders	80	39	28	13	281	247	91
Rangers	80	38	32	10	308	284	86
Flames	80	35	32	13	282	269	83
Washington	80	27	40	13	261	293	67

Smythe Division

	GP	W	L	T	GF	GA	PTS
Chicago	80	34	27	19	241	250	87
St. Louis	80	34	34	12	266	278	80
Vancouver	80	27	37	16	256	281	70
Edmonton	80	28	39	13	301	322	69
Winnipeg	80	20	49	11	214	314	51
Rockies	80	19	48	13	234	308	51

* top four teams in each division qualified for the playoffs

Finals

May 13	Islanders 4 at Philadelphia 3 (Denis Potvin 4:07 OT)
May 15	Islanders 3 at Philadelphia 8
May 17	Philadelphia 2 at Islanders 6
May 19	Philadelphia 2 at Islanders 5
May 22	Islanders 3 at Philadelphia 6
May 24	Philadelphia 4 at Islanders 5 (Bob Nystrom 7:11 OT)

Islanders won Stanley Cup best-of-seven 4–2

1980–1981

PRINCE OF WALES CONFERENCE
Adams Division

	GP	W	L	T	GF	GA	PTS
Buffalo	80	39	20	21	327	250	99
Boston	80	37	30	13	316	272	87
North Stars	80	35	28	17	291	263	87
Quebec	80	30	32	18	314	318	78
Toronto	80	28	37	15	322	367	71

Norris Division

	GP	W	L	T	GF	GA	PTS
Canadiens	80	45	22	13	332	232	103
Los Angeles	80	43	24	13	337	290	99
Pittsburgh	80	30	37	13	302	345	73
Hartford	80	21	41	18	292	372	60
Detroit	80	19	43	18	252	339	56

CLARENCE CAMPBELL CONFERENCE
Patrick Division

	GP	W	L	T	GF	GA	PTS
Islanders	80	48	18	14	355	260	110
Philadelphia	80	41	24	15	313	249	97
Calgary	80	39	27	14	329	298	92
Rangers	80	30	36	14	312	317	74
Washington	80	26	36	18	286	317	70

Smythe Division

St. Louis	80	45	18	17	352	281	107
Chicago	80	31	33	16	304	315	78
Vancouver	80	28	32	20	289	301	76
Edmonton	80	29	35	16	328	327	74
Rockies	80	22	45	13	258	344	57
Winnipeg	80	9	57	14	246	400	32

Finals

May 12	North Stars 3 at Islanders 6
May 14	North Stars 3 at Islanders 6
May 17	Islanders 7 at North Stars 5
May 19	Islanders 2 at North Stars 4
May 21	North Stars 1 at Islanders 5

Islanders won Stanley Cup best-of-seven 4–1

1981–1982

CLARENCE CAMPBELL CONFERENCE

Norris Division

	GP	W	L	T	GF	GA	PTS
North Stars	80	37	23	20	346	288	94
Winnipeg	80	33	33	14	319	332	80
St. Louis	80	32	40	8	315	349	72
Chicago	80	30	38	12	332	363	72
Toronto	80	20	44	16	298	380	56
Detroit	80	21	47	12	270	351	54

Smythe Division

Edmonton	80	48	17	15	417	295	111
Vancouver	80	30	33	17	290	286	77
Calgary	80	29	34	17	334	345	75
Los Angeles	80	24	41	15	314	369	63
Rockies	80	18	49	13	241	362	49

PRINCE OF WALES CONFERENCE
Adams Division

Canadiens	80	46	17	17	360	223	109
Boston	80	43	27	10	323	285	96
Buffalo	80	39	26	15	307	273	93
Quebec	80	33	31	16	356	345	82
Hartford	80	21	41	18	264	351	60

Patrick Division

Islanders	80	54	16	10	385	250	118
Rangers	80	39	27	14	316	306	92
Philadelphia	80	38	31	11	325	313	87
Pittsburgh	80	31	36	13	310	337	75
Washington	80	26	41	13	319	338	65

Stanley Cup Finals

May 8	Vancouver 5 at Islanders 6 (Mike Bossy 19:58 OT)
May 11	Vancouver 4 at Islanders 6
May 13	Islanders 3 at Vancouver 0 [Smith]
May 16	Islanders 3 at Vancouver 1

Islanders won best-of-seven finals 4–0

1982–1983

CLARENCE CAMPBELL CONFERENCE
Norris Division

	GP	W	L	T	GF	GA	PTS
Chicago	80	47	23	10	338	268	104
North Stars	80	40	24	16	321	290	96
Toronto	80	28	40	12	293	330	68
St. Louis	80	25	40	15	285	316	65
Detroit	80	21	44	15	263	344	57

Smythe Division

Edmonton	80	47	21	12	424	315	106
Calgary	80	32	34	14	321	317	78
Vancouver	80	30	35	15	303	309	75
Winnipeg	80	33	39	8	311	333	74
Los Angeles	80	27	41	12	308	365	66

PRINCE OF WALES CONFERENCE

Adams Division

Boston	80	50	20	10	327	228	110
Canadiens	80	42	24	14	350	286	98
Buffalo	80	38	29	13	318	285	89
Quebec	80	34	34	12	343	336	80
Hartford	80	19	54	7	261	403	45

Patrick Division

Philadelphia	80	49	23	8	326	240	106
Islanders	80	42	26	12	302	226	96
Washington	80	39	25	16	306	283	94
Rangers	80	35	35	10	306	287	80
New Jersey	80	17	49	14	230	338	48
Pittsburgh	80	18	53	9	257	394	45

Stanley Cup Finals

May 10	Islanders 2 at Edmonton 0 [Smith]
May 12	Islanders 6 at Edmonton 3
May 14	Edmonton 1 at Islanders 5
May 17	Edmonton 2 at Islanders 4

Islanders won best-of-seven finals 4–0

1983–1984

CLARENCE CAMPBELL CONFERENCE

Norris Division

	GP	W	L	T	GF	GA	PTS
North Stars	80	39	31	10	345	344	88
St. Louis	80	32	41	7	293	316	71
Detroit	80	31	42	7	298	323	69
Chicago	80	30	42	8	277	311	68
Toronto	80	26	45	9	303	387	61

Smythe Division

	GP	W	L	T	GF	GA	PTS
Edmonton	80	57	18	5	446	314	119
Calgary	80	34	32	14	311	314	82
Vancouver	80	32	39	9	306	328	73
Winnipeg	80	31	38	11	340	374	73
Los Angeles	80	23	44	13	309	376	59

PRINCE OF WALES CONFERENCE

Adams Division

	GP	W	L	T	GF	GA	PTS
Boston	80	49	25	6	336	261	104
Buffalo	80	48	25	7	315	257	103
Quebec	80	42	28	10	360	278	94
Canadiens	80	35	40	5	286	295	75
Hartford	80	28	42	10	288	320	66

Patrick Division

	GP	W	L	T	GF	GA	PTS
Islanders	80	50	26	4	357	269	104
Washington	80	48	27	5	308	226	101
Philadelphia	80	44	26	10	350	290	98
Rangers	80	42	29	9	314	304	93
New Jersey	80	17	56	7	231	350	41
Pittsburgh	80	16	58	6	254	390	38

* five-minute sudden-death overtime introduced for regular-season games

Stanley Cup Finals

May 10	Edmonton 1 at Islanders 0 [Fuhr]
May 12	Edmonton 1 at Islanders 6
May 15	Islanders 2 at Edmonton 7
May 17	Islanders 2 at Edmonton 7
May 19	Islanders 2 at Edmonton 5

Edmonton won best-of-seven finals 4–1

1984–1985

CLARENCE CAMPBELL CONFERENCE

Norris Division

	GP	W	L	T	GF	GA	PTS
St. Louis	80	37	31	12	299	288	86
Chicago	80	38	35	7	309	299	83
Detroit	80	27	41	12	313	357	66
North Stars	80	25	43	12	268	321	62
Toronto	80	20	52	8	253	358	48

Smythe Division

Edmonton	80	49	20	11	401	298	109
Winnipeg	80	43	27	10	358	332	96
Calgary	80	41	27	12	363	302	94
Los Angeles	80	34	32	14	339	326	82
Vancouver	80	25	46	9	284	401	59

PRINCE OF WALES CONFERENCE

Adams Division

Canadiens	80	41	27	12	309	262	94
Quebec	80	41	30	9	323	275	91
Buffalo	80	38	28	14	290	237	90
Boston	80	36	34	10	303	287	82
Hartford	80	30	41	9	268	318	69

Patrick Division

Philadelphia	80	53	20	7	348	241	113
Washington	80	46	25	9	322	240	101
Islanders	80	40	34	6	345	312	86
Rangers	80	26	44	10	295	345	62
New Jersey	80	22	48	10	264	346	54
Pittsburgh	80	24	51	5	276	385	53

Stanley Cup Finals

May 21	Edmonton 1 at Philadelphia 4
May 23	Edmonton 3 at Philadelphia 1
May 25	Philadelphia 3 at Edmonton 4
May 28	Philadelphia 3 at Edmonton 5
May 30	Philadelphia 3 at Edmonton 8

Edmonton won best-of-seven finals 4–1

1985–1986

CLARENCE CAMPBELL CONFERENCE

Norris Division

	GP	W	L	T	GF	GA	PTS
Chicago	80	39	33	8	351	349	86
North Stars	80	38	33	9	327	305	85
St. Louis	80	37	34	9	302	291	83
Toronto	80	25	48	7	311	386	57
Detroit	80	17	57	6	266	415	40

Smythe Division

Edmonton	80	56	17	7	426	310	119
Calgary	80	40	31	9	354	315	89
Winnipeg	80	26	47	7	295	372	59
Vancouver	80	23	44	13	282	333	59
Los Angeles	80	23	49	8	284	389	54

PRINCE OF WALES CONFERENCE
Adams Division

Quebec	80	43	31	6	330	289	92
Canadiens	80	40	33	7	330	280	87
Boston	80	37	31	12	311	288	86
Hartford	80	40	36	4	332	302	84
Buffalo	80	37	37	6	296	291	80

Patrick Division

Philadelphia	80	53	23	4	335	241	110
Washington	80	50	23	7	315	272	107
Islanders	80	39	29	12	327	284	90
Rangers	80	36	38	6	280	276	78
Pittsburgh	80	34	38	8	313	305	76
New Jersey	80	28	49	3	300	374	59

Stanley Cup Finals

May 16	Canadiens 2 at Calgary 5
May 18	Canadiens 3 at Calgary 2 (Brian Skrudland 0:09 OT)
May 20	Calgary 3 at Canadiens 5
May 22	Calgary 0 at Canadiens 1 [Roy]
May 24	Canadiens 4 at Calgary 3

Canadiens won best-of-seven finals 4–1

1986–1987

CLARENCE CAMPBELL CONFERENCE

Norris Division

	GP	W	L	T	GF	G	PTS
St. Louis	80	32	33	15	281	293	79
Detroit	80	34	36	10	260	274	78
Chicago*	80	29	37	14	290	310	72
Toronto	80	32	42	6	286	319	70
North Stars	80	30	40	10	296	314	70

Smythe Division

	GP	W	L	T	GF	G	PTS
Edmonton	80	50	24	6	372	284	106
Calgary	80	46	31	3	318	289	95
Winnipeg	80	40	32	8	279	271	88
Los Angeles	80	31	41	8	318	341	70
Vancouver	80	29	43	8	282	314	66

PRINCE OF WALES CONFERENCE

Adams Division

	GP	W	L	T	GF	G	PTS
Hartford	80	43	30	7	287	270	93
Canadiens	80	41	29	10	277	241	92
Boston	80	39	34	7	301	276	85
Quebec	80	31	39	10	267	276	72
Buffalo	80	28	44	8	280	308	64

Patrick Division

	GP	W	L	T	GF	G	PTS
Philadelphia	80	46	26	8	310	245	100
Washington	80	38	32	10	285	278	86
Islanders	80	35	33	12	279	281	82
Rangers	80	34	38	8	307	323	76
Pittsburgh	80	30	38	12	297	290	72
New Jersey	80	29	45	6	293	368	64

* Chicago changed spelling of nickname from Black Hawks to Blackhawks at
  start of season

Stanley Cup Finals

May 17	Philadelphia 2 at Edmonton 4
May 20	Philadelphia 2 at Edmonton 3 (Jari Kurri 6:50 OT)
May 22	Edmonton 3 at Philadelphia 5
May 24	Edmonton 4 at Philadelphia 1
May 26	Philadelphia 4 at Edmonton 3
May 28	Edmonton 2 at Philadelphia 3
May 31	Philadelphia 1 at Edmonton 3

Edmonton won best-of-seven finals 4–3

1987–1988

CLARENCE CAMPBELL CONFERENCE

Norris Division

	GP	W	L	T	GF	GA	PTS
Detroit	80	41	28	11	322	269	93
St. Louis	80	34	38	8	278	294	76
Chicago	80	30	41	9	284	326	69
Toronto	80	21	49	10	273	345	52
North Stars	80	19	48	13	242	349	51

Smythe Division

Calgary	80	48	23	9	397	305	105
Edmonton	80	44	25	11	363	288	99
Winnipeg	80	33	36	11	292	310	77
Los Angeles	80	30	42	8	318	359	68
Vancouver	80	25	46	9	272	320	59

PRINCE OF WALES CONFERENCE

Adams Division

Canadiens	80	45	22	13	298	238	103
Boston	80	44	30	6	300	251	94
Buffalo	80	37	32	11	283	305	85
Hartford	80	35	38	7	249	267	77
Quebec	80	32	43	5	271	306	69

Patrick Division

Islanders	80	39	31	10	308	267	88
Washington	80	38	33	9	281	249	85
Philadelphia	80	38	33	9	292	282	85
New Jersey	80	38	36	6	295	296	82
Rangers	80	36	34	10	300	283	82
Pittsburgh	80	36	35	9	319	316	81

Stanley Cup Finals

May 18	Boston 1 at Edmonton 2
May 20	Boston 2 at Edmonton 4
May 22	Edmonton 6 at Boston 3
May 24	Edmonton 3 at Boston 3*
May 26	Boston 3 at Edmonton 6

* game suspended because of power failure but statistics count (if necessary, this game would have been made up at the end of the series)

Edmonton won best-of-seven finals 4–0

1988–1989
CLARENCE CAMPBELL CONFERENCE
Norris Division

	GP	W	L	T	GF	GA	PTS
Detroit	80	34	34	12	313	316	80
St. Louis	80	33	35	12	275	285	78
North Stars	80	27	37	16	258	278	70
Chicago	80	27	41	12	297	335	66
Toronto	80	28	46	6	259	342	62

Smythe Division

Calgary	80	54	17	9	354	226	117
Los Angeles	80	42	31	7	376	335	91
Edmonton	80	38	34	8	325	306	84
Vancouver	80	33	39	8	251	253	74
Winnipeg	80	26	42	12	300	355	64

PRINCE OF WALES CONFERENCE

Adams Division

Canadiens	80	53	18	9	315	218	115
Boston	80	37	29	14	289	256	88
Buffalo	80	38	35	7	291	299	83
Hartford	80	37	38	5	299	290	79
Quebec	80	27	46	7	269	342	61

Patrick Division

Washington	80	41	29	10	305	259	92
Pittsburgh	80	40	33	7	347	349	87
Rangers	80	37	35	8	310	307	82
Philadelphia	80	36	36	8	307	285	80
New Jersey	80	27	41	12	281	325	66
Islanders	80	28	47	5	265	325	61

Stanley Cup Finals

May 14	Canadiens 2 at Calgary 3
May 17	Canadiens 4 at Calgary 2
May 19	Calgary 3 at Canadiens 4 (Ryan Walter 38:08 OT)
May 21	Calgary 4 at Canadiens 2
May 23	Canadiens 2 at Calgary 3
May 25	Calgary 4 at Canadiens 2

Calgary won best-of-seven finals 4–2

1989–1990
CLARENCE CAMPBELL CONFERENCE
Norris Division

	GP	W	L	T	GF	GA	PTS
Chicago	80	41	33	6	316	294	88
St. Louis	80	37	34	9	295	279	83
Toronto	80	38	38	4	337	358	80
North Stars	80	36	40	4	284	291	76
Detroit	80	28	38	14	288	323	70

Smythe Division

	GP	W	L	T	GF	GA	PTS
Calgary	80	42	23	15	348	265	99
Edmonton	80	38	28	14	315	283	90
Winnipeg	80	37	32	11	298	290	85
Los Angeles	80	34	39	7	338	337	75
Vancouver	80	25	41	14	245	306	64

PRINCE OF WALES CONFERENCE
Adams Division

	GP	W	L	T	GF	GA	PTS
Boston	80	46	25	9	289	232	101
Buffalo	80	45	27	8	286	248	98
Canadiens	80	41	28	11	288	234	93
Hartford	80	38	33	9	275	268	85
Quebec	80	12	61	7	240	407	31

Patrick Division

	GP	W	L	T	GF	GA	PTS
Rangers	80	36	31	13	279	267	85
New Jersey	80	37	34	9	295	288	83
Washington	80	36	38	6	284	275	78
Islanders	80	31	38	11	281	288	73
Pittsburgh	80	32	40	8	318	359	72
Philadelphia	80	30	39	11	290	297	71

Stanley Cup Finals

May 15	Edmonton 3 at Boston 2 (Petr Klima 55:13 OT)
May 18	Edmonton 7 at Boston 2
May 20	Boston 2 at Edmonton 1
May 22	Boston 1 at Edmonton 5
May 24	Edmonton 4 at Boston 1

Edmonton won best-of-seven finals 4–1

1990–1991

CLARENCE CAMPBELL CONFERENCE

Norris Division

	GP	W	L	T	GF	GA	PTS
Chicago	80	49	23	8	284	211	106
St. Louis	80	47	22	11	310	250	105
Detroit	80	34	38	8	273	298	76
North Stars	80	27	39	14	256	266	68
Toronto	80	23	46	11	241	318	57

Smythe Division

Los Angeles	80	46	24	10	340	254	102
Calgary	80	46	26	8	344	263	100
Edmonton	80	37	37	6	272	272	80
Vancouver	80	28	43	9	243	315	65
Winnipeg	80	26	43	11	260	288	63

Prince of Wales Conference

Adams Division

Boston	80	44	24	12	299	264	100
Canadiens	80	39	30	11	273	249	89
Buffalo	80	31	30	19	292	278	81
Hartford	80	31	38	11	238	276	73
Quebec	80	16	50	14	236	354	46

Patrick Division

Pittsburgh	80	41	33	6	342	305	88
Rangers	80	36	31	13	297	265	85
Washington	80	37	36	7	258	258	81
New Jersey	80	32	33	15	272	264	79
Philadelphia	80	33	37	10	252	267	76
Islanders	80	25	45	10	223	290	60

Stanley Cup Finals

May 15	Minnesota 5 at Pittsburgh 4
May 17	Minnesota 1 at Pittsburgh 4
May 19	Pittsburgh 1 at Minnesota 3
May 21	Pittsburgh 5 at Minnesota 3
May 23	Minnesota 4 at Pittsburgh 6
May 25	Pittsburgh 8 at Minnesota 0 [Barrasso]

Pittsburgh won best-of-seven finals 4–2

1991–1992
CLARENCE CAMPBELL CONFERENCE
Norris Division

	GP	W	L	T	GF	GA	PTS
Detroit	80	43	25	12	320	256	98
Chicago	80	36	29	15	257	236	87
St. Louis	80	36	33	11	279	266	83
North Stars	80	32	42	6	246	278	70
Toronto	80	30	43	7	234	294	67

Smythe Division

Vancouver	80	42	26	12	285	250	96
Los Angeles	80	35	31	14	287	296	84
Edmonton	80	36	34	10	295	297	82
Winnipeg	80	33	32	15	251	244	81
Calgary	80	31	37	12	296	305	74
San Jose	80	17	58	5	219	359	39

PRINCE OF WALES CONFERENCE
Adams Division

Canadiens	80	41	28	11	267	207	93
Boston	80	36	32	12	270	275	84
Buffalo	80	31	37	12	289	299	74
Hartford	80	26	41	13	247	283	65
Quebec	80	20	48	12	255	318	52

Patrick Division

Rangers	80	50	25	5	321	246	105
Washington	80	45	27	8	330	275	98
Pittsburgh	80	39	32	9	343	308	87
New Jersey	80	38	31	11	289	259	87
Islanders	80	34	35	11	291	299	79
Philadelphia	80	32	37	11	252	273	75

Stanley Cup Finals

May 26	Chicago 4 at Pittsburgh 5
May 28	Chicago 1 at Pittsburgh 3
May 30	Pittsburgh 1 at Chicago 0 [Barrasso]
June 1	Pittsburgh 6 at Chicago 5

Pittsburgh won best-of-seven finals 4–0

1992–1993

CLARENCE CAMPBELL CONFERENCE
Norris Division

	GP	W	L	T	GF	GA	PTS
Chicago	84	47	25	12	279	230	106
Detroit	84	47	28	9	369	280	103
Toronto	84	44	29	11	288	241	99
St. Louis	84	37	36	11	282	278	85
North Stars	84	36	38	10	272	293	82
Tampa Bay	84	23	54	7	245	332	53

Smythe Division

Vancouver	84	46	29	9	346	278	101
Calgary	84	43	30	11	322	282	97
Los Angeles	84	39	35	10	338	340	88
Winnipeg	84	40	37	7	322	320	87
Edmonton	84	26	50	8	242	337	60
San Jose	84	11	71	2	218	414	24

PRINCE OF WALES CONFERENCE

Adams Division

Boston	84	51	26	7	332	268	109
Quebec	84	47	27	10	351	300	104
Canadiens	84	48	30	6	326	280	102
Buffalo	84	38	36	10	335	297	86
Hartford	84	26	52	6	284	369	58
Ottawa	84	10	70	4	202	395	24

Patrick Division

Pittsburgh	84	56	21	7	367	268	119
Washington	84	43	34	7	325	286	93
Islanders	84	40	37	7	335	297	87
New Jersey	84	40	37	7	308	299	87
Philadelphia	84	36	37	11	319	319	83
Rangers	84	34	39	11	304	308	79

Stanley Cup Finals

June 1	Los Angeles 4 at Canadiens 1
June 3	Los Angeles 2 at Canadiens 3 (Eric Desjardins 0:51 OT)
June 5	Canadiens 4 at Los Angeles 3 (John LeClair 0:34 OT)
June 7	Canadiens 3 at Los Angeles 2 (John LeClair 14:37 OT)
June 9	Los Angeles 1 at Canadiens 4

Canadiens won best-of-seven finals 4–1

1993–1994

WESTERN CONFERENCE
Central Division

	GP	W	L	T	GF	GA	PTS
Detroit	84	46	30	8	356	275	100
Toronto	84	43	29	12	280	243	98
Dallas	84	42	29	13	286	265	97
St. Louis	84	40	33	11	270	283	91
Chicago	84	39	36	9	254	240	87
Winnipeg	84	24	51	9	245	344	57

Pacific Division

	GP	W	L	T	GF	GA	PTS
Calgary	84	42	29	13	302	256	97
Vancouver	84	41	40	3	279	276	85
San Jose	84	33	35	16	252	265	82
Anaheim	84	33	46	5	229	251	71
Los Angeles	84	27	45	12	294	322	66
Edmonton	84	25	45	14	261	305	64

EASTERN CONFERENCE
Northeast Division

	GP	W	L	T	GF	GA	PTS
Pittsburgh	84	44	27	13	299	285	101
Boston	84	42	29	13	289	252	97
Canadiens	84	41	29	14	283	248	96
Buffalo	84	43	32	9	282	218	95
Quebec	84	34	42	8	277	292	76
Hartford	84	27	48	9	227	288	63
Ottawa	84	14	61	9	201	397	37

Atlantic Division

Rangers	84	52	24	8	299	231	112
New Jersey	84	47	25	12	306	220	106
Washington	84	39	35	10	277	263	88
Islanders	84	36	36	12	282	264	84
Florida	84	33	34	17	233	233	83
Philadelphia	84	35	39	10	294	314	80
Tampa Bay	84	30	43	11	224	251	71

* the top eight teams in each conference qualified for the playoffs

Stanley Cup Finals

May 31   Vancouver 3 at Rangers 2 (Greg Adams 19:26 OT)
June 2   Vancouver 1 at Rangers 3
June 4   Rangers 5 at Vancouver 1
June 7   Rangers 4 at Vancouver 2
June 9   Vancouver 6 at Rangers 3
June 11   Rangers 1 at Vancouver 4
June 14   Vancouver 2 at Rangers 3
Rangers won best-of-seven finals 4–3

1994–1995

WESTERN CONFERENCE

Central Division

	GP	W	L	T	GF	GA	PTS
Detroit	48	33	11	4	180	117	70
St. Louis	48	28	15	5	178	135	61
Chicago	48	24	19	5	156	115	53
Toronto	48	21	19	8	135	146	50
Dallas 48	17	23	8	136	135	42	
Winnipeg	48	16	25	7	157	177	39

Pacific Division

Calgary	48	24	17	7	163	135	55
Vancouver	48	18	18	12	153	148	48
San Jose	48	19	25	4	129	161	42
Los Angeles	48	16	23	9	142	174	41
Edmonton	48	17	27	4	136	183	38
Anaheim	48	16	27	5	125	164	37

EASTERN CONFERENCE

Northeast Division

Quebec	48	30	13	5	185	134	65
Pittsburgh	48	29	16	3	181	158	61
Boston	48	27	18	3	150	127	57
Buffalo	48	22	19	7	130	119	51
Hartford	48	19	24	5	127	141	43
Canadiens	48	18	23	7	125	148	43
Ottawa	48	9	34	5	116	174	23

Atlantic Division

Philadelphia	48	28	16	4	150	132	60
New Jersey	48	22	18	8	136	121	52
Washington	48	22	18	8	136	120	52
Rangers	48	22	23	3	139	134	47
Florida	48	20	22	6	115	127	46
Tampa Bay	48	17	28	3	120	144	37
Islanders	48	15	28	5	126	158	35

Stanley Cup Finals

June 17	New Jersey 2 at Detroit 1
June 20	New Jersey 4 at Detroit 2
June 22	Detroit 2 at New Jersey 5
June 24	Detroit 2 at New Jersey 5

New Jersey won best-of-seven finals 4–0

1995–1996

WESTERN CONFERENCE
Central Division

	GP	W	L	T	GF	GA	PTS
Detroit	82	62	13	7	325	181	131
Chicago	82	40	28	14	273	220	94
Toronto	82	34	36	12	247	252	80
St. Louis	82	32	34	16	219	248	80
Winnipeg	82	36	40	6	275	291	78
Dallas	82	26	42	14	227	280	66

Pacific Division

	GP	W	L	T	GF	GA	PTS
Colorado	82	47	25	10	326	240	104
Calgary	82	34	37	11	241	240	79
Vancouver	82	32	35	15	278	278	79
Anaheim	82	35	39	8	234	247	78
Edmonton	82	30	44	8	240	304	68
Los Angeles	82	24	40	18	256	302	66
San Jose	82	20	55	7	252	357	47

EASTERN CONFERENCE
Northeast Division

	GP	W	L	T	GF	GA	PTS
Pittsburgh	82	49	29	4	362	284	102
Boston	82	40	31	11	282	269	91
Canadiens	82	40	32	10	265	248	90
Hartford	82	34	39	9	237	259	77
Buffalo	82	33	42	7	247	262	73
Ottawa	82	18	59	5	191	291	41

Atlantic Division

Philadelphia	82	45	24	13	282	208	103
Rangers	82	41	27	14	272	237	96
Florida	82	41	31	10	254	234	92
Washington	82	39	32	11	234	204	89
Tampa Bay	82	38	32	12	238	248	88
New Jersey	82	37	33	12	215	202	86
Islanders	82	22	50	10	229	315	54

Stanley Cup Finals

June 4	Florida 1 at Colorado 3
June 6	Florida 1 at Colorado 8
June 8	Colorado 3 at Florida 2
June 10	Colorado 1 at Florida 0 (Uwe Krupp 44:31 OT) [Roy]

Colorado won best-of seven finals 4–0

1996–1997

WESTERN CONFERENCE

Central Division

	GP	W	L	T	GF	GA	PTS
Dallas	82	48	26	8	252	198	104
Detroit	82	38	26	18	253	197	94
Phoenix	82	38	37	7	240	243	83
St. Louis	82	36	35	11	236	239	83
Chicago	82	34	35	13	223	210	81
Toronto	82	30	44	8	230	273	68

Pacific Division

Colorado	82	49	24	9	277	205	107
Anaheim	82	36	33	13	245	233	85
Edmonton	82	36	37	9	252	247	81
Vancouver	82	35	40	7	257	273	77
Calgary	82	32	41	9	214	239	73
Los Angeles	82	28	43	11	214	268	67
San Jose	82	27	47	8	211	278	62

EASTERN CONFERENCE
Northeast Division

Buffalo	82	40	30	12	237	208	92
Pittsburgh	82	38	36	8	285	280	84
Ottawa	82	31	36	15	226	234	77
Canadiens	82	31	36	15	249	276	77
Hartford	82	32	39	11	226	256	75
Boston	82	26	47	9	234	300	61

Atlantic Division

New Jersey	82	45	23	14	231	182	104
Philadelphia	82	45	24	13	274	217	103
Florida	82	35	28	19	221	201	89
Rangers	82	38	34	10	258	231	86
Washington	82	33	40	9	214	231	75
Tampa Bay	82	32	40	10	217	247	74
Islanders	82	29	41	12	240	250	70

Stanley Cup Finals

May 31	Detroit 4 at Philadelphia 2
June 3	Detroit 4 at Philadelphia 2
June 5	Philadelphia 1 at Detroit 6
June 7	Philadelphia 1 at Detroit 2

Detroit won best-of-seven finals 4–0

997–98

WESTERN CONFERENCE

Central Division

	GP	W	L	T	GF	GA	PTS
Dallas	82	49	22	11	242	167	109
Detroit	82	44	23	15	250	196	103
St. Louis	82	45	29	8	256	204	98
Phoenix	82	35	35	12	224	227	82
Chicago	82	30	39	13	192	199	73
Toronto	82	30	43	9	194	237	69

Pacific Division

	GP	W	L	T	GF	GA	PTS
Colorado	82	39	26	17	231	205	95
Los Angeles	82	38	33	11	227	225	87
Edmonton	82	35	37	10	215	224	80
San Jose	82	34	38	10	210	216	78
Calgary	82	26	41	15	217	252	67
Anaheim	82	26	43	13	205	261	65
Vancouver	82	25	43	14	224	273	64

EASTERN CONFERENCE

Northeast Division

	GP	W	L	T	GF	GA	PTS
Pittsburgh	82	40	24	18	228	188	98
Boston	82	39	30	13	221	194	91
Buffalo	82	36	29	17	211	187	89
Canadiens	82	37	32	13	235	208	87
Ottawa	82	34	33	15	193	20	83
Carolina	82	33	41	8	200	219	74

Atlantic Division

New Jersey	82	48	23	11	225	166	107
Philadelphia	82	42	29	11	242	193	95
Washington	82	40	30	12	219	202	92
Islanders	82	30	41	11	212	225	71
Rangers	82	25	39	18	197	231	68
Florida	82	24	43	15	203	256	63
Tampa Bay	82	17	55	10	151	269	44

Stanley Cup Finals

June 9	Washington 1 at Detroit 2
June 11	Washington 4 at Detroit 5 (Kris Draper 15:24 OT)
June 13	Detroit 2 at Washington 1
June 16	Detroit 4 at Washington 1

Detroit won best-of-seven finals 4–0

1998–99

EASTERN CONFERENCE

Northeast Division

	GP	W	L	T	GF	GA	PTS
Ottawa	82	44	23	15	239	179	103
Toronto	82	45	30	7	268	231	97
Boston	82	39	30	13	214	181	91
Buffalo	82	37	28	17	207	175	91
Canadiens	82	32	39	11	184	209	75

Atlantic Division

New Jersey	82	47	24	11	248	196	105
Philadelphia	82	37	26	19	231	196	93
Pittsburgh	82	38	30	14	242	225	90
Rangers	82	33	38	11	217	227	77
Islanders	82	24	48	10	194	244	58

Southeast Division

Carolina	82	34	30	18	210	202	86
Florida	82	30	34	18	210	228	78
Washington	82	31	45	6	200	218	68
Tampa Bay	82	19	54	9	179	292	47

WESTERN CONFERENCE

Central Division

Detroit	82	43	32	7	245	202	93
St. Louis	82	37	32	13	237	209	87
Chicago	82	29	41	12	202	248	70
Nashville	82	28	47	7	190	261	63

Pacific Division

Dallas	82	51	19	12	236	168	114
Phoenix	82	39	31	12	205	197	90
Anaheim	82	35	34	13	215	206	83
San Jose	82	31	33	18	196	191	80
Los Angeles	82	32	45	5	189	222	69

Northwest Division

Colorado	82	44	28	10	239	205	98
Edmonton	82	33	37	12	230	226	78
Calgary	82	30	40	12	211	234	72
Vancouver	82	23	47	12	192	258	58

Stanley Cup Finals

June 8	Buffalo 3 at Dallas 2 (Jason Woolley 15:30 OT)
June 10	Buffalo 2 at Dallas 4
June 12	Dallas 2 at Buffalo 1
June 15	Dallas 1 at Buffalo 2
June 17	Buffalo 0 at Dallas 2 [Belfour]
June 19	Dallas 2 at Buffalo 1 (Brett Hull 54:51 OT)

Dallas won best-of-seven finals 4–2

1999–2000

EASTERN CONFERENCE
Northeast Division

	GP	W	L	T	OTL	GF	GA	PTS
Toronto	82	45	30	7	3	246	222	100
Ottawa	82	41	30	11	2	244	210	95
Buffalo	82	35	36	11	4	213	204	85
Canadiens	82	35	38	9	4	196	194	83
Boston	82	24	39	19	6	210	248	73

Atlantic Division

	GP	W	L	T	OTL	GF	GA	PTS
Philadelphia	82	45	25	12	3	237	179	105
New Jersey	82	45	29	8	5	251	203	103
Pittsburgh	82	37	37	8	6	241	236	88
Rangers	82	29	42	12	3	218	246	73
Islanders	82	24	49	9	1	194	275	58

Southeast Division

	GP	W	L	T	OTL	GF	GA	PTS
Washington	82	44	26	12	2	227	194	102
Florida	82	43	33	6	6	244	209	98
Carolina	82	37	35	10	0	217	216	84
Tampa Bay	82	19	54	9	7	204	309	54
Atlanta	82	14	61	7	4	170	313	39

WESTERN CONFERENCE
Central Division

	GP	W	L	T	OTL	GF	GA	PTS
St. Louis	82	51	20	11	1	248	165	114
Detroit	82	48	24	10	2	278	210	108
Chicago	82	33	39	10	2	242	245	78
Nashville	82	28	47	7	7	199	240	70

Northwest Division

Colorado	82	42	29	11	1	233	201	96
Edmonton	82	32	34	16	8	226	212	88
Vancouver	82	30	37	15	8	227	237	83
Calgary	82	31	41	10	5	211	256	77

Pacific Division

Dallas	82	43	29	10	6	211	184	102
Los Angeles	82	39	31	12	4	245	228	94
Phoenix	82	39	35	8	4	232	228	90
San Jose	82	35	37	10	7	225	214	87
Anaheim	82	34	36	12	3	217	227	83

Stanley Cup Finals

May 30	Dallas 3 at New Jersey 7
June 1	Dallas 2 at New Jersey 1
June 3	New Jersey 2 at Dallas 1
June 5	New Jersey 3 at Dallas 1
June 8	Dallas 1 at New Jersey 0 (Mike Modano 46:21 OT) [Belfour]
June 10	New Jersey 2 at Dallas 1 (Jason Arnott 28:20 OT)

New Jersey won best-of-seven finals 4–2

2000–01

EASTERN CONFERENCE
Northeast Division

	GP	W	L	T	OTL	GF	GA	PTS
Ottawa	82	48	21	9	4	274	205	109
Buffalo	82	46	30	5	1	218	184	98
Toronto	82	37	29	11	5	232	207	90
Boston	82	36	30	8	8	227	249	88
Montreal	82	28	40	8	6	206	232	70

Atlantic Division

	GP	W	L	T	OTL	GF	GA	PTS
New Jersey	82	48	19	12	3	295	195	111
Philadelphia	82	43	25	11	3	240	207	100
Pittsburgh	82	42	28	9	3	281	256	96
Rangers	82	33	43	5	1	250	290	72
Islanders	82	21	51	7	3	185	268	52

Southeast Division

	GP	W	L	T	OTL	GF	GA	PTS
Washington	82	41	27	10	4	233	211	96
Carolina	82	38	32	9	3	212	225	88
Florida	82	22	38	13	9	200	246	66
Atlanta	82	23	45	12	2	211	289	60
Tampa Bay	82	24	47	6	5	201	280	59

WESTERN CONFERENCE
Central Division

	GP	W	L	T	OTL	GF	GA	PTS
Detroit	82	49	20	9	4	253	202	111
St. Louis	82	43	22	12	5	249	195	103
Nashville	82	34	36	9	3	186	200	80
Chicago	82	29	40	8	5	210	246	71
Columbus	82	28	39	9	6	190	233	71

Northwest Division

Colorado	82	52	16	10	4	270	192	118
Edmonton	82	39	28	12	3	243	222	93
Vancouver	82	36	28	11	7	239	238	90
Calgary	82	27	36	15	4	197	236	73
Minnesota	82	25	39	13	5	168	210	68

Pacific Division

Dallas	82	48	24	8	2	241	187	106
San Jose	82	40	27	12	3	217	192	95
Los Angeles	82	38	28	13	3	252	228	92
Phoenix	82	35	27	17	3	214	212	90
Anaheim	82	25	41	11	5	188	245	66

Stanley Cup Finals

May 26	New Jersey 0 at Colorado 5 [Roy]
May 29	New Jersey 2 at Colorado 1
May 31	Colorado 3 at New Jersey 1
June 2	Colorado 2 at New Jersey 3
June 4	New Jersey 4 at Colorado 1
June 7	Colorado 4 at New Jersey 0 [Roy]
June 9	New Jersey 1 at Colorado 3

Colorado won best-of-seven 4–3

2001–02

EASTERN CONFERENCE
Northeast Division

	GP	W	L	T	OTL	GF	GA	PTS
Boston	82	43	24	6	9	236	201	101
Toronto	82	43	25	10	4	249	207	100
Ottawa	82	39	27	9	7	243	208	94
Montreal	82	36	31	12	3	207	209	87
Buffalo	82	35	35	11	1	213	200	82

Atlantic Division

	GP	W	L	T	OTL	GF	GA	PTS
Philadelphia	82	42	27	10	3	234	192	97
Islanders	82	42	28	8	4	239	220	96
New Jersey	82	41	28	9	4	205	187	95
Rangers	82	36	38	4	4	227	258	80
Pittsburgh	82	28	41	8	5	198	249	69

Southeast Division

	GP	W	L	T	OTL	GF	GA	PTS
Carolina	82	35	26	16	5	217	217	91
Washington	82	36	33	11	2	228	240	85
Tampa Bay	82	27	40	11	4	178	219	69
Florida	82	22	44	10	6	180	250	60
Atlanta	82	19	47	11	5	187	288	54

WESTERN CONFERENCE
Central Division

	GP	W	L	T	OTL	GF	GA	PTS
Detroit	82	51	17	10	4	251	187	116
St. Louis	82	43	27	8	4	227	188	98
Chicago	82	41	27	13	1	216	207	96
Nashville	82	28	41	13	0	196	230	69
Columbus	82	22	47	8	5	164	255	57

Pacific Division

San Jose	82	44	27	8	3	248	199	99
Phoenix	82	40	27	9	6	228	210	95
Los Angeles	82	40	27	11	4	214	190	95
Dallas	82	36	28	13	5	215	213	90
Anaheim	82	29	42	8	3	175	198	69

Northwest Division

Colorado	82	42	28	8	1	212	169	99
Vancouver	82	42	30	7	3	254	211	94
Edmonton	82	38	28	12	4	205	182	92
Calgary	82	32	35	12	3	201	220	79
Minnesota	82	26	35	12	9	195	238	73

Stanley Cup Finals

June 4	Carolina 3 at Detroit 2
June 6	Carolina 1 at Detroit 3
June 8	Detroit 3 at Carolina 2
June 10	Detroit 3 at Carolina 0
June 13	Carolina 1 at Detroit 3

Detroit wins Stanley Cup best-of-seven 4–1

2002–03

EASTERN CONFERENCE

Northeast Division

	GP	W	L	T	OTL	GF	GA	PTS
Ottawa	82	52	21	8	1	263	182	113
Toronto	82	44	28	7	3	236	208	98
Boston	82	36	31	11	4	245	237	87
Montreal	82	30	35	8	9	206	234	77
Buffalo	82	27	37	10	8	190	219	72

Atlantic Division

New Jersey	82	46	20	10	6	216	166	108
Philadelphia	82	45	20	13	4	211	166	107
Islanders	82	35	34	11	2	224	231	83
Rangers	82	32	36	10	4	210	231	78
Pittsburgh	82	27	44	6	5	189	255	65

Southeast Division

Tampa Bay	82	36	25	16	5	219	210	93
Washington	82	39	29	8	6	224	220	92
Atlanta	82	31	39	7	5	226	284	74
Florida	82	24	36	13	9	176	237	70
Carolina	82	22	43	11	6	171	240	61

WESTERN CONFERENCE

Central Division

Detroit	82	48	20	10	4	269	203	110
St. Louis	82	41	24	11	6	253	222	99
Chicago	82	30	33	13	6	207	226	79
Nashville	82	27	35	13	7	183	206	74
Columbus	82	29	42	8	3	213	263	69

Pacific Division

Dallas	82	46	17	15	4	245	169	111
Anaheim	82	40	27	9	6	203	193	95
Los Angeles	82	33	37	6	6	203	221	78
Phoenix	82	31	35	11	5	204	230	78
San Jose	82	28	37	9	8	214	239	73

Northwest Division

Colorado	82	42	19	13	8	251	194	105
Vancouver	82	45	23	13	1	264	208	104
Minnesota	82	42	29	10	1	198	178	95
Edmonton	82	36	26	11	9	231	230	92
Calgary	82	29	36	13	4	186	228	75

Stanley Cup Finals

May 27	Anaheim 0 at New Jersey 3 [Brodeur]
May 29	Anaheim 0 at New Jersey 3 [Brodeur]
May 31	New Jersey 2 at Anaheim 3 (Ruslan Salei 6:59 OT)
June 2	New Jersey 0 at Anaheim 1 (Steve Thomas 0:39 OT) [Giguere]
June 5	Anaheim 3 at New Jersey 6
June 7	New Jersey 2 at Anaheim 5
June 9	Anaheim 0 at New Jersey 3 [Brodeur]

New Jersey won best-of-seven finals 4–3

2003–2004

EASTERN CONFERENCE
Atlantic Division

	GP	W	L	T	OTL	PTS	GF	GA
Philadelphia	82	40	21	15	6	101	229	186
New Jersey	82	43	25	12	2	100	213	164
Islanders	82	38	29	11	4	91	237	210
Rangers	82	27	40	7	8	69	206	250
Pittsburgh	82	23	47	8	4	58	190	303

Northeast Division

Boston	82	41	19	15	7	104	209	188
Toronto	82	45	24	10	3	103	242	204
Ottawa	82	43	23	10	6	102	262	189
Montreal	82	41	30	7	4	93	208	192
Buffalo	82	37	34	7	4	85	220	221

Southeast Division

Tampa Bay	82	46	22	8	6	106	245	192
Atlanta	82	33	37	8	4	78	214	243
Carolina	82	28	34	14	6	76	172	209
Florida	82	28	35	15	4	75	188	221
Washington	82	23	46	10	3	59	186	253

WESTERN CONFERENCE
Central Division

Detroit	82	48	21	11	2	109	255	189
St. Louis	82	39	30	11	2	91	191	198
Nashville	82	38	29	11	4	91	216	217
Columbus	82	25	45	8	4	62	177	238
Chicago	82	20	43	11	8	59	188	259

Northwest Division

Vancouver	82	43	24	10	5	101	235	194
Colorado	82	40	22	13	7	100	236	198
Calgary	82	42	30	7	3	94	200	176
Edmonton	82	36	29	12	5	89	221	208
Minnesota	82	30	29	20	3	83	188	183

Pacific Division

San Jose	82	43	21	12	6	104	219	183
Dallas	82	41	26	13	2	97	194	175
Los Angeles	82	28	29	16	9	81	205	217
Anaheim	82	29	35	10	8	76	184	213
Phoenix	82	22	36	18	6	68	188	245

Note: overtime losses (OTL) are worth one point in the standings and are not included in the loss column (L)

Stanley Cup Finals

May 25	Calgary 4 at Tampa Bay 1
May 27	Calgary 1 at Tampa Bay 4
May 29	Tampa Bay 0 at Calgary 3 [Kiprusoff]
May 31	Tampa Bay 1 at Calgary 0 (Richards 2:48 1st) [Khabibulin]
June 3	Calgary 3 at Tampa Bay 2 (Saprykin 14:40 OT)
June 5	Tampa Bay 3 at Calgary 2 (St. Louis 20:33 OT)
June 7	Calgary 1 at Tampa Bay 2

Tampa Bay wins Stanley Cup best-of-seven 4–3

NHL AWARDS

Art Ross Trophy

1917–18	Joe Malone	Montreal Canadiens (48 points)
1918–19	Newsy Lalonde	Montreal Canadiens (32 points)
1919–20	Joe Malone	Quebec Bulldogs (49 points)
1920–21	Newsy Lalonde	Montreal Canadiens (43 points)
1921–22	Punch Broadbent	Ottawa Senators (46 points)
1922–23	Babe Dye	Toronto St. Pats (37 points)
1923–24	Cy Denneny	Ottawa Senators (24 points)
1924–25	Babe Dye	Toronto St. Pats (46 points)
1925–26	Nels Stewart	Montreal Maroons (42 points)
1926–27	Bill Cook	New York Rangers (37 points)
1927–28	Howie Morenz	Montreal Canadiens (51 points)
1928–29	Ace Bailey	Toronto Maple Leafs (32 points)
1929–30	Cooney Weiland	Boston Bruins (73 points)
1930–31	Howie Morenz	Montreal Canadiens (51 points)
1931–32	Busher Jackson	Toronto Maple Leafs (53 points)
1932–33	Bill Cook	New York Rangers (50 points)
1933–34	Charlie Conacher	Toronto Maple Leafs (52 points)
1934–35	Charlie Conacher	Toronto Maple Leafs (57 points)
1935–36	Sweeney Schriner	New York Americans (45 points)
1936–37	Sweeney Schriner	New York Americans (46 points)
1937–38	Gordie Drillon	Toronto Maple Leafs (52 points)
1938–39	Toe Blake	Montreal Canadiens (47 points)
1939–40	Milt Schmidt	Boston Bruins (52 points)
1940–41	Bill Cowley	Boston Bruins (62 points)
1941–42	Bryan Hextall	New York Rangers (56 points)
1942–43	Doug Bentley	Chicago Black Hawks (73 points)
1943–44	Herb Cain	Boston Bruins (82 points)
1944–45	Elmer Lach	Montreal Canadiens (80 points)
1945–46	Max Bentley	Chicago Black Hawks (61 points)
1946–47	Max Bentley	Chicago Black Hawks (72 points)

1947–48	Elmer Lach	Montreal Canadiens (61 points)
1948–49	Roy Conacher	Chicago Black Hawks (68 points)
1949–50	Ted Lindsay	Detroit Red Wings (78 points)
1950–51	Gordie Howe	Detroit Red Wings (86 points)
1951–52	Gordie Howe	Detroit Red Wings (86 points)
1952–53	Gordie Howe	Detroit Red Wings (95 points)
1953–54	Gordie Howe	Detroit Red Wings (81 points)
1954–55	Bernie Geoffrion	Montreal Canadiens (75 points)
1955–56	Jean Beliveau	Montreal Canadiens (88 points)
1956–57	Gordie Howe	Detroit Red Wings (89 points)
1957–58	Dickie Moore	Montreal Canadiens (84 points)
1958–59	Dickie Moore	Montreal Canadiens (96 points)
1959–60	Bobby Hull	Chicago Black Hawks (81 points)
1960–61	Bernie Geoffrion	Montreal Canadiens (95 points)
1961–62	Bobby Hull	Chicago Black Hawks (84 points)
1962–63	Gordie Howe	Detroit Red Wings (86 points)
1963–64	Stan Mikita	Chicago Black Hawks (89 points)
1964–65	Stan Mikita	Chicago Black Hawks (87 points)
1965–66	Bobby Hull	Chicago Black Hawks (97 points)
1966–67	Stan Mikita	Chicago Black Hawks (97 points)
1967–68	Stan Mikita	Chicago Black Hawks (87 points)
1968–69	Phil Esposito	Boston Bruins (126 points)
1969–70	Bobby Orr	Boston Bruins (120 points)
1970–71	Phil Esposito	Boston Bruins (152 points)
1971–72	Phil Esposito	Boston Bruins (133 points)
1972–73	Phil Esposito	Boston Bruins (130 points)
1973–74	Phil Esposito	Boston Bruins (145 points)
1974–75	Bobby Orr	Boston Bruins (135 points)
1975–76	Guy Lafleur	Montreal Canadiens (125 points)
1976–77	Guy Lafleur	Montreal Canadiens (136 points)
1977–78	Guy Lafleur	Montreal Canadiens (132 points)
1978–79	Bryan Trottier	New York Islanders (134 points)
1979–80	Marcel Dionne	Los Angeles Kings (137 points)
1980–81	Wayne Gretzky	Edmonton Oilers (164 points)

1981–82	Wayne Gretzky	Edmonton Oilers (212 points)
1982–83	Wayne Gretzky	Edmonton Oilers (196 points)
1983–84	Wayne Gretzky	Edmonton Oilers (205 points)
1984–85	Wayne Gretzky	Edmonton Oilers (208 points)
1985–86	Wayne Gretzky	Edmonton Oilers (215 points)
1986–87	Wayne Gretzky	Edmonton Oilers (183 points)
1987–88	Mario Lemieux	Pittsburgh Penguins (168 points)
1988–89	Mario Lemieux	Pittsburgh Penguins (199 points)
1989–90	Wayne Gretzky	Los Angeles Kings (142 points)
1990–91	Wayne Gretzky	Los Angeles Kings (163 points)
1991–92	Mario Lemieux	Pittsburgh Penguins (131 points)
1992–93	Mario Lemieux	Pittsburgh Penguins (160 points)
1993–94	Wayne Gretzky	Los Angeles Kings (130 points)
1994–95	Jaromir Jagr	Pittsburgh Penguins (70 points)
1995–96	Mario Lemieux	Pittsburgh Penguins (161 points)
1996–97	Mario Lemieux	Pittsburgh Penguins (122 points)
1997–98	Jaromir Jagr	Pittsburgh Penguins (102 points)
1998–99	Jaromir Jagr	Pittsburgh Penguins (127 points)
1999–00	Jaromir Jagr	Pittsburgh Penguins (96 points)
2000–01	Jaromir Jagr	Pittsburgh Penguins (121 points)
2001–02	Jarome Iginla	Calgary Flames (96 points)
2002–03	Peter Forsberg	Colorado Avalanche (106 points)
2003–04	Martin St. Louis	Tampa Bay Lightning (94 points)
2004–05	no winner	
2005–06	Joe Thornton	Boston Bruins/San Jose Sharks (125 points)

Hart Trophy

1923–24	Frank Nighbor	Ottawa Senators
1924–25	Billy Burch	Hamilton Tigers
1925–26	Nels Stewart	Montreal Maroons
1926–27	Herb Gardiner	Montreal Canadiens
1927–28	Howie Morenz	Montreal Canadiens
1928–29	Roy Worters	New York Americans

1929–30	Nels Stewart	Montreal Maroons
1930–31	Howie Morenz	Montreal Canadiens
1931–32	Howie Morenz	Montreal Canadiens
1932–33	Eddie Shore	Boston Bruins
1933–34	Aurel Joliat	Montreal Canadiens
1934–35	Eddie Shore	Boston Bruins
1935–36	Eddie Shore	Boston Bruins
1936–37	Babe Siebert	Montreal Canadiens
1937–38	Eddie Shore	Boston Bruins
1938–39	Toe Blake	Montreal Canadiens
1939–40	Ebbie Goodfellow	Detroit Red Wings
1940–41	Bill Cowley	Boston Bruins
1941–42	Tom Anderson	Brooklyn Americans
1942–43	Bill Cowley	Boston Bruins
1943–44	Babe Pratt	Toronto Maple Leafs
1944–45	Elmer Lach	Montreal Canadiens
1945–46	Max Bentley	Chicago Black Hawks
1946–47	Maurice Richard	Montreal Canadiens
1947–48	Buddy O'Connor	New York Rangers
1948–49	Sid Abel	Detroit Red Wings
1949–50	Chuck Rayner	New York Rangers
1950–51	Milt Schmidt	Boston Bruins
1951–52	Gordie Howe	Detroit Red Wings
1952–53	Gordie Howe	Detroit Red Wings
1953–54	Al Rollins	Chicago Black Hawks
1954–55	Ted Kennedy	Toronto Maple Leafs
1955–56	Jean Beliveau	Montreal Canadiens
1956–57	Gordie Howe	Detroit Red Wings
1957–58	Gordie Howe	Detroit Red Wings
1958–59	Andy Bathgate	New York Rangers
1959–60	Gordie Howe	Detroit Red Wings
1960–61	Bernie Geoffrion	Montreal Canadiens
1961–62	Jacques Plante	Montreal Canadiens
1962–63	Gordie Howe	Detroit Red Wings

1963–64	Jean Beliveau	Montreal Canadiens
1964–65	Bobby Hull	Chicago Black Hawks
1965–66	Bobby Hull	Chicago Black Hawks
1966–67	Stan Mikita	Chicago Black Hawks
1967–68	Stan Mikita	Chicago Black Hawks
1968–69	Phil Esposito	Boston Bruins
1969–70	Bobby Orr	Boston Bruins
1970–71	Bobby Orr	Boston Bruins
1971–72	Bobby Orr	Boston Bruins
1972–73	Bobby Clarke	Philadelphia Flyers
1973–74	Phil Esposito	Boston Bruins
1974–75	Bobby Clarke	Philadelphia Flyers
1975–76	Bobby Clarke	Philadelphia Flyers
1976–77	Guy Lafleur	Montreal Canadiens
1977–78	Guy Lafleur	Montreal Canadiens
1978–79	Bryan Trottier	New York Islanders
1979–80	Wayne Gretzky	Edmonton Oilers
1980–81	Wayne Gretzky	Edmonton Oilers
1981–82	Wayne Gretzky	Edmonton Oilers
1982–83	Wayne Gretzky	Edmonton Oilers
1983–84	Wayne Gretzky	Edmonton Oilers
1984–85	Wayne Gretzky	Edmonton Oilers
1985–86	Wayne Gretzky	Edmonton Oilers
1986–87	Wayne Gretzky	Edmonton Oilers
1987–88	Mario Lemieux	Pittsburgh Penguins
1988–89	Wayne Gretzky	Edmonton Oilers
1989–90	Mark Messier	Edmonton Oilers
1990–91	Brett Hull	St. Louis Blues
1991–92	Mark Messier	New York Rangers
1992–93	Mario Lemieux	Pittsburgh Penguins
1993–94	Sergei Fedorov	Detroit Red Wings
1994–95	Eric Lindros	Philadelphia Flyers
1995–96	Mario Lemieux	Pittsburgh Penguins
1996–97	Dominik Hasek	Buffalo Sabres

1997–98	Dominik Hasek	Buffalo Sabres
1998–99	Jaromir Jagr	Pittsburgh Penguins
1999–00	Chris Pronger	St. Louis Blues
2000–01	Joe Sakic	Colorado Avalanche
2001–02	Jose Theodore	Montreal Canadiens
2002–03	Peter Forsberg	Colorado Avalanche
2003–04	Martin St. Louis	Tampa Bay Lightning
2004–05	no winner	
2005–06	Joe Thornton	Boston Bruins/San Jose Sharks

Lady Byng Trophy

1924–25	Frank Nighbor	Ottawa Senators
1925–26	Frank Nighbor	Ottawa Senators
1926–27	Billy Burch	New York Americans
1927–28	Frank Boucher	New York Rangers
1928–29	Frank Boucher	New York Rangers
1929–30	Frank Boucher	New York Rangers
1930–31	Frank Boucher	New York Rangers
1931–32	Joe Primeau	Toronto Maple Leafs
1932–33	Frank Boucher	New York Rangers
1933–34	Frank Boucher	New York Rangers
1934–35	Frank Boucher	New York Rangers
1935–36	Doc Romnes	Chicago Black Hawks
1936–37	Marty Barry	Detroit Red Wings
1937–38	Gordie Drillon	Toronto Maple Leafs
1938–39	Clint Smith	New York Rangers
1939–40	Bobby Bauer	Boston Bruins
1940–41	Bobby Bauer	Boston Bruins
1941–42	Syl Apps	Toronto Maple Leafs
1942–43	Max Bentley	Chicago Black Hawks
1943–44	Clint Smith	Chicago Black Hawks
1944–45	Bill Mosienko	Chicago Black Hawks
1945–46	Toe Blake	Montreal Canadiens
1946–47	Bobby Bauer	Boston Bruins

1947–48	Buddy O'Connor	New York Rangers
1948–49	Bill Quackenbush	Detroit Red Wings
1949–50	Edgar Laprade	New York Rangers
1950–51	Red Kelly	Detroit Red Wings
1951–52	Sid Smith	Toronto Maple Leafs
1952–53	Red Kelly	Detroit Red Wings
1953–54	Red Kelly	Detroit Red Wings
1954–55	Sid Smith	Toronto Maple Leafs
1955–56	Dutch Reibel	Detroit Red Wings
1956–57	Andy Hebenton	New York Rangers
1957–58	Camille Henry	New York Rangers
1958–59	Alex Delvecchio	Detroit Red Wings
1959–60	Don McKenney	Boston Bruins
1960–61	Red Kelly	Toronto Maple Leafs
1961–62	Dave Keon	Toronto Maple Leafs
1962–63	Dave Keon	Toronto Maple Leafs
1963–64	Kenny Wharram	Chicago Black Hawks
1964–65	Bobby Hull	Chicago Black Hawks
1965–66	Alex Delvecchio	Detroit Red Wings
1966–67	Stan Mikita	Chicago Black Hawks
1967–68	Stan Mikita	Chicago Black Hawks
1968–69	Alex Delvecchio	Detroit Black Hawks
1969–70	Phil Goyette	St. Louis Blues
1970–71	John Bucyk	Boston Bruins
1971–72	Jean Ratelle	New York Rangers
1972–73	Gilbert Perreault	Buffalo Sabres
1973–74	John Bucyk	Boston Bruins
1974–75	Marcel Dionne	Detroit Red Wings
1975–76	Jean Ratelle	New York Rangers/Boston Bruins
1976–77	Marcel Dionne	Los Angeles Kings
1977–78	Butch Goring	Los Angeles Kings
1978–79	Bob MacMillan	Atlanta Flames
1979–80	Wayne Gretzky	Edmonton Oilers
1980–81	Rick Kehoe	Pittsburgh Penguins

1981–82	Rick Middleton	Boston Bruins
1982–83	Mike Bossy	New York Islanders
1983–84	Mike Bossy	New York Islanders
1984–85	Jari Kurri	Edmonton Oilers
1985–86	Mike Bossy	New York Islanders
1986–87	Joe Mullen	Calgary Flames
1987–88	Mats Naslund	Montreal Canadiens
1988–89	Joe Mullen	Calgary Flames
1989–90	Brett Hull	St. Louis Blues
1990–91	Wayne Gretzky	Los Angeles Kings
1991–92	Wayne Gretzky	Los Angeles Kings
1992– 93	Pierre Turgeon	New York Islanders
1993–94	Wayne Gretzky	Los Angeles Kings
1994–95	Ron Francis	Pittsburgh Penguins
1995–96	Paul Kariya	Mighty Ducks of Anaheim
1996–97	Paul Kariya	Mighty Ducks of Anaheim
1997–98	Ron Francis	Pittsburgh Penguins
1998–99	Wayne Gretzky	New York Rangers
1999–00	Pavol Demitra	St. Louis Blues
2000–01	Joe Sakic	Colorado Avalanche
2001–02	Ron Francis	Carolina Hurricanes
2002–03	Alexander Mogilny	Toronto Maple Leafs
2003–04	Brad Richards	Tampa Bay Lightning
2004–05	no winner	
2005–06	Pavel Datsyuk	Detroit Red Wings

Vezina Trophy

1926–27	George Hainsworth	Montreal Canadiens (1.47 GAA)
1927–28	George Hainsworth	Montreal Canadiens (1.05 GAA)
1928–29	George Hainsworth	Montreal Canadiens (0.92 GAA)
1929–30	Tiny Thompson	Boston Bruins (2.19 GAA)
1930–31	Roy Worters	New York Americans (1.61 GAA)
1931–32	Charlie Gardiner	Chicago Black Hawks (1.85 GAA)
1932–33	Tiny Thompson	Boston Bruins (1.76 GAA)

1933–34	Charlie Gardiner	Chicago Black Hawks (1.63 GAA)
1934–35	Lorne Chabot	Chicago Black Hawks (1.80 GAA)
1935–36	Tiny Thompson	Boston Bruins (1.68 GAA)
1936–37	Normie Smith	Detroit Red Wings (2.05 GAA)
1937–38	Tiny Thompson	Boston Bruins (1.80 GAA)
1938–39	Frank Brimsek	Boston Bruins (1.56 GAA)
1939–40	Dave Kerr	New York Rangers (1.54 GAA)
1940–41	Turk Broda	Toronto Maple Leafs (2.00 GAA)
1941–42	Frank Brimsek	Boston Bruins (2.35 GAA)
1942–43	Johnny Mowers	Detroit Red Wings (2.47 GAA)
1943–44	Bill Durnan	Montreal Canadiens (2.18 GAA)
1944–45	Bill Durnan	Montreal Canadiens (2.42 GAA)
1945–46	Bill Durnan	Montreal Canadiens (2.60 GAA)
1946–47	Bill Durnan	Montreal Canadiens (2.30 GAA)
1947–48	Turk Broda	Toronto Maple Leafs (2.38 GAA)
1948–49	Bill Durnan	Montreal Canadiens (2.10 GAA)
1949–50	Bill Durnan	Montreal Canadiens (2.20 GAA)
1950–51	Al Rollins	Toronto Maple Leafs (1.77 GAA)
1951–52	Terry Sawchuk	Detroit Red Wings (1.90 GAA)
1952–53	Terry Sawchuk	Detroit Red Wings (1.90 GAA)
1953–54	Harry Lumley	Toronto Maple Leafs (1.86 GAA)
1954–55	Terry Sawchuk	Detroit Red Wings (1.96 GAA)
1955–56	Jacques Plante	Montreal Canadiens (1.86 GAA)
1956–57	Jacques Plante	Montreal Canadiens (2.00 GAA)
1957–58	Jacques Plante	Montreal Canadiens (2.11 GAA)
1958–59	Jacques Plante	Montreal Canadiens (2.16 GAA)
1959–60	Jacques Plante	Montreal Canadiens (2.54 GAA)
1960–61	Johnny Bower	Toronto Maple Leafs (2.50 GAA)
1961–62	Jacques Plante	Montreal Canadiens (2.37 GAA)
1962–63	Glenn Hall	Chicago Black Hawks (2.47 GAA)
1963–64	Charlie Hodge	Montreal Canadiens (2.26 GAA)
1964–65	Terry Sawchuk	Toronto Maple Leafs (2.56 GAA)
	Johnny Bower	Toronto Maple Leafs (2.38 GAA)

1965–66	Gump Worsley	Montreal Canadiens (2.36 GAA)
	Charlie Hodge	Montreal Canadiens (2.58 GAA)
1966–67	Glenn Hall	Chicago Black Hawks (2.38 GAA)
	Denis Dejordy	Chicago Black Hawks (2.46 GAA)
1967–68	Gump Worsley	Montreal Canadiens (1.98 GAA)
	Rogie Vachon	Montreal Canadiens (2.48 GAA)
1968–69	Jacques Plante	St. Louis Blues (1.96 GAA)
	Glenn Hall	St. Louis Blues (2.17 GAA)
1969–70	Tony Esposito	Chicago Black Hawks (2.17 GAA)
1970–71	Ed Giacomin	New York Rangers (2.16 GAA)
	Gilles Villemure	New York Rangers (2.30 GAA)
1971–72	Tony Esposito	Chicago Black Hawks (1.77 GAA)
	Gary Smith	Chicago Black Hawks (2.42 GAA)
1972–73	Ken Dryden	Montreal Canadiens (2.26 GAA)
1973–74	Bernie Parent	Philadelphia Flyers (1.89 GAA)
	Tony Esposito	Chicago Black Hawks (2.04 GAA)
1974–75	Bernie Parent	Philadelphia Flyers (2.03 GAA)
1975–76	Ken Dryden	Montreal Canadiens (2.03 GAA)
1976–77	Ken Dryden	Montreal Canadiens (2.14 GAA)
	Michel Larocque	Montreal Canadiens (2.09 GAA)
1977–78	Ken Dryden	Montreal Canadiens (2.05 GAA)
	Michel Larocque	Montreal Canadiens (2.67 GAA)
1978–79	Ken Dryden	Montreal Canadiens (2.30 GAA)
	Michel Larocque	Montreal Canadiens (2.84 GAA)
1979–80	Bob Sauve	Buffalo Sabres (2.36 GAA)
	Don Edwards	Buffalo Sabres (2.57 GAA)
1980–81	Richard Sevigny	Montreal Canadiens (2.40 GAA)
	Dennis Herron	Montreal Canadiens (3.50 GAA)
	Michel Larocque	Montreal Canadiens (3.03 GAA)
1981–82	Billy Smith	New York Islanders (2.97 GAA)
1982–83	Pete Peeters	Boston Bruins (2.36 GAA)
1983–84	Tom Barrasso	Buffalo Sabres (2.84 GAA)
1984–85	Pelle Lindbergh	Philadelphia Flyers (3.02 GAA)
1985–86	John Vanbiesbrouck	New York Rangers (3.32 GAA)

1986–87	Ron Hextall	Philadelphia Flyers (3.00 GAA)
1987–88	Grant Fuhr	Edmonton Oilers (3.43 GAA)
1988–89	Patrick Roy	Montreal Canadiens (2.47 GAA)
1989–90	Patrick Roy	Montreal Canadiens (2.53 GAA)
1990–91	Ed Belfour	Chicago Blackhawks (2.47 GAA)
1991–92	Patrick Roy	Montreal Canadiens (2.36 GAA)
1992–93	Ed Belfour	Chicago Blackhawks (2.59 GAA)
1993–94	Dominik Hasek	Buffalo Sabres (1.95 GAA)
1994–95	Dominik Hasek	Buffalo Sabres (2.11 GAA)
1995–96	Jim Carey	Washington Capitals (2.26 GAA)
1996–97	Dominik Hasek	Buffalo Sabres (2.27 GAA)
1997–98	Dominik Hasek	Buffalo Sabres (2.09 GAA)
1998–99	Dominik Hasek	Buffalo Sabres (1.87 GAA)
1999–00	Olaf Kolzig	Washington Capitals (2.24 GAA)
2000–01	Dominik Hasek	Buffalo Sabres (2.11 GAA)
2001–02	Jose Theodore	Montreal Canadiens (2.11 GAA)
2002–03	Martin Brodeur	New Jersey Devils (2.02 GAA)
2003–04	Martin Brodeur	New Jersey Devils (2.62 GAA)
2004–05	no winner	
2005–06	Miikka Kiprusoff	Calgary Flames (2.07 GAA)

Calder Memorial Trophy

1932–33	Carl Voss	Detroit Red Wings
1933–34	Russ Blinco	Montreal Maroons
1934–35	Sweeney Schriner	New York Americans
1935–36	Mike Karakas	Chicago Black Hawks
1936–37	Syl Apps	Toronto Maple Leafs
1937–38	Cully Dahlstrom	Chicago Black Hawks
1938–39	Frank Brimsek	Boston Bruins
1939–40	Kilby MacDonald	New York Rangers
1940–41	John Quilty	Montreal Canadiens
1941–42	Grant Warwick	New York Rangers
1942–43	Gaye Stewart	Toronto Maple Leafs
1943–44	Gus Bodnar	Toronto Maple Leafs

1944–45	Frank McCool	Toronto Maple Leafs
1945–46	Edgar Laprade	New York Rangers
1946–47	Howie Meeker	Toronto Maple Leafs
1947–48	Jim McFadden	Detroit Red Wings
1948–49	Pentti Lund	New York Rangers
1949–50	Jack Gelineau	Boston Bruins
1950–51	Terry Sawchuk	Detroit Red Wings
1951–52	Bernie Geoffrion	Montreal Canadiens
1952–53	Gump Worsley	New York Rangers
1953–54	Camille Henry	New York Rangers
1954–55	Ed Litzenberger	Chicago Black Hawks
1955–56	Glenn Hall	Detroit Red Wings
1956–57	Larry Regan	Boston Bruins
1957–58	Frank Mahovlich	Toronto Maple Leafs
1958–59	Ralph Backstrom	Montreal Canadiens
1959–60	Bill Hay	Chicago Black Hawks
1960–61	Dave Keon	Toronto Maple Leafs
1961–62	Bobby Rousseau	Montreal Canadiens
1962–63	Kent Douglas	Toronto Maple Leafs
1963–64	Jacques Laperriere	Montreal Canadiens
1964–65	Roger Crozier	Detroit Red Wings
1965–66	Brit Selby	Toronto Maple Leafs
1966–67	Bobby Orr	Boston Bruins
1967–68	Derek Sanderson	Boston Bruins
1968–69	Danny Grant	Minnesota North Stars
1969–70	Tony Esposito	Chicago Black Hawks
1970–71	Gilbert Perreault	Buffalo Sabres
1971–72	Ken Dryden	Montreal Canadiens
1972–73	Steve Vickers	New York Rangers
1973–74	Denis Potvin	New York Islanders
1974–75	Eric Vail	Atlanta Flames
1975–76	Bryan Trottier	New York Islanders
1976–77	Willi Plett	Atlanta Flames
1977–78	Mike Bossy	New York Islanders

1978–79	Bobby Smith	Minnesota North Stars
1979–80	Raymond Bourque	Boston Bruins
1980–81	Peter Stastny	Quebec Nordiques
1981–82	Dale Hawerchuk	Winnipeg Jets
1982–83	Steve Larmer	Chicago Black Hawks
1983–84	Tom Barrasso	Buffalo Sabres
1984–85	Mario Lemieux	Pittsburgh Penguins
1985–86	Gary Suter	Calgary Flames
1986–87	Luc Robitaille	Los Angeles Kings
1987–88	Joe Nieuwendyk	Calgary Flames
1988–89	Brian Leetch	New York Rangers
1989–90	Sergei Makarov	Calgary Flames
1990–91	Ed Belfour	Chicago Blackhawks
1991–92	Pavel Bure	Vancouver Canucks
1992–93	Teemu Selanne	Winnipeg Jets
1993–94	Martin Brodeur	New Jersey Devils
1994–95	Peter Forsberg	Quebec Nordiques
1995–96	Daniel Alfredsson	Ottawa Senators
1996–97	Bryan Berard	New York Islanders
1997–98	Sergei Samsonov	Boston Bruins
1998–99	Chris Drury	Colorado Avalanche
1999–00	Scott Gomez	New Jersey Devils
2000–01	Evgeni Nabokov	San Jose Sharks
2001–02	Danny Heatley	Atlanta Thrashers
2002–03	Barret Jackman	St. Louis Blues
2003–04	Andrew Raycroft	Boston Bruins
2004–05	no winner	
2005–06	Alexander Ovechkin	Washington Capitals

James Norris Trophy

1953–54	Red Kelly	Detroit Red Wings
1954–55	Doug Harvey	Montreal Canadiens
1955–56	Doug Harvey	Montreal Canadiens
1956–57	Doug Harvey	Montreal Canadiens

1957–58	Doug Harvey	Montreal Canadiens
1958–59	Tom Johnson	Montreal Canadiens
1959–60	Doug Harvey	Montreal Canadiens
1960–61	Doug Harvey	Montreal Canadiens
1961–62	Doug Harvey	Montreal Canadiens
1962–63	Pierre Pilote	Chicago Black Hawks
1963–64	Pierre Pilote	Chicago Black Hawks
1964–65	Pierre Pilote	Chicago Black Hawks
1965–66	Jacques Laperriere	Montreal Canadiens
1966–67	Harry Howell	New York Rangers
1967–68	Bobby Orr	Boston Bruins
1968–69	Bobby Orr	Boston Bruins
1969–70	Bobby Orr	Boston Bruins
1970–71	Bobby Orr	Boston Bruins
1971–72	Bobby Orr	Boston Bruins
1972–73	Bobby Orr	Boston Bruins
1973–74	Bobby Orr	Boston Bruins
1974–75	Bobby Orr	Boston Bruins
1975–76	Denis Potvin	New York Islanders
1976–77	Larry Robinson	Montreal Canadiens
1977–78	Denis Potvin	New York Islanders
1978–79	Denis Potvin	New York Islanders
1979–80	Larry Robinson	Montreal Canadiens
1980–81	Randy Carlyle	Pittsburgh Penguins
1981–82	Doug Wilson	Chicago Black Hawks
1982–83	Rod Langway	Washington Capitals
1983–84	Rod Langway	Washington Capitals
1984–85	Paul Coffey	Edmonton Oilers
1985–86	Paul Coffey	Edmonton Oilers
1986–87	Raymond Bourque	Boston Bruins
1987–88	Raymond Bourque	Boston Bruins
1988–89	Chris Chelios	Montreal Canadiens
1989–90	Raymond Bourque	Boston Bruins
1990–91	Raymond Bourque	Boston Bruins

1991–92	Brian Leetch	New York Rangers
1992–93	Chris Chelios	Chicago Blackhawks
1993–94	Raymond Bourque	Boston Bruins
1994–95	Paul Coffey	Detroit Red Wings
1995–96	Chris Chelios	Chicago Blackhawks
1996–97	Brian Leetch	New York Rangers
1997–98	Rob Blake	Los Angeles Kings
1998–99	Al MacInnis	St. Louis Blues
1999–00	Chris Pronger	St. Louis Blues
2000–01	Nicklas Lidstrom	Detroit Red Wings
2001–02	Nicklas Lidstrom	Detroit Red Wings
2002–03	Nicklas Lidstrom	Detroit Red Wings
2003–04	Scott Niedermayer	New Jersey Devils
2004–05	no winner	
2005–06	Nicklas Lidstrom	Detroit Red Wings

Lester Patrick Trophy

1965–66	Jack Adams
1966–67	Gordie Howe
	Charles F. Adams
	James Norris, Sr.
1967–68	Tommy Lockhart
	Walter A. Brown
	Gen. John R. Kilpatrick
1968–69	Bobby Hull
	Ed Jeremiah
1969–70	Eddie Shore
	Jim Hendy
1970–71	Bill Jennings
	John B. Sollenberger
	Terry Sawchuk
1971–72	Clarence Campbell
	John A. Kelly
	Cooney Weiland
	James D. Norris

1972–73	Walter Bush, Jr.
1973–74	Alex Delvecchio
	Murray Murdoch
	Weston W. Adams Sr.
	Charles L. Crovat
1974–75	Donald M. Clark
	Bill Chadwick
	Tommy Ivan
1975–76	Stan Mikita
	George Leader
	Bruce A. Norris
1976–77	Johnny Bucyk
	Murray Armstrong
	John Mariucci
1977–78	Phil Esposito
	Tom Fitzgerald
	William T. Tutt
	Bill Wirtz
1978–79	Bobby Orr
1979–80	Bobby Clarke
	Ed Snider
	Fred Shero
	1980 U.S. Olympic Hockey Team
1980–81	Charles M. Schulz
1981–82	Emile Francis
1982–83	Bill Torrey
1983–84	John A. Ziegler Jr.
	Art Ross
1984–85	Jack Butterfield
	Arthur M. Wirtz
1985–86	John MacInnes
	Jack Riley
1986–87	Hobey Baker
	Frank Mathers

1987–88	Keith Allen
	Fred Cusick
	Bob Johnson
1988–89	Dan Kelly
	Lou Nanne
	Lynn Patrick
	Bud Poile
1989–90	Len Ceglarski
1990–91	Rod Gilbert
	Mike Ilitch
1991–92	Al Arbour
	Art Berglund
	Lou Lamoriello
1992–93	Frank Boucher
	Red Dutton
	Bruce McNall
	Gil Stein
1993–94	Wayne Gretzky
	Robert Ridder
1994–95	Joe Mullen
	Brian Mullen
	Bob Fleming
1995–96	George Gund
	Ken Morrow
	Milt Schmidt
1996–97	Seymour H. Knox III
	Bill Cleary
	Pat LaFontaine
1997–98	Peter Karmanos
	Neal Broten
	John Mayasich
	Max McNab
1998–99	Harry Sinden
	1998 U.S. Olympic Women's Hockey Team

1999–00	Mario Lemieux
	Craig Patrick
	Lou Vairo
2000–01	Scotty Bowman
	David Poile
	Gary Bettman
2001–02	1960 U.S. Olympic Team
	Herb Brooks
	Larry Pleau
2002–03	Ray Bourque
	Ron DeGregorio
	Willie O'Ree
2003–04	Mike Emrick
	John Davidson
	Ray Miron
2004–05	none

Conn Smythe Trophy

1964–65	Jean Beliveau	Montreal Canadiens
1965–66	Roger Crozier	Detroit Red Wings
1966–67	Dave Keon	Toronto Maple Leafs
1967–68	Glenn Hall	St. Louis Blues
1968–69	Serge Savard	Montreal Canadiens
1969–70	Bobby Orr	Boston Bruins
1970–71	Ken Dryden	Montreal Canadiens
1971–72	Bobby Orr	Boston Bruins
1972–73	Yvan Cournoyer	Montreal Canadiens
1973–74	Bernie Parent	Philadelphia Flyers
1974–75	Bernie Parent	Philadelphia Flyers
1975–76	Reggie Leach	Philadelphia Flyers
1976–77	Guy Lafleur	Montreal Canadiens
1977–78	Larry Robinson	Montreal Canadiens
1978–79	Bob Gainey	Montreal Canadiens
1979–80	Bryan Trottier	New York Islanders

1980–81	Butch Goring	New York Islanders
1981–82	Mike Bossy	New York Islanders
1982–83	Billy Smith	New York Islanders
1983–84	Mark Messier	Edmonton Oilers
1984–85	Wayne Gretzky	Edmonton Oilers
1985–86	Patrick Roy	Montreal Canadiens
1986–87	Ron Hextall	Philadelphia Flyers
1987–88	Wayne Gretzky	Edmonton Oilers
1988–89	Al MacInnis	Calgary Flames
1989–90	Bill Ranford	Edmonton Oilers
1990–91	Mario Lemieux	Pittsburgh Penguins
1991–92	Mario Lemieux	Pittsburgh Penguins
1992–93	Patrick Roy	Montreal Canadiens
1993–94	Brian Leetch	New York Rangers
1994–95	Claude Lemieux	New Jersey Devils
1995–96	Joe Sakic	Colorado Avalanche
1996–97	Mike Vernon	Detroit Red Wings
1997–98	Steve Yzerman	Detroit Red Wings
1998–99	Joe Nieuwendyk	Dallas Stars
1999–00	Scott Stevens	New Jersey Devils
2000–01	Patrick Roy	Colorado Avalanche
2001–02	Nicklas Lidstrom	Detroit Red Wings
2002–03	J-S Giguere	Mighty Ducks of Anaheim
2003–04	Brad Richards	Tampa Bay Lightning
2004–05	no winner	
2005–06	Cam Ward	Carolina Hurricanes

Bill Masterton Trophy

1967–68	Claude Provost	Montreal Canadiens
1968–69	Ted Hampson	Oakland Seals
1969–70	Pit Martin	Chicago Black Hawks
1970–71	Jean Ratelle	New York Rangers
1971–72	Bobby Clarke	Philadelphia Flyers
1972–73	Lowell MacDonald	Pittsburgh Penguins

1973–74	Henri Richard	Montreal Canadiens
1974–75	Don Luce	Buffalo Sabres
1975–76	Rod Gilbert	New York Rangers
1976–77	Ed Westfall	New York Islanders
1977–78	Butch Goring	Los Angeles Kings
1978–79	Serge Savard	Montreal Canadiens
1979–80	Al MacAdam	Minnesota North Stars
1980–81	Blake Dunlop	St. Louis Blues
1981–82	Glenn Resch	Colorado Rockies
1982–83	Lanny McDonald	Calgary Flames
1983–84	Brad Park	Detroit Red Wings
1984–85	Anders Hedberg	New York Rangers
1985–86	Charlie Simmer	Boston Bruins
1986–87	Doug Jarvis	Hartford Whalers
1987–88	Bob Bourne	Los Angeles Kings
1988–89	Tim Kerr	Philadelphia Flyers
1989–90	Gord Kluzak	Boston Bruins
1990–91	Dave Taylor	Los Angeles Kings
1991–92	Mark Fitzpatrick	New York Islanders
1992–93	Mario Lemieux	Pittsburgh Penguins
1993–94	Cam Neely	Boston Bruins
1994–95	Pat LaFontaine	Buffalo Sabres
1995–96	Gary Roberts	Calgary Flames
1996–97	Tony Granato	San Jose Sharks
1997–98	Jamie McLennan	St. Louis Blues
1998–99	John Cullen	Tampa Bay Lightning
1999–00	Ken Daneyko	New Jersey Devils
2000–01	Adam Graves	New York Rangers
2001–02	Saku Koivu	Montreal Canadiens
2002–03	Steve Yzerman	Detroit Red Wings
2003–04	Bryan Berard	Chicago Blackhawks
2004–05	no winner	
2005–06	Teemu Selanne	Mighty Ducks of Anaheim

Jack Adams Award

1973–74	Fred Shero	Philadelphia Flyers
1974–75	Bob Pulford	Los Angeles Kings
1975–76	Don Cherry	Boston Bruins
1976–77	Scotty Bowman	Montreal Canadiens
1977–78	Bobby Kromm	Detroit Red Wings
1978–79	Al Arbour	New York Islanders
1979–80	Pat Quinn	Philadelphia Flyers
1980–81	Red Berenson	St. Louis Blues
1981–82	Tom Watt	Winnipeg Jets
1982–83	Orval Tessier	Chicago Black Hawks
1983–84	Bryan Murray	Washington Capitals
1984–85	Mike Keenan	Philadelphia Flyers
1985–86	Glen Sather	Edmonton Oilers
1986–87	Jacques Demers	Detroit Red Wings
1987–88	Jacques Demers	Detroit Red Wings
1988–89	Pat Burns	Montreal Canadiens
1989–90	Bob Murdoch	Winnipeg Jets
1990–91	Brian Sutter	St. Louis Blues
1991–92	Pat Quinn	Vancouver Canucks
1992–93	Pat Burns	Toronto Maple Leafs
1993–94	Jacques Lemaire	New Jersey Devils
1994–95	Marc Crawford	Quebec Nordiques
1995–96	Scotty Bowman	Detroit Red Wings
1996–97	Ted Nolan	Buffalo Sabres
1997–98	Pat Burns	Boston Bruins
1998–99	Jacques Martin	Ottawa Senators
1999–00	Joel Quenneville	St. Louis Blues
2000–01	Bill Barber	Philadelphia Flyers
2001–02	Bob Francis	Phoenix Coyotes
2002–03	Jacques Lemaire	Minnesota Wild
2003–04	John Tortorella	Tampa Bay Lightning
2004–05	no winner	
2005–06	Lindy Ruff	Buffalo Sabres

Lester B. Pearson Award

1970–71	Phil Esposito	Boston Bruins
1971–72	Jean Ratelle	New York Rangers
1972–73	Bobby Clarke	Philadelphia Flyers
1973–74	Phil Esposito	Boston Bruins
1974–75	Bobby Orr	Boston Bruins
1975–76	Guy Lafleur	Montreal Canadiens
1976–77	Guy Lafleur	Montreal Canadiens
1977–78	Guy Lafleur	Montreal Canadiens
1978–79	Marcel Dionne	Los Angeles Kings
1979–80	Marcel Dionne	Los Angeles Kings
1980–81	Mike Liut	St. Louis Blues
1981–82	Wayne Gretzky	Edmonton Oilers
1982–83	Wayne Gretzky	Edmonton Oilers
1983–84	Wayne Gretzky	Edmonton Oilers
1984–85	Wayne Gretzky	Edmonton Oilers
1985–86	Mario Lemieux	Pittsburgh Penguins
1986–87	Wayne Gretzky	Edmonton Oilers
1987–88	Mario Lemieux	Pittsburgh Penguins
1988–89	Steve Yzerman	Detroit Red Wings
1989–90	Mark Messier	Edmonton Oilers
1990–91	Brett Hull	St. Louis Blues
1991–92	Mark Messier	New York Rangers
1992–93	Mario Lemieux	Pittsburgh Penguins
1993–94	Sergei Fedorov	Detroit Red Wings
1994–95	Eric Lindros	Philadelphia Flyers
1995–96	Mario Lemieux	Pittsburgh Penguins
1996–97	Dominik Hasek	Buffalo Sabres
1997–98	Dominik Hasek	Buffalo Sabres
1998–99	Jaromir Jagr	Pittsburgh Penguins
1999–00	Jaromir Jagr	Pittsburgh Penguins
2000–01	Joe Sakic	Colorado Avalanche
2001–02	Jarome Iginla	Calgary Flames
2002–03	Markus Naslund	Vancouver Canucks

2003–04	Martin St. Louis	Tampa Bay Lightning
2004–05	no winner	
2005–06	Jaromir Jagr	New York Rangers

Frank J. Selke Trophy

1977–78	Bob Gainey	Montreal Canadiens
1978–79	Bob Gainey	Montreal Canadiens
1979–80	Bob Gainey	Montreal Canadiens
1980–81	Bob Gainey	Montreal Canadiens
1981–82	Steve Kasper	Boston Bruins
1982–83	Bobby Clarke	Pittsburgh Penguins
1983–84	Doug Jarvis	Washington Capitals
1984–85	Craig Ramsay	Buffalo Sabres
1985–86	Troy Murray	Chicago Black Hawks
1986–87	Dave Poulin	Philadelphia Flyers
1987–88	Guy Carbonneau	Montreal Canadiens
1988–89	Guy Carbonneau	Montreal Canadiens
1989–90	Rick Meagher	St. Louis Blues
1990–91	Dirk Graham	Chicago Blackhawks
1991–92	Guy Carbonneau	Montreal Canadiens
1992–93	Doug Gilmour	Toronto Maple Leafs
1993–94	Sergei Fedorov	Detroit Red Wings
1994–95	Ron Francis	Pittsburgh Penguins
1995–96	Sergei Fedorov	Detroit Red Wings
1996–97	Michael Peca	Buffalo Sabres
1997–98	Jere Lehtinen	Dallas Stars
1998–99	Jere Lehtinen	Dallas Stars
1999–00	Steve Yzerman	Detroit Red Wings
2000–01	John Madden	New Jersey Devils
2001–02	Michael Peca	New York Islanders
2002–03	Jere Lehtinen	Dallas Stars
2003–04	Kris Draper	Detroit Red Wings
2004–05	no winner	
2005–06	Rod Brind 'Amour	Carolina Hurricanes

William M. Jennings Trophy

1981–82	Rick Wamsley & Denis Herron	Montreal Canadiens
1982–83	Rollie Melanson & Billy Smith	New York Islanders
1983–84	Al Jensen & Pat Riggin	Washington Capitals
1984–85	Tom Barrasso & Bob Sauve	Buffalo Sabres
1985–86	Bob Froese & Darren Jensen	Philadelphia Flyers
1986–87	Patrick Roy & Brian Hayward	Montreal Canadiens
1987–88	Patrick Roy & Brian Hayward	Montreal Canadiens
1988–89	Patrick Roy & Brian Hayward	Montreal Canadiens
1989–90	Andy Moog & Reggie Lemelin	Boston Bruins
1990–91	Ed Belfour	Chicago Blackhawks
1991–92	Patrick Roy	Montreal Canadiens
1992–93	Ed Belfour	Chicago Blackhawks
1993–94	Dominik Hasek & Grant Fuhr	Buffalo Sabres
1994–95	Ed Belfour	Chicago Blackhawks
1995–96	Chris Osgood & Mike Vernon	Detroit Red Wings
1996–97	Martin Brodeur & Mike Dunham	New Jersey Devils
1997–98	Martin Brodeur	New Jersey Devils
1998–99	Ed Belfour & Roman Turek	Dallas Stars
1999–00	Roman Turek	St. Louis Blues
2000–01	Dominik Hasek	Buffalo Sabres
2001–02	Patrick Roy	Colorado Avalanche
2002–03	Martin Brodeur	New Jersey Devils
	Roman Cechmanek	Philadelphia Flyers
	Robert Esche	Philadelphia Flyers
2003–04	Martin Brodeur	New Jersey Devils
2004–05	no winner	
2005–06	Miikka Kiprusoff	Calgary Flames

King Clancy Memorial Trophy

1987–88	Lanny McDonald	Calgary Flames
1988–89	Bryan Trottier	New York Islanders
1989–90	Kevin Lowe	Edmonton Oilers

1990–91	Dave Taylor	Los Angeles Kings
1991–92	Raymond Bourque	Boston Bruins
1992–93	Dave Poulin	Boston Bruins
1993–94	Adam Graves	New York Rangers
1994–95	Joe Nieuwendyk	Calgary Flames
1995–96	Kris King	Winnipeg Jets
1996–97	Trevor Linden	Vancouver Canucks
1997–98	Kelly Chase	St. Louis Blues
1998–99	Rob Ray	Buffalo Sabres
1999–00	Curtis Joseph	Toronto Maple Leafs
2000–01	Shjon Podein	Colorado Avalanche
2001–02	Ron Francis	Carolina Hurricanes
2002–03	Brendan Shanahan	Detroit Red Wings
2003–04	Jarome Iginla	Calgary Flames
2004–05	no winner	
2005–06	Olaf Kolzig	Washington Capitals

Rocket Richard Trophy

1998–99	Teemu Selanne	Mighty Ducks of Anaheim (47 goals)
1999–00	Pavel Bure	Florida Panthers (58 goals)
2000–01	Pavel Bure	Florida Panthers (59 goals)
2001–02	Jarome Iginla	Calgary Flames (52 goals)
2002–03	Milan Hejduk	Colorado Avalanche (50 goals)
2003–04	Rick Nash	Columbus Blue Jackets (41 goals)
	Jarome Iginla	Calgary Flames (41 goals)
	Ilya Kovalchuk	Atlanta Thrashers (41 goals)
2004–05	no winner	
2005–06	Jonathan Cheechoo	San Jose Sharks (56 goals)

HOCKEY HALLS OF FAME

Hockey Hall of Fame 2006 elections, June 28, 2006

First-time eligible players: Tom Barrasso, Pavel Bure, Ken Daneyko, Kevin Dineen, Doug Gilmour, Adam Graves, Phil Housley, Kirk Muller, Mike Richter, Patrick Roy

Other notable players still eligible: Glenn Anderson, Dino Ciccarelli

Inductees:

Players
Dick Duff

One of the most successful players of the 1960s, Duff won Stanley Cups with the two great dynasties of that decade, Toronto and Montreal. He won with the Leafs in 1962 and 1963, but the following year he was traded to the New York Rangers in a blockbuster deal. Later traded to Montreal, Duff won four more championships—1965, 1966, 1968, and 1969. In all, he played 1,030 games and recorded nearly 600 points.

Patrick Roy

Goalie Patrick Roy is the only three-time winner of the Conn Smythe Trophy. He won his first Stanley Cup in 1986 as a rookie in Montreal, and won again in 1993 with another mediocre team that featured his spectacular goaltending. After being traded to Colorado, he won two more Cups, the first in 1996 and again in 2002. He is the all-time leader in regular-season games played (1,029) and wins (551) and playoff games played (247) and wins (151).

Builders
Herb Brooks

Brooks coached USA to a stunning gold medal at the 1980 Olympics in Lake Placid. The "Miracle on Ice" included a 4–3 win over the Soviet Union. Brooks later coached three teams in the NHL—New Jersey,

Minnesota and New York Rangers—and finished his career by guiding USA to a silver medal at the 2002 Olympics in Salt Lake City.

Harley Hotchkiss
Hotchkiss was one of a group that brought NHL hockey to Calgary from Atlanta in 1979. The team went on to play in the Stanley Cup finals in 1986 and three years later won the sacred trophy, defeating Montreal on Forum ice. He was later instrumental in the league and players reaching an historic agreement featuring a salary cap in the summer of 2005.

Hockey Hall of Fame Honoured Members
(member, category, year inducted)

Sid Abel—Player, 1969
Charles Adams—Builder, 1960
Jack Adams—Player, 1959
Weston Adams—Builder, 1972
Frank Ahearn—Builder, 1962
Bunny Ahearne—Builder, 1977
Sir Montagu Allan—Builder, 1945
Keith Allen—Builder, 1992
Syl Apps—Player, 1961
Al Arbour—Builder, 1996
George Armstrong—Player, 1975
Neil Armstrong—Official, 1991
John Ashley—Official, 1981
Ace Bailey—Player, 1975
Dan Bain—Player, 1945
Hobey Baker—Player, 1945
Harold Ballard—Builder, 1977
Bill Barber—Player, 1990
Marty Barry—Player, 1965

Andy Bathgate—Player, 1978
Bobby Bauer—Player, 1996
Father David Bauer—Builder, 1989
Jean Beliveau—Player, 1972
Clint Benedict—Player, 1965
Doug Bentley—Player, 1964
Max Bentley—Player, 1966
Jack Bickell—Builder, 1978
Toe Blake—Player, 1966
Leo Boivin—Player, 1986
Dickie Boon—Player, 1952
Mike Bossy—Player, 1991
Butch Bouchard—Player, 1966
Frank Boucher—Player, 1958
George Boucher—Player, 1960
Ray Bourque—Player, 2004
Johnny Bower—Player, 1976
Russell Bowie—Player, 1945
Scotty Bowman—Builder, 1991

Frank Brimsek—Player, 1966

Punch Broadbent—Player, 1962

Turk Broda—Player, 1967

Herb Brooks—Builder, 2006

George Brown—Builder, 1961

Walter Brown—Builder, 1962

Frank Buckland—Builder, 1975

Johnny Bucyk—Player, 1981

Billy Burch—Player, 1974

Walter Bush—Builder, 2000

Jack Butterfield—Builder, 1980

Frank Calder—Builder, 1947

Harry Cameron—Player, 1962

Angus Campbell—Builder, 1964

Clarence Campbell—Builder, 1966

Joe Cattarinich—Builder, 1977

Bill Chadwick—Official, 1964

Gerry Cheevers—Player, 1985

King Clancy—Player, 1958

Dit Clapper—Player, 1947

Bobby Clarke—Player, 1987

Sprague Cleghorn—Player, 1958

Paul Coffey—Player, 2004

Neil Colville—Player, 1967

Charlie Conacher—Player, 1961

Lionel Conacher—Player, 1994

Roy Conacher—Player, 1998

Alex Connell—Player, 1958

Bill Cook—Player, 1952

Bun Cook—Player, 1995

Murray Costello—Builder, 2005

Art Coulter—Player, 1974

Yvan Cournoyer—Player, 1982

Bill Cowley—Player, 1968

Rusty Crawford—Player, 1962

John D'Amico—Official, 1993

Leo Dandurand—Builder, 1963

Jack Darragh—Player, 1962

Scotty Davidson—Player, 1950

Hap Day—Player, 1961

Alex Delvecchio—Player, 1977

Cy Denneny—Player, 1959

Frank Dilio—Builder, 1964

Marcel Dionne—Player, 1992

Gord Drillon—Player, 1975

Graham Drinkwater—Player, 1950

Ken Dryden—Player, 1983

George Dudley—Builder, 1958

Dick Duff—Player, 2006

Woody Dumart—Player, 1992

Tommy Dunderdale—Player, 1974

James Dunn—Builder, 1968

Bill Durnan—Player, 1964

Red Dutton—Player, 1958

Babe Dye—Player, 1970

Chaucer Elliott—Official, 1961

Tony Esposito—Player, 1988

Phil Esposito—Player, 1984

Art Farrell—Player, 1965

Bernie Federko—Player, 2002

Slava Fetisov—Player, 2001

Fern Flaman—Player, 1990

Cliff Fletcher—Builder, 2004

Frank Foyston—Player, 1958

Emile Francis—Builder, 1982

Frank Fredrickson—Player, 1958

Grant Fuhr—Player, 2003

Bill Gadsby—Player, 1970

Bob Gainey—Player, 1992
Chuck Gardiner—Player, 1945
Herb Gardiner—Player, 1958
Jimmy Gardner—Player, 1962
Mike Gartner—Player, 2001
Bernie Geoffrion—Player, 1972
Eddie Gerard—Player, 1945
Ed Giacomin—Player, 1987
Dr. Jack Gibson—Builder, 1976
Rod Gilbert—Player, 1982
Clark Gillies—Player, 2002
Billy Gilmour—Player, 1962
Moose Goheen—Player, 1952
Ebbie Goodfellow—Player, 1963
Tommy Gorman—Builder, 1963
Michel Goulet—Player, 1998
Mike Grant—Player, 1950
Shorty Green—Player, 1962
Wayne Gretzky—Player, 1999
Si Griffis—Player, 1950
Frank Griffiths—Builder, 1993
George Hainsworth—Player, 1961
Glenn Hall—Player, 1975
Joe Hall—Player, 1961
William Hanley—Builder, 1986
Doug Harvey—Player, 1973
Dale Hawerchuk—Player, 2001
Charles Hay—Builder, 1974
George Hay—Player, 1958
George Hayes—Official, 1988
Jim Hendy—Builder, 1968
Riley Hern—Player, 1962
Bobby Hewitson—Official, 1963
Foster Hewitt—Builder, 1965

William Hewitt—Builder, 1947
Bryan Hextall—Player, 1969
Harry Holmes—Player, 1972
Tom Hooper—Player, 1962
Red Horner—Player, 1965
Tim Horton—Player, 1977
Harley Hotchkiss—Builder, 2006
Gordie Howe—Player, 1972
Syd Howe—Player, 1965
Harry Howell—Player, 197
Bobby Hull—Player, 1983
Fred Hume—Builder, 1962
Bouse Hutton—Player, 1962
Harry Hyland—Player, 1962
Mike Ilitch—Builder, 2003
Punch Imlach—Builder, 1984
Mickey Ion—Official, 1961
Dick Irvin—Player, 1958
Tommy Ivan—Builder, 1974
Harvey Jackson—Player, 1971
William Jennings—Builder, 1975
Bob Johnson—Builder, 1992
Moose Johnson—Player, 1952
Ching Johnson—Player, 1958
Tom Johnson—Player, 1970
Aurel Joliat—Player, 1947
Gordon Juckes—Builder, 1979
Duke Keats—Player, 1958
Red Kelly—Player, 1969
Ted Kennedy—Player, 1966
Dave Keon—Player, 1986
Valeri Kharlamov—Player, 2005
Gen. John Reed Kilpatrick—
  Builder, 1960

Brian Kilrea—Builder, 2003

Seymour Knox—Builder, 1993

Jari Kurri—Player, 2001

Elmer Lach—Player, 1966

Guy Lafleur—Player, 1988

Pat LaFontaine—Player, 2003

Newsy Lalonde—Player, 1950

Rod Langway—Player, 2002

Jacques Laperriere—Player, 1987

Guy Lapointe—Player, 1993

Edgar Laprade—Player, 1993

Jack Laviolette—Player, 1962

George Leader—Builder, 1969

Robert LeBel—Builder, 1970

Hugh Lehman—Player, 1958

Jacques Lemaire—Player, 1984

Mario Lemieux—Player, 1997

Percy LeSueur—Player, 1961

Herbie Lewis—Player, 1989

Ted Lindsay—Player, 1966

Tommy Lockhart—Builder, 1965

Paul Loicq—Builder, 1961

Harry Lumley—Player, 1980

Mickey MacKay—Player, 1952

Frank Mahovlich—Player, 1981

Joe Malone—Player, 1950

Sylvio Mantha—Player, 1960

John Mariucci—Builder, 1985

Jack Marshall—Player, 1965

Frank Mathers—Builder, 1992

Steamer Maxwell—Player, 1962

Lanny McDonald—Player, 1992

Frank McGee—Player, 1945

Billy McGimsie—Player, 1962

Major Frederic McLaughlin—
Builder, 1963

George McNamara—Player, 1958

Stan Mikita—Player, 1983

Jake Milford—Builder, 1984

Hon. Hartland Molson—
Builder, 1973

Dickie Moore—Player, 1974

Paddy Moran—Player, 1958

Howie Morenz—Player, 1945

Scotty Morrison—Builder, 1999

Bill Mosienko—Player, 1965

Joe Mullen—Player, 2000

Larry Murphy—Player, 2004

Monsignor Athol Murray—
Builder, 1998

Cam Neely—Player, 2005

Roger Neilson—Builder, 2002

Francis Nelson—Builder, 1947

Frank Nighbor—Player, 1947

Reg Noble—Player, 1962

Bruce A. Norris—Builder, 1969

James Norris Jr.—Builder, 1962

James Norris Sr.—Builder, 1958

William Northey—Builder, 1947

Ambrose O'Brien—Builder, 1962

Buddy O'Connor—Player, 1988

Harry Oliver—Player, 1967

Bert Olmstead—Player, 1985

Brian O'Neill—Builder, 1994

Bobby Orr—Player, 1979

Fred Page—Builder, 1993

Bernie Parent—Player, 1984

Brad Park—Player, 1988

Craig Patrick—Builder, 2001
Frank Patrick—Builder, 1958
Lester Patrick—Player, 1947
Lynn Patrick—Player, 1980
Matt Pavelich—Official, 1987
Gilbert Perreault—Player, 1990
Tommy Phillips—Player, 1945
Allan Pickard—Builder, 1958
Pierre Pilote—Player, 1975
Rudy Pilous—Builder, 1985
Didier Pitre—Player, 1962
Jacques Plante—Player, 1978
Bud Poile—Builder, 1990
Sam Pollock—Builder, 1978
Denis Potvin—Player, 1991
Babe Pratt—Player, 1966
Joe Primeau—Player, 1963
Marcel Pronovost—Player, 1978
Bob Pulford—Player, 1991
Harvey Pulford—Player, 1945
Bill Quackenbush—Player, 1976
Frank Rankin—Player, 1961
Jean Ratelle—Player, 1985
Sen. Donat Raymond—
    Builder, 1958
Chuck Rayner—Player, 1973
Ken Reardon—Player, 1966
Henri Richard—Player, 1979
Maurice Richard—Player, 1961
George Richardson—Player, 1950
Gordon Roberts—Player, 1971
John Ross Robertson—
    Builder, 1947
Claude Robinson—Builder, 1947

Larry Robinson—Player, 1995
Mike Rodden—Official, 1962
Art Ross—Player, 1945
Philip D. Ross—Builder, 1976
Patrick Roy—Player, 2006
Blair Russel—Player, 1965
Ernie Russell—Player, 1965
Jack Ruttan—Player, 1962
Dr. Gunther Sabetzki—
    Builder, 1995
Borje Salming—Player, 1996
Glen Sather—Builder, 1997
Denis Savard—Player, 2000
Serge Savard—Player, 1986
Terry Sawchuk—Player, 1971
Fred Scanlan—Player, 1965
Milt Schmidt—Player, 1961
Sweeney Schriner—Player, 1962
Earl Seibert—Player, 1963
Oliver Seibert—Player, 1961
Frank Selke—Builder, 1960
Eddie Shore—Player, 1947
Steve Shutt—Player, 1993
Babe Siebert—Player, 1964
Joe Simpson—Player, 1962
Harry Sinden—Builder, 1983
Darryl Sittler—Player, 1989
Cooper Smeaton—Official, 1961
Alf Smith—Player, 1962
Billy Smith—Player, 1993
Clint Smith—Player, 1991
Frank Smith—Builder, 1962
Hooley Smith—Player, 1972
Tommy Smith—Player, 1973

Conn Smythe—Builder, 1958
Ed Snider—Builder, 1988
Allan Stanley—Player, 1981
Barney Stanley—Player, 1962
Peter Stastny—Player, 1998
Jack Stewart—Player, 1964
Lord Stanley of Preston—
    Builder, 1945
Nels Stewart—Player, 1962
Red Storey—Official, 1967
Bruce Stuart—Player, 1961
Hod Stuart—Player, 1945
Capt. James T. Sutherland—
    Builder, 1947
Anatoli Tarasov—Builder, 1974
Cyclone Taylor—Player, 1947
Tiny Thompson—Player, 1959
Bill Torrey—Builder, 1995
Vladislav Tretiak—Player, 1989
Harry Trihey—Player, 1950
Bryan Trottier—Player, 1997
Lloyd Turner—Builder, 1958

William Tutt—Builder, 1978
Frank Udvari—Official, 1973
Norm Ullman—Player, 1982
Andy Van Hellemond—
    Official, 1999
Georges Vezina—Player, 1945
Carl Voss—Builder, 1974
Fred Waghorne—Builder, 1961
Jack Walker—Player, 1960
Marty Walsh—Player, 1962
Harry E. Watson—Player, 1962
Harry Watson—Player, 1994
Cooney Weiland—Player, 1971
Harry Westwick—Player, 1962
Fred Whitcroft—Player, 1962
Phat Wilson—Player, 1962
Arthur Wirtz—Builder, 1971
Bill Wirtz—Builder, 1976
Gump Worsley—Player, 1980
Roy Worters—Player, 1969
John Ziegler—Builder, 1987

IIHF Hall of Fame
(player, nationality, year inducted)

Guido Adamec (Czech Republic),
    2005
John "Bunny" Ahearne (Great
    Britain), 1997
Ernest Aljancic Sr. (Slovenia), 2002
Helmut Balderis (Latvia), 1998
Rudi Ball (Germany), 2004

Father David Bauer (Canada), 1997
Curt Berglund (Sweden), 2003
Sven Bergqvist (Sweden), 1999
Lars Bjorn (Sweden), 1998
Vsevolod Bobrov (USSR), 1997
Roger Bourbonnais (Canada), 1999
Herb Brooks (USA), 1999

Walter Brown (USA), 1997

Vlastimil Bubnik
(Czechoslovakia), 1997

Mike Buckna (Canada), 2004

Enrico Calcaterra (Italy), 1999

Ferdinand Cattini
(Switzerland), 1998

Hans Cattini (Switzerland), 1998

Arkady Chernyshev (Russia), 1999

Bill Christian (USA), 1998

Bill Cleary (USA), 1997

Gerry Cosby (USA), 1997

Jim Craig (USA), 1999

Mike Curran (USA), 1999

Ove Dahlberg (Sweden), 2004

Vitali Davydov (Russia), 2004

Jaroslav Drobny
(Czechoslovakia), 1997

Vladimir Dzurilla (Slovakia), 1998

Rudolf Eklow (Sweden), 1999

Carl Erhardt (Great Britain), 1998

Slava Fetisov (Russia), 2005

Anatoli Firsov (Russia), 1998

Josef Golonka (Slovakia), 1998

Wayne Gretzky (Canada), 2000

Arne Grunander (Sweden), 1997

Henryk Gruth (Poland), 2006

Bengt-Ake Gustafsson (Sweden),
2003

Karel Gut (Czechoslovakia), 1998

Anders Hedberg (Sweden), 1997

Heinz Henschel (Germany), 2003

William Hewitt (Canada), 1998

Ivan Hlinka (Czech Republic), 2002

Jiri Holecek (Czech Republic), 1998

Jiri Holik (Czech Republic), 1999

Derek Holmes (Canada), 1999

Leif Holmqvist (Sweden), 1999

Ladislav Horsky (Slovakia), 2004

Fran Huck (Canada), 1999

Jorgen Hviid (Denmark), 2005

Gustav Jaenecke (Germany), 1998

Tore Johannessen (Norway), 1999

Mark Johnson (USA), 1999

Marshall Johnston (Canada), 1998

Tomas Jonsson (Sweden), 2000

Gord Juckes (Canada), 1997

Timo Jutila (Finland), 2003

Yuri Karandin (Russia), 2004

Tsutomu Kawabuchi (Japan), 2004

Matti Keinonen (Finland), 2002

Valeri Kharlamov (Russia), 1998

Anatoli Khorozov (Ukraine), 2006

Udo Kiessling (Germany), 2000

Dave King (Canada), 2001

Josef Kompalla (Germany), 2003

Vladimir Kostka
(Czechoslovakia), 1997

Erich Kuhnhackl (Germany), 1997

Jari Kurri (Finland), 2000

Viktor Kuzkin (Russia), 2005

Jacques Lacarriere (France), 1998

Bob Lebel (Canada), 1997

Harry Lindblad (Finland), 1999

Vic Lindquist (Canada), 1997

Paul Loicq (Belgium), 1997

Hakan Loob (Sweden), 1998

Cesar Luthi (Switzerland), 1998

Oldrich Machac (Czech Republic), 1999

Barry MacKenzie (Canada), 1999

Sergei Makarov (Russia), 2001

Josef Malecek (Czech Republic), 2003

Alexander Maltsev (Russia), 1999

Louis Magnus (France), 1997

Pekka Marjamaki (Finland), 1998

Seth Martin (Canada), 1997

Vladimir Martinec (Czech Republic), 2001

John Mayasich (USA), 1997

Boris Mayorov (Russia), 1999

Jack McCartan (USA), 1998

Jack McLeod (Canada), 1999

Boris Mikhailov (Russia), 2000

Lou Nanne (USA), 2004

Mats Naslund (Sweden), 2005

Vaclav Nedomansky (Czechoslovakia), 1997

Kent Nilsson (Sweden), 2006

Nisse Nilsson (Sweden), 2002

Lasse Oksanen (Finland), 1999

Terry O'Malley (Canada), 1998

Eduard Pana (Romania), 1998

Gyorgy Pasztor (Hungary), 2001

Peter Patton (Great Britain), 2002

Vladimir Petrov (Russia), 2006

Ronald Pettersson (Sweden), 2004

Frantisek Pospisil (Czech Republic), 1999

Sepp Puschnig (Austria), 1999

Alexander Ragulin (USSR), 1997

Hans Rampf (Germany), 2001

Gord Renwick (Canada), 2002

Bob Ridder (USA), 1998

Jack Riley (USA), 1998

Gunther Sabetzki (Germany), 1997

Borje Salming (Sweden), 1998

Alois Schloder (Germany), 2005

Harry Sinden (Canada), 1997

Nikolai Sologubov (Russia), 2004

Andrei Starovoitov (Russia), 1997

Jan Starsi (Slovakia), 1999

Peter Stastny (Slovakia), 2000

Ulf Sterner (Sweden), 2001

Roland Stoltz (Sweden), 1999

Arne Stromberg (Sweden), 1998

Goran Stubb (Finland), 2000

Miroslav Subrt (Czech Republic), 2004

Anatoli Tarasov (Russia), 1997

Frantisek Tikal (Czech Republic), 2004

Viktor Tikhonov (Russia), 1998

Shoichi Tomita (Japan), 2006

Richard "Bibi" Torriani (Switzerland), 1997

Vladislav Tretiak (Russia), 1997

Hal Trumble (USA), 1999

Yoshiaki Tsutsumi (Japan), 1999

Sven Tumba (Sweden), 1997

Thayer Tutt (USA), 2002

Xaver Unsinn (Germany), 1998

Jorma Valtonen (Finland), 1999

Valeri Vasiliev (Russia), 1998

Juhani Wahlsten (Finland), 2006

Walter Wasservogel (Austria), 1997
Harry Watson (Canada), 1998
Unto Wiitala (Finland), 2003
Alexander Yakushev (Russia), 2003
Urpo Ylonen (Finland), 1997

Vldimir Yurzinov (Russia), 2002
Vladimir Zabrodsky
 (Czechoslovakia), 1997
Joachim Ziesche (Germany), 1999

United States Hockey Hall of Fame Members
(year inducted in brackets)

Taffy Abel (1973)
Oscar Almquist (1983)
Hobey Baker (1973)
Earl Bartholome (1977)
Amo Bessone (1992)
Pete Bessone (1978)
Bob Blake (1985)
Henry Boucha (1995)
Frank Brimsek (1973)
Herb Brooks (1990)
Neal Broten (2000)
George Brown (1973)
Walter Brown (1973)
Walter Bush (1980)
Joseph Cavanagh, Jr. (1994)
Len Ceglarski (1992)
Bill Chadwick (1974)
John Chase (1973)
Ray Chiasson (1974)
Bill Christian (1984)
Dave Christian (2001)
Roger Christian (1989)
Don Clark (1978)

James Claypool (1995)
Bill Cleary (1976)
Bob Cleary (1981)
Tony Conroy (1975)
Paul Coppo (2004)
John Cunniff (2003)
Mike Curran (1998)
Cully Dahlstrom (1973)
Vic Desjardins (1974)
Richard Desmond (1988)
Bob Dill (1979)
Dick Dougherty (2003)
Doug Everett (1974)
Robbie Ftorek (1991)
James Fullerton (1992)
Mark Fusco (2002)
Scott Fusco (2002)
Serge Gambucci (1996)
John Garrison (1973)
Jack Garrity (1986)
Doc Gibson (1973)
Moose Goheen (1973)
Malcolm Gordon (1973)

Wally Grant (1994)

Austie Harding (1975)

Ned Harkness (1994)

Vic Heyliger (1974)

Charlie Holt (1997)

Phil Housley (2004)

Mark Howe (2003)

Willard Ikola (1990)

Mike Ilitch (2004)

Stewrt Inglehart (1975)

William Jennings (1981)

Ed Jeremiah (1973)

Bob Johnson (1991)

Mark Johnson (2004)

Paul Johnson (2001)

Virgil Johnson (1974)

Nick Kahler (1980)

Mike Karakas (1973)

Jack Kelley (1974)

Snooks Kelley (1993)

Jack Kirrane, Jr. (1987)

Pat LaFontaine (2003)

Dave Langevin (1993)

Rod Langway (1999)

Joe Linder (1975)

Tom Lockhart (1973)

Myles Lane (1973)

Reed Larson (1996)

Sam LoPresti (1973)

John Mariucci (1973)

Calvin Marvin (1982)

John Matchefts (1991)

Bruce Mather (1998)

John Mayasich (1976)

Jack McCartan (1983)

Billy Moe (1974)

Ken Morrow (1995)

Fred Moseley (1975)

Joe Mullen (1998)

Muzz Murray (1987)

Lou Nanne (1998)

Hub Nelson (1978)

Bill Nyrop (1997)

Eddie Olson (1977)

George Owen (1973)

Doug Palazzari (2000)

Ding Palmer (1973)

Bob Paradise (1989)

Craig Patrick (1996)

Larry Pleau (2000)

Connie Pleban (1990)

Fido Purpur (1974)

Mike Ramsey (2001)

Bob Ridder (1976)

Bill Riley (1977)

Jack Riley (1979)

Joe Riley (2002)

Gordie Roberts (1999)

Doc Romnes (1973)

Dick Rondeau (1985)

Larry Ross (1988)

Charles Schulz (1993)

Tim Sheehy (1997)

Bill Stewart (1982)

Cliff Thomspon (1973)

Hal Trumble (1985)

Thayer Tutt (1973)

Sid Watson (1999)

Tommy Williams (1981)

Ralph Winsor (1973)

Bill Wirtz (1984)

Coddy Winters (1973)

Doug Woog (2002)

Lyle Wright (1973)

Ken Yackel (1986)

1960 U.S. Olympic Team (2000)

1980 U.S. Olympic Team (2003)

2006 OLYMPIC WINTER GAMES RESULTS

TORINO, ITALY February 10–26, 2006

Results, Men
Final Placings
Gold Medal	Sweden
Silver Medal	Finland
Bronze Medal	Czech Republic
Fourth Place	Russia
Fifth Place	Slovakia
Sixth Place	Switzerland
Seventh Place	Canada
Eighth Place	USA
Ninth Place	Kazakhstan
Tenth Place	Germany
Eleventh Place	Italy
Twelfth Place	Latvia

Tournament MVP   Antero Niittymaki (FIN)

Directorate Awards
Best Goalie	Antero Niittymaki (FIN)
Best Defenceman	Kenny Jonsson (SWE)
Best Forward	Teemu Selanne (FIN)

Media All-Star Team
Goal	Antero Niittymaki (FIN)
Defence	Nicklas Lidstrom (SWE), Kimmo Timonen (FIN)
Forward	Teemu Selanne (FIN), Saku Koivu (FIN), Alexander Ovechkin (RUS)

FINAL STANDINGS
Group A

	GP	W	L	T	GF	GA	P
Finland	5	5	0	0	19	2	10
Switzerland	5	2	1	2	10	12	6
Canada	5	3	2	0	15	9	6
Czech Republic	5	2	3	0	14	12	4
Germany	5	0	3	2	7	16	2
Italy	5	0	3	2	9	23	2

February 15	Canada 7/Italy 2
	Finland 5/Switzerland 0
	Czech Republic 4/Germany 1
February 16	Canada 5/Germany 1
	Finland 6/Italy 0
	Switzerland 3/Czech Republic 2
February 18	Switzerland 2/Canada 0
	Germany 3/Italy 3
	Finland 4/Czech Republic 2
February 19	Finland 2/Canada 0
	Germany 2/Switzerland 2
	Czech Republic 4/Italy 1
February 21	Canada 3/Czech Republic 2
	Switzerland 3/Italy 3
	Finland 2/Germany 0

Group B

	GP	W	L	T	GF	GA	P
Slovakia	5	5	0	0	18	8	10
Russia	5	4	1	0	23	11	8
Sweden	5	3	2	0	15	12	6
USA	5	1	3	1	13	13	3
Kazakhstan	5	1	4	0	9	16	2
Latvia	5	0	4	1	11	29	1

February 15	Sweden 7/Kazakhstan 2
	Slovakia 5/Russia 3
	Latvia 3/USA 3
February 16	Russia 5/Sweden 0
	Slovakia 6/Latvia 3
	USA 4/Kazakhstan 1
February 18	Russia 1/Kazakhstan 0
	Sweden 6/Latvia 1
	Slovakia 2/USA 1
February 19	Russia 9/Latvia 2
	Slovakia 2/Kazakhstan 1
	Sweden 2/USA 1
February 21	Kazakhstan 5/Latvia 2
	Slovakia 3/Sweden 0
	Russia 5/USA 4

PLAYOFFS
Quarterfinals

February 22	Russia 2/Canada 0
	Sweden 6/Switzerland 2
	Finland 4/USA 3
	Czech Republic 3/Slovakia 1

Semifinals

| February 24 | Finland 4/Russia 0 |
| | Sweden 7/Czech Republic 2 |

Bronze Medal Game

| February 25 | Czech Republic 3/Russia 0 |

Gold Medal Game

| February 26 | Sweden 3/Finland 2 |

Results, Women

Final Placings

Gold Medal	Canada
Silver Medal	Sweden
Bronze Medal	USA
Fourth Place	Finland
Fifth Place	Germany
Sixth Place	Russia
Seventh Place	Switzerland
Eighth Place	Italy

Tournament MVP   Hayley Wickenheiser (CAN)

Directorate Awards

Best Goalie	Kim Martin (SWE)
Best Defenceman	Angela Ruggiero (USA)
Best Forward	Hayley Wickenheiser (CAN)

All-Star Team

Goal	Kim Martin (SWE)
Defence	Carla MacLeod (CAN), Angela Ruggiero (USA)
Forward	Hayley Wickenheiser (CAN), Gillian Apps (CAN), Maria Rooth (SWE)

Group A

	GP	W	L	T	GF	GA	P
Canada	3	3	0	0	36	1	6
Sweden	3	2	1	0	15	9	4
Russia	3	1	2	0	6	16	2
Italy	3	0	3	0	1	32	0

February 11   Canada 16/Italy 0
Sweden 3/Russia 1

February 12   Canada 12/Russia 0
February 13   Sweden 11/Italy 0
February 14   Canada 8/Sweden 1
                 Russia 5/Italy 1

Group B

	GP	W	L	T	GF	GA	P
USA	3	3	0	0	18	3	6
Finland	3	2	1	0	10	7	4
Germany	3	1	2	0	2	9	2
Switzerland	3	0	3	0	1	12	0

February 11   Finland 3/Germany 0
                 USA 6/Switzerland 0
February 12   USA 5/Germany 0
February 13   Finland 4/Switzerland 0
February 14   Germany 2/Switzerland 1
                 USA 7/Finland 3

Placement Games

February 17   Russia 6/Switzerland 2
                 Germany 5/Italy 2

Seventh Place Game

February 20   Switzerland 11/Italy 0

Fifth Place Game

February 20   Germany 1/Russia 0 (OT/SO)

PLAYOFFS
Semifinals
February 17   Canada 6/Finland 0
                    Sweden 3/USA 2 (OT/SO)

Bronze Medal Game
February 20   USA 4/Finland 0

Gold Medal Game
February 20   Canada 4/Sweden 1

PRO CLASSICS RESULTS

1972 Summit Series
Canada/Moscow, September 2–28, 1972

	GP	W	L	T	GF	GA	P
Canada	8	4	3	1	31	32	9
Soviet Union	8	3	4	1	32	31	7

Results

Game 1	September 2	Montreal	Soviet Union 7/Canada 3
Game 2	September 4	Toronto	Canada 4/Soviet Union 1
Game 3	September 6	Winnipeg	Canada 4/Soviet Union 4
Game 4	September 8	Vancouver	Soviet Union 5/Canada 3

Exhibition	September 16	Stockholm	Canada 4/Swedish Nationals 1
Exhibition	September 17	Stockholm	Canada 4/Swedish Nationals 4

Game 5	September 22	Moscow	Soviet Union 5/Canada 4
Game 6	September 24	Moscow	Canada 3/Soviet Union 2
Game 7	September 26	Moscow	Canada 4/Soviet Union 3
Game 8	September 28	Moscow	Canada 6/Soviet Union 5

(Paul Henderson scores series winner at 19:26 of 3rd)

Exhibition	September 30	Prague	Canada 3/Czech Nationals 3

1976 Canada Cup
Canada, September 2–15, 1976
Series MVP: Bobby Orr (Canada)

Team MVPs

Canada	Rogie Vachon
Czechoslovakia	Milan Novy
Soviet Union	Alexander Maltsev
Sweden	Borje Salming
United States	Robbie Ftorek
Finland	Matti Hagman

Final Standings Round Robin

	GP	W	L	T	GF	GA	P
Canada	5	4	1	0	22	6	8
Czechoslovakia	5	3	1	1	19	9	7
Soviet Union	5	2	2	1	23	14	5
Sweden	5	2	2	1	16	18	5
United States	5	1	3	1	14	21	3
Finland	5	1	4	0	16	42	2

Results

September 2	Ottawa	Canada 11/Finland 2
September 3	Toronto	Sweden 5/United States 2
	Montreal	Czechoslovakia 5/Soviet Union 3
September 5	Montreal	Canada 4/United States 2
	Montreal	Soviet Union 3/Sweden 3
	Toronto	Czechoslovakia 8/Finland 0
September 7	Toronto	Canada 4/Sweden 0
	Montreal	Soviet Union 11/Finland 3
	Philadelphia	Czechoslovakia 4/United States 4

September 9	Montreal	Czechoslovakia 1/Canada 0
	Winnipeg	Finland 8/Sweden 6
	Philadelphia	Soviet Union 5/United States 0
September 11	Toronto	Canada 3/Soviet Union 1
	Quebec City	Sweden 2/Czechoslovakia 1
	Montreal	United States 6/Finland 3

FINALS (best two-of-three)

September 13	Toronto	Canada 6/Czechoslovakia 0
September 15	Montreal	Canada 5/Czechoslovakia 4
		(Sittler 11:33 OT)

1981 Canada Cup

Canada, September 1–13, 1981
Tournament MVP: Vladislav Tretiak
Team Canada MVP: Mike Bossy

All-Star Team

Goal	Vladislav Tretiak (Soviet Union)
Defence	Alexei Kasatonov (Soviet Union)
	Arnold Kadlec (Czechoslovakia)
Forward	Gil Perreault (Canada)
	Mike Bossy (Canada)
	Sergei Shepelev (Soviet Union)

Final Standings Round Robin

	GP	W	L	T	GF	GA	P
Canada	5	4	0	1	32	13	9
Soviet Union	5	3	1	1	20	13	7
Czechoslovakia	5	2	1	2	21	13	6
United States	5	2	2	1	17	19	5
Sweden	5	1	4	0	13	20	2
Finland	5	0	4	1	6	31	1

Results

September 1	Edmonton	Canada 9/Finland 0
	Edmonton	United States 3/Sweden 1
	Winnipeg	Czechoslovakia 1/Soviet Union 1
September 3	Edmonton	Canada 8/United States 3
	Edmonton	Czechoslovakia 7/Finland 1
	Winnipeg	Soviet Union 6/Sweden 3
September 5	Winnipeg	Canada 4/Czechoslovakia 4
	Winnipeg	Sweden 5/Finland 0
	Edmonton	Soviet Union 4/United States 1
September 7	Montreal	Canada 4/Sweden 3
	Winnipeg	Soviet Union 6/Finland 1
	Montreal	United States 6/Czechoslovakia 2
September 9	Montreal	Canada 7/Soviet Union 3
	Ottawa	Czechoslovakia 7/Sweden 1
	Montreal	Finland 4/United States 4

Semifinals

September 11	Montreal	Canada 4/United States 1
	Ottawa	Soviet Union 4/Czechoslovakia 1

Finals

September 13 Montreal Soviet Union 8/Canada 1

1984 Canada Cup

Canada, September 1–18, 1984

Tournament MVP: John Tonelli

All-Star Team

Goal Vladimir Myshkin (Soviet Union)

Defence Paul Coffey (Canada)
Rod Langway (United States)

Forward Wayne Gretzky (Canada)
John Tonelli (Canada)
Sergei Makarov (Soviet Union)

Final Standings Round Robin

	GP	W	L	T	GF	GA	P
Soviet Union	5	5	0	0	22	7	10
United States	5	3	1	1	21	13	7
Sweden	5	3	2	0	15	16	6
Canada	5	2	2	1	23	18	5
West Germany	5	0	4	1	13	29	1
Czechoslovakia	5	0	4	1	10	21	1

Results

September 1 Montreal Canada 7/West Germany 2
Halifax United States 7/Sweden 1

September 2 Montreal Soviet Union 3/Czechoslovakia 0

September 3 Montreal Canada 4/United States 4

September 4	London	Czechoslovakia 4/West Germany 4
	Calgary	Soviet Union 3/Sweden 2
September 6	Vancouver	Sweden 4/Canada 2
	Edmonton	Soviet Union 8/West Germany 1
	Buffalo	United States 3 /Czechoslovakia 2
September 8	Calgary	Canada 7/Czechoslovakia 2
	Calgary	Sweden 4/West Germany 2
	Edmonton	Soviet Union 2/United States 1
September 10	Edmonton	Soviet Union 6/Canada 3
	Vancouver	Sweden 4/Czechoslovakia 2
	Calgary	United States 6/West Germany 4

Semifinals

September 12	Edmonton	Sweden 9/United States 2
September 13	Calgary	Canada 3/Soviet Union 2
		(Bossy 12:29 OT)

Finals (best two-of-three)

| September 16 | Calgary | Canada 5/Sweden 2 |
| September 18 | Edmonton | Canada 6/Sweden 5 |

1987 Canada Cup
Canada, August 28–September 15, 1987

Tournament All-Star Team

Goal	Grant Fuhr (Canada)
Defence	Ray Bourque (Canada)
	Viacheslav Fetisov (Soviet Union)

Forward   Mario Lemieux (Canada)
           Wayne Gretzky (Canada)
           Vladimir Krutov (Soviet Union)

Final Standings Round Robin

	GP	W	L	T	GF	GA	P
Canada	5	3	0	2	19	13	8
Soviet Union	5	3	1	1	22	13	7
Sweden	5	3	2	0	17	14	6
Czechoslovakia	5	2	2	1	12	15	5
United States	5	2	3	0	13	14	4
Finland	5	0	5	0	9	23	0

Results

August 28	Calgary	Canada 4/Czechoslovakia 4
	Hartford	United States 4/Finland 1
August 29	Calgary	Sweden 5/Soviet Union 3
August 30	Hamilton	Canada 4/Finland 1
August 31	Regina	Soviet Union 4/Czechoslovakia 0
	Hamilton	United States 5/Sweden 2
September 2	Halifax	Soviet Union 7/Finland 4
	Hamilton	Canada 3/United States 2
	Regina	Sweden 4/Czechoslovakia 0
September 4	Hartford	Soviet Union 5/United States 1
	Sydney	Czechoslovakia 5/Finland 2
	Montreal	Canada 5/Sweden 3
September 6	Sydney	Sweden 3/Finland 1
	Sydney	Czechoslovakia 3/United States 1
	Hamilton	Canada 3/Soviet Union 3

| September 8 | Hamilton | Soviet Union 4/Sweden 2 |
| | Montreal | Canada 5/Czechoslovakia 3 |

Finals (best two-of-three)

September 11	Montreal	Soviet Union 6/Canada 5
		(Semak 5:33 OT)
September 13	Hamilton	Canada 6/Soviet Union 5
		(Mario Lemieux 30:07 OT)
September 15	Hamilton	Canada 6/Soviet Union 5
		(Lemieux scores winner at
		18:34 of 3rd)

1991 Canada Cup
Canada, August 31–September 16, 1991
Tournament All-Star Team

Goal	Bill Ranford (Canada)
Defence	Al MacInnis (Canada)
	Chris Chelios (United States)
Forward	Wayne Gretzky (Canada)
	Jeremy Roenick (United States)
	Mats Sundin (Sweden)

Final Standings Round Robin

	GP	W	L	T	GF	GA	P
Canada	5	3	0	2	21	11	8
United States	5	4	1	0	19	15	8
Finland	5	2	2	1	10	13	5
Sweden	5	2	3	0	13	17	4
Soviet Union	5	1	3	1	14	14	3
Czechoslovakia	5	1	4	0	11	18	2

Results

August 31	Toronto	Canada 2/Finland 2
	Saskatoon	Czechoslovakia 5/Soviet Union 2
	Pittsburgh	United States 6/Sweden 3
September 2	Hamilton	Canada 6/United States 3
	Montreal	Sweden 3/Soviet Union 2
	Saskatoon	Finland 1/Czechoslovakia 0
September 5	Toronto	Canada 4/Sweden 1
	Hamilton	Soviet Union 6/Finland 1
	Detroit	United States 4/Czechoslovakia 2
September 7	Montreal	Canada 6/Czechoslovakia 2
	Toronto	Finland 3/Sweden 1
	Chicago	United States 2/Soviet Union 1
September 9	Quebec City	Canada 3/Soviet Union 3
	Toronto	Sweden 5/Czechoslovakia 2
	Chicago	United States 4/Finland 3

Semifinals

| September 11 | Hamilton | United States 7/Finland 3 |
| September 12 | Toronto | Canada 4/Sweden 0 |

Finals (best two-of-three)

| September 14 | Montreal | Canada 4/United States 1 |
| September 16 | Hamilton | Canada 4/United States 2 |

1996 World Cup Of Hockey
Canada/Europe/United States, August 26–September 14, 1996

FINAL STANDINGS ROUND ROBIN
North American Pool

	GP	W	L	T	GF	GA	P
United States	3	3	0	0	19	8	6
Canada	3	2	1	0	11	10	4
Russia	3	1	2	0	12	14	2
Slovakia	3	0	3	0	9	19	0

European Pool

	GP	W	L	T	GF	GA	P
Sweden	3	3	0	0	14	3	6
Finland	3	2	1	0	17	11	4
Germany	3	1	2	0	11	15	2
Czech Republic	3	0	3	0	4	17	0

Results

August 26	Stockholm	Sweden 6/Germany 1
August 27	Helsinki	Finland 7/Czech Republic 3
August 28	Helsinki	Finland 8/Germany 3
	Prague	Sweden 3/Czech Republic 0
	Vancouver	Canada 5/Russia 3
August 31	Philadelphia	United States 5/Canada 3
	Garmisch	Germany 7/Czech Republic 1
	Montreal	Russia 7/Slovakia 4
September 1	Ottawa	Canada 3/Slovakia 2
	Stockholm	Sweden 5/Finland 2

| September 2 | New York | United States 5/Russia 2 |
| September 3 | New York | United States 9/Slovakia 3 |

Quarterfinals

| September 5 | Montreal | Canada 4/Germany 1 |
| September 6 | Ottawa | Russia 5/Finland 0 |

Semifinals

| September 7 | Philadelphia | Canada 3/Sweden 2 (Fleury 39:47 OT) |
| September 8 | Ottawa | United States 5/Russia 2 |

Finals (best two-of-three)

September 10	Philadelphia	Canada 4/United States 3 (Yzerman 19:53 OT)
September 12	Montreal	United States 5/Canada 2
September 14	Montreal	United States 5/Canada 2

World Cup of Hockey 2004

August 30–September 14, 2004

Tournament MVP: Vincent Lecavalier (CAN)

All-Tournament Team

Goal	Martin Brodeur (CAN)
Defence	Adam Foote (CAN)
	Kimmo Timonen (FIN)
Forward	Vincent Lecavalier (CAN)
	Fredrik Modin (SWE)
	Saku Koivu (FIN)

PRELIMINARY ROUND STANDINGS
European Pool

	GP	W	L	T	GF	GA	P
Finland*	3	2	0	1	11	4	5
Sweden	3	2	0	1	13	9	5
Czech Republic	3	1	2	0	10	10	2
Germany	3	0	3	0	4	15	0

*given superior ranking based on goals differential

August 30	Helsinki	Finland 4/Czech Republic 0
August 31	Stockholm	Sweden 5/Germany 2
September 1	Stockholm	Sweden 4/Czech Republic 3
September 2	Cologne	Finland 3/Germany 0
September 3	Prague	Czech Republic 7/Germany 2
September 4	Helsinki	Finland 4/Sweden 4 (5:00 OT)

North American Pool

	GP	W	L	T	GF	GA	P
Canada	3	3	0	0	10	3	6
Russia	3	2	1	0	9	6	4
USA	3	1	2	0	5	6	2
Slovakia	3	0	3	0	4	13	0

August 31	Montreal	Canada 2/USA 1
September 1	Montreal	Canada 5/Slovakia 1
September 2	St. Paul	Russia 3/USA 1
September 3	St. Paul	USA 3/Slovakia 1
September 4	Toronto	Canada 3/Russia 1
September 5	Toronto	Russia 5/Slovakia 2

Quarterfinals

September 6	Helsinki	Finland 2/Germany 1
September 7	Stockholm	Czech Republic 6/Sweden 1
September 7	St. Paul	USA 5/Russia 2
September 8	Toronto	Canada 5/Slovakia 1

Semifinals

September 11	St. Paul	Finland 2/USA 1
September 12	Toronto	Canada 4/Czech Republic 3
		(Vincent Lecavalier 3:45 OT)

Finals

| September 14 | Toronto | Canada 3/Finland 2 |

THE GAMES OF THE VII OLYMPIAD

ANTWERP, BELGIUM, April 23–September 12, 1920
(Winter Olympics held April 23–29, 1920)

FINAL PLACINGS

GOLD MEDAL	Canada
SILVER MEDAL	United States
BRONZE MEDAL	Czechoslovakia
Fourth Place	Sweden

THE FIRST OLYMPIC WINTER GAMES

CHAMONIX, FRANCE, January 25–February 5, 1924

FINAL PLACINGS

GOLD MEDAL	Canada
SILVER MEDAL	United States
BRONZE MEDAL	Great Britain
Fourth Place	Sweden
Fifth Place	Czechoslovakia
(tie)	France
Seventh Place	Belgium
(tie)	Switzerland

THE SECOND OLYMPIC WINTER GAMES

ST. MORITZ, SWITZERLAND, February 11–20, 1928

FINAL PLACINGS

GOLD MEDAL	Canada
SILVER MEDAL	Sweden
BRONZE MEDAL	Switzerland
Fourth Place	Great Britain
Fifth Place	France
Sixth Place	Czechoslovakia

Seventh Place	Belgium
(tie)	Austria
Ninth Place	Poland
Tenth Place	Germany
Eleventh Place	Hungary

THE THIRD OLYMPIC WINTER GAMES

LAKE PLACID, NEW YORK February 4–13, 1932

FINAL PLACINGS

GOLD MEDAL	Canada
SILVER MEDAL	United States
BRONZE MEDAL	Germany
Fourth Place	Poland

THE FOURTH OLYMPIC WINTER GAMES

GARMISCH–PARTENKIRCHEN, GERMANY February 6–16, 1936

FINAL PLACINGS

GOLD MEDAL	Great Britain
SILVER MEDAL	Canada
BRONZE MEDAL	United States
Fourth Place	Czechoslovakia
Fifth Place	Germany
(tie)	Sweden
Seventh Place	Austria
(tie)	Hungary
Ninth Place	Italy
(tie)	France
(tie)	Japan
(tie)	Poland
Thirteenth Place	Belgium
(tie)	Latvia
(tie)	Switzerland

THE FIFTH OLYMPIC WINTER GAMES

ST. MORITZ, SWITZERLAND January 30–February 8, 1948

FINAL PLACINGS

GOLD MEDAL	Canada
SILVER MEDAL	Czechoslovakia
BRONZE MEDAL	Switzerland
Fourth Place	Sweden
Fifth Place	Great Britain
Sixth Place	Poland
Seventh Place	Austria
Eighth Place	Italy

THE SIXTH OLYMPIC WINTER GAMES

OSLO, NORWAY February 15–25, 1952

FINAL PLACINGS

GOLD MEDAL	Canada
SILVER MEDAL	United States
BRONZE MEDAL	Sweden
Fourth Place	Czechoslovakia
Fifth Place	Switzerland
Sixth Place	Poland
Seventh Place	Finland
Eighth Place	West Germany
Ninth Place	Norway

THE SEVENTH OLYMPIC WINTER GAMES

CORTINA d'AMPEZZO, ITALY January 26–February 4, 1956

FINAL PLACINGS

GOLD MEDAL	Soviet Union
SILVER MEDAL	United States
BRONZE MEDAL	Canada
Fourth Place	Sweden
Fifth Place	Czechoslovakia

Sixth Place	Germany
Seventh Place	Italy
Eighth Place	Poland
Ninth Place	Switzerland
Tenth Place	Austria

THE EIGHTH OLYMPIC WINTER GAMES

SQUAW VALLEY, CALIFORNIA February 19–28, 1960

FINAL PLACINGS

GOLD MEDAL	United States
SILVER MEDAL	Canada
BRONZE MEDAL	Soviet Union
Fourth Place	Czechoslovakia
Fifth Place	Sweden
Sixth Place	Germany
Seventh Place	Finland
Eighth Place	Japan
Ninth Place	Australia

THE NINTH OLYMPIC WINTER GAMES

INNSBRUCK, AUSTRIA January 29–February 9, 1964

FINAL PLACINGS

GOLD MEDAL	Soviet Union
SILVER MEDAL	Sweden
BRONZE MEDAL	Czechoslovakia
Fourth Place	Canada
Fifth Place	United States
Sixth Place	Finland
Seventh Place	Germany
Eighth Place	Switzerland
Ninth Place	Poland
Tenth Place	Norway
Eleventh Place	Japan

Twelfth Place	Romania
Thirteenth Place	Austria
Fourteenth Place	Yugoslavia
Fifteenth Place	Italy
Sixteenth Place	Hungary

THE TENTH OLYMPIC WINTER GAMES

GRENOBLE, FRANCE February 6–17, 1968

FINAL PLACINGS

GOLD MEDAL	Soviet Union
SILVER MEDAL	Czechoslovakia
BRONZE MEDAL	Canada
Fourth Place	Sweden
Fifth Place	Finland
Sixth Place	United States
Seventh Place	West Germany
Eighth Place	East Germany
Ninth Place	Yugoslavia
Tenth Place	Japan
Eleventh Place	Norway
Twelfth Place	Romania
Thirteenth Place	Austria
Fourteenth Place	France

THE ELEVENTH OLYMPIC WINTER GAMES

SAPPORO, JAPAN February 5–12, 1972

FINAL PLACINGS

GOLD MEDAL	Soviet Union
SILVER MEDAL	United States
BRONZE MEDAL	Czechoslovakia
Fourth Place	Sweden
Fifth Place	Finland
Sixth Place	Poland
Seventh Place	West Germany

Eighth Place	Norway
Ninth Place	Japan
Tenth Place	Switzerland
Eleventh Place	Yugoslavia

THE TWELFTH OLYMPIC WINTER GAMES

INNSBRUCK, AUSTRIA February 4–13, 1976

FINAL PLACINGS

GOLD MEDAL	Soviet Union
SILVER MEDAL	Czechoslovakia
BRONZE MEDAL	West Germany
Fourth Place	Finland
Fifth Place	United States
Sixth Place	Poland
Seventh Place	Romania
Eighth Place	Austria
Ninth Place	Japan
Tenth Place	Yugoslavia
Eleventh Place	Switzerland
(tie)	Norway
Thirteenth Place	Bulgaria

THE THIRTEENTH OLYMPIC WINTER GAMES

LAKE PLACID, NEW YORK February 13–24, 1980

FINAL PLACINGS

GOLD MEDAL	United States
SILVER MEDAL	Soviet Union
BRONZE MEDAL	Sweden
Fourth Place	Finland
Fifth Place	Czechoslovakia
Sixth Place	Canada
Seventh Place	Poland
Eighth Place	Romania
Ninth Place	Netherlands

(tie)	Norway
Eleventh Place	West Germany
(tie)	Yugoslavia
Thirteenth Place	Japan

THE FOURTEENTH OLYMPIC WINTER GAMES

SARAJEVO, YUGOSLAVIA February 7–19, 1984

FINAL PLACINGS

GOLD MEDAL	Soviet Union
SILVER MEDAL	Czechoslovakia
BRONZE MEDAL	Sweden
Fourth Place	Canada
Fifth Place	West Germany
Sixth Place	Finland
Seventh Place	United States
Eighth Place	Poland
Ninth Place	Italy
Tenth Place	Norway
Eleventh Place	Austria
(tie)	Yugoslavia

THE FIFTEENTH OLYMPIC WINTER GAMES

CALGARY, ALBERTA February 13–28, 1988

FINAL PLACINGS

GOLD MEDAL	Soviet Union
SILVER MEDAL	Finland
BRONZE MEDAL	Sweden
Fourth Place	Canada
Fifth Place	West Germany
Sixth Place	Czechoslovakia
Seventh Place	United States
Eighth Place	Switzerland
Ninth Place	Austria
Tenth Place	Poland

Eleventh Place France
Twelfth Place Norway

THE SIXTEENTH OLYMPIC WINTER GAMES

ALBERTVILLE, FRANCE February 8–23, 1992

FINAL PLACINGS

GOLD MEDAL   Unified Team
SILVER MEDAL   Canada
BRONZE MEDAL   Czechoslovakia
Fourth Place   United States
Fifth Place   Sweden
Sixth Place   Germany
Seventh Place   Finland
Eighth Place   France
Ninth Place   Norway
Tenth Place   Switzerland
Eleventh Place   Poland
Twelfth Place   Italy

THE SEVENTEENTH OLYMPIC WINTER GAMES

LILLEHAMMER, NORWAY February 13–27, 1994

FINAL PLACINGS

GOLD MEDAL   Sweden
SILVER MEDAL   Canada
BRONZE MEDAL   Finland
Fourth Place   Russia
Fifth Place   Czech Republic
Sixth Place   Slovakia
Seventh Place   Germany
Eighth Place   United States
Ninth Place   Italy
Tenth Place   France
Eleventh Place   Norway
Twelfth Place   Austria

THE EIGHTEENTH OLYMPIC WINTER GAMES

NAGANO, JAPAN, February 7–22, 1998 (Men);
February 8–17, 1998 (Women)

FINAL PLACINGS: MEN

GOLD MEDAL	Czech Republic
SILVER MEDAL	Russia
BRONZE MEDAL	Finland
Fourth Place	Canada
Fifth Place (tie)	Sweden
	United States
	Belarus
	Kazakhstan
Ninth Place	Germany
Tenth Place	Slovakia
Eleventh Place	France
Twelfth Place	Italy
Thirteenth Place	Japan
Fourteenth Place	Austria

FINAL PLACINGS: WOMEN

GOLD MEDAL	United States
SILVER MEDAL	Canada
BRONZE MEDAL	Finland
Fourth Place	China
Fifth Place	Sweden
Sixth Place	Japan

THE NINETEENTH OLYMPIC WINTER GAMES

SALT LAKE CITY, UTAH, February 9–24, 2002 (Men);
February 11–21, 2002 (Women)

FINAL PLACINGS: MEN

GOLD MEDAL	Canada
SILVER MEDAL	United States
BRONZE MEDAL	Russia

Fourth Place	Belarus
Fifth Place	Sweden
Sixth Place	Finland
Seventh Place	Czech Republic
Eighth Place	Germany
Ninth Place	Latvia
Tenth Place	Ukraine
Eleventh Place	Switzerland
Twelfth Place	Austria
Thirteenth Place	Slovakia
Fourteenth Place	France

FINAL PLACINGS: WOMEN

GOLD MEDAL	Canada
SILVER MEDAL	United States
BRONZE MEDAL	Sweden
Fourth Place	Finland
Fifth Place	Russia
Sixth Place	Germany
Seventh Place	China
Eighth Place	Kazakhstan

* for the Twentieth Olympic Winter Games (2006), see section beginning p. 443

ALL WORLD CHAMPIONSHIPS PLACINGS

January 31–February 10, 1930

Chamonix, France/Berlin, Germany/Vienna, Austria

GOLD MEDAL	Canada
SILVER MEDAL	Germany
BRONZE MEDAL	Switzerland
Fourth Place	Austria
Fifth Place	Poland
Sixth Place (tie)	Czechoslovakia
	France
	Hungary
	Japan
Tenth Place (tie)	Belgium
	Great Britain
	Italy

March 1–8, 1931

Krynica, Poland

GOLD MEDAL	Canada
SILVER MEDAL	United States
BRONZE MEDAL	Austria
Fourth Place	Poland
Fifth Place	Czechoslovakia
Sixth Place	Sweden
Seventh Place	Hungary
Eighth Place	Great Britain
Ninth Place	France
Tenth Place	Romania

February 18–26, 1933

Prague, Czechoslovakia

GOLD MEDAL	United States
SILVER MEDAL	Canada
BRONZE MEDAL	Czechoslovakia
Fourth Place	Austria
Fifth Place (tie)	Germany
	Switzerland
Seventh Place (tie)	Hungary
	Poland
Ninth Place	Romania
Tenth Place	Latvia
Eleventh Place	Italy
Twelfth Place	Belgium

February 3–11, 1934

Milan, Italy

GOLD MEDAL	Canada
SILVER MEDAL	United States
BRONZE MEDAL	Germany
Fourth Place	Switzerland
Fifth Place	Czechoslovakia
Sixth Place	Hungary
Seventh Place	Austria
Eighth Place	Great Britain
Ninth Place	Italy
Tenth Place	Romania
Eleventh Place	France
Twelfth Place	Belgium

January 19–27, 1935

Davos, Switzerland

GOLD MEDAL	Canada
SILVER MEDAL	Switzerland
BRONZE MEDAL	Great Britain
Fourth Place	Czechoslovakia
Fifth Place	Sweden
Sixth Place	Austria
Seventh Place	France
Eighth Place	Italy
Ninth Place	Germany
Tenth Place	Poland
Eleventh Place (tie)	Hungary
	Romania
Thirteenth Place	Latvia
Fourteenth Place	Belgium
	Netherlands

February 17–27, 1937

London, Great Britain

GOLD MEDAL	Canada
SILVER MEDAL	Great Britain
BRONZE MEDAL	Switzerland
Fourth Place	Germany
Fifth Place	Hungary
Sixth Place	Czechoslovakia
Seventh Place	France
Eighth Place	Poland
Ninth Place (tie)	Norway
	Romania
	Sweden

February 11–20, 1938

Prague, Czechoslovakia

GOLD MEDAL	Canada
SILVER MEDAL	Great Britain
BRONZE MEDAL	Czechoslovakia
Fourth Place	Germany
Fifth Place	Sweden
Sixth Place	Switzerland
Seventh Place (tie)	Hungary
	Poland
	United States
Tenth Place (tie)	Austria
	Latvia
	Lithuania
Thirteenth Place (tie)	Norway
	Romania

February 3–12, 1939

Basel/Zurich, Switzerland

GOLD MEDAL	Canada
SILVER MEDAL	United States
BRONZE MEDAL	Switzerland
Fourth Place	Czechoslovakia
Fifth Place	Germany
Sixth Place	Poland
Seventh Place	Hungary
Eighth Place	Great Britain
Ninth Place	Italy
Tenth Place	Latvia
Eleventh Place (tie)	Belgium
	Netherlands
Thirteenth Place	Finland
	Yugoslavia

February 15–23, 1947

Prague, Czechoslovakia

GOLD MEDAL	Czechoslovakia
SILVER MEDAL	Sweden
BRONZE MEDAL	Austria
Fourth Place	Switzerland
Fifth Place	United States
Sixth Place	Poland
Seventh Place	Romania
Eighth Place	Belgium

February 12–20, 1949

Stockholm, Sweden

GOLD MEDAL	Czechoslovakia
SILVER MEDAL	Canada
BRONZE MEDAL	United States
Fourth Place	Sweden
Fifth Place	Switzerland
Sixth Place	Austria
Seventh Place	Finland
Eighth Place	Norway
Ninth Place	Belgium
Tenth Place	Denmark

March 13–22, 1950

London, Great Britain

GOLD MEDAL	Canada
SILVER MEDAL	United States
BRONZE MEDAL	Switzerland
Fourth Place	Great Britain
Fifth Place	Sweden
Sixth Place	Norway

Seventh Place	Belgium
Eighth Place	Netherlands
Ninth Place	France

March 9–17, 1951

Paris, France

GOLD MEDAL	Canada
SILVER MEDAL	Sweden
BRONZE MEDAL	Switzerland
Fourth Place	Norway
Fifth Place	Great Britain
Sixth Place	United States
Seventh Place	Finland

March 6–15, 1953

Zurich/Basel, Switzerland

GOLD MEDAL	Sweden
SILVER MEDAL	West Germany
BRONZE MEDAL	Switzerland
Fourth Place	Czechoslovakia

February 26–March 7, 1954

Stockholm, Sweden

GOLD MEDAL	Soviet Union
SILVER MEDAL	Canada
BRONZE MEDAL	Sweden
Fourth Place	Czechoslovakia
Fifth Place	West Germany
Sixth Place	Finland
Seventh Place	Switzerland
Eighth Place	Norway

February 25–March 6, 1955

Dusseldorf, West Germany

GOLD MEDAL	Canada
SILVER MEDAL	Soviet Union
BRONZE MEDAL	Czechoslovakia
Fourth Place	United States
Fifth Place	Sweden
Sixth Place	West Germany
Seventh Place	Poland
Eighth Place	Switzerland
Ninth Place	Finland

February 24–March 5, 1957

Moscow, Soviet Union

GOLD MEDAL	Sweden
SILVER MEDAL	Soviet Union
BRONZE MEDAL	Czechoslovakia
Fourth Place	Finland
Fifth Place	West Germany
Sixth Place	Poland
Seventh Place	Austria
Eighth Place	Japan

To protest the suppression of the Hungarian revolution by Soviet forces, Canadian Prime Minister Louis St. Laurent refused to allow a Canadian team to travel to Moscow to play at the World Championships.

February 25–March 9, 1958

Oslo, Norway

GOLD MEDAL	Canada
SILVER MEDAL	Soviet Union
BRONZE MEDAL	Sweden

Fourth Place	Czechoslovakia
Fifth Place	United States
Sixth Place	Finland
Seventh Place	Norway
Eighth Place	Poland

March 9–15, 1959

Prague, Czechoslovakia

GOLD MEDAL	Canada
SILVER MEDAL	Soviet Union
BRONZE MEDAL	Czechoslovakia
Fourth Place	United States
Fifth Place	Sweden
Sixth Place	Finland
Seventh Place	West Germany
Eighth Place	Norway
Ninth Place	East Germany
Tenth Place	Italy
Eleventh Place	Poland
Twelfth Place	Switzerland
Thirteenth Place	Romania
Fourteenth Place	Hungary
Fifteenth Place	Austria

March 1–12, 1961

Geneva/Lausanne, Switzerland

GOLD MEDAL	Canada
SIVER MEDAL	Czechoslovakia
BRONZE MEDAL	Soviet Union
Fourth Place	Sweden
Fifth Place	East Germany
Sixth Place	United States

Seventh Place	Finland
Eighth Place	West Germany

May 8–18, 1962

Colorado Springs, United States

GOLD MEDAL	Sweden
SILVER MEDAL	Canada
BRONZE MEDAL	United States
Fourth Place	Finland
Fifth Place	Norway
Sixth Place	West Germany
Seventh Place	Switzerland
Eighth Place	Great Britain

March 7–17, 1963

Stockholm, Sweden

GOLD MEDAL	Soviet Union
SILVER MEDAL	Sweden
BRONZE MEDAL	Czechoslovakia
Fourth Place	Canada
Fifth Place	Finland
Sixth Place	East Germany
Seventh Place	West Germany
Eighth Place	United States

March 3–14, 1965

Tampere, Finland

GOLD MEDAL	Soviet Union
SILVER MEDAL	Czechoslovakia
BRONZE MEDAL	Sweden
Fourth Place	Canada
Fifth Place	East Germany

Sixth Place   United States
Seventh Place   Finland
Eighth Place   Norway

March 3–14, 1966

Ljubljana, Yugoslavia

GOLD MEDAL   Soviet Union
SILVER MEDAL   Czechoslovakia
BRONZE MEDAL   Canada
Fourth Place   Sweden
Fifth Place   East Germany
Sixth Place   United States
Seventh Place   Finland
Eighth Place   Poland

March 18–29, 1967

Vienna, Austria

GOLD MEDAL   Soviet Union
SILVER MEDAL   Sweden
BRONZE MEDAL   Canada
Fourth Place   Czechoslovakia
Fifth Place   United States
Sixth Place   Finland
Seventh Place   West Germany
Eighth Place   East Germany

March 15–30, 1969

Stockholm, Sweden

GOLD MEDAL   Soviet Union
SILVER MEDAL   Sweden
BRONZE MEDAL   Czechoslovakia
Fourth Place   Canada

| Fifth Place | Finland |
| Sixth Place | United States |

To protest the ineligibility of professionals from the World Championship according to IIHF rules, Canada did not compete in IIHF sanctioned tournaments from 1970 through 1976.

March 14–30, 1970

Stockholm, Sweden

GOLD MEDAL	Soviet Union
SILVER MEDAL	Sweden
BRONZE MEDAL	Czechoslovakia
Fourth Place	Finland
Fifth Place	East Germany
Sixth Place	Poland

March 19–April 3, 1971

Bern/Geneva/Switzerland

GOLD MEDAL	Soviet Union
SILVER MEDAL	Czechoslovakia
BRONZE MEDAL	Sweden
Fourth Place	Finland
Fifth Place	East Germany
Sixth Place	United States

April 7–22, 1972

Prague, Czechoslovakia

GOLD MEDAL	Czechoslovakia
SILVER MEDAL	Soviet Union
BRONZE MEDAL	Sweden
Fourth Place	Finland
Fifth Place	East Germany
Sixth Place	Switzerland

March 31–April 15, 1973

Moscow, Soviet Union

GOLD MEDAL	Soviet Union
SILVER MEDAL	Sweden
BRONZE MEDAL	Czechoslovakia
Fourth Place	Finland
Fifth Place	Poland
Sixth Place	East Germany

April 5–20, 1974

Helsinki, Finland

GOLD MEDAL	Soviet Union
SILVER MEDAL	Czechoslovakia
BRONZE MEDAL	Sweden
Fourth Place	Finland
Fifth Place	Poland
Sixth Place	East Germany

April 3–19, 1975

Munich/Dusseldorf, West Germany

GOLD MEDAL	Soviet Union
SILVER MEDAL	Czechoslovakia
BRONZE MEDAL	Sweden
Fourth Place	Finland
Fifth Place	Poland
Sixth Place	United States

April 8–25, 1976

Katowice, Poland

GOLD MEDAL	Czechoslovakia
SILVER MEDAL	Soviet Union

BRONZE MEDAL	Sweden
Fourth Place	United States
Fifth Place	Finland
Sixth Place	West Germany
Seventh Place	Poland
Eighth Place	East Germany

April 21–May 8, 1977

Vienna, Austria

GOLD MEDAL	Czechoslovakia
SILVER MEDAL	Sweden
BRONZE MEDAL	Soviet Union
Fourth Place	Canada
Fifth Place	Finland
Sixth Place	United States
Seventh Place	West Germany
Eighth Place	Romania

April 25–May 8, 1978

Prague, Czechoslovakia

GOLD MEDAL	Soviet Union
SILVER MEDAL	Czechoslovakia
BRONZE MEDAL	Canada
Fourth Place	Sweden
Fifth Place	West Germany
Sixth Place	USA
Seventh Place	Finland
Eighth Place	East Germany

April 14–27, 1979

Moscow, Soviet Union

GOLD MEDAL	Soviet Union
SILVER MEDAL	Czechoslovakia
BRONZE MEDAL	Sweden
Fourth Place	Canada
Fifth Place	Finland
Sixth Place	West Germany
Seventh Place	United States
Eighth Place	Poland

April 12–26, 1981

Gothenburg/Stockholm, Sweden

GOLD MEDAL	Soviet Union
SILVER MEDAL	Sweden
BRONZE MEDAL	Czechoslovakia
Fourth Place	Canada
Fifth Place	United States
Sixth Place	Finland
Seventh Place	West Germany
Eighth Place	Netherlands

April 15–29, 1982

Helsinki/Tampere, Finland

GOLD MEDAL	Soviet Union
SILVER MEDAL	Czechoslovakia
BRONZE MEDAL	Canada
Fourth Place	Sweden
Fifth Place	Finland
Sixth Place	West Germany
Seventh Place	Italy
Eighth Place	United States

April 16–May 2, 1983

Dortmund/Dusseldorf/Munich, West Germany

GOLD MEDAL	Soviet Union
SILVER MEDAL	Czechoslovakia
BRONZE MEDAL	Canada
Fourth Place	Sweden
Fifth Place	East Germany
Sixth Place	West Germany
Seventh Place	Finland
Eighth Place	Italy

April 17–May 3, 1985

Prague, Czechoslovakia

GOLD MEDAL	Czechoslovakia
SILVER MEDAL	Canada
BRONZE MEDAL	Soviet Union
Fourth Place	United States
Fifth Place	Finland
Sixth Place	Sweden
Seventh Place	East Germany
Eighth Place	West Germany

April 12–28, 1986

Moscow, Soviet Union

GOLD MEDAL	Soviet Union
SILVER MEDAL	Sweden
BRONZE MEDAL	Canada
Fourth Place	Finland
Fifth Place	Czechoslovakia
Sixth Place	United States
Seventh Place	East Germany
Eighth Place	Poland

April 17–May 3, 1987

Vienna, Austria

GOLD MEDAL	Soviet Union
SILVER MEDAL	Czechoslovakia
BRONZE MEDAL	Sweden
Fourth Place	Canada
Fifth Place	West Germany
Sixth Place	Finland
Seventh Place	United States
Eighth Place	Switzerland

April 15–May 1, 1989

Stockholm, Sweden

GOLD MEDAL	Soviet Union
SILVER MEDAL	Canada
BRONZE MEDAL	Czechoslovakia
Fourth Place	Sweden
Fifth Place	Finland
Sixth Place	United States
Seventh Place	West Germany
Eighth Place	Poland

April 16–May 2, 1990

Bern, Switzerland

GOLD MEDAL	Soviet Union
SILVER MEDAL	Sweden
BRONZE MEDAL	Czechoslovakia
Fourth Place	Canada
Fifth Place	United States
Sixth Place	Finland
Seventh Place	West Germany
Eighth Place	Norway

April 14–May 5, 1991

Helsinki, Finland

GOLD MEDAL	Sweden
SILVER MEDAL	Canada
BRONZE MEDAL	Soviet Union
Fourth Place	United States
Fifth Place	Finland
Sixth Place	Czechoslovakia
Seventh Place	Switzerland
Eight Place	Germany

April 28–May 10, 1992

Prague/Bratislava, Czechoslovakia

GOLD MEDAL	Sweden
SILVER MEDAL	Finland
BRONZE MEDAL	Czechoslovakia
Fourth Place	Switzerland
Fifth Place	Russia
Sixth Place	Germany
Seventh Place	United States
Eighth Place	Canada
Ninth Place	Italy
Tenth Place	Norway
Eleventh Place	France
Twelfth Place	Poland

April 18–May 2, 1993

Munich, Germany

GOLD MEDAL	Russia
SILVER MEDAL	Sweden
BRONZE MEDAL	Czech Republic
Fourth Place	Canada

Fifth Place   Germany
Sixth Place   United States
Seventh Place   Finland
Eighth Place   Italy
Ninth Place   Austria
Tenth Place   France
Eleventh Place   Norway
Twelfth Place   Switzerland

April 25–May 8, 1994

Bolzano, Italy

GOLD MEDAL   Canada
SILVER MEDAL   Finland
BRONZE MEDAL   Sweden
Fourth Place   United States
Fifth Place   Russia
Sixth Place   Italy
Seventh Place   Czech Republic
Eighth Place   Austria
Ninth Place   Germany
Tenth Place   France
Eleventh Place   Norway
Twelfth Place   Great Britain

April 23–May 7, 1995

Stockholm/Gavle, Sweden

GOLD MEDAL   Finland
SILVER MEDAL   Sweden
BRONZE MEDAL   Canada
Fourth Place   Czech Republic
Fifth Place   Russia
Sixth Place   United States
Seventh Place   Italy

Eighth Place   France
Ninth Place   Germany
Tenth Place   Norway
Eleventh Place   Austria
Twelfth Place   Switzerland

April 21–May 5, 1996

Vienna, Austria

GOLD MEDAL   Czech Republic
SILVER MEDAL   Canada
BRONZE MEDAL   United States
Fourth Place   Russia
Fifth Place   Finland
Sixth Place   Sweden
Seventh Place   Italy
Eighth Place   Germany
Ninth Place   Norway
Tenth Place   Slovakia
Eleventh Place   France
Twelfth Place   Austria

April 26–May 14, 1997

Helsinki/Tampere/Turku, Finland

GOLD MEDAL   Canada
SILVER MEDAL   Sweden
BRONZE MEDAL   Czech Republic
Fourth Place   Russia
Fifth Place   Finland
Sixth Place   United States
Seventh Place   Latvia
Eighth Place   Italy
Ninth Place   Slovakia

Tenth Place	France
Eleventh Place	Germany
Twelfth Place	Norway

May 1–17, 1998

Zurich, Switzerland

GOLD MEDAL	Sweden
SILVER MEDAL	Finland
BRONZE MEDAL	Czech Republic
Fourth Place	Switzerland
Fifth Place	Russia
Sixth Place	Canada
Seventh Place	Slovakia
Eighth Place	Belarus
Ninth Place	Latvia
Tenth Place	Italy
Eleventh Place	Germany
Twelfth Place	United States

May 1–16, 1999

Oslo/Hamar/Lillehammer, Norway

GOLD MEDAL	Czech Republic
SILVER MEDAL	Finland
BRONZE MEDAL	Sweden
Fourth Place	Canada
Fifth Place	Russia
Sixth Place	United States
Seventh Place	Slovakia
Eighth Place	Switzerland
Ninth Place	Belarus
Tenth Place	Austria
Eleventh Place	Latvia

Twelfth Place	Norway
Thirteenth Place	Italy
Fourteenth Place	Ukraine
Fifteenth Place	France
Sixteenth Place	Japan

April 29–May 14, 2000

St. Petersburg, Russia

GOLD MEDAL	Czech Republic
SILVER MEDAL	Slovakia
BRONZE MEDAL	Finland
Fourth Place	Canada
Fifth Place	United States
Sixth Place	Switzerland
Seventh Place	Sweden
Eighth Place	Latvia
Ninth Place	Belarus
Tenth Place	Norway
Eleventh Place	Russia
Twelfth Place	Italy
Thirteenth Place	Austria
Fourteenth Place	Ukraine
Fifteenth Place	France
Sixteenth Place	Japan

April 28–May 13, 2001

Hanover/Cologne/Nuremberg, Germany

GOLD MEDAL	Czech Republic
SILVER MEDAL	Finland
BRONZE MEDAL	Sweden
Fourth Place	United States
Fifth Place	Canada

Sixth Place   Russia
Seventh Place   Slovakia
Eighth Place   Germany
Ninth Place   Switzerland
Tenth Place   Ukraine
Eleventh Place   Austria
Twelfth Place   Italy
Thirteenth Place   Latvia
Fourteenth Place   Belarus
Fifteenth Place   Norway
Sixteenth Place   Japan

April 26–May 11, 2002

Gothenburg/Karlstad/Jonkoping, Sweden

GOLD MEDAL   Slovakia
SILVER MEDAL   Russia
BRONZE MEDAL   Sweden
Fourth Place   Finland
Fifth Place   Czech Republic
Sixth Place   Canada
Seventh Place   United States
Eighth Place   Germany
Ninth Place   Ukraine
Tenth Place   Switzerland
Eleventh Place   Latvia
Twelfth Place   Austria
Thirteenth Place   Slovenia
Fourteenth Place   Poland
Fifteenth Place   Italy
Sixteenth Place   Japan

April 27–May 11, 2003

Helsinki/Tampere/Turku, Finland

GOLD MEDAL	Canada
SILVER MEDAL	Sweden
BRONZE MEDAL	Slovakia
Fourth Place	Czech Republic
Fifth Place	Finland
Sixth Place	Germany
Seventh Place	Russia
Eighth Place	Switzerland
Ninth Place	Latvia
Tenth Place	Austria
Eleventh Place	Denmark
Twelfth Place	Ukraine
Thirteenth Place	United States
Fourteenth Place	Belarus
Fifteenth Place	Slovenia
Sixteenth Place	Japan

April 24–May 9, 2004

Prague/Ostrava, Czech Republic

GOLD MEDAL	Canada
SILVER MEDAL	Sweden
BRONZE MEDAL	United States
Fourth Place	Slovakia
Fifth Place	Czech Republic
Sixth Place	Finland
Seventh Place	Latvia
Eighth Place	Switzerland
Ninth Place	Germany
Tenth Place	Russia
Eleventh Place	Austria

Twelfth Place	Denmark
Thirteenth Place	Kazakhstan
Fourteenth Place	Ukraine
Fifteenth Place	Japan
Sixteenth Place	France

April 30–May 15, 2005

Vienna/Innsbruck, Austria

GOLD MEDAL	Czech Republic
SILVER MEDAL	Canada
BRONZE MEDAL	Russia
Fourth Place	Sweden
Fifth Place	Slovakia
Sixth Place	United States
Seventh Place	Finland
Eighth Place	Switzerland
Ninth Place	Latvia
Tenth Place	Belarus
Eleventh Place	Ukraine
Twelfth Place	Kazakhstan
Thirteenth Place	Slovenia
Fourteenth Place	Denmark
Fifteenth Place	Germany
Sixteenth Place	Austria

WORLD JUNIOR CHAMPIONSHIPS, 1977–2006

ALL MEDAL WINNERS BY CUMULATIVE STANDINGS (1977–2006)

Country	Gold	Silver	Bronze	Total
Canada	12	6	4	22
Soviet Union	9	3	2	14
Finland	2	4	6	12
Sweden	1	6	4	11
Czechoslovakia	0	5	6	11
Russia	3	4	3	10
United States	1	1	2	4
Czech Republic	2	0	1	3
Slovakia	0	0	1	1
Switzerland	0	0	1	1

1977 WORLD JUNIOR CHAMPIONSHIPS

CZECHOSLOVAKIA, DECEMBER 22, 1976–JANUARY 2, 1977

FINAL PLACINGS

GOLD MEDAL	Soviet Union
SILVER MEDAL	Canada
BRONZE MEDAL	Czechoslovakia
Fourth Place	Finland
Fifth Place	Sweden
Sixth Place	West Germany
Seventh Place	United States
Eighth Place	Poland*

* relegated to 'B' pool for 1978

ALL-STAR TEAM

Goal   Alexander Tyznych (Soviet Union)

Defence   Risto Siltanen (Finland)
            Lubos Oslizlo (Czechoslovakia)

Forward   Dale McCourt (Canada)
            Bengt-Ake Gustafsson (Sweden)
            Igor Rómasin (Soviet Union)

DIRECTORATE AWARDS

BEST GOALIE   Jan Hrabak (Czechoslovakia)
BEST DEFENCEMAN   Viacheslav Fetisov (Soviet Union)
BEST FORWARD   Dale McCourt (Canada)

1978 WORLD JUNIOR CHAMPIONSHIPS

CANADA, DECEMBER 22, 1977–JANUARY 3, 1978

FINAL PLACINGS

GOLD MEDAL   Soviet Union
SILVER MEDAL   Sweden
BRONZE MEDAL   Canada
Fourth Place   Czechoslovakia
Fifth Place   United States
Sixth Place   Finland
Seventh Place   West Germany
Eighth Place   Switzerland*

* promoted from 'B' pool in 1977; relegated to 'B' pool for 1979

ALL-STAR TEAM

Goal	Alexander Tyznych (Soviet Union)
Defence	Risto Siltanen (Finland)
	Viacheslav Fetisov (Soviet Union)
Forward	Wayne Gretzky (Canada)
	Mats Naslund (Sweden)
	Anton Stastny (Czechoslovakia)

DIRECTORATE AWARDS

BEST GOALIE	Alexander Tyzhnych (Soviet Union)
BEST DEFENCEMAN	Viacheslav Fetisov (Soviet Union)
BEST FORWARD	Wayne Gretzky (Canada)

1979 WORLD JUNIOR CHAMPIONSHIPS

SWEDEN, DECEMBER 27, 1978–JANUARY 3, 1979

FINAL PLACINGS

GOLD MEDAL	Soviet Union
SILVER MEDAL	Sweden
BRONZE MEDAL	Czechoslovakia
Fourth Place	Finland
Fifth Place	Canada
Sixth Place	United States
Seventh Place	West Germany
Eighth Place	Norway*

* promoted from 'B' pool in 1978; relegated to 'B' pool for 1980

ALL-STAR TEAM

Goal   Pelle Lindbergh (Sweden)

Defence   Ivan Cerny (Czechoslovakia)
            Alexei Kasatonov (Soviet Union)

Forward   Anatoli Tarasov (Soviet Union)
            Thomas Steen (Sweden)
            Vladimir Krutov (Soviet Union)

DIRECTORATE AWARDS

BEST GOALIE   Pelle Lindbergh (Sweden)
BEST DEFENCEMAN   Alexei Kasatonov (Soviet Union)
BEST FORWARD   Vladimir Krutov (Soviet Union)

1980 WORLD JUNIOR CHAMPIONSHIPS

FINLAND, DECEMBER 27, 1979–JANUARY 2, 1980

FINAL PLACINGS

GOLD MEDAL   Soviet Union
SILVER MEDAL   Finland
BRONZE MEDAL   Sweden
Fourth Place   Czechoslovakia
Fifth Place   Canada
Sixth Place   West Germany
Seventh Place   United States
Eighth Place   Switzerland*

* promoted from 'B' pool in 1979; relegated to 'B' pool for 1981

ALL-STAR TEAM

Goal	Jari Paavola (Finland)
Defence	Reijo Ruotsalainen (Finland)
	Tomas Jonsson (Sweden)
Forward	Hakan Loob (Sweden)
	Igor Larionov (Soviet Union)
	Vladimir Krutov (Soviet Union)

DIRECTORATE AWARDS

BEST GOALIE	Jari Paavola (Finland)
BEST DEFENCEMAN	Reijo Ruotsalainen (Finland)
BEST FORWARD	Vladimir Krutov (Soviet Union)

1981 WORLD JUNIOR CHAMPIONSHIPS

WEST GERMANY, DECEMBER 27, 1980–JANUARY 2, 1981

FINAL PLACINGS

GOLD MEDAL	Sweden
SILVER MEDAL	Finland
BRONZE MEDAL	Soviet Union
Fourth Place	Czechoslovakia
Fifth Place	West Germany
Sixth Place	United States
Seventh Place	Canada
Eighth Place	Austria*

* promoted from 'B' pool in 1980; relegated to 'B' pool for 1982

ALL-STAR TEAM

Goal   Lars Eriksson (Sweden)

Defence   Miloslav Horava (Czechoslovakia)
            Hakan Nordin (Sweden)

Forward   Ari Lahteenmaki (Finland)
            Patrik Sundstrom (Sweden)
            Jan Erixon (Sweden)

DIRECTORATE AWARDS

BEST GOALIE   Lars Eriksson (Sweden)
BEST DEFENCEMAN   Miloslav Horava (Czechoslovakia)
BEST FORWARD   Patrik Sundstrom (Sweden)

1982 WORLD JUNIOR CHAMPIONSHIPS

UNITED STATES, DECEMBER 22, 1981–JANUARY 2, 1982
(some games played in Canada)

FINAL PLACINGS

GOLD MEDAL   Canada
SILVER MEDAL   Czechoslovakia
BRONZE MEDAL   Finland
Fourth Place   Soviet Union
Fifth Place   Sweden
Sixth Place   United States
Seventh Place   West Germany
Eighth Place   Switzerland*

* promoted from 'B' pool in 1981; relegated to 'B' pool for 1983

ALL-STAR TEAM

Goal   Mike Moffat (Canada)

Defence   Gord Kluzak (Canada)
            Ilya Biakin (Soviet Union)

Forward   Mike Moller (Canada)
            Petri Skriko (Finland)
            Vladimir Ruzicka (Czechoslovakia)

DIRECTORATE AWARDS

BEST GOALIE   Mike Moffat (Canada)
BEST DEFENCEMAN   Gord Kluzak (Canada)
BEST FORWARD   Petri Skriko (Finland)

1983 WORLD JUNIOR CHAMPIONSHIPS

SOVIET UNION, DECEMBER 26, 1982–JANUARY 4, 1983

FINAL PLACINGS

GOLD MEDAL   Soviet Union
SILVER MEDAL   Czechoslovakia
BRONZE MEDAL   Canada
Fourth Place   Sweden
Fifth Place   United States
Sixth Place   Finland
Seventh Place   West Germany
Eighth Place   Norway*

* promoted from 'B' pool in 1982; relegated to 'B' pool for 1984

ALL-STAR TEAM

| Goal | Matti Rautiainen (Finland) |

Defence   Ilya Biakin (Soviet Union)
          Simo Saarinen (Finland)

Forward   Tomas Sandstrom (Sweden)
          Vladimir Ruzicka (Czechoslovakia)
          German Volgin (Soviet Union)

DIRECTORATE AWARDS

BEST GOALIE	Dominik Hasek (Czechoslovakia)
BEST DEFENCEMAN	Ilya Biakin (Soviet Union)
BEST FORWARD	Tomas Sandstrom (Sweden)

1984 WORLD JUNIOR CHAMPIONSHIPS

SWEDEN, DECEMBER 25, 1983–JANUARY 3, 1984

FINAL PLACINGS

GOLD MEDAL	Soviet Union
SILVER MEDAL	Finland
BRONZE MEDAL	Czechoslovakia
Fourth Place	Canada
Fifth Place	Sweden
Sixth Place	United States
Seventh Place	West Germany
Eighth Place	Switzerland*

* promoted from 'B' pool in 1983; relegated to 'B' pool for 1985

ALL-STAR TEAM

Goal	Evgeny Belosheikin (Soviet Union)
Defence	Alexei Gusarov (Soviet Union)
	Frantisek Musil (Czechoslovakia)
Forward	Petr Rosol (Czechoslovakia)
	Raimo Helminen (Finland)
	Nikolai Borschevsky (Soviet Union)

DIRECTORATE AWARDS

BEST GOALIE	Alan Perry (United States)
BEST DEFENCEMAN	Alexei Gusarov (Soviet Union)
BEST FORWARD	Raimo Helminen (Finland)

1985 WORLD JUNIOR CHAMPIONSHIPS

FINLAND, DECEMBER 23, 1984–JANUARY 1, 1985

FINAL PLACINGS

GOLD MEDAL	Canada
SILVER MEDAL	Czechoslovakia
BRONZE MEDAL	Soviet Union
Fourth Place	Finland
Fifth Place	Sweden
Sixth Place	United States
Seventh Place	West Germany
Eighth Place	Poland*

* promoted from 'B' pool in 1984; relegated to 'B' pool for 1986

ALL-STAR TEAM

Goal	Timo Lehkonen (Finland)
Defence	Bobby Dollas (Canada)
	Mikhail Tatarinov (Soviet Union)
Forward	Mikko Makela (Finland)
	Michal Pivonka (Czechoslovakia)
	Esa Tikkanen (Finland)

DIRECTORATE AWARDS

BEST GOALIE	Craig Billington (Canada)
BEST DEFENCEMAN	Vesa Salo (Finland)
BEST FORWARD	Michal Pivonka (Czechoslovakia)

1986 WORLD JUNIOR CHAMPIONSHIPS

CANADA, DECEMBER 26, 1985–JANUARY 4, 1986

FINAL PLACINGS

GOLD MEDAL	Soviet Union
SILVER MEDAL	Canada
BRONZE MEDAL	United States
Fourth Place	Czechoslovakia
Fifth Place	Sweden
Sixth Place	Finland
Seventh Place	Switzerland*
Eighth Place	West Germany**

* promoted from 'B' pool in 1985
** relegated to 'B' pool for 1987

ALL-STAR TEAM

Goal	Evgeny Belosheikin (Soviet Union)
Defence	Sylvain Cote (Canada)
	Mikhail Tatarinov (Soviet Union)
Forward	Shayne Corson (Canada)
	Igor Viazmikin (Soviet Union)
	Michal Pivonka (Czechoslovakia)

DIRECTORATE AWARDS

BEST GOALIE	Evgeny Belosheikin (Soviet Union)
BEST DEFENCEMAN	Mikhail Tatarinov (Soviet Union)
BEST FORWARD	Jim Sandlak (Canada)

1987 WORLD JUNIOR CHAMPIONSHIPS

CZECHOSLOVAKIA, DECEMBER 26, 1986–JANUARY 4, 1987

FINAL PLACINGS

GOLD MEDAL	Finland
SILVER MEDAL	Czechoslovakia
BRONZE MEDAL	Sweden
Fourth Place	United States
Fifth Place	Poland*
Sixth PLace	Switzerland**

Canada and the Soviet Union were disqualified

* promoted from 'B' pool in 1986
** relegated to 'B' pool for 1988

ALL-STAR TEAM

Goal   Sam Lindstahl (Sweden)

Defence   Jiri Latal (Czechoslovakia)
            Brian Leetch (United States)

Forward   Ulf Dahlen (Sweden)
            Juraj Jurik (Czechoslovakia)
            Scott Young (United States)

DIRECTORATE AWARDS

BEST GOALIE   Markus Ketterer (Finland)
BEST DEFENCEMAN   Calle Johansson (Sweden)
BEST FORWARD   Robert Kron (Czechoslovakia)

1988 WORLD JUNIOR CHAMPIONSHIPS

RUSSIA, DECEMBER 26, 1987–JANUARY 4, 1988

FINAL PLACINGS

GOLD MEDAL   Canada
SILVER MEDAL   Soviet Union
BRONZE MEDAL   Finland
Fourth Place   Czechosloavkia
Fifth Place   Sweden
Sixth Place   United States
Seventh Place   West Germany*
Eighth Place   Poland**

* promoted from 'B' pool in 1987
** relegated to 'B' pool for 1989

ALL-STAR TEAM

Goal	Jimmy Waite (Canada)
Defence	Greg Hawgood (Canada)
	Teppo Numminen (Finland)
Forward	Theoren Fleury (Canada)
	Alexander Mogilny (Soviet Union)
	Petr Hrbek (Czechoslovakia)

DIRECTORATE AWARDS

BEST GOALIE	Jimmy Waite (Canada)
BEST DEFENCEMAN	Teppo Numminen (Finland)
BEST FORWARD	Alexander Mogilny (Soviet Union)

1989 WORLD JUNIOR CHAMPIONSHIPS

UNITED STATES, DECEMBER 26, 1988–JANUARY 4, 1989

FINAL PLACINGS

GOLD MEDAL	Soviet Union
SILVER MEDAL	Sweden
BRONZE MEDAL	Czechoslovakia
Fourth Place	Canada
Fifth Place	United States
Sixth Place	Finland
Seventh Place	Norway*
Eighth Place	West Germany**

* promoted from 'B' pool in 1988
** relegated to 'B' pool for 1990

ALL-STAR TEAM

Goal	Alexei Ivashkin (Soviet Union)
Defence	Rickard Persson (Sweden)
	Milan Tichy (Czechoslovakia)
Forward	Niklas Eriksson (Sweden)
	Pavel Bure (Soviet Union)
	Jeremy Roenick (United States)

DIRECTORATE AWARDS

BEST GOALIE	Alexei Ivashkin (Soviet Union)
BEST DEFENCEMAN	Rickard Persson (Sweden)
BEST FORWARD	Pavel Bure (Soviet Union)

1990 WORLD JUNIOR CHAMPIONSHIPS

FINLAND, DECEMBER 26, 1989–JANUARY 4, 1990

FINAL PLACINGS

GOLD MEDAL	Canada
SILVER MEDAL	Soviet Union
BRONZE MEDAL	Czechoslovakia
Fourth Place	Finland
Fifth Place	Sweden
Sixth Place	Norway
Seventh Place	United States
Eighth Place	Poland*

* promoted from 'B' pool in 1989; relegated to 'B' pool for 1991

ALL-STAR TEAM

Goal	Stephane Fiset (Canada)
Defence	Alexander Godynyuk (Soviet Union)
	Jiri Slegr (Czechoslovakia)
Forward	Dave Chyzowski (Canada)
	Jaromir Jagr (Czechoslovakia)
	Robert Reichel (Czechoslovakia)

DIRECTORATE AWARDS

BEST GOALIE	Stephane Fiset (Canada)
BEST DEFENCEMAN	Alexander Godynyuk (Soviet Union)
BEST FORWARD	Robert Reichel (Czechoslovakia)

1991 WORLD JUNIOR CHAMPIONSHIPS

CANADA, DECEMBER 26, 1990–JANUARY 4, 1991

FINAL PLACINGS

GOLD MEDAL	Canada
SILVER MEDAL	Soviet Union
BRONZE MEDAL	Czechoslovakia
Fourth Place	United States
Fifth Place	Finland
Sixth Place	Sweden
Seventh Place	Switzerland*
Eighth Place	Norway**

* promoted from 'B' pool in 1990
** relegated to 'B' pool for 1992

ALL-STAR TEAM

Goal   Pauli Jaks (Switzerland)

Defence   Dmitri Yushkevich (Soviet Union)
              Scott Lachance (United States)

Forward   Mike Craig (Canada)
              Eric Lindros (Canada)
              Martin Rucinsky (Czechoslovakia)

DIRECTORATE AWARDS

BEST GOALIE   Pauli Jaks (Switzerland)
BEST DEFENCEMAN   Jiri Slegr (Czechoslovakia)
BEST FORWARD   Eric Lindros (Canada)

1992 WORLD JUNIOR CHAMPIONSHIPS

GERMANY, DECEMBER 26, 1991–JANUARY 4, 1992

FINAL PLACINGS

GOLD MEDAL   Commonwealth of Independent States
SILVER MEDAL   Sweden
BRONZE MEDAL   United States
Fourth Place   Finland
Fifth Place   Czechoslovakia
Sixth Place   Canada
Seventh Place   Germany*
Eighth Place   Switzerland**

* promoted from 'B' pool in 1991
** relegated to 'B' pool for 1993

ALL-STAR TEAM

Goal   Mike Dunham (United States)

Defence   Scott Niedermayer (Canada)
           Janne Gronvall (Finland)

Forward   Alexei Kovalev (CIS)
           Michael Nylander (Sweden)
           Peter Ferraro (United States)

DIRECTORATE AWARDS

BEST GOALIE	Mike Dunham (United States)
BEST DEFENCEMAN	Darius Kasparaitis (CIS)
BEST FORWARD	Michael Nylander (Sweden)

1993 WORLD JUNIOR CHAMPIONSHIPS

SWEDEN, DECEMBER 26, 1992–JANUARY 4, 1993

FINAL PLACINGS

GOLD MEDAL	Canada
SILVER MEDAL	Sweden
BRONZE MEDAL	Czech Republic
Fourth Place	United States
Fifth Place	Finland
Sixth Place	Russia
Seventh Place	Germany
Eighth place	Japan*

* promoted from 'B' pool in 1992; relegated to 'B' pool for 1994

ALL-STAR TEAM

Goal   Manny Legace (Canada)

Defence   Brent Tully (Canada)
            Kenny Jonsson (Sweden)

Forward   Paul Kariya (Canada)
            Markus Naslund (Sweden)
            Peter Forsberg (Sweden)

DIRECTORATE AWARDS

BEST GOALIE   Manny Legace (Canada)
BEST DEFENCEMAN   Janne Gronvall (Finland)
BEST FORWARD   Peter Forsberg (Sweden)

1994 WORLD JUNIOR CHAMPIONSHIPS

CZECH REPUBLIC, DECEMBER 26, 1993–JANUARY 4, 1994

FINAL PLACINGS

GOLD MEDAL   Canada
SILVER MEDAL   Sweden
BRONZE MEDAL   Russia
Fourth Place   Finland
Fifth Place   Czech Republic
Sixth Place   United States
Seventh Place   Germany
Eighth Place   Switzerland*

* promoted from 'B' pool in 1993; relegated to 'B' pool for 1995

ALL-STAR TEAM

Goal	Evgeny Riabchikov (Russia)
Defence	Kenny Jonsson (Sweden)
	Kimmo Timonen (Finland)
Forward	Niklas Sundstrom (Sweden)
	Valeri Bure (Russia)
	David Vyborny (Czech Republic)

DIRECTORATE AWARDS

BEST GOALIE	Jamie Storr (Canada)
BEST DEFENCEMAN	Kenny Jonsson (Sweden)
BEST FORWARD	Niklas Sundstrom (Sweden)

1995 WORLD JUNIOR CHAMPIONSHIPS

CANADA, DECEMBER 26, 1994–JANUARY 4, 1995

FINAL PLACINGS

GOLD MEDAL	Canada
SILVER MEDAL	Russia
BRONZE MEDAL	Sweden
Fourth Place	Finland
Fifth Place	United States
Sixth Place	Czech Republic
Seventh Place	Germany
Eighth Place	Ukraine*

* promoted from 'B' pool in 1994

Note: no team was relegated to 'B' pool from this year's tournament because in 1996 the 'A' pool expanded to ten teams and a new round-robin format

ALL-STAR TEAM

Goal   Igor Karpenko (Ukraine)

Defence   Bryan McCabe (Canada)
            Anders Eriksson (Sweden)

Forward   Jason Allison (Canada)
            Eric Daze (Canada)
            Marty Murray (Canada)

DIRECTORATE AWARDS

BEST GOALIE   Evgeny Tarasov (Russia)
BEST DEFENCEMAN   Bryan McCabe (Canada)
BEST FORWARD   Marty Murray (Canada)

1996 WORLD JUNIOR CHAMPIONSHIPS

UNITED STATES, DECEMBER 26, 1995–JANUARY 4, 1996

FINAL PLACINGS

GOLD MEDAL   Canada
SILVER MEDAL   Sweden
BRONZE MEDAL   Russia
Fourth Place   Czech Republic
Fifth Place   United States
Sixth Place   Finland
Seventh Place   Slovakia*
Eighth Place   Germany
Ninth Place   Switzerland*
Tenth Place   Ukraine**

* promoted from 'B' pool in 1995
** relegated to 'B' pool for 1997

ALL-STAR TEAM

Goal	Jose Theodore (Canada)
Defence	Nolan Baumgartner (Canada)
	Mattias Ohlund (Sweden)
Forward	Jarome Iginla (Canada)
	Johan Davidsson (Sweden)
	Alexei Morozov (Russia)

DIRECTORATE AWARDS

BEST GOALIE	Jose Theodore (Canada)
BEST DEFENCEMAN	Mattias Ohlund (Sweden)
BEST FORWARD	Jarome Iginla (Canada)

1997 WORLD JUNIOR CHAMPIONSHIPS

SWITZERLAND, DECEMBER 26, 1996–JANUARY 4, 1997

FINAL PLACINGS

GOLD MEDAL	Canada
SILVER MEDAL	United States
BRONZE MEDAL	Russia
Fourth Place	Czech Republic
Fifth Place	Finland
Sixth Place	Slovakia
Seventh Place	Switzerland
Eighth Place	Sweden
Ninth Place	Germany
Tenth Place	Poland*

* promoted from 'B' pool in 1996; relegated to 'B' pool for 1998

ALL-STAR TEAM

Goal   Brian Boucher (United States)

Defence   Chris Phillips (Canada)
            Mark Streit (Switzerland)

Forward   Christian Dube (Canada)
            Sergei Samsonov (Russia)
            Michael York (United States)

DIRECTORATE AWARDS

BEST GOALIE   Marc Denis (Canada)
BEST DEFENCEMAN   Joseph Corvo (United States)
BEST FORWARD   Alexei Morozov (Russia)

1998 WORLD JUNIOR CHAMPIONSHIPS

FINLAND, DECEMBER 25, 1997–JANUARY 3, 1998

FINAL PLACINGS

GOLD MEDAL   Finland
SILVER MEDAL   Russia
BRONZE MEDAL   Switzerland
Fourth Place   Czech Republic
Fifth Place   United States
Sixth Place   Sweden
Seventh Place   Kazakhstan*
Eighth Place   Canada
Ninth Place   Slovakia
Tenth Place   Germany**

* promoted from 'B' pool in 1997
** relegated to 'B' pool for 1999

ALL-STAR TEAM

Goal   David Aebischer (Switzerland)

Defence   Pierre Hedin (Sweden)
            Andrei Markov (Russia)

Forward   Olli Jokinen (Finland)
            Eero Somervuori (Finland)
            Maxim Balmochnykh (Russia)

DIRECTORATE AWARDS
BEST GOALIE   David Aebischer (Switzerland)
BEST DEFENCEMAN   Pavel Skrbek (Czech Republic)
BEST FORWARD   Olli Jokinen (Finland)

1999 WORLD JUNIOR CHAMPIONSHIPS
CANADA, DECEMBER 26, 1998–JANUARY 5, 1999

FINAL PLACINGS
GOLD MEDAL   Russia
SILVER MEDAL   Canada
BRONZE MEDAL   Slovakia
Fourth Place   Sweden
Fifth Place   Finland
Sixth Place   Kazakhstan
Seventh Place   Czech Republic
Eighth Place   United States
Ninth Place   Switzerland
Tenth Place   Belarus*

* promoted from 'B' pool in 1998; relegated to 'B' pool for 2000

ALL-STAR TEAM

Goal   Roberto Luongo (Canada)

Defence   Vitali Vishnevsky (Russia)
            Brian Campbell (Canada)

Forward   Daniel Tkachuk (Canada)
            Brian Gionta (United States)
            Maxim Balmochnykh (Russia)

DIRECTORATE AWARDS

BEST GOALIE   Roberto Luongo (Canada)
BEST DEFENCEMAN   Maxim Afinigenov (Russia)
BEST FORWARD   Vitali Vishnevski (Russia)

2000 WORLD JUNIOR CHAMPIONSHIPS

SWEDEN, DECEMBER 25, 1999–JANUARY 4, 2000

FINAL PLACINGS

GOLD MEDAL	Czech Republic
SILVER MEDAL	Russia
BRONZE MEDAL	Canada
Fourth Place	United States
Fifth Place	Sweden
Sixth Place	Switzerland
Seventh Place	Finland
Eighth Place	Kazakhstan
Ninth Place	Slovakia
Tenth Place	Ukraine*

* promoted from 'B' pool in 1999; demoted to 'B' pool for 2001

ALL-STAR TEAM

Goal	Rick DiPietro (United States)
Defence	Mathieu Biron (Canada)
	Alexander Rjasantsev (Russia)
Forward	Milan Kraft (Czech Republic)
	Alexei Tereschenko (Russia)
	Evgeny Muratov (Russia)

DIRECTORATE AWARDS

BEST GOALIE	Rick DiPietro (United States)
BEST DEFENCEMAN	Alexander Rjasantsev (Russia)
BEST FORWARD	Milan Kraft (Czech Republic)

2001 WORLD JUNIOR CHAMPIONSHIPS

RUSSIA, DECEMBER 26, 2000–JANUARY 5, 2001

FINAL PLACINGS

GOLD MEDAL	Czech Republic
SILVER MEDAL	Finland
BRONZE MEDAL	Canada
Fourth Place	Sweden
Fifth Place	United States
Sixth Place	Switzerland
Seventh Place	Russia
Eighth Place	Slovakia
Ninth Place	Belarus*
Tenth Place	Kazakhstan**

* promoted from 'B' pool in 2000
** demoted to 'B' pool for 2002

ALL-STAR TEAM

Goal   Ari Ahonen (Finland)

Defence   Rostislav Klesla (Czech Republic)
          Tuukka Mantyla (Finland)

Forward   Jason Spezza (Canada)
          Jani Rita (Finland)
          Pavel Brendl (Czech Republic)

DIRECTORATE AWARDS

BEST GOALIE   Tomas Duba (Czech Republic)
BEST DEFENCEMAN   Rostislav Klesla (Czech Republic)
BEST FORWARD   Pavel Brendl (Czech Republic)

2002 WORLD JUNIOR CHAMPIONSHIPS

CZECH REPUBLIC, DECEMBER 25, 2001–JUANUARY 4, 2002

FINAL PLACINGS

GOLD MEDAL   Russia
SILVER MEDAL   Canada
BRONZE MEDAL   Finland
Fourth Place   Switzerland
Fifth Place   United States
Sixth Place   Sweden
Seventh Place   Czech Republic
Eighth Place   Slovakia
Ninth Place   Belarus
Tenth Place   France*

* promoted from 2001; demoted for 2003

ALL-STAR TEAM

Goal	Pascal Leclaire (Canada)
Defence	Jay Bouwmeester (Canada)
	Igor Knyazev (Russia)
Forward	Mike Cammalleri (Canada)
	Marek Svatos (Canada)
	Stanislav Chistov (Russia)

DIRECTORATE AWARDS

BEST GOALIE	Kari Lehtonen (Finland)
BEST DEFENCEMAN	Igor Knyazev (Russia)
BEST FORWARD	Mike Cammalleri (Canada)

2003 WORLD JUNIOR CHAMPIONSHIPS

CANADA, DECEMBER 26, 2002–JANUARY 5, 2003

FINAL PLACINGS

GOLD MEDAL	Russia
SILVER MEDAL	Canada
BRONZE MEDAL	Finland
Fourth Place	United States
Fifth Place	Slovakia
Sixth Place	Czech Republic
Seventh Place	Switzerland
Eighth Place	Sweden
Ninth Place	Germany*
Tenth Place	Belarus**

* promoted from 2002
** demoted for 2004

ALL-STAR TEAM

Goal   Marc-Andre Fleury (Canada)

Defence   Carlo Colaiacovo (Canada)
            Joni Pitkanen (Finland)

Forward   Scottie Upshall (Canada)
            Igor Grigorenko (Russia)
            Yuri Trubachev (Russia)

DIRECTORATE AWARDS

BEST GOALIE   Marc-Andre Fleury (Canada)
BEST DEFENCEMAN   Joni Pitkanen (Finland)
BEST FORWARD   Igor Grigorenko (Russia)

2004 WORLD JUNIOR CHAMPIONSHIPS

FINLAND, DECEMBER 26, 2003–JANUARY 6, 2004

FINAL PLACINGS

GOLD MEDAL   United States
SILVER MEDAL   Canada
BRONZE MEDAL   Finland
Fourth Place   Czech Republic
Fifth Place   Russia
Sixth Place   Slovakia
Seventh Place   Sweden
Eighth Place   Switzerland
Ninth Place   Austria*
Tenth Place   Ukraine**

* promoted from 2003
** demoted for 2005

ALL-STAR TEAM

Goal	Al Montoya (United States)
Defence	Dion Phaneuf (Canada)
	Sami Lepisto (Finland)
Forward	Jeff Carter (Canada)
	Valtteri Filppula (Finland)
	Zach Parise (United States)

DIRECTORATE AWARDS

BEST GOALIE	Al Montoya (United States)
BEST DEFENCEMAN	Sami Lepisto (Finland)
BEST FORWARD	Zach Parise (United States)

2005 WORLD JUNIOR CHAMPIONSHIP

UNITED STATES, December 25, 2004–January 4, 2005

FINAL PLACINGS

GOLD MEDAL	Canada
SILVER MEDAL	Russia
BRONZE MEDAL	Czech Republic
Fourth Place	United States
Fifth Place	Finland
Sixth Place	Sweden
Seventh Place	Slovakia
Eighth Place	Switzerland
Ninth Place	Germany*
Tenth Place	Belarus*

* promoted from 2004; demoted for 2006

ALL-STAR TEAM

Goal   Marek Schwarz (Czech Republic)

Defence   Dion Phaneuf (Canada)
            Gary Suter (United States)

Forward   Patrice Bergeron (Canada)
            Jeff Carter (Canada)
            Alexander Ovechkin (Russia)

DIRECTORATE AWARDS

BEST GOALIE   Marek Schwarz (Czech Republic)
BEST DEFENCEMAN   Dion Phaneuf (Canada)
BEST FORWARD   Alexander Ovechkin (Russia)

2006 WORLD JUNIOR CHAMPIONSHIP

CANADA, December 26, 2005–January 5, 2006

FINAL PLACINGS

GOLD MEDAL   Canada
SILVER MEDAL   Russia
BRONZE MEDAL   Finland
Fourth Place   United States
Fifth Place   Sweden
Sixth Place   Czech Republic
Seventh Place   Switzerland
Eighth Place   Slovakia
Ninth Place   Latvia*
Tenth Place   Norway*

* promoted from 2005; demoted for 2007

ALL-STAR TEAM

Goal	Tuukka Rask (Finland)
Defence	Luc Bourdon (Canada)
	Jack Johnson (United States)
Forward	Steve Downie (Canada)
	Evgeni Malkin (Russia)
	Lauri Tukonen (Finland)

DIRECTORATE AWARDS

BEST GOALIE	Tuukka Rask (Finland)
BEST DEFENCEMAN	Marc Staal (Canada)
BEST FORWARD	Evgeni Malkin (Russia)

WOMEN'S HOCKEY

WORLD WOMEN'S CHAMPIONSHIPS RESULTS

1990 Women's World Championships

CANADA, March 19–25, 1990

FINAL PLACINGS

GOLD	Canada
SILVER	United States
BRONZE	Finland
Fourth Place	Sweden
Fifth Place	Switzerland
Sixth Place	Norway
Seventh Place	Germany
Eighth Place	Japan

1992 Women's World Championships

FINLAND, April 20–26, 1992

FINAL PLACINGS

GOLD	Canada
SILVER	United States
BRONZE	Finland
Fourth Place	Sweden
Fifth Place	China
Sixth Place	Norway
Seventh Place	Denmark
Eighth Place	Switzerland

DIRECTORATE AWARDS

BEST GOALIE	Annica Ahlen (Sweden)
BEST DEFENCEMAN	Geraldine Heaney (Canada)
BEST FORWARD	Cammi Granato (United States)

1994 Women's World Championships

UNITED STATES, April 11–17, 1994

FINAL PLACINGS

GOLD	Canada
SILVER	United States
BRONZE	Finland
Fourth Place	China
Fifth Place	Sweden
Sixth Place	Norway
Seventh Place	Switzerland
Eighth Place	Germany

DIRECTORATE AWARDS

BEST GOALIE	Erin Whitten (United States)
BEST DEFENCEMAN	Geraldine Heaney (Canada)
BEST FORWARD	Riikka Nieminen (Finland)

1997 Women's World Championships

CANADA, March 31–April 6, 1997

FINAL PLACINGS

GOLD	Canada
SILVER	United States
BRONZE	Finland
Fourth Place	China
Fifth Place	Sweden
Sixth Place	Russia

Seventh Place   Switzerland
Eighth Place   Norway

DIRECTORATE AWARDS
None awarded

1999 Women's World Championships

FINLAND, March 8–14, 1999

FINAL PLACINGS
GOLD   Canada
SILVER   United States
BRONZE   Finland
Fourth Place   Sweden
Fifth Place   China
Sixth Place   Russia
Seventh Place   Germany
Eighth Place   Switzerland

DIRECTORATE AWARDS
BEST GOALIE   Sami Jo Small (Canada)
BEST DEFENCEMAN   Kirsi Hanninen (Finland)
BEST FORWARD   Jenny Schmidgall (United States)

2000 Women's World Championships

CANADA, April 3–9, 2000

FINAL PLACINGS
GOLD   Canada
SILVER   United States
BRONZE   Finland
Fourth Place   Sweden
Fifth Place   Russia
Sixth Place   China

Seventh Place   Germany
Eighth Place   Japan

DIRECTORATE AWARDS
BEST GOALIE   Sami Jo Small (Canada)
BEST DEFENCEMAN   Angela Ruggiero (United States)
BEST FORWARD   Katja Riipi (Finland)

2001 Women's World Championships

UNITED STATES, April 2–8, 2001

FINAL PLACINGS
GOLD   Canada
SILVER   United States
BRONZE   Russia
Fourth Place   Finland
Fifth Place   Sweden
Sixth Place   Germany
Seventh Place   China
Eighth Place   Kazakhstan

DIRECTORATE AWARDS
BEST GOALIE   Kim St. Pierre (Canada)
BEST DEFENCEMAN   Karyn Bye (United States)
BEST FORWARD   Jennifer Botterill (Canada)
MVP   Jennifer Botterill (Canada)

2003 World Championships

CHINA, April 3–9, 2003

CANCELLED DUE TO SARS OUTBREAK

2004 World Championships

CANADA, March 30–April 6, 2004

FINAL PLACINGS

GOLD MEDAL	Canada
SILVER MEDAL	United States
BRONZE MEDAL	Finland
Fourth Place	Sweden
Fifth Place	Russia
Sixth Place	Germany
Seventh Place	China
Eighth Place	Switzerland
Ninth Place	Japan

DIRECTORATE AWARDS

BEST GOALIE	Kim St. Pierre (Canada)
BEST DEFENCEMAN	Angela Ruggiero (United States)
BEST FORWARD	Jayna Hefford (Canada)
MVP	Jennifer Botterill (Canada)

ALL-STAR TEAM

Goal	Pam Dreyer (United States)
Defence	Gunilla Andersson (Sweden), Angela Ruggiero (United States)
Forward	Jayna Hefford (Canada), Jennifer Botterill (Canada), Natalie Darwitz (United States)

2005 World Championships

SWEDEN, April 2–9, 2005

FINAL PLACINGS

GOLD MEDAL	United States
SILVER MEDAL	Canada
BRONZE MEDAL	Sweden
Fourth Place	Finland

Fifth Place	Germany
Sixth Place	China
Seventh Place	Kazakhstan
Eighth Place	Russia

DIRECTORATE AWARDS

BEST GOALIE	Chanda Gunn (United States)
BEST DEFENCEMAN	Angela Ruggiero (United States)
BEST FORWARD	Jayna Hefford (Canada)
MVP	Krissy Wendell (United States)

ALL-STAR TEAM

Goalie	Natalya Turnova (Kazakhstan)
Defence	Cheryl Pounder (Canada), Angela Ruggiero (United States)
Forward	Hayley Wickenheiser (Canada), Maria Rooth (Sweden), Krissy Wendell (United States)

NATIONAL WOMEN'S HOCKEY LEAGUE ALL-TIME STANDINGS

1999–2000
Eastern Division

	GP	W	L	T	GF	GA	P
Sainte Julie Pantheres	35	20	8	7	109	68	47
Montreal Wingstar	35	18	7	10	116	62	46
Ottawa Raiders	35	9	20	6	61	109	24
Laval Le Mistral	35	7	23	5	78	177	19

Western Division

	GP	W	L	T	GF	GA	P
Beatrice Aeros	40	35	3	2	217	37	72
Brampton Thunder	40	29	5	6	208	64	64
Mississauga Chiefs	40	21	13	6	133	79	48
Clearnet Lightning	40	4	33	3	44	249	11
Scarborough Sting	40	3	34	3	49	170	9

CHAMPIONSHIP FINALS

March 18   Sainte Julie Pantheres 2/Beatrice Aeros 2
March 19   Beatrice Aeros 1/Sainte Julie Pantheres 0
Beatrice wins championship 3–1 in points

2000–2001

Eastern Division

	GP	W	L	T	GF	GA	P
Montreal Wingstar	40	30	6	4	163	63	64
Sainte Julie Pantheres	40	22	15	3	168	102	47
Ottawa Raiders	40	11	25	4	78	150	26
Laval Le Mistral	40	5	33	2	68	261	12

Western Division

	GP	W	L	T	GF	GA	P
Beatrice Aeros	40	35	2	3	222	46	73
Brampton Thunder	40	30	7	3	223	82	63
Mississauga Ice Bears	40	21	16	3	107	97	45
Toronto Sting	40	8	29	3	82	168	19
Clearnet Lightning	40	5	34	1	77	219	11
Vancouver Griffins	18	14	4	0	91	43	28

CHAMPIONSHIP FINALS

Beatrice Aeros 2/Sainte Julie Pantheres 2
Beatrice Aeros 8/Sainte Julie Pantheres 1
Beatrice wins championship 3–1 in points

2001–2002

Eastern Division

	GP	W	L	T	GF	GA	P
Ottawa Raiders	30	14	10	6	71	72	34
Montreal Wingstar	30	11	14	5	66	78	27
Le Cheyenne de la Metropol	30	11	15	4	73	85	26

Western Division

	G	W	L	T	OTL	GF	GA	PTS
Beatrice Aeros	30	23	2	5		149	39	51
Mississauga Ice Bears	30	12	10	8		82	81	32
Brampton Thunder	30	8	14	8		73	97	24
TELUS Lightning	30	4	18	8		59	120	16

Pacific Division

	G	W	L	T	OTL	GF	GA	PTS
Vancouver Griffins	31	27	4	0		84	14	54

CHAMPIONSHIP FINALS
Beatrice Aeros 3/Brampton Thunder 2 (OT)

2002–03
Eastern Division

	GP	W	L	T	OTL	GF	GA	P
Montreal Wingstar	36	18	15	3	0	83	81	39
Ottawa Raiders	36	13	20	1	2	96	122	29
Quebec Avalanche	36	10	20	5	1	87	120	26

Central Division

	GP	W	L	T	OTL	GF	GA	P
Beatrice Aeros	36	32	3	1	0	201	54	65
Brampton Thunder	36	27	9	0	0	152	71	54
Mississauga Ice Bears	36	19	13	3	1	122	111	42
TELUS Lightning	36	0	34	1	1	54	236	2

Western Division

	GP	W	L	T	OTL	GF	GA	P
Calgary X-Treme	24	23	1	0	0	144	37	46
Vancouver Griffins	24	10	13	0	1	82	92	21
Edmonton Chimos	24	3	20	0	1	35	132	7

CHAMPIONSHIP FINALS
Calgary X-Treme 3/Beatrice Aeros 0

'003–04

astern Division

	G	W	L	T	OTL	GF	GA	PTS
Montreal Axion	36	20	10	5	1	113	84	46
Ottawa Raiders	36	9	23	4	0	85	144	22
Quebec Avalanche	36	4	28	2	2	65	163	12

Central Division

	G	W	L	T	OTL	GF	GA	PTS
Toronto Aeros	36	33	2	1	0	197	42	67
Brampton Thunder	36	28	6	2	0	190	72	58
Oakville Ice	36	17	17	2	0	118	99	36
TELUS Lightning	36	8	28	0	0	66	224	16

Western Division

	G	W	L	T	OTL	GF	GA	PTS
Calgary X-Treme	12	11	1	0	0	64	9	22
Edmonton Chimos	12	1	11	0	0	9	64	2

CHAMPIONSHIP FINALS

Calgary X-Treme 5/Brampton Thunder 4 (OT/SO)

2004–05

Eastern Division

	G	W	L	T	OTL	GF	GA	PTS
Montreal Axion	36	24	9	2	1	140	85	51
Ottawa Raiders	36	14	19	2	1	101	128	31
Quebec Avalanche	36	5	25	4	2	53	132	16

Central Division

	G	W	L	T	OTL	GF	GA	PTS
Brampton Thunder	36	30	3	2	1	165	70	63
Toronto Aeros	36	24	6	4	2	142	68	54
Oakville Ice	36	13	15	6	2	97	99	34
TELUS Lightning	36	4	28	4	0	72	189	12

CHAMPIONSHIP FINALS
Toronto Aeros 5/Montreal Axion 4 (OT)

2005–06
Eastern Division

	G	W	L	T	OTL	GF	GA	PTS
Ottawa Raiders	36	21	8	4	3	122	77	49
Montreal Axion	36	14	17	3	2	100	122	33
Quebec Avalanche	36	4	28	2	2	58	135	12

Central Division

	G	W	L	T	OTL	GF	GA	PTS
Durham Lightning	36	23	6	5	2	107	74	53
Brampton Thunder	36	19	12	5	0	113	97	43
Oakville Ice	36	20	14	1	1	118	100	42
Toronto Aeros	36	13	17	4	2	114	127	32

CHAMPIONSHIP FINALS
April 15   Montreal 1/Brampton 0